Common Word Commands

Command	Key Combination	Menu Item
Annotation, Insert	Alt-I, *then* A	Insert/Annotation
Annotation Window, Open/Close	Alt-V, *then* A	View/Annotations
Bookmark, Assign to Selection	Alt-I, *then* M *or* Ctrl-Shift-F5	Insert/Bookmark
Border, Add to Paragraph, Picture, or Cell	Alt-T, *then* B	Format/Border
Break: Page, Column, or Section	Alt-I, *then* B	Insert/Break
Bulleted List, Create	Alt-O, *then* B	Tools/Bullets and Numbering
Calculate	Alt-O, *then* C	Tools/Calculate
Character, Format	Alt-T, *then* C	Format/Character
Close All Windows for Current Document	Alt-F, *then* C	File/Close
Close Document Window	Alt-hyphen, *then* C *or* Ctrl-F4	Document Control/Close
Close Word Window (Exit Program)	Alt-Spacebar, *then* C, Alt-F, *then* X, *or* Alt-F4	Word Control/Close *or* File/Exit
Columns, Format	Alt-T, *then* O	Format/Columns
Compare Versions of Document	Alt-O, *then* V	Tools/Compare Versions
Copy Selection to Clipboard	Alt-E, *then* C, Ctrl-C, *or* Ctrl-Ins	Edit/Copy
Customize Word Features	Alt-O, *then* O	Tools/Options
Cut Selection to Clipboard	Alt-E, *then* T, Ctrl-X, *or* Shift-Del	Edit/Cut
Date and Time, Insert	Alt-I, *then* T	Insert/Date and Time
Draft Document View	Alt-V, *then* D	View/Draft
Exit Program	Alt-Spacebar, *then* C, Alt-F, *then* X, *or* Alt-F4	Word Control/Close *or* File/Exit
Field, Insert	Alt-I, *then* D	Insert/Field
Fields, Show Codes/Results	Alt-V, *then* C	View/Field Codes
Find Document	Alt-F, *then* F	File/Find File
Find Text or Formatting	Alt-E, *then* F	Edit/Find
Footnote, Insert Reference	Alt-I, *then* N	Insert/Footnote
Footnote Window, Open/Close	Alt-V, *then* F	View/Footnotes
Format Character	Alt-T, *then* C	Format/Character
Format Paragraph	Alt-T, *then* P	Format/Paragraph
Frame, Insert	Alt-I, *then* F	Insert/Frame
Frame, Format	Alt-T, *then* F	Format/Frame
Glossary Entry, Define or Insert	Alt-E, *then* O	Edit/Glossary
Go to Position in Document	Alt-E, *then* G *or* F5	Edit/Go To
Grammar, Check	Alt-O, *then* G	Tools/Grammar
Header or Footer, Edit	Alt-V, *then* H	View/Header/Footer

Computer users are not all alike.
Neither are SYBEX books.

We know our customers have a variety of needs. They've told us so. And because we've listened, we've developed several distinct types of books to meet the needs of each of our customers. What are you looking for in computer help?

If you're looking for the basics, try the **ABC's** series. You'll find short, unintimidating tutorials and helpful illustrations. For a more visual approach, select **Teach Yourself**, featuring screen-by-screen illustrations of how to use your latest software purchase.

Mastering and **Understanding** titles offer you a step-by-step introduction, plus an in-depth examination of intermediate-level features, to use as you progress.

Our **Up & Running** series is designed for computer-literate consumers who want a no-nonsense overview of new programs. Just 20 basic lessons, and you're on your way.

We also publish two types of reference books. Our **Instant References** provide quick access to each of a program's commands and functions. SYBEX **Encyclopedias** and **Desktop References** provide a *comprehensive reference* and explanation of all of the commands, features and functions of the subject software.

Sometimes a subject requires a special treatment that our standard series don't provide. So you'll find we have titles like **Advanced Techniques, Handbooks, Tips & Tricks,** and others that are specifically tailored to satisfy a unique need.

We carefully select our authors for their in-depth understanding of the software they're writing about, as well as their ability to write clearly and communicate effectively. Each manuscript is thoroughly reviewed by our technical staff to ensure its complete accuracy. Our production department makes sure it's easy to use. All of this adds up to the highest quality books available, consistently appearing on best-seller charts worldwide.

You'll find SYBEX publishes a variety of books on every popular software package. Looking for computer help? Help Yourself to SYBEX.

For a complete catalog of our publications:

SYBEX Inc.
2021 Challenger Drive, Alameda, CA 94501
Tel: (510) 523-8233/(800) 227-2346 Telex: 336311
Fax: (510) 523-2373

Mastering Microsoft Word
for Windows, Version 2.0

Mastering Microsoft® Word
for Windows,™ Version 2.0

Second Edition

Michael J. Young

SYBEX® San Francisco ■ Paris ■ Düsseldorf ■ Soest

Acquisitions Editor: Dianne King
Editors: D. Robert and L. Settembrini
Technical Reviewer: Maryann Brown
Word Processors: Ann Dunn and Susan Trybull
Chapter Art: Alissa Feinberg
Screen Graphics: Cuong Le
Typesetter: Elizabeth Newman
Proofreaders/Production Assistants: Rhonda Holmes and Janet Boone
Indexer: Ted Laux
Cover Designer: Ingalls + Associates
Cover Photographer: Mark Johann

SYBEX is a registered trademark of SYBEX Inc.

Library of Congress Card Number: 91-67384
ISBN: 0-7821-1012-6

Manufactured in the United States of America
10 9 8 7 6

Acknowledgments

I would like to thank all of the people at Sybex who made writing the second edition of this book possible, especially Editor-in-Chief Rudolph Langer and Acquisitions Editor Dianne King for sponsoring the project, and all the other people whose names appear at the front of the book. I would also like to thank Microsoft Corporation for supplying early releases of the program. Finally, I would like to thank the developers at Microsoft, who did a superb job writing the latest version of Word for Windows.

Contents at a Glance

Table of Contents

xviii

Introduction

WORD FOR WINDOWS IS A WORD PROCESSING program designed specifically for the Microsoft Windows operating environment. While providing all of the sophisticated features offered by traditional text-mode word processors, such as Microsoft Word for DOS, it also takes full advantage of the graphics interface provided by Windows, allowing you to view and control the precise printed appearance of your document. In addition, as a Windows application, it permits close interaction with other Windows programs, such as spreadsheets and graphics applications.

Word for Windows is ideal both for writing simple documents and for creating complex camera-ready art; in other words, it is easy to use for standard word processing tasks, but it also provides many of the features of dedicated desktop publishing applications. Its large number of features, however, can make learning the program a challenging task. This book is designed to help you quickly learn the basic word processing tasks, so that you can rapidly become a productive user of Word for Windows, and to provide thorough explanations of Word's more advanced features to help you take full advantage of the program.

The book provides tutorial exercises, step-by-step procedures, and many examples. It also contains discussions to help you *understand* Word's features, many of which are complex, subtle, and confusing even to users experienced with word processing.

AN OVERVIEW OF THE BOOK

The book is divided into five parts. Part I provides a fast, basic tutorial introduction. Parts II and III present the information most users need to create, alter, format, and print real-world papers, chapters, and reports. Parts IV and V discuss more advanced features and methods, which can save you time and extend your word processing abilities to create and manage more complex documents and collections of documents.

The tutorial introduction in **Part I** covers the basic tasks of creating, formatting, and printing a simple short document. By working through the exercises given in the two chapters in this part, you will gain a clear overview of Word's features and you will begin to use the program productively.

Part II, on editing, focuses on the techniques for creating the document *content*. In this part, you will learn how to enter and revise the text and graphics that constitute longer documents. You will learn how to use program features that help you enter, correct, and organize document text, and you will learn how to add special elements to your document, such as headers, footnotes, and indexes.

Part III, on formatting, explains how to control the printed *appearance* of your document, and how to produce the final printed copy. You will learn how to assign formatting features to each level of your document, ranging from the entire document to individual characters. You will also learn how to preview and print the document, and how to generate form letters.

Part IV discusses document templates (a template is the basic framework from which a document derives its shape, style, and repetitive elements), and the timesaving features that can be assigned to them. You will learn how to speed up your work by defining styles, storing text within glossaries, and automating tasks using macros. You will also learn how to customize the program's own menus, keyboard commands, and other features.

Part V focuses on techniques for working with larger or more complex documents, and for creating documents in conjunction with other writers or editors. You will learn how to edit or view the document as an outline, how to add annotations and mark revisions, how

You should finish working through this book before customizing the Word program, since the descriptions in the book refer to the initial *default* Word features.

to manage collections of documents, and how to add elements to your documents from other Windows applications using Object Linking and Embedding (OLE).

CONVENTIONS USED

The sequence of topics in this book follows generally from simple to complex, and along the way we often mention or introduce topics that could easily take up full chapters on their own. Because a great many of the features you will be working with are interrelated, the problem arises of having to repeat information about these features in many different places. Of course, without totally abandoning the procedure at hand, it would not be possible to launch into a full explanation of these topics every time the occasion arises. Instead, we use special margin notes (with the traditional "pointing finger" motif, as you saw above) to refer you to the chapters where the related topics are presented.

Other margin notes offer special tips (the "checkmark" note) and warnings (the "alarm" note).

To help you find the topic or feature you are looking for, we have used boldface type within chapter sections to highlight the first occurrences of commands, options, buttons, and keystrokes. Text and other data that you are expected to type are shown in a different typeface altogether. Finally, with the special "Fast Track" sections at the head of selected discussions, you can jump right into working with the feature being presented, or simply jog your memory concerning the basic steps.

NEW FEATURES OF VERSION 2.0

This edition of *Mastering Microsoft Word for Windows* covers only version 2.0. If you are still using version 1.0 or 1.1, the first thing you should do is to upgrade to version 2.0 so that you can take advantage of its many new features.

The following is a summary of some of the important new features of version 2.0:

- A customizable "Toolbar," which allows you to perform a wide variety of tasks with a single click of the mouse.

- Quick insertion of bulleted or numbered lists, using any of a wide variety of bullet or number styles.

- Insertion of symbol characters.

- Envelope printing.

- "Drag and Drop," which allows you to copy and move selected blocks of text to their new locations simply by dragging them with the mouse.

- A grammar checker.

- "Help for WordPerfect Users" (see Chapter 23), which enables you to use WordPerfect keystrokes to access equivalent features in Word, and offers optional instruction on learning the Word approach to using those features.

- Changing margins, page size, or page orientation for portions of the document from *within* the document.

- Applying shading to paragraphs.

- The ability to zoom the document view, so that you can examine and edit the document at any level of magnification.

- A simplified print merge procedure.

- Using keystrokes to assign styles.

- Inserting charts, graphics, equations, and other objects that are created and edited by other applications, using Object Linking and Embedding (OLE). The Word package also now includes several utility programs for creating and editing "embeddable" objects, such as graphs, equations, and simple drawings.

REQUIREMENTS FOR USING WORD FOR WINDOWS

To use Word for Windows version 2.0, you will need the following hardware and software:

- An IBM-compatible microcomputer, with an 80286 or later-model processor

- Microsoft Windows, version 3.0 or higher
- At least 1 megabyte of RAM. (Two or more megabytes are recommended, and in fact are *required* if you expect to run Word on a network or in conjunction with other programs.)
- One hard disk drive, and one double-sided floppy disk drive
- An EGA or higher-resolution monitor and adapter. (The monitor and adapter must be compatible with Windows 3.0.)
- A Microsoft or compatible mouse or pointing device.

Before using Word for Windows, you should be familiar with basic Windows techniques, such as:

- Maximizing, minimizing, and restoring a window
- Moving a window on the screen
- Adjusting the size of a window
- Working with dialog boxes

If you need more information on any of these methods, see the *Microsoft Windows User's Guide* (especially the chapter titled "Basic Skills"). Another way to learn some of these basic skills is to run the tutorial program that comes with Word for Windows.

Also, this book occasionally refers to the *Microsoft Word User's Guide* and the *Microsoft Word for Windows Technical Reference*. The *User's Guide* is supplied with the Word for Windows package, and the *Technical Reference* can be obtained from Microsoft or through a bookstore.

Part

1

The Ten Minute Version

These first two chapters are designed to give you a fast overview of Word for Windows. By following the step-by-step instructions given here, you will learn in their simplest form the most essential word processing tasks: creating, saving, and printing a document. You will learn each task by actually performing it.

1: **Creating a Document**

2: **Editing, Previewing, and Printing the Document**

1

Creating a Document

IN THIS CHAPTER, YOU WILL CREATE A VERY SIMPLE
Word for Windows *document*. A document is a body of text—possibly
including graphics or other data—that you create using the Word for
Windows program. Once you have created a document in Word,
you can revise it, print it, and store it in a disk file. After the document has been stored in a disk file, you can later *open* it in Word (that
is, read it from the disk back into the program) to make further revisions or print additional copies.

First you will learn how to start Word for Windows and type a
short block of text into a new document window. You will discover
how to designate separate paragraphs and how to correct minor typing errors. Then you will save the document and exit from the program. In Chapter 2, you will open this same document, make several
revisions to it, preview its printed appearance, and, finally, print it.

INSTALLING AND STARTING WORD FOR WINDOWS

The basic hardware
and software
requirements for install-
ing the program are
outlined in the Introduc-
tion under the heading
"Requirements for Using
Word for Windows."

The current version of Word for Windows is designed to run
within Microsoft Windows version 3.0 or later. Before you can install
the program, you must install Windows itself on your hard disk, following the instructions provided by the *Microsoft Windows User's Guide*.

Once you have installed Windows, you can install Word for Windows using *Setup,* the automated installation program that is provided
with the Word package; complete instructions are given in Appendix A.
The installation program will add a program group to your Program
Manager window. To run Word, perform the following two steps:

1. If it is not already open, open the Word program group by
   double-clicking on the group icon,

Word for Windows 2.0

or by highlighting the icon and pressing Enter. Once the Word group has been opened, you will see the icons for several of the programs that are supplied with the Word package:

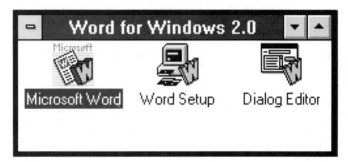

2. To start the program, double-click on the Microsoft Word icon,

or highlight the icon and press Enter.

THE OPENING WINDOW

When Word for Windows begins running, you will see a window similar to that illustrated in Figure 1.1. This is the *default* window, the one that appears the first time you run the program. Your window may differ somewhat from the illustration—for example, an element such as the ''Toolbar'' or horizontal scroll bar might be missing at

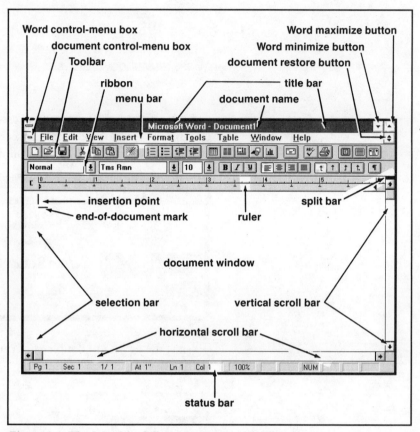

Figure 1.1: The Word for Windows opening window

first—but don't worry about it; it simply means that the program has been customized in some way. You will see shortly how to make some of these customizations.

As you work through the chapters of this book, you will learn about each of the parts of this screen. For easy reference, this same illustration is also printed on the inside front cover of the book.

For now, the most important part of this window is the large rectangular area labeled *document window*. This is the area in which Word displays the contents of the document you are creating or modifying. The window is initially blank, since at this point Word begins by

In Chapter 3, you will see how to have Word automatically open an existing document when it first runs.

opening a new (empty) document. As you can see in the *title bar* above the document window, the new document is temporarily named **Document1**; when you save the document as described later in the chapter, you will assign it a permanent name.

Although the document window does not yet display text, it does contain two important objects: the *end-of-document mark* and the *insertion point*. The end-of-document mark is a short horizontal line that appears directly after the last character in the document. The insertion point is a blinking vertical line that marks the point where the characters you type will be inserted into the document. The insertion point is where most of the action takes place within the Word program. As you will see later, in addition to inserting characters, you can also delete characters, change the appearance of characters, mark blocks of text, and perform many other tasks at the insertion point. You can move the insertion point throughout the document. You cannot, however, move it beyond the end-of-document mark, since there is nothing contained beyond this mark.

USING THE PROGRAM MENUS AND SIMPLIFYING THE WINDOW

Before entering text into the new document, you can practice using the program menus by reducing some of the clutter in the Word window—by removing several window elements that are not yet needed. The first step is to remove the *ribbon*. (See Figure 1.1 for the location of the ribbon; if the ribbon is not currently displayed in your window, skip this procedure.)

1. Pull down the **View** menu on the menu bar.

2. The **Ribbon** item should have a checkmark next to it, indicating that the ribbon is currently displayed. While holding down the mouse button, drag the highlight down to the **Ribbon** command, and release the mouse button, as illustrated in Figure 1.2. This eliminates the checkmark. The **View** menu will disappear and the ribbon will be removed.

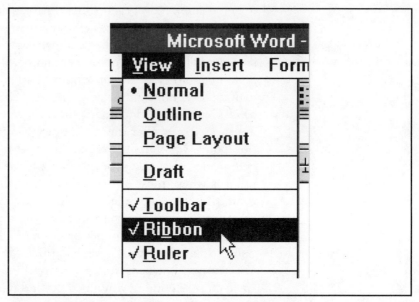

Figure 1.2: Choosing the Ribbon item on the View menu

If you later want to restore the ribbon, you would perform this same procedure again, because choosing the Ribbon command on the View menu *toggles* the ribbon—from on to off and off to on.

Next, remove the *ruler* by choosing the **Ruler** item on the **View** menu, using the same general procedure that was just described.

The settings you have just made will be saved until you explicitly change them, even if you close the current document or quit Word.

ENTERING TEXT

In a moment you will begin by typing in the text shown in Figure 1.3, using the computer keyboard as if it were a typewriter. For example, to type uppercase letters—or any upper character on keys with two characters—you type while holding down the Shift key.

Now begin typing the first paragraph, remembering not to press the Enter (◄─┘) key at the end of the line. *Type the text exactly as shown; in Chapter 2 you will correct the misspellings and make several other revisions to this document.* When you have completed typing the first paragraph

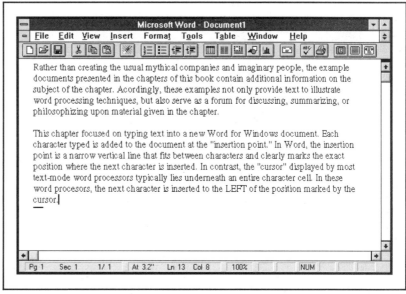

Figure 1.3: An example document for you to type into your own Document1

(that is, when you have typed through the words **in the chapter.**), press Enter to end the paragraph. Before typing the second paragraph, press ◄─┘ again so that there will be a blank line between the two paragraphs; this blank line is actually a separate paragraph that contains no characters.

Notice that as you type each character, it is inserted into the document at the current position of the insertion point, and that the insertion point instantly moves to the right, marking the position where the next character will be inserted.

If you've never used a word processor before, be aware of an important difference between using a typewriter and using a word processor (like Word): When using a word processor, you should not press the Enter key at the end of each line. Press it only to end a paragraph. As you approach the end of the first line in the document window, simply continue typing as if the line extended forever to the right. When you type a word that is too long to fit at the end of the current line, Word automatically moves the word—together with the insertion point—down to the beginning of the next line. This feature is known as *automatic word wrap*.

When you are typing your document, each line may break at a different point than illustrated in Figure 1.3. The exact position at which Word breaks a line (through automatic word wrap) depends upon margins and the number of characters that can be displayed on a line using the current type font.

The instructions in this chapter assume that you are in the *insert mode* rather than in the *overtype mode*. If the letters **OVR** appear on the status bar at the bottom of the screen, indicating that the overtype mode is active, press the Ins key once to restore the insert mode. (See Chapter 3 for an explanation of the overtype mode.)

If you make a mistake of your own while typing the text, you can correct it by using the Backspace key. Each time you press Backspace, Word erases the character immediately preceding the insertion point and moves the insertion point one character position back. If you continue to hold down the Backspace key, this action is automatically repeated so that you can erase an entire series of previously typed characters. (In following chapters you will learn much more efficient ways to correct large errors.)

In the same manner, type in the second paragraph to complete the document. Remember to use quotation marks around the words **insertion point** and **cursor**, and to emphasize the word **LEFT** by using all capital letters. (In Chapter 16, you will learn other, more effective ways to emphasize characters, using techniques such as italics or boldface.)

SAVING THE DOCUMENT

While you are creating a document, your work is stored only in the computer's temporary memory. Before quitting Word, therefore, you should save the document in a file on disk. (If you forget to do this and begin to quit the program, Word will *ask* if you want to save the document.) It is especially important to save the document you created in this chapter, since you will be using it in the next chapter.

To save the document, choose the **Save** command on the **File** menu (from now on, this command will be referred to as the **File/Save** command; similar notation will be used for other menu commands).

Alternatively, you can issue the Save command by simply clicking the **Save button** on the **Toolbar**:

If the Toolbar is not currently visible, you can make it appear by choosing the **View/Toolbar** menu command.

The Toolbar, which consists of a row of buttons at the top of the window (see Figure 1.1), is a new feature in Word. By simply clicking the appropriate button in the Toolbar, you can instantly execute any of a wide variety of Word commands. You will find all the buttons illustrated, together with descriptions, on the inside covers of this book. In Chapter 23, you will learn how to customize the Toolbar in such a way that you can include only buttons for the commands you use most often.

Once you have chosen the File/Save command or have clicked the Save button from the Toolbar, Word will display a *dialog box* requesting the name of the file in which the document is to be stored (Figure 1.4). A dialog box is a window that Word displays to obtain additional information. You must supply a file name the first time you

Word will display this dialog box only the first time you choose the File/Save command or click the Save button in the Toolbar; thereafter, it will immediately save the file under the same name. If you later want to change the name under which the document is stored, use the **File/Save As** command instead.

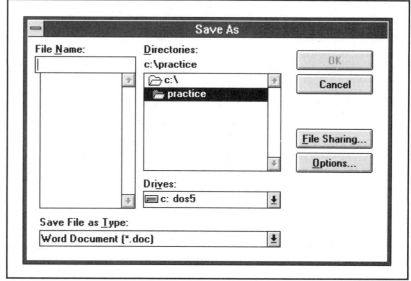

Figure 1.4: The dialog box displayed when you first save a new file

save the document because the name appearing on the title bar, **Document1**, is only temporary. Once the dialog box appears, perform the following steps:

See Appendix B for an explanation of DOS drives and directories.

1. In the **Drives:** list box, choose the disk drive on which you want to store the document. If the drive you want doesn't appear, click on the arrow at the right end of the box to open a

list of all drives on your system, then click the desired drive. This drive then becomes the current Word drive.

You do not need to perform step 2 if the name of the directory in which you want to save the document is already displayed above the Directories list (that is, if it is already the current directory).

2. In the **Directories:** list box, double-click on the disk directory in which you want to save the document.

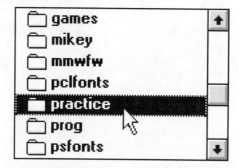

The name of the current directory is displayed above the Directories list box. When you double-click on the name of a directory in the list box, it becomes the current Word directory, and the view in the Directories box changes to show the parent of the current directory (if any), the current directory itself, and all subdirectories belonging to the current directory. If you do not initially see the directory in which you want to store your document, you can navigate through the directories on your disk by choosing parent directories or subdirectories until you find the desired directory.

3. Type the document name into the **File Name:** text box, as follows:

File Name:

`EXAMPLE.DOC`

4. Click the OK button, or press Enter.

You do not need to include an *extension*—the optional one to three final letters that follow a period—in the name you specify when saving a file. If you do not provide an extension, Word automatically adds the extension **.DOC**. For example, if you type **TABBY**, Word will name the document **TABBY.DOC**.

5. For now, simply click the OK button or press Enter to quickly save the document.

Once you click OK or press Enter, Word will display another dialog box requesting *summary information*. Filling in these fields is completely optional. The summary information associated with a document is used primarily to make it easier to find and identify documents (using the **File/Find File** command, discussed in Chapter 26). Note that Word will request summary information only the first time you choose the File/Save command or click the Save button from the Toolbar. If you later want to change this information, choose the **File/Summary Info** command (also explained in Chapter 26).

Word will now save the document in a disk file named EXAMPLE.DOC within the requested directory, and will remove the dialog box. Notice that after you perform the Save operation, the file name you assigned now appears on the window title bar.

If you decide not to save the document while the dialog box is still open, click the **Cancel** button or press **Esc**. In general, pressing the Esc key will remove a dialog box or menu without performing any action, or will interrupt a process such as printing a document.

HELP!

Before proceeding further in your exploration of Word for Windows, you might want to learn about the program's help facility. By using the help feature, you can discover how to use many of Word's functions without referring to the printed documentation.

If you are a Word-Perfect user, you'll find that Word's special "Help for WordPerfect Users" (presented in Chapter 23) enables you to use standard Word-Perfect keystrokes to access the equivalent Word feature and offers optional instruction on learning the Word approach to using those features.

The easiest way to access help is to simply press the **F1** key. When you press this key, a window will appear that contains information pertaining to whatever task you are currently performing; Word for Windows help is therefore described as *context sensitive*. For example, to display information on the File/Save command, just highlight Save on the File menu and then press F1. Similarly, if the Open dialog box (that is, the one displayed when you select the File/Open command) is open when you press F1, the help window will display information on the fields within this dialog box. If no particular command is in progress when you press F1, a general index of help topics will appear in the help window, as illustrated in Figure 1.5.

If you press F1 when the help window is already active, the window will display information on how to use the help facility itself. In summary, all you have to remember to obtain help is to press F1.

EXITING FROM WORD FOR WINDOWS

Once you have saved your document, you can exit from the Word for Windows program. To quit Word, choose the **Exit** command from the **File** menu.

Alternatively, you can terminate the program by opening the **Word control menu** (in the upper left-hand corner of the window—see Figure 1.1)

and choosing the **Close** command.

You can also quit the program by double-clicking on the **Word control-menu box.**

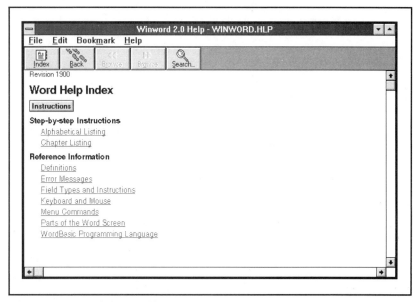

Figure 1.5: Word's help utility

2

Editing, Previewing,
and Printing the Document

IN CHAPTER 1, YOU CREATED A NEW DOCUMENT BY entering text in much the same manner as you would type a paper using a typewriter. In this chapter, you will learn one of the great advantages of using a word processor such as Word for Windows: the ability to revise an existing document, freely inserting, deleting, or changing characters.

You will begin by running Word and opening the example document you created in Chapter 1. You will then make several revisions to this document by moving the insertion point to the appropriate locations and then deleting or inserting characters. Next, you will save the revised version. Finally, you will preview the printed appearance of the document and produce a printed copy.

OPENING THE DOCUMENT

If Windows is not currently running, start it by typing **win** at the DOS prompt. Run Word for Windows by double-clicking on the Microsoft Word icon in the Windows Program Manager, as described in Chapter 1. As before, when Word begins it will automatically open a new, empty document. This time, however, rather than entering text into a new document, you will *open* the document (EXAMPLE.DOC) you created in the previous chapter:

1. Choose the **File/Open** menu command or click on the **Open button** in the Toolbar:

Word will display the Open dialog box, illustrated in Figure 2.1.

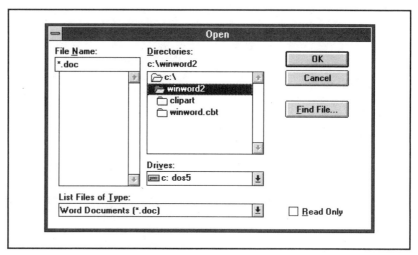

Figure 2.1: The Open dialog box

2. If the letter for the disk drive containing EXAMPLE.DOC doesn't appear in the **Drives:** box, click on the arrow at the right end of the box to open a list of all drives on your system. Then, click on the desired drive.

3. If EXAMPLE.DOC does not already appear in the **File Name:** list box, choose the disk directory containing this document by double-clicking on the directory name in the **Directories:** list box.

   As explained in the previous chapter, if the directory containing your document is not listed in the Directories list box, you must navigate through the directory system, by choosing either parent directories or subdirectories, until you locate the desired directory. Each time you select a new directory, all of the document files contained in that directory are listed in the File Name list box, as illustrated in Figure 2.2.

4. Once you have selected the appropriate directory, the file name **EXAMPLE.DOC** will appear in the File Name list box. To open this document, simply double-click on the name.

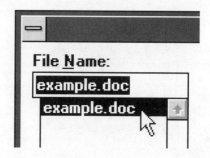

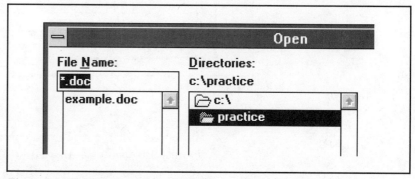

Figure 2.2: The Directories: and File Name: list boxes

Once you open the document you created in the last chapter, the new, empty document will be abandoned, and your document will appear in its place. The window should appear as it was when you saved it in Chapter 1. In the next section, you will make several changes to the document; the original and revised versions are illustrated in Figure 2.3.

(Remember that the exact location of the line breaks in your document depends upon the printer that is installed as well as the printer fonts that are available.)

MAKING THE REVISIONS

As you saw in Chapter 1, the insertion point marks the position in the document where characters are inserted or deleted. Accordingly,

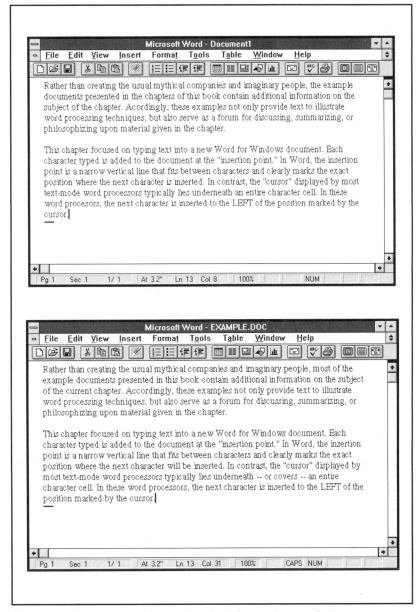

Figure 2.3: The original (top) and revised (bottom) example documents

making a revision normally requires the following two steps:

1. Move the insertion point to the place in the document you want to change.

2. Delete and/or insert characters as required to make the change.

This section discusses these two procedures individually, and then gives step-by-step instructions for revising the example document.

MOVING THE INSERTION POINT

This section describes two methods for moving the insertion point: using the arrow keys and using the mouse.

If you will be using the arrow keys on the numeric keypad (the set of number keys at the right side of the keyboard), make sure that the keypad is not in the Num Lock state. Num Lock is indicated by the word **NUM** on the right side of the Word status bar; you can turn it off by pressing the Num Lock key once.

Pressing an arrow key moves the insertion point one character position in the corresponding direction. Holding down an arrow key causes the insertion point to continue moving, character by character, or line by line. Using the arrow keys is a convenient method for moving the insertion point a short distance; it can be quite slow, however, for moving horizontally across an entire line or vertically through an entire paragraph.

Chapter 3 presents several other methods for efficiently moving the insertion point in longer documents as well as techniques for scrolling the document if the text does not fit entirely within the window.

Using the mouse is a faster method for moving the insertion point a distance greater than a few characters. While the mouse pointer is within the document window, it has an I-beam shape:

Rather than creating the usual

Simply move the mouse pointer to the location in the document where you would like to place the insertion point, and press the left mouse button. The insertion point will instantly appear at the designated position. You can't position the insertion point beyond the last character in the document.

INSERTING AND DELETING CHARACTERS

Chapter 5 presents other, more efficient methods for deleting larger amounts of text.

Once you have moved the insertion point to the desired location, you are ready to make changes to the document. You can delete existing characters using either the Backspace key or the Del key. As you saw in Chapter 1, pressing the **Backspace** key deletes the character immediately preceding the insertion point and moves the insertion point one character space back. Pressing the **Del** key erases the character immediately following the insertion point. Remember that holding down either Backspace or Del causes the erasing action to repeat automatically.

To insert one or more new characters at the insertion point, simply look to make sure that **OVR**—the overwrite mode indicator—does not appear in the status bar (if it does, toggle it back to insert mode by pressing the Ins key) and start typing.

To make the first revision, move the insertion point immediately in front of the words **the example documents** in the first sentence. Type the words

most of

followed by a space character.

Next, move the insertion point in front of the words **the chapters of this book contain**..., also in the first paragraph. Now press the Del key repeatedly to erase the words **the chapters of**.

Notice that as you erase or insert characters, Word maintains the paragraph margins, automatically adjusting line breaks as necessary.

Now place the insertion point in front of **chapter. Acordingly, these examples,** and add the word

current

followed by a space character. Also, move the insertion point a few characters forward and add a second **c** to the word incorrectly spelled **Acordingly.**

Moving to the second paragraph, place the insertion point immediately after the word **is** in the expression **is inserted,** near the middle of the paragraph. Press the Backspace key twice to erase the **is**, and then type the words

will be

(not followed by a space).

Finally, move the insertion point in front of the expression **an entire character cell** near the end of the second paragraph, and insert

-- or covers --

followed by a space.

You have now finished revising the document. Compare your result with the completed document shown in Figure 2.3.

SAVING THE DOCUMENT

Whenever you are working on a document, it is a good idea to save it frequently to prevent losing work in the event of a computer failure; in Chapter 23 you will learn how to have Word save your document automatically at periodic intervals.

Before continuing, save the document by choosing the **File/Save** command, or by clicking the **Save button** in the Toolbar

as described in Chapter 1. Since you have already assigned the document a permanent name (EXAMPLE.DOC), Word will save the document without prompting you for a file name or document summary information.

If you want to take a break before previewing and printing the document, you can quit Word by double-clicking the Word control menu box.

PREVIEWING THE DOCUMENT FOR PRINTING

Chapter 17 provides a summary of all the document views provided by Word.

Now you will see some tangible results from the efforts you have expended so far. Word for Windows provides several alternative document views. A *document view* is a particular way of looking at and working with a document. When you start Word and open a document, you begin in the *normal,* or editing, view, which is the default view you have seen in these first two chapters. In normal view, although the characters and paragraphs are usually displayed as they will be printed, you cannot see the page margins, multiple columns, or elements such as headers and footers.

In this section, you will see another document view, known as *Print Preview*, which allows you to view the overall printed appearance of each page of the document.

If you are not already running Word, start the program and open EXAMPLE.DOC. You should see the example document in normal view. Now switch into Print Preview by choosing the **Print Preview** command from the **File** menu. This new view of the document is illustrated in Figure 2.4.

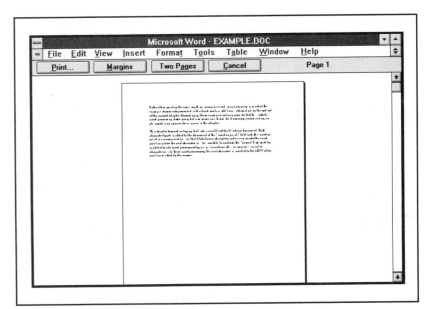

Figure 2.4: The Print Preview view of our example document

To view one page in the Print Preview window, click the **One Page** button; to view two pages, click the **Two Pages** button. See Chapter 17 for complete details on Print Preview, as well as the zoom feature that allows you to preview a page and continue to edit it.

In Print Preview, you can see a representation of one or two entire document pages as they will be printed. Although the individual characters are too small to read, this view shows you the overall composition of the page. As you will see in Part III, Print Preview is especially valuable when you have added headers or footers, or when you have placed text or graphics at specific positions on the page. You cannot perform normal editing tasks such as inserting or deleting characters while in Print Preview; however, as you will also see in Part III, you can adjust the positions of various objects on the page so that you can refine the final page layout.

To exit from Print Preview and return to normal view, click the Cancel button or press the Esc key.

When you are creating a more complex document, you will normally go into Print Preview just before printing the document to verify that the page layout is correct and to make any necessary layout adjustments.

PRINTING THE DOCUMENT

You can print the document while you are still in Print Preview, or after you have returned to normal view.

- To print from Print Preview mode, choose the **File/Print** command, click the **Print button on the Toolbar**, or simply press **P**.

- To print from the normal editing view, choose the **File/Print** command.

Make sure the printer is connected to the computer and is turned on before issuing the print command.

Once you have chosen the print command, Word will display the Print dialog box, which is shown in Figure 2.5. At the top of this dialog box you will see the name of the *default* Windows printer, which is the printer that currently receives all printed output from Windows applications, and the name of the port to which this printer is attached.

The Print dialog box allows you to specify several printing options. For now, however, simply click the OK button, or press Enter, to accept the default options and to begin printing. Word will remove the dialog box and will print your document.

You supply the name of the default printer when you install Windows. To change the default printer, you must run the Windows Control Panel and choose the **Printers** item. (See the *Microsoft Windows User's Guide* for instructions.)

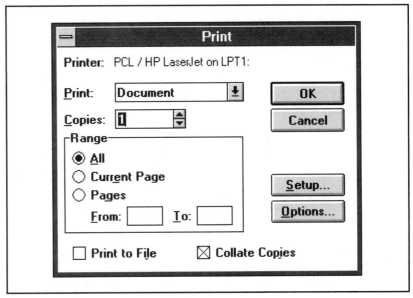

Figure 2.5: The Print dialog box

As an alternative method, from normal view you can simply click the **Print button** on the Toolbar:

If you click the Print button, Word will start printing the document immediately, using the default printing options, *without* displaying the Print dialog box.

While printing, Word displays a message box indicating the name of the printer and the document it is printing; you can stop the print job by clicking the Cancel button within the message box, or by pressing Esc. (Depending on how much of the print job has already been sent to your printer's buffer, however, the document may still print through to the end.)

The printed document is illustrated in Figure 2.6. See Chapter 17 for more information on printing, especially if you have any difficulties printing your document.

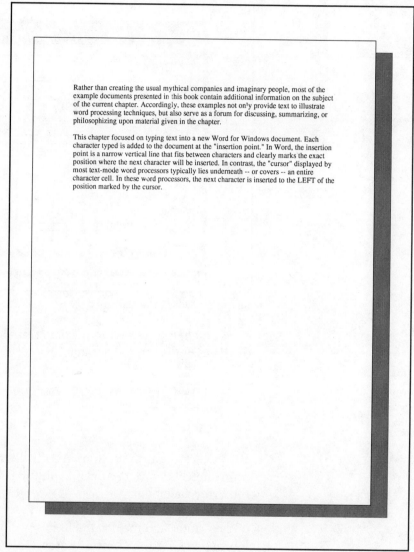

Figure 2.6: The printed example document

Part
II

Word's Writing and Editing Features

This part of the book focuses on techniques for creating the *content* of your documents. The chapters in this part show you how to enter and revise text, graphics, tables of information, headers, and footers. They also explain how to check your spelling and grammar, how to find synonyms, and how to automatically generate indexes, tables of contents, and footnotes.

3

Basic Editing Skills

CHAPTER 3

IN THIS CHAPTER, YOU WILL LEARN FUNDAMENTAL Word for Windows editing skills: how to create a new document or open an existing one, how to enter text and perform minor revisions, and how to save a document in a disk file. If you worked through the tutorial in Part I of this book, you will already be familiar with some of these techniques; this chapter, however, treats these topics in much greater detail.

CREATING A NEW DOCUMENT

To create a new document, use either of the following methods:

- Start Word by clicking on the **Microsoft Word icon** that was added to the Windows Program Manager when you installed the program.

- If Word is already running, choose **File/New** or click the **New button** on the Toolbar.

If you already have a document open when you create a new document through the File/New command, *both* documents will be open simultaneously in Word. See Chapter 26 for information on techniques for managing multiple document windows within Word.

As you saw in Chapter 1, you can open a new document when you start Word. You can also open a new document at any time you are running Word (provided that you have not exceeded the limit of nine open windows) by choosing the **File/New** menu command. You might, for example, be working on an existing document and decide that you want to open a new document. When you create a new document through the File/New command, Word displays the New dialog box (Figure 3.1), which prompts you for the name of the *document template* to be associated with the new document.

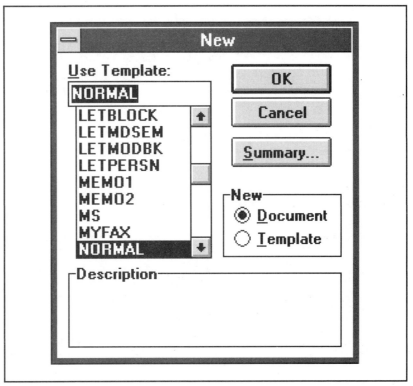

Figure 3.1: The New dialog box, displayed by File/New

In Chapter 19 you will learn how to create and use templates and how to alter NORMAL.DOT. While you are working through the exercises in this book, however, you should use the NORMAL.DOT template, and not make any modifications to it, since the descriptions of program features in the book are based upon the default values initially assigned to this template.

A template is a file that serves as the framework upon which a document is built; each template helps you create a particular type of document, such as a letter, a memo, a brochure, or various other documents. Notice that Word initially selects the template **NORMAL.DOT**, which contains the standard (default) program values. For the exercises in this chapter, simply click the OK button in the New dialog box or press Enter to accept NORMAL.DOT as the template for the document you create. It will then have a standard set of formatting styles, menu designs, and other features.

As an alternative method for creating a new document, you can simply click the **New button** on the Toolbar:

When you click this button, Word immediately opens a new document, based upon the NORMAL.DOT template, *without displaying the New dialog box*.

When Word opens the new document, it assigns it a temporary name (**Document1** if it is the first document you have opened, **Document2** if it is the second, and so on).

OPENING AN EXISTING DOCUMENT

To open an existing Word document, use one of the following methods:

- Start Word by double-clicking on the name of a Word document file displayed in the Windows File Manager.

- Start Word by double-clicking on a special Microsoft Word program icon that you have added to the Windows Program Manager, and to which you have assigned a specific document name (in the command line).

- If Word is already running, choose **File/New** or click on the **Open button** in the Toolbar, and then select the desired document from the Open dialog box.

You can open an existing document either when you run Word for Windows, or at any time after the program has already started. This section describes these two methods.

STARTING WORD AND
OPENING A DOCUMENT SIMULTANEOUSLY

You can start Word and automatically open an existing document by selecting the document name directly from the Windows File Manager. The procedure is as follows:

For complete information on using the Windows File Manager, see the chapter "File Manager" in *Microsoft Windows User's Guide*.

1. Run the Windows File Manager.

2. Open the directory containing the desired Word document.

3. Double-click the name of the document you would like to open, or highlight the name and press Enter. The file must have the .DOC extension.

Word will begin running and will automatically open the selected document. Note that for this method to work, the line

    doc = winword.exe   ^.doc

must be in the EXTENSIONS section of your WIN.INI file. The Word setup program should have added this line for you.

As an alternative method for starting Word, you can add to the Windows Program Manager a special Microsoft Word icon with the name of a document that you access frequently.

For information on using the Program Manager, see the chapter titled "Program Manager" in *Microsoft Windows User's Guide.*

When you double-click this icon, Word will start running and will simultaneously open the specified document. The procedure is as follows:

1. Run the Windows Program Manager.

2. Activate the window for the program group to which you want to add the new icon (i.e., make sure the window is open and its border is highlighted).

3. Choose the **File/New** command from the Program Manager menu.

4. The Program Manager will display a dialog box. Make sure that the **Program Item** option is selected and click on OK.

(An individual icon in the Program Manager is known as a *program item.*)

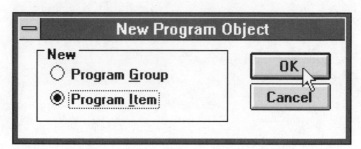

5. The Program Manager will display the Program Item Properties dialog box (Figure 3.2), which allows you to specify the item's icon label and the command to run the new item. Type into this dialog box's **Description:** box the label (in this case the name of the file) you would like displayed with the Microsoft Word icon in the Program Manager.

See Appendix B for an explanation of file path names.

6. Into the same dialog box's **Command Line:** box, type **winword** followed by a space and then the name of the document you want to open. You must specify the full path name for the document, so that the Program Manager can locate it regardless of the current directory. When you click the OK button or press Enter, the new icon will be added to the Program Manager. You can create any number of such Program Manager items as a way of organizing and rapidly accessing your most important documents.

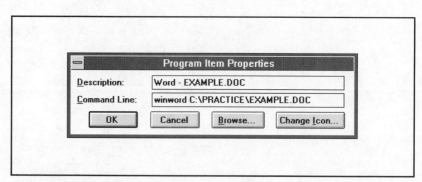

Figure 3.2: Specifying properties for a new Program Manager icon

You can also create a Program Manager icon for running Word and automatically opening the document that was last opened when you previously ran the program. To do this, type winword /mfile1 into the **Command Line:** box of the Program Item Properties dialog box. Be sure to leave a space between winword and /mfile.

OPENING A DOCUMENT FROM WITHIN WORD

 If you do not close the current document before opening a new document through the File/Open command, *both* documents will be open simultaneously in Word. See Chapter 26 for information on techniques for managing multiple document windows in Word.

There are three methods for opening an existing document within Word:

- You can use the Open dialog box
- You can choose a document from the File menu
- You can use the File/Find File menu command.

Method 1: Using the Open Dialog Box

To access the Open dialog box, either choose the **File/Open** menu command or click the **Open button** from the Toolbar:

The Open dialog box is illustrated in Figure 3.3. To open a document, perform the following steps:

1. Make sure that the letter for the disk drive containing the document appears in the **Drives:** box. If it doesn't, click the arrow at the right end of the box to open a list of all drives on your system, and click on the desired drive. This drive will then become the *current* Word drive.

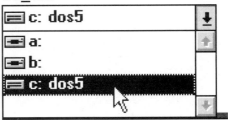

Drives:

c: dos5

a:

b:

c: dos5

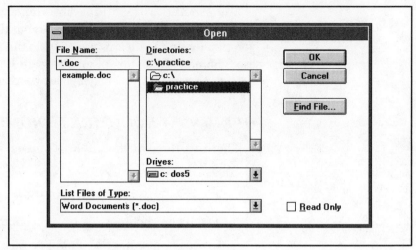

Figure 3.3: The Open dialog box

2. If you do not see the name of the desired document in the **File
   Name:** list box, choose the disk directory that contains this
   document by double-clicking on the directory name in the
   Directories: list box.

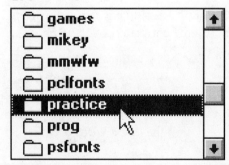

When you double-click on the name of a directory in the
Directories list box, it becomes the current Word directory
(the name of the current directory is displayed above the list
box). The view in the Directories box then changes to show
the parent of the current directory (if any), the current directory, and all subdirectories belonging to the current directory.

Also, each time you select a new directory, all of the document files contained in that directory are listed in the File Name list box. If you do not initially see the directory containing the desired document, you can navigate through the directory system by choosing parent directories or subdirectories until you find the appropriate one.

3. Once you have selected the correct directory, double-click the name of the desired document in the **File Name:** list box.

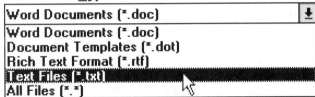

You can also view—and possibly open—files with extensions other than .DOC by choosing the desired type of file from the **List Files of Type:** list.

When you choose an item from this list, the File Name list immediately displays any files matching the selected description that are contained within the current directory. If the file is of a type that can be opened or converted by Word, you can then open one of these files in the same manner as opening a .DOC file. In the next section, you will learn more about opening files that are not in standard Word document format.

The **Read Only** option in the File/Open dialog box is a safeguard that prevents you from modifying the original copy of a document.

If you select this option, Word will open the file and allow you to freely make editing changes. However, you will not be able to save such a document under its original name. If you have changed the document and want to save the modified version, use the **File/Save As** command to save a *copy* of the document under a new name, thus leaving the original version intact.

If you know the name and location of the document you want to open, you can type its name (include the path specification if it is not in the current Word directory) into the **File Name:** text box. See Appendix B for information on specifying path names.

To list files having a specified extension, you can also type the * wild-card character followed by the extension (such as .TXT) directly into the **File Name:** text box.

Method 2: Choosing from a List in the File Menu

If the document you want to open is one that has been open recently, you can use this faster method of opening an existing document. The File menu automatically displays the names of the four most recently opened or saved files in a numbered list at the bottom of the menu. To open one of these files, simply choose the corresponding menu item.

Method 3: Using Find File

You can also access the Find File feature by clicking the **Find button** within the **File/ Open** dialog box.

You can also open a document by means of **File/Find File,** which allows you to search for documents that meet a wide variety of criteria, and to preview the document contents. Once you have located the desired document(s), you can open or print as many as you want. The Find File command is described in detail in Chapter 26.

OPENING A DOCUMENT
CREATED BY ANOTHER PROGRAM

Word must also convert documents that were created by earlier versions of Word. Word, however, *automatically* makes the appropriate conversion, without displaying the Convert File dialog box.

In addition to standard Word for Windows document files, you can open files created by text editors or other word-processing programs. To open such a file, follow the same procedure used for opening a standard Word document. Word will detect that the file is not in standard Word for Windows document format, and will automatically display the Convert File dialog box, illustrated in Figure 3.4. The dialog box lists a variety of file formats, and Word highlights the most appropriate format based upon its analysis of the file (if it doesn't recognize the format, it selects **Text Only**). If Word makes the wrong guess, you should select the correct format description for the document you are opening.

When you save a document you have converted, the original file format will be lost (Word will issue a warning). To preserve the original file, use the **File/ Save As** command to save the document under a new name.

Click OK or press Enter when you are ready to open the file. The program then reads the file and converts it to standard Word for Windows document format; it does *not* work with the file in its original format. Note that the choice of file formats you can read (listed in the Convert File dialog box) depends upon which *converters* have been installed on your computer. The Word package comes with a large set of converters; when you first run the Word *Setup* program, you have a choice of which of these to install. You can run the *Setup* program

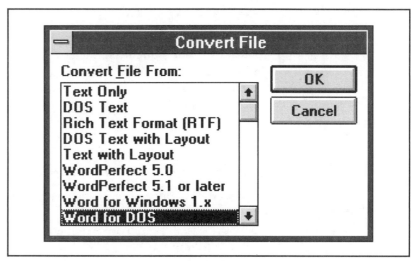

Figure 3.4: The Convert File dialog box

again, at any time, to install additional converters that are supplied with Word or that you have obtained from other sources.

PERFORMING SIMPLE WORD-PROCESSING OPERATIONS

To perform simple word-processing operations:

- Press **Ctrl-Enter** to force a page break within a document.
- Enter foreign language characters or symbols with **Insert/Symbol**.
- Reverse your last editing action by choosing **Edit/Undo**, by pressing **Ctrl-Z**, or by clicking the **Undo button** from the Toolbar. Repeat your last editing action by choosing **Edit/Repeat** or by pressing **F4**.

INSERTING TABS

The Tab key moves the insertion point to the next tab stop, and causes the subsequent character that is typed to be aligned at this stop. (See Chapter 15 for information on setting and using tab stops.) Note, however, that using tabs to create tables of side-by-side information is an obsolete method under Word; employing Word's table feature, described in Chapter 8, is a much easier technique.

PREVENTING LINE BREAKS

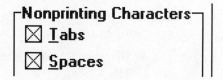 Word may insert a line break following a hyphen. See the first section of Chapter 17 to learn how to instruct Word when and when not to break certain words (specifically, using *optional* and *nonbreaking* hyphens).

As Word performs automatic word wrap, it may insert a line break between any two words (Word places on each line the maximum number of words that can fit between the text margins). If you want to prevent Word from breaking a line between two particular words, you can insert a *nonbreaking* space between these words. You enter a nonbreaking space by typing the **Ctrl-Shift-spacebar** key combination.

Normally, a tab character appears on the screen as one or more spaces, and a nonbreaking space appears as a single space. You can differentiate these two characters by choosing the **Tools/Options** command and then selecting **View** in the **Category:** list within the Options dialog box. The **Tabs** item in the **Nonprinting Characters:** box displays special tab symbols at every tab occurrence, and the **Spaces** item makes both space characters *and* nonbreaking spaces visible.

```
┌─Nonprinting Characters─┐
  ☒ Tabs
  ☒ Spaces
```

Figure 3.5 shows these special characters.

CREATING TEXT BREAKS

As explained in Chapter 1, while you are typing text, you can press the **Enter** key to create a new paragraph. Word will begin inserting characters on a new line, within a new paragraph.

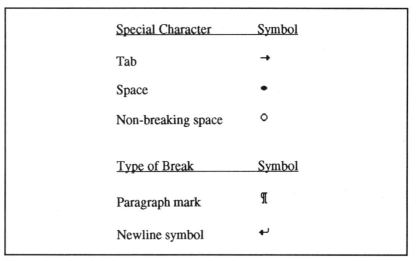

Figure 3.5: Special characters and text breaks

You can press **Shift-Enter** to generate a line break *within* a paragraph. Although this keystroke may seem to have the same effect as pressing Enter, the significant distinction is that all characters you subsequently type will share the paragraph *formatting* that applies to the preceding characters. (Paragraph formatting is explained in Chapter 15.)

When you press Shift-Enter, Word enters a character into the document known as a *newline* (see Figure 3.5). Normally, this character is invisible. However, if you choose the **Tools/Options** command, select the **View** item from the **Category:** list, and check the **Paragraph Marks** item in the dialog box, Word will make the character visible.

You can create a *hard page break* by pressing **Ctrl-Enter**. A hard page break forces Word to begin printing any following characters on a new page. A hard page break is indicated by a tight dotted line extending across the document.

This line comes immediately before a hard page break inserted by pressing **Ctrl-Enter**.

This line comes immediately after a hard page break.

You can also insert a hard page break by choosing the **Insert/Break** menu command, and then selecting the **Page Break** item within the dialog box that Word displays.

Finally, you can insert a hard page break by formatting the paragraph with the **Page Break Before** option, as explained in Chapter 15.

When Word prepares a document for previewing or printing, it automatically divides it into separate pages (a process known as *pagination*). The division between each of these pages is known as a *soft page break*. Like a hard page break, a soft page break is indicated by a dotted line extending across the document; there is a bit less space above the soft page break's dotted line, however, though the dots themselves are spaced further apart.

> This line comes immediately before a soft page break inserted by Word.
> This line comes immediately after a soft page break.

Two other types of document breaks, *column breaks* and *section breaks*, are discussed in Chapter 14.

If you change the formatting or content of the document, the next time Word paginates it will automatically adjust the position of soft page breaks as necessary to maintain the correct document page length. In contrast, Word will not change the position of a hard page break, though you can always manually delete or move a hard page break. (In Chapter 17, you will see how to quickly adjust the position of page breaks within the Print Preview document view.)

To practice entering the different types of characters discussed so far in this section, try to create the short document shown in Figure 3.6. Begin by choosing the **Tools/Options** menu command, select the **View** icon from the **Category:** list, and check the **All** item (if it is not already checked). This will make *all* characters visible on the screen as you type them.

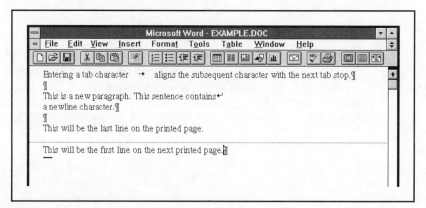

Figure 3.6: An exercise in entering characters

ENTERING SPECIAL SYMBOLS

In addition to the characters pictured on the keyboard, you can enter a wide variety of special characters and symbols into your document. To insert one of these characters, perform the following steps:

1. Place the insertion point at the position in your document where you want to insert the symbol.

2. Choose the **Insert/Symbol** command. Word will display a dialog box showing a wide variety of symbols.

3. If you do not see the symbol you want, choose another *font* (set of characters) from the list labeled **Symbols From:** at the top of the dialog box.

Each time you select a different font within this list, Word displays the entire set of characters belonging to the font. The set of fonts that appears in the list depends upon which fonts you have installed within Windows.

4. Double-click the symbol you want. Word will remove the dialog box and insert the symbol into your document at the position of the insertion point.

Note that Word automatically adjusts the size of the symbol to match the size of the surrounding text.

You can also insert special symbols into your document by entering its ASCII code. Table 3.1 lists some of the useful symbols that can be inserted in this manner. This technique is important, since several of the symbols in Table 3.1 (for example, the em and en dash) cannot usually be inserted using the **Insert/Symbol** menu command (they are typically not included in any of the Windows fonts). Use the following procedure:

1. Make sure that the Num Lock state is active (if the **NUM** indicator does not appear on the status bar, press the Num Lock key).

To see the symbol in your document, the **Field Codes** option on the **View** menu must be disabled (unchecked). Otherwise, you will see the instructions that *generate* the symbol, rather than the symbol itself.

Table 3.1: Several Useful ANSI Characters

SYMBOL:	KEYSTROKE:	DESCRIPTION:
'	Alt-0145	Single opening quotation mark
'	Alt-0146	Single closing quotation mark
"	Alt-0147	Double opening quotation mark
"	Alt-0148	Double closing quotation mark
•	Alt-0149	Bullet
—	Alt-0151	Em dash
–	Alt-0150	En dash
¢	Alt-0162	Cent sign
©	Alt-0169	Copyright symbol
¼	Alt-0188	One-quarter
½	Alt-0189	One-half
¾	Alt-0190	Three-quarters

2. While holding down the **Alt** key, type the number **0** followed by the code given in Table 3.1. You must use the numeric keypad to type the numbers. For example, you can insert a bullet character by typing **0149** on the numeric keypad while holding down Alt.

UNDOING, REDOING, AND REPEATING YOUR EDITING ACTIONS

Undoing and Redoing

In previous versions of Word, the keystroke for issuing the Undo command was Alt-Backspace. You can still use this keystroke if you wish; it is not listed on the menu, however.

The **Undo** command provides another way to correct not only typing errors but also many other types of mistakes made while working with Word. When you issue the Undo command, Word reverses the effect of your most recent action (provided that the action *is* reversible). To issue the Undo command, choose **Edit/Undo**, press **Ctrl-Z**, or click the **Undo button** on the Toolbar.

Ctrl-Z and the Undo button immediately undo the last action, unless the action is not reversible. If the action is not reversible, Word simply beeps.

When you choose the Undo command from the Edit menu, however, you will notice that the menu item (which is at the top of the menu) is labeled with the name of the action that will be reversed. For example, if you have just typed several characters, the label will read *Undo Typing*, or if you have just deleted some characters with the Del key, the label will be *Undo Edit Clear*. If the action cannot be reversed, the label will read *Can't Undo* followed by the name of your last action. Thus, the Edit/Undo method can be more useful than Ctrl-Z or the Toolbar's Undo button in that you can verify exactly which actions cannot be reversed. It is also helpful in situations where you may be uncertain what your last action was!

The Undo command itself is among the reversible Word actions. Therefore, if you choose the Undo command to reverse an action, and then immediately choose Undo again, you will reverse the undoing, thereby restoring the effect of the original action (in other words, redoing it, and the menu label will read *Undo Undo*). For example, if you move the insertion point, type a sentence, and then issue the Undo command, the sentence will be erased. If you immediately issue the Undo command again, the sentence will be restored. If you continue to choose Undo, the sentence will alternately be erased and restored.

The Undo command in Word for Windows reverses only the immediately preceding action, in contrast to some text editors that continue to reverse prior editing actions one by one as you repeat the Undo command.

Repeating Your Actions

The **Repeat** command enables you to repeat your last editing or formatting action. Note, however, that just as not every action is reversible through the Undo command, not every action is repeatable through the Repeat command. You issue this command by pressing **F4** or by choosing **Edit/Repeat**.

When you press F4, the last action is immediately repeated (provided that the action *is* repeatable). If the action is not repeatable, Word simply beeps.

The Repeat command displayed on the Edit menu identifies the action that will be repeated. For example, if you had just typed some characters, the title would read *Repeat Typing,* and if you had just deleted a character by pressing Del, the title would be *Repeat Edit Clear.* If the previous action cannot be repeated, the command will read *Can't Repeat* followed by the name of your last action. The Edit/ Repeat method is therefore more useful than the F4 method in situations where you may be uncertain whether the last action can be repeated, or if you are not sure exactly what action will be repeated when you issue the Repeat command.

SAVING A DOCUMENT

To save a document, use one of the following methods:

- To save the document you are working on under its current name, choose the **File/Save** command, or click the **Save button** in the Toolbar.

- To save the document under a new name, leaving the original document file intact on the disk, choose the **File/ Save As** command, or press **F12** or **Alt-F2**, and enter the new name.

- You can also use the **File/Save As** command if you want to save a copy of the document in a different format, or if you want to protect the document or change the save options.

- Choose the **File/Save All** command to save all modified documents that are currently open, as well as any modified templates associated with an open document.

It is important to remember that while you are creating or modifying a document, your work is saved only in the computer's temporary memory until you explicitly save the document in a disk file.

Each time you save the document, the current document contents are written to a permanent file on the disk. If the power is interrupted, or if the computer stops operating due to a software or hardware problem, data stored in temporary memory is lost; data written to a disk file, however, is preserved.

In Chapters 1 and 2, you learned the basic method for saving a Word document. In this section, you will learn additional information concerning the three commands Word provides for saving documents—**Save**, **Save As**, and **Save All**—and the options available with these commands.

THE SAVE COMMAND

Normally, when you want to save the document you are working on, you simply issue the Save command. This command can be issued by choosing the **File/Save**, by pressing **Shift-F12** or **Alt-Shift-F2**, or by clicking the **Save button** on the Toolbar.

If the document has already been saved, the Save command immediately saves it under its current name, which is the name that appears on the title bar. In this case, Word displays a message in the status bar, but does not prompt you for further information.

If, however, you are saving a new document for the first time, the Save command performs two special actions. First, it actually activates the *Save As* command (described in the next section). As you will see, the Save As command prompts you to specify a document name. You must provide a name because Word recognizes that the name it initially assigns to a new file (a name such as Document1 or Document2) is only temporary.

Second, before the Save As command saves the new document, it displays a dialog box prompting you for document *summary information*. As you will see in Chapter 26, summary information is used primarily for helping you retrieve the document later. You do not *need* to

You can add or revise the document summary information at any time the document is open by choosing **File/Summary Info**. See Chapter 26 for a discussion on maintaining and using document summary information.

supply any of this information to save the file; in fact, for our purposes at this time, when Word displays the summary information dialog box you should simply click the OK button or press Enter to complete the saving process.

THE SAVE AS COMMAND

You will already be familiar with the operation of the Save As command from Part I because the Save As command is automatically invoked when you first save a new document. You might also want to choose this command, rather than the Save command, in the following situations:

- When you want to save a copy of the document under a new name.

- When you want to save a copy of the document in a different format (such as pure text, or the format used by another word processor).

- When you want to select one or more of the options that control the way Word saves documents.

Each of these uses for the Save As command will be discussed shortly.

You can issue the Save As command by choosing **File/Save As** or by pressing the **F12** or **Alt-F2** keystroke. Word will display the dialog box shown in Figure 3.7.

If you have previously saved the document, the name you assigned will appear in the **File Name:** text box at the top of the dialog window. If you simply click the OK button or press Enter, the Save As command will have the same effect as the Save command; that is, it will immediately save the document under its existing name.

If the document is being saved for the first time, the text box will be empty and you *must* enter a file name.

If you enter a new name or specify a different directory, Word will create a *copy* of the document under the new name or in the new location, leaving the original document file unchanged. Word will also display the new name within the title bar, and will use this name whenever you subsequently save the document.

The Save As command is thus useful for creating an exact copy of a document under a new name, *or a copy under the same name but within a new directory.* You can also use it to preserve copies of various versions

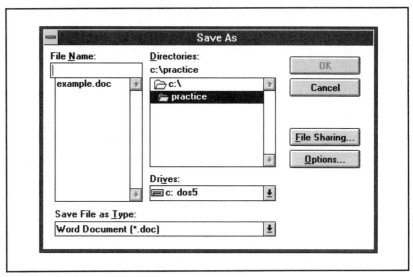

Figure 3.7: The Save As dialog box

of a document. Each time you create a new document version, you can use the Save As command to save it under a new name.

When you double-click on the name of a directory in the **Directories:** list box, it becomes the current Word directory, the name of which is displayed above the list box. Setting the current directory in the Save As dialog box affects the current directory used by other commands, such as Open. Also, the directory you set will be remembered the next time you use the Save As command.

If you do not include an extension in the name you specify when saving a file, Word automatically adds the extension .DOC. If the document name and location you specify is the same as that of an existing file, Word will ask you if you want to replace the original file. Don't click OK unless you are sure you want to erase the original file.

Also, the first time you save a document under a new name, Word will prompt you for document summary information, as described previously. As mentioned, you should forgo the summary information at this point until you learn more of its uses, which will be detailed in Chapter 26.

Finally, before you click the OK button or press Enter, thereby dismissing the Save As dialog box, you might want to choose one or more of the options discussed in the following sections.

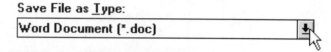

Saving in a Different Format

Just as Word allows you to open and convert files having various formats, it also permits you to save a copy of a file in one of a variety of different formats. To create a copy of the document you are working on in a specific format, use the Save As command to specify the file name and location, as described previously in this section. Before clicking the OK button or pressing Enter, however, choose the desired format from the **Save File As Type:** list at the bottom of the dialog. (Word initially selects the Word Document format, which saves the document as a current-version Word for Windows document file.)

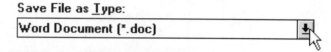
Save File as **T**ype:

Word Document (*.doc)

The formats that you will see in this list depend upon which converters you have installed. As you saw in the section on how to open documents, when you first run the Word *Setup* program you have a choice of which converters to install. You can run the *Setup* program again, at any time, to install additional converters.

File Sharing

The **File Sharing** button in the Save As dialog box allows you to control access to the document you are saving. You can assign a *password* to the document so that no one will be able to open the document without entering the password, and you can *lock* the document so that other users will be able to open and read it but will not be able to modify it. To control document access, click the **File Sharing** button before saving the file.

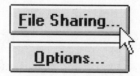

Word will display the File Sharing dialog box, illustrated in Figure 3.8.

When you install a given converter, for example the one for WordStar 4.0, it will be available for both opening and saving a file in the supported format.

When you save a document in a format other than the current-version Word for Windows document format, you *must* specify a new file name or directory; Word does not allow you to overwrite the original Word document with the document copy in the new format. Otherwise, if you later issue the Save command, the document is saved under its original name and in standard Word format. Saving a document in a different format merely makes a copy of the document having the specified format; it does not affect the name or format of the document that is still open in Word.

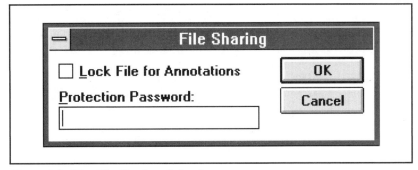

Figure 3.8: The File Sharing dialog box

To assign a password, do the following:

1. Type the desired password into the **Protection Password:** box. As you type the password, Word displays a series of * characters rather than the letters you type (in case someone is looking over your shoulder!).

2. Click the OK button. Word now displays the Confirm Password dialog box.

3. Type the password again, and click OK.

Once you close the file, neither you nor anyone else will be able to open the document without supplying the password you specified. You can change or remove the password at any time the document is open by repeating the procedure outlined above. To remove the password, simply delete the contents of the Protection Password box.

If you select the **Lock for Annotations** option in the File Sharing dialog box, Word preserves the original document content, while allowing one or more reviewers running their own copies of Word for Windows on their own computers to read and comment on the manuscript. This works because when a document is saved Word stores the name of the author together with the document text. (Unless you change it in the Summary Information dialog box, Word assumes the author is the same as the program user, since the user entered this name when he or she installed the program. If a document is locked, Word allows you to modify it only if the name of the author stored with the document matches the name of the program user.

Annotations are notes that you append to specific locations in a document. They are discussed in Chapter 25.

Specifying Save Options

The **Options** button in the Save As dialog box enables you to set several options that affect the way Word saves documents.

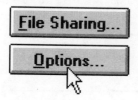

Word will open the Options dialog box, and allow you to set the following options:

- **Always Create Backup Copy**
- **Allow Fast Saves**
- **Prompt for Summary Information**
- **Automatic Save**

Whatever settings you select here will affect not only the current save operation, but all future saves, until you explicitly change the option(s) again. These four options can also be set by issuing the **Tools/Options** command and then selecting the **Save** icon in the **Category:** list. They are described in detail in Chapter 23.

THE SAVE ALL COMMAND

Document templates and the items that may be assigned to them are discussed in Chapter 19.

When you choose **File/Save All**, Word saves *all* open documents that have unsaved changes, as well as any document template that you have modified while working with a document. A document template is modified whenever you add, delete, or change a macro, a glossary entry, a keyboard assignment, a menu assignment, a Toolbar button, or a style (when you have chosen the Add to Template option).

When you issue the Save All command, Word prompts you before saving each unsaved item. The same sequence of prompts occurs as when you quit the program without saving a modified document or template.

4

Navigating
through a Document

CHAPTER 4

AS YOU HAVE SEEN, THE INSERTION POINT MARKS the location in the document where the insertion or deletion of characters takes place. Once you have entered text into a new document, or once you have opened an existing document, you need to be able to move the insertion point efficiently to any position in the text.

This chapter explains each of the following methods that Word provides for moving the insertion point or scrolling the document within the window:

- Using the keyboard
- Using the mouse
- Using the Go To command
- Other methods

The chapter concludes with an explanation of the status bar at the bottom of the window, which shows you the current location of the insertion point within the document.

USING THE KEYBOARD

To navigate through a document using the keyboard:

- Use the **arrow keys** to move character by character, or line by line.
- Press **PgUp** or **PgDn** to move up or down in the document by one "page" (the number of lines that can fit within the window).
- Use any of the other key combinations listed in Table 4.1.

In Chapter 2, you saw how to use the arrow keys to move the insertion point one character position at a time in the desired direction. Word provides several other simple keystrokes for quickly moving the insertion point to various positions in the document. These keystrokes are summarized in Table 4.1.

Table 4.1: Keystrokes for Moving the Insertion Point

PRESS THIS KEY:	TO MOVE TO:
←	Previous character
→	Following character
↑	Previous line
↓	Following line
Ctrl-←	Previous word
Ctrl-→	Next word
Home	Beginning of line
End	End of line
Ctrl-↑	Previous paragraph
Ctrl-↓	Following paragraph
Ctrl-PgUp	First character in window
Ctrl-PgDn	Last character in window
PgUp	Previous page
PgDn	Following page
Ctrl-Home	Beginning of document
Ctrl-End	End of document

As you can see in the table, pressing the PgUp key moves you toward the beginning of the document by one "page"—page being defined as the amount of document that can fit within the current height of the document window. Similarly, the PgDn key moves you toward the end of the document by one page.

The Go To command, described later in the chapter, also allows you to move to various document positions using keyboard commands.

USING THE MOUSE

To navigate through a document using the mouse:

- Use the **vertical scroll bar** to scroll toward the beginning or end of the document.
- Use the **horizontal scroll bar** to scroll toward the left or right edge of the document. (This only works if the entire document width doesn't fit in the window.)
- Use the position of the **scroll box** in the vertical scroll bar to gauge your relative position within a large document.

You can use the mouse to scroll vertically through the document by means of the vertical scroll bar, and horizontally through the document by means of the horizontal scroll bar. When you first install Word, both of these bars are displayed. You can hide either the vertical or the horizontal scroll bar by choosing **Tools/Options**, then selecting the **View** icon from the **Category:** list, and unchecking the **Vertical Scroll Bar** or **Horizontal Scroll Bar** option.

Table 4.2 summarizes vertical scrolling techniques with the mouse, and Table 4.3 summarizes horizontal scrolling techniques.

A couple of important notes about scrolling: First, a "page" is the amount of document that can fit within the current vertical dimension of the document window. Second, normally you can scroll left only until you reach the left margin; however, if you press the Shift

Table 4.2: Vertical Scroll Bar Techniques

PERFORM THIS ACTION:	TO SCROLL:
Click up arrow	One line up
Click down arrow	One line down
Click scroll bar above scroll box	One page up
Click scroll bar below scroll box	One page down
Drag scroll box	To any relative position

Table 4.3: Horizontal Scroll Bar Techniques

PERFORM THIS ACTION:	TO SCROLL:
Click left arrow	Several columns to the left
Click left arrow while holding down the Shift key	Left into the margin area
Click right arrow	Several columns to the right
Click scroll bar to left of scroll box	One page toward the left margin
Click scroll bar to right of scroll box	One page toward the right margin
Drag scroll box	To any relative horizontal position

key while clicking the left scroll bar arrow, you can continue scrolling into the left margin. (You might need to scroll into the left margin to view a paragraph that has been assigned a negative left indent—that is, a paragraph that extends into the left margin. Setting indents is described in Chapter 15.)

Scrolling with a scroll bar causes Word to display a different portion of the document within the window. *Scroll bar actions, however, do not move the position of the insertion point.* If you have scrolled away from the insertion point and then type a character, the view in the window will instantly scroll back to the portion of the document containing the insertion point (and the new character). You can use these features to your advantage; the following typical scenario shows how you could quickly view another document position without losing the current position of the insertion point:

1. You are entering text into a document, and want to temporarily view a previous section of the document.

2. You click the vertical scroll bar above the scroll box to move up through the document, one "page" at a time. After clicking three times, you find the portion of the document you want to see. The insertion point will no longer be visible within the window.

3. To return to your original position, you type a character (the next character you were going to type, or any other character). Word instantly jumps back to the portion of the document containing the insertion point.

4. You resume entering text, or delete the character that brought you back to the insertion point and then continue with your work.

As you can see, the insertion point is not always located within the portion of the document displayed in the window. The insertion point, however, will instantly move to the first character position currently within the window if you press an arrow key or issue any command that moves the insertion point, such as Edit/Go To. For example, if you scroll the document vertically so that the insertion point is no longer visible, and then press the right-arrow key, the insertion point will initially move to the first character position in the window (in the upper left corner) and will then move one character position to the right.

USING THE GO TO COMMAND

The Go To command moves the insertion point to a precise location in the document. There are two ways to issue the Go To command. First, you can choose **Edit/Go To**, and Word will display the dialog box shown in Figure 4.1. Type the desired target location into the text box—using one of the methods described in this section—or choose one of the *bookmarks* (explained later in this section) to send the insertion point directly to a position you have previously defined as a target location.

Alternatively, you can press **F5** and type the desired location or bookmark name at the prompt that Word displays within the status bar.

(Pressing F5 twice displays the same dialog box activated by the Edit/ Go To menu command.)

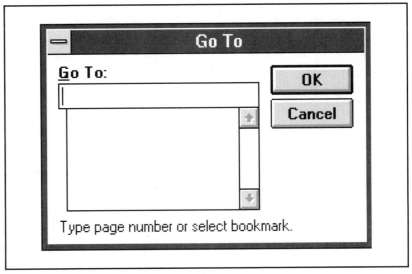

Figure 4.1: The Edit/Go To dialog box

If you have issued the **Search** command (explained in Chapter 6) since the last time you issued the Go To command, the **Shift-F4** keystroke will repeat the Search command rather than the Go To command.

If you decide after moving elsewhere in the document that you want to return to the location specified in the last Go To command, you can accomplish this immediately by pressing **Shift-F4**.

SPECIFYING THE TARGET LOCATION

Whether you have chosen the Edit/Go To menu command or have pressed the F5 key, you can express the desired target location by specifying one or more of the following document features:

- Page
- Section
- Line
- Percentage of the document
- Footnote
- Annotation
- Bookmark
- A combination of elements

When specifying a location, do **not** type a space between the **p, s, l, %, f,** or **a** character and the associated number.

Go to a Page

To go to a specific page in the document, type **p** followed immediately by the page number, or simply type the page number by itself. For example, to go to page 5, type **p5** or **5**. (To go to the very *next* page, simply type **p** or leave the specification field blank.) When you press Enter (or click the OK button in the Go To dialog box), Word will immediately place the insertion point at the first character position within the specified page.

Note that before you can go to a specified page in a document, the document must be *paginated*, or divided into pages. If the automatic pagination feature is enabled, Word will automatically paginate the document while you work on it. (This feature is normally enabled when you first install Word; see Chapter 23 for instructions on turning the feature on or off.) If automatic pagination is not enabled, the document is paginated when you print it, or when you issue the **Tools/Repaginate Now** menu command, discussed in Chapter 17. The document will also be paginated up to the page you are currently viewing when you activate the **Print Preview** or **Page View** mode, also discussed in Chapter 17.

When you specify a page number, the Go To command simply counts pages from the beginning of the document. It does not necessarily conform to printed page numbers in headers or footers (discussed in Chapter 10). For example, although you may have specified that printed page numbers begin with 100 on the first page of the document, the Go To command still regards the first page as number 1.

To go to a location a specified number of pages *after* the current page, type a + (plus symbol) in front of the page number. To go to a page a specified number of pages *before* the current page, type a - (minus symbol or hyphen) in front of the page number. For example, to move five pages forward in the document, type **p + 5** or simply **+ 5**.

Go to a Section

To go to a specified document section, type **s** followed by the section number. (To go to the very *next* section, simply type **s**.) To go to a section a given number of sections *after* the current section, type a + (plus) in front of the section number. To go to a section a given number of sections *before* the current section, type a - (minus or hyphen) in front of the number.

When you specify a section with the Go To command, Word will place the insertion point at the *first character position* within that section.

Go to a Line

To go to a specific line within the document, type l (the letter ''el'') followed by the line number. To move a given number of lines toward the end of the document, type a + (plus) in front of the line number, and to move a given number of lines toward the beginning of the document, type a - (minus or hyphen) in front of the line number.

When going to a specific line, the Go To command simply counts lines from the beginning of the document (the first line in the document is number 1). It ignores any line numbering you may have enabled for one or more document sections that do not necessarily start with 1. Word places the insertion point at the first character position within the specified line.

Go to a Location a Given Percentage through the Document

You can also move to a point that is a given percentage of the way through the document by typing % followed by the percentage. For example, to go to a point midway through the document, type %50. The % sign can also *follow* the number; for example, 50%.

Go to a Footnote or Annotation

To go to a footnote, type f followed by the number of the footnote, and to go to an annotation, type a followed by the number of the annotation. The Go To command numbers footnotes and annotations from the beginning of the document, including *all* footnotes or annotations. It ignores the numbers assigned to specific footnotes or annotations.

You can also move to a footnote or annotation a given number of footnotes or annotations *after* the current one by typing a + (plus) in front of the number, and you can move a specific number of footnotes or annotations toward the *beginning* of the document by typing a - (minus or hyphen) in front of the number.

Go to a Bookmark

Using bookmarks, you can tag an entire set of document locations, and then go instantly to any one of them. A bookmark is a name that you assign to a specific document position. To assign a bookmark, place the insertion point at the desired location, choose the **Insert/ Bookmark** menu command, type the name you want to assign the bookmark, and click the OK button or press Enter. Figure 4.2 shows the Bookmark dialog box.

A bookmark name must begin with a letter; it can contain only letters, numbers, or underlines (_); and it must be from 1 to 20 characters in length.

The dialog box also displays a list containing any bookmarks that have already been assigned. Selecting one of these bookmarks displays its name in the box at the top of the list. You can delete the bookmark by clicking the **Delete button**.

Alternatively, you can bypass the Bookmark dialog box and assign a bookmark to the current position of the insertion point in your document by pressing **Ctrl-Shift-F5** and typing the bookmark name at the prompt that appears within the status bar (following the same rules just stated for typing a bookmark name into the Insert/ Bookmark dialog box).

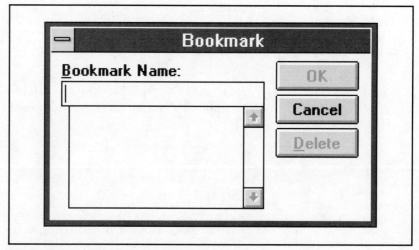

Figure 4.2: The Bookmark dialog box

Once you have defined a bookmark, you can quickly move the insertion point to the corresponding document position by issuing the Go To command and typing the bookmark name when prompted for the target location. Alternatively, if the Go To dialog box is displayed, you can just double-click the bookmark name.

Note that you can also assign a bookmark to an entire block of characters, rather than to a single insertion-point position. To make such an assignment, you must first *select* the block, and then assign the bookmark as just explained. (Techniques for selecting text are discussed in Chapter 5.) If you specify a bookmark that refers to a block of text, the Go To command will select that block rather than simply moving the insertion point to a position within the block.

Go to a Location Specified as a Combination of Elements

When specifying a target location for the Go To command, you can *combine* any of the elements discussed previously in this section, subject to the following two rules:

1. If you specify a bookmark or document percentage (%), you cannot also specify a page, line, or other element.

2. The specification may contain only *one* of the following elements: line (l), footnote (f), or annotation (a). (Specifying more than one of these elements would make no sense.)

To understand how multiple elements combine, it is useful to divide the elements into the following three levels:

Level 1:   Section

Level 2:   Page

Level 3:   Line, Footnote, or Annotation

This division is based upon the fact that a section can contain pages, and a page can contain lines, footnotes, or annotations.

Here are some examples of how you can combine elements:

s2p5   Go to the fifth page from the beginning of section 2 of the document.

p5l8	Go to the eighth line on page 5 of the document (the pages are counted from the beginning of the document).
s3f5	Go to the fifth footnote from the beginning of section 3 of the document.
s2p5l3	Go to the third line on the fifth page of section 2 of the document.

When you specify a number, the Go To command always counts from the beginning of the document, section, or page (depending on the specification) and ignores any numbering you may have *assigned* to an element (such as the page numbers or footnote numbers that will appear on the printed document copy).

As you saw in the previous sections of this chapter, when you specify a single element the Go To command always counts from the beginning of the document. For example, p5 means the fifth page from the beginning of the document. If, however, you include a higher-level element in the specification, the Go To command counts from the beginning of the higher-level element. For example, s2p5 means the fifth page from the beginning of section 2 (regardless of the page number that might appear on the printed page).

A final guideline: you can include the + or - symbol (to specify a relative move) in a combined specification, but only for the highest-level element. Thus, the expression s-2p3 is allowed (meaning the third page in the section that comes two sections before the current section); but, the expression s2p-3 is not allowed.

THE GO BACK COMMAND (SHIFT-F5)

Pressing Shift-F5 moves the insertion point back to its *previous location*, that is, the most recent position where an action, such as one of the following, occurred:

- You inserted or deleted characters.
- You issued a Go To command.
- The insertion point was positioned via a Go To command.
- You saved the document.

If you press Shift-F5 again, the insertion point will move to the next most recent position. Each subsequent press will continue to move the insertion point to prior positions. Word, however, remembers only three locations before the present one; therefore, on the fourth consecutive press of Shift-F5, the insertion point is returned to the location where Shift-F5 was first pressed.

One very useful application for the Go Back command is when you first open an existing document, to bring you to the point in the document where you last issued a Save command before closing the document or exiting from Word.

OTHER NAVIGATION METHODS

To move efficiently to specific positions in a document, or to increase the speed of scrolling:

- Issue the **Edit/Find** command to move to the first occurrence of a specific sequence of characters or character formatting.

- Choose **View/Draft** to enable draft view. In draft view, character formatting and graphics are not displayed, and scrolling is faster.

- Choose the **View/Outline** to enable outline view, which gives you an overview of your document, and allows you to move rapidly to any topic in the text.

- Choose **Tools/Options** and select the **View button** in the **Category:** list. You can then set window options for increasing the efficiency of scrolling through the document.

This section summarizes the following additional ways to move the insertion point to specific document positions, or to enhance the efficiency of scrolling through a document:

- Using the Edit/Find command

- Employing other document views

- Choosing efficient display options

Most of these methods are discussed in detail in other chapters of the book.

EDIT/FIND

The Edit/Find command allows you to search for a particular sequence of characters, or for a particular format, within the document. The command moves you to the first occurrence of the characters or format, and highlights it. Chapter 6 discusses Edit/Find in detail.

You can also use this command or the **Tools/Revision Marks** command to search for *revision marks* in your document. Revision marks are discussed in Chapter 25.

DRAFT AND OUTLINE VIEW

See Chapter 17 for a summary of all the document views provided by Word.

You saw in Chapter 2 that Word provides several alternative document views, which are different ways of looking at and working with your document. The default document view is called *normal* view. In Chapter 2, you also saw the *print preview* document view. Two other document views are mentioned here because they can help you navigate through your document: *draft view* and *outline view*.

Normally, Word displays characters and paragraph formatting so that the document's appearance on the screen is quite similar to its printed appearance; in general, Word for Windows abides by the WYSIWYG—what you see is what you get—rule. However, displaying various fonts and other features required to simulate the printed document is time-consuming. You can increase the speed of scrolling through the document by switching into *draft view*. In draft view, all characters are displayed using a single typeface and character size (employing a font known as the *system font*). Also, all character enhancements, such as bold and italic, are displayed as simple underlined characters. Furthermore, draft view eliminates the time-consuming display of graphics. Draft view is especially valuable for slower computer models.

As you will see in Chapter 17, you can also save time when *printing* your document by selecting the **Draft** option in the **File/Print** dialog box.

To activate draft view, choose **View/Draft**. To deactivate draft view, choose this menu item again.

In *outline view,* you can hide or reveal entire blocks of text in your document. Outline view not only affords you an overview of the structure of your document, but also allows you to move instantly to any desired topic within the document. Outline view is discussed in detail in Chapter 24.

DISPLAY OPTIONS FOR EFFICIENT SCROLLING

By choosing **Tools/Options** and selecting the **View** button in the **Category:** list, you can set a number of options that affect the way a document is displayed in the window. These options are illustrated in Figure 4.3.

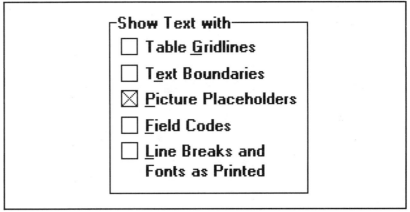

Figure 4.3: The **Show Text with area of the** View/Preferences dialog box

Making the following settings can increase the speed of scrolling through a document:

1. Do *not* select the **Line Breaks and Fonts as Printed** option. This way, Word will not have to calculate the printed length of each line and insert line breaks at the exact positions where they will occur on the printed page.

2. Select the **Picture Placeholders** option. Word will then display any graphic image you have inserted into your document as an empty box (the same size as the graphic), rather than engaging in the time-consuming process of fully drawing the graphic each time it appears within the document window.

3. Do *not* select the **Table Gridlines** option. Word will then be relieved of the task of drawing lines around each cell of any table that appears within the document window.

THE STATUS BAR

The status bar displayed at the bottom of the window can help you navigate through a document by showing you the current position of the insertion point. The relevant status bar fields are labeled in Figure 4.4.

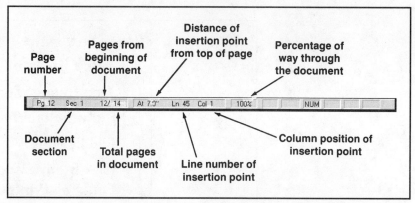

Figure 4.4: Status bar fields showing your current document position

The following is an explanation of each of these fields, going from left to right along the status bar:

Pg   The number of the page containing the insertion point. If you have included a page number in a header or footer, the page number in the Pg field is the number that would be printed for the current page. By default, page numbering begins with 1 at the beginning of the current section.

Sec   The number of the document section that contains the insertion point. Sections are always numbered beginning with 1 at the start of the document. See Chapter 14 for an explanation of sections.

c/t   The first number, *c*, is the number of the current page, and the second number, *t*, is the total number of pages in the document. Word derives both of these numbers by simply counting pages *from the beginning of the document*. These numbers are not necessarily the same as page numbers printed in headers and footers (which may not start from 1). Thus, the number c might not equal the Pg field.

At The distance of the insertion point from the top edge of the page.

Ln The number of the line containing the insertion point. Lines are numbered starting at the beginning of the current page.

Col The column containing the insertion point. Columns are numbered beginning with 1 at the leftmost position within the paragraph, and increase by 1 with each character position to the right.

Note that the page numbers displayed in the status bar are not necessarily accurate unless the document has recently been paginated, as described previously in this chapter (in the section ''Go to a Page'').

5

Using Block
Editing Commands

CHAPTER 5

IN THIS CHAPTER, YOU WILL LEARN HOW TO manipulate entire *blocks* of text and graphics, ranging from single characters to an entire document.

To work with a block, you must first *select* (or highlight) it. You can then delete it, copy it, or move it to another location. Each procedure is described in this chapter in detail. Also, selecting a block of text is often the first step in applying formatting, which is discussed in Part III.

SELECTING TEXT AND GRAPHICS

Many editing and formatting commands involve two distinct steps: selecting the text or graphic and manipulating the selection. For example, to delete a line, you first select all characters on the line and then press **Del**.

When you select a block of data, Word highlights the selection on the screen. For example, if your system normally displays black on white, a selected block will appear as white on black.

It is important to distinguish the *insertion point* from the *selection*. As you have seen, the insertion point (or cursor) is the *position* where characters are inserted into the document. A selection is a highlighted area that *encompasses* at least one character. These two elements cannot be present at the same time.

Word provides many techniques for selecting text or graphics. Choose the one that is most efficient for the size of block you want to select. The techniques are divided into those that use the keyboard and those that use the mouse.

Although this chapter frequently refers to blocks of text, the techniques given here can be used to manipulate text, graphics, or a combination of the two. When performing a block-editing command, a graphic image (called a *picture*) is treated as a single character.

In this chapter it is assumed that you are in one of the standard editing views (that is, *normal* and *page layout* view). The *outline* document view provides many special, highly efficient ways of working with blocks and is discussed in Chapter 24.

See Chapter 8 for an explanation of the techniques for selecting within a Word *table*.

SELECTING WITH THE KEYBOARD

Use one of the following methods to select text with the keyboard:

- Hold down **Shift** and press an arrow key to select text character by character or line by line.

- Hold down **Shift** and press **Home, End, PgUp**, or **PgDn** to quickly select larger blocks.

- Press **F8** repeatedly to select progressively larger blocks of text.

- Press **Ctrl-5** (5 on the keypad) to select the entire document.

- Press **Ctrl-Shift-F8** to enter column-select mode.

You can label a frequently used selection using a *bookmark*. Assign the selection a bookmark as explained in Chapter 4. Then, when you choose **Edit/Go To** and specify the bookmark, Word will select the entire block.

The easiest way to select a small block of text is to press an arrow key while holding down the Shift key. First, position the insertion point at one end of the block of text you want to select. Then, hold down **Shift** and press the appropriate arrow key—repeatedly if necessary—to select the desired area. The right-arrow key extends the selection to the right, while the left-arrow key extends it to the left.

If you press the down-arrow key while holding down Shift, Word moves the insertion point down one line and selects *all* characters in between.

Try the following to practice selecting:

1. Open a new document and type in the text shown in Figure 5.1.

2. Create the selection shown in Figure 5.1 by placing the cursor in front of the word **you** on the third line. While holding down Shift, press the down-arrow key once and then hold down the right-arrow key until the highlight encompasses the comma following the word **line**. Your screen should now look like Figure 5.1.

3. Cancel the selection by pressing any arrow key.

Keep this document on your screen; in a moment you'll use it to practice some other editing techniques.

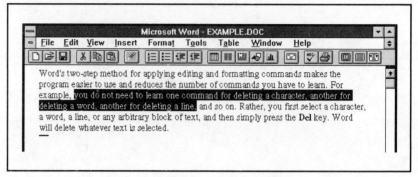

Figure 5.1: A sample paragraph showing selected text

Pressing the up-arrow key along with Shift moves the insertion point up one line, and, like the down-arrow key, selects all characters that fall between. If you want to select a *rectangular* block of text, use one of the column selection techniques discussed in the section "Selecting Rectangular Blocks."

As an alternative to selecting text or graphics with Shift, you can press **F8** to turn on *extend-selection* mode. When you activate this mode, the letters **EXT** appear in the status bar, and pressing one of the direction keys will extend the selection as if Shift were held down. Pressing F8 twice will select the word containing the insertion point. Successively, pressing F8 will select the entire sentence, the paragraph, the section, and finally, the whole document. To turn off extend-selection mode, press **Esc**. It will turn off automatically if you execute an editing or formatting command.

Use the practice document you just created to try out extend-selection mode.

1. Place the cursor in front of the word **you** and press F8 once.

2. Press the down-arrow key once and then hold down the right-arrow key until the selection covers the comma following the word **line**.

3. Remove the selection by pressing Esc and then an arrow key.

Keep the document on your screen.

When extend-selection mode is active, you can type a letter to expand the selection to the next occurrence of that letter. For example, if you press F8 and then type the character **a**, Word will select all text or graphics from the current insertion point through the first occurrence of the letter **a**. Type **a** again to further extend the selection. When you are finished, press Esc to turn off extend-selection mode.

Finally, you can use any of the following keystrokes to select the entire document:

- **Ctrl-5** (5 on the numeric keypad)
- **Ctrl-Home**, then **Ctrl-Shift-End**
- **Ctrl-End**, then **Ctrl-Shift-Home**

You can also choose **Edit/Select All**.

Selecting Rectangular Blocks

 See the section "Deleting a Column of Text" for a practice exercise illustrating column selection.

To select a rectangular block of text of more than one line, you must first activate *column-selection* mode by pressing **Ctrl-Shift-F8**. When this mode is active, the words **COL** appear in the status bar, and pressing an arrow key extends a rectangular selection in the corresponding direction. Unlike the selection methods described above, column selection does *not* include all text between the starting and ending positions, but only the text that falls within a rectangular block.

Like extend-selection mode, column-selection mode is terminated when you issue an editing or formatting command or press **Esc**.

Table 5.1 summarizes keyboard-selection methods.

SELECTING WITH THE MOUSE

Use one of the following methods to select text with the mouse:

- Hold down the **left mouse button,** and drag the highlight over the text you want to select.
- Click on one end of the block you want to select, then click on the other end while holding down **Shift** (the **Shift-Click** method).
- **Double-click** to select a whole word or click while pressing **Ctrl** to select an entire sentence.

- Click or drag the mouse pointer in the **selection bar** to quickly select larger blocks of text. The selection bar is the window area to the left of the text; the mouse pointer is an arrow in this area.

- To select the entire document, click in the selection bar while holding down **Ctrl.**

- To select a **column** of text, hold down the **right mouse button** and drag the highlight.

Table 5.1: Keyboard Methods for Selecting Text or Graphics

TO SELECT	PRESS
Following character	Shift-→, or F8 then →
Preceding character	Shift-←, or F8 then ←
Following line	Shift-↓, or F8 then ↓
Preceding line	Shift-↑, or F8 then ↑
Through end of line	Shift-End, or F8 then End
Through beginning of line	Shift-Home, or F8 then Home
Through following page	Shift-PgDn, or F8 then PgDn
Through preceding page	Shift-PgUp, or F8 then PgUp
Current word	F8 twice
Current sentence	F8 three times
Current paragraph	F8 four times
Current section	F8 five times
Entire document	F8 six times, or Ctrl-5 (on numeric keypad), or Ctrl-Home then Ctrl-Shift-End
Through a given character	F8 then character
Rectangular block	Ctrl-Shift-F8, then arrow key, Home, End, PgUp, or PgDn

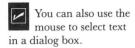 You can also use the mouse to select text in a dialog box.

To select a block with the mouse, place the mouse pointer at either end of the desired block, press the left mouse button, and while holding down the button, drag the highlight over the area you want to select. Notice that when you drag the highlight up or down in the document, Word includes all text on each line that falls in between. To select a rectangular block spanning more than one line, use the mouse column-selection technique described later in the chapter.

Alternatively, you can select by clicking one end of the desired block, and then holding down the **Shift** key while clicking the other end. If you need to scroll the document to reach the other end of the block, use a scroll bar rather than a keyboard command so you do not inadvertently move the insertion point before marking the opposite end of the block. You can also click the start of the block, press **F8**, and then click the end of the block.

To quickly select an entire word, double-click the word. To quickly select an entire sentence, click the sentence while pressing **Ctrl.**

Using the Selection Bar

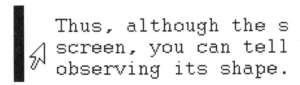 If the *style name area* is displayed, as explained in Chapter 20, the selection bar is between the style name area and the document text.

You can use the mouse in conjunction with the *selection bar* to quickly select various block sizes. When the mouse pointer is within this area, it becomes an arrow pointing up and to the right.

```
Thus, although the s
screen, you can tell
observing its shape.
```

Thus, you always can tell when the pointer is in the selection bar by observing its shape.

To select a single line, click in the selection bar to the left of the line. To select a series of lines, place the pointer next to the first or last line and hold down the left mouse button while dragging the highlight over the desired lines. To select a single paragraph, double-click in the selection bar anywhere next to the paragraph. To select a series of paragraphs, double-click in the selection bar and, while holding down the left button, drag the highlight over the desired paragraphs.

Finally, to select the entire document, click anywhere in the selection bar while pressing **Ctrl.**

Unless otherwise stated, click with the *left* mouse button.

Using the practice document you created earlier in this chapter, follow these steps to try selecting with the mouse:

1. Create the selection shown in Figure 5.1 using the mouse. Place the pointer immediately in front of the word **you** on the third line. Click and drag the highlight to the comma following the word **line**. Remove the selection by clicking anywhere in the document.

2. Create the same selection using the following alternative mouse method: Click immediately in front of the word **you** on the third line, and, while holding down Shift, click to the right of the comma following the word **line**. Remove the selection by clicking anywhere in the document.

You can also use the mouse to select a rectangular-shaped block of text. First, place the mouse pointer on one corner of the area you want to select. Then, while holding down the **right mouse button,** drag the highlight to the opposite corner.

Table 5.2 summarizes the methods for selecting text or graphics using the mouse.

CANCELING THE SELECTION

Once you have selected a block, Word will display a selection rather than an insertion point. Even after you have issued a command, the selection remains marked on the screen (unless, you have deleted the block). You can remove the selection and restore the insertion point by performing an action that moves or positions the insertion point. For example, you can press an arrow key or PgUp, or click within the text.

If you press a character, such as an **A**, the result depends upon whether the **Typing Replaces Selection** option is enabled; this option is described in the next section.

DELETING, MOVING, AND COPYING

In this section, you will learn how to delete, move, and copy a selected block.

Table 5.2: Methods for Selecting Text or Graphics with the Mouse

TO SELECT	USE THE MOUSE TO
A series of characters in the document	Click and drag to highlight the entire block *or* click one end of the block and then the other while pressing Shift
A word	Double-click the word
A sentence	Click the sentence while pressing Ctrl
A line	Click in the selection bar to the left of line
A series of lines	Click and drag in the selection bar
A paragraph	Double-click in the selection bar next to the paragraph
A series of paragraphs	Double-click the selection bar and drag
Entire document	Click in the selection bar while pressing Ctrl
A rectangular block (a column selection)	Click and drag with the *right* mouse button

DELETING THE SELECTION

To delete a block of text or graphics you have selected:

- Press Del.

- If the **Typing Replaces Selection** option is enabled, you can simply begin typing characters; the selected block will be replaced by the new characters.

The Undo command is discussed in Chapter 3.

You can delete any size block by selecting it and pressing **Del.**

Once you have deleted a portion of your document with Del, you can restore it only by issuing Undo immediately. As a precaution, therefore, if you are deleting a large block you might want to *cut* it to the Clipboard, as described in the next section, rather than deleting it. Data stored in the Clipboard can easily be inserted back into the document.

The Typing Replaces Selection Option

When you first install Word, the **Typing Replaces Selection** option is initially enabled. If a selection is marked when you press a character key (such as **A**, **?**, or Tab), Word deletes the selected block and inserts the character in its place. Also, pressing **Backspace** will delete the selected data, in the same manner as pressing Del.

You can turn off the **Typing Replaces Selection** option by issuing the **Tools/Options** command, selecting the **General** icon in the **Category:** list, and removing the check from the **Typing Replaces Selection** item.

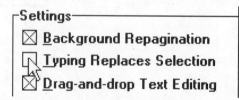

If this option is disabled, and you type a character while a selection is marked, Word inserts the character *in front of* the text that was selected. Also, pressing backspace does *not* delete the selected data; rather, it places the insertion point to the left of the block.

Deleting a Column of Text

By deleting a column selection, you can quickly eliminate a portion of several lines. The exercise below illustrates using this technique to remove the numbers from a list of items within a document.

1. Open a new document and type in the text, as shown in Figure 5.2.

2. Place the insertion point in front of the **1**.

3. Enable column selection by pressing **Ctrl-Shift-F8**.

4. Use the arrow keys to move the highlight over the numbers and space characters in front of the lines of text. Your screen will look like Figure 5.2.

Since an editing operation can radically change a document (you could easily delete an entire document with a few commands!), remember that you can reverse your last editing command through **Edit/Undo** or by pressing **Alt-Backspace**. You must, however, issue the Undo command *immediately after* performing the action you want to reverse.

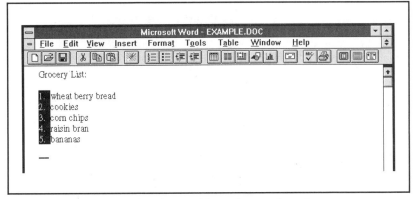

Figure 5.2: The sample document with a column selected

5. Press **Del.** The numbers and leading spaces will be deleted, and the remaining portions of the lines will move to the left margin. Your screen should now look like Figure 5.3.

You can also select the column of text using the mouse, as described previously in the chapter.

COPYING AND MOVING USING THE CLIPBOARD

To copy or move using the Clipboard:

1. Select the text or graphics you want to copy or move.

2. To copy, issue the **Edit/Copy** command, press **Ctrl-C,** or click the **Copy button** in the Toolbar. To move, issue the **Edit/Cut** command, press **Ctrl-X,** or click the **Cut button** on the Toolbar.

3. Place the insertion point at the desired target location.

4. Choose **Edit/Paste**, press **Ctrl-V,** or click the **Paste button** on the Toolbar.

Once you have selected a portion of your document, you can move or copy it to another location by using the Windows *Clipboard*. The Clipboard is a facility that Windows maintains for temporarily storing and transferring selections of text or graphics.

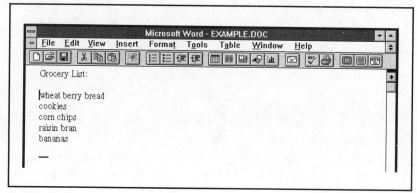

Figure 5.3: Deleting a column of text

In Word, you access the Clipboard through the following three commands:

- Cut

- Copy

- Paste

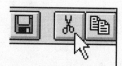

> The Clipboard can hold only one data selection. When you add a selection through the Cut or Copy command, it *replaces* the selection currently held in the Clipboard.

> You can also use the following keystrokes, supported by former versions of Word: **Shift-Del** to cut, **Ctrl-Ins** to copy, and **Shift-Ins** to paste.

The *Cut* command stores the current selection in the Clipboard and deletes it from your document. You issue this command by choosing **Edit/Cut,** by pressing **Ctrl-X,** or by clicking the **Cut button** on the Toolbar:

The selection remains in the Clipboard until you store a new selection. You can also use this command to delete a selection or move it to another location. If nothing is selected, the Cut command is displayed in gray letters on the menu and cannot be chosen.

The *Copy* command also stores the current selection in the Clipboard, but does *not* remove it from your document. You issue this command by choosing **Edit/Copy,** by pressing **Ctrl-C,** or by clicking the **Copy button** on the Toolbar:

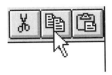

If there is nothing selected, the Copy command is displayed in gray letters on the menu and cannot be chosen.

The *Paste* command inserts the contents of the Clipboard into your document at the insertion point. You issue this command by choosing **Edit/Paste**, by pressing **Ctrl-V**, or by clicking the **Paste button** on the Toolbar:

After pasting, the selection *remains* in the Clipboard and can be pasted into additional locations. If the Clipboard is empty, the Paste command is displayed in gray letters and cannot be chosen.

You can use the Cut or Copy command together with the Paste command to move or copy a selection to another location.

To *move* the selection, issue the Cut command, position the insertion point at the desired new location, and issue the Paste command.

To *copy* the selection, issue the Copy command, place the insertion point where you would like to insert the copy, and issue the Paste command.

Since the selection remains in the Clipboard after you have pasted it, you can insert the selection into additional locations after moving or copying it.

Not only can you use the Clipboard to move and copy data within a document, you can also use it to exchange data among documents. For example, you can copy a block of data from one document into the Clipboard, switch to another document, and paste the data into the second document. The second document need not even be open when you copy the data into the Clipboard.

Because the Clipboard is accessible to all applications running under Windows, you can use it to exchange data between a Word

If you have stored a large selection in the Clipboard, Word will ask you if you want to save the data when quitting Word. Unless you answer yes, the Clipboard's contents will be lost. When you quit Windows, the Clipboard's contents are always lost unless you explicitly saved them in a file.

document and a file in another application. For example, you could copy a block of text from a Word document and paste it into a file in the Windows Notepad editor. Or, you could cut a drawing from Windows Paintbrush and paste it into a Word document (pasting graphics is discussed in Chapter 9). The only requirement for exchanging data between applications is that the source application must provide the Clipboard data in a format that the receiving application can process. In general, if **Edit/Paste** is available in the receiving application (that is, not displayed in gray letters), then the Clipboard contains data that the application can handle.

Accessing the Clipboard

The Clipboard window displays the contents of the Clipboard. This can be useful if you want to determine exactly what is contained in the Clipboard before pasting it into a document.

You can directly access the Clipboard at any time. To access it from within Word, choose **Run** from the Word control menu or press **Alt-Spacebar** and then **u**. Word will display a dialog box. Select the **Clipboard** item and then click the OK button or press Enter. The Windows Clipboard window will appear, as shown in Figure 5.4.

To close the Clipboard window and return to Word, double-click the control menu box in the upper-left corner of the Clipboard window, or press **Alt-Spacebar** and then **c**.

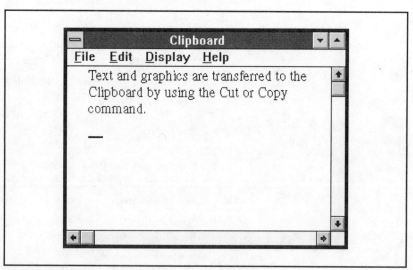

Figure 5.4: The Windows Clipboard window

MOVING AND COPYING WITHOUT USING THE CLIPBOARD

Use any of the following methods to move or copy a selection without involving the Clipboard:

- Press **F2** to move the selection.
- Press **Shift-F2** to copy the selection.
- To move the selection to the position of the mouse pointer, click the **right mouse button** while pressing **Ctrl**.
- To copy the selection to the position of the mouse pointer, click the **right mouse button** while pressing **Ctrl-Shift**.
- To move, copy, or link the selection, place the mouse pointer on the selection, press the **right mouse button**, drag the dotted insertion point to the target location, and release the button.

Word provides several methods for moving or copying data that do not use the Clipboard. An advantage of these techniques is that you can avoid deleting the contents of the Clipboard. A disadvantage is that once you have completed the move or copy operation, you cannot reinsert additional copies. Also, in bypassing the Clipboard. you cannot exchange data with other Windows applications.

Using the Keyboard

You can also use the Word glossary to move or copy a block of text or graphics.

You can *move* a selection by pressing **F2**. You can either select the block and then indicate the target location or vice versa. Follow these steps:

1. Select the block you want to move.

2. Press F2. The insertion point will become a *dotted* vertical line.

3. Move the dotted insertion point to the location where you want to move the text, using the keyboard or mouse.

4. Press Enter, and Word will move the selected block. (Press Esc to cancel the operation.)

You can *copy* a selection by pressing **Shift-F2.** You can either select the block and then indicate the target location, or vice versa. These techniques are the same as those described for *moving* a block, except that you press Shift-F2 rather than F2.

You can use these methods to move or copy a block from one Word document to another, provided that both documents are open at the time you issue the command.

Using the Mouse

You can use the mouse to move or copy a block without involving the Clipboard. To move a selection, use the following procedure:

1. Select the block.

2. Position the mouse pointer where you want to move the selection.

3. Click the *right* mouse button while pressing **Ctrl.**

To copy a selection, follow these steps:

1. Select the block.

2. Position the mouse pointer where you want to copy the selection.

3. Click the *right* mouse button while pressing **Ctrl-Shift.**

Again, to move or copy a selection from one document to another and bypass the Clipboard, both documents must be open.

Alternatively, you can use the new *drag and drop* method. The drag and drop method allows you to move, copy, or *link* a block of text or graphics. Linking is like copying, except that the source and copy remain connected; if you change the source, the change will be reflected in the copy. Linking data within documents is discussed later in the chapter in the section "Using the Paste Special Command." To move, copy or link a selection, do the following:

1. Select the block you want to move, copy, or link.

2. Move the mouse pointer into the highlighted area. Note that the pointer changes from an I-beam to an arrow.

```
the highlighted area, pr
it a dotted square and do
```

3. Press the *right* mouse button. Note that a dotted square and a dotted insertion point appear together with the mouse pointer.

4. While holding down the *right* button, drag the dotted insertion point to where you want to move the block.

```
document .
```

Note that if you drag the pointer to the edge of the window, the document scrolls automatically.

5. When the insertion point is positioned at the target location, release the button. A small menu will immediately appear.

```
Copy
Move
Link
```

6. Choose the desired action by clicking on it or highlighting it and pressing Enter. You can cancel the operation by pressing Esc.

If you want to *move* the selection, use the following, shorter method:

1. Select the block you want to move.

2. Place the mouse pointer within the highlighted area and press the *left* mouse button.

3. Drag the dotted insertion point to the target location.

4. Release the button. Word will move the selection without displaying a menu.

COPYING FORMATTING

The drag and drop technique is convenient for moving, copying, or linking selections over short distances in a single document. You cannot, however, use it to exchange data between different documents and it is inconvenient for transferring data in a long document.

You can copy the *formatting* of a selection without copying the text. However, you must use the mouse to do this. Character formatting is discussed in Chapter 16 and paragraph formatting in Chapter 15. Follow these steps:

1. Select the text with the *source* formatting.

2. If you want to copy *character* formatting, place the mouse pointer on the destination character. If you want to copy *paragraph* formatting, place the mouse pointer in the selection bar adjacent to the destination paragraph.

3. Click the left mouse button while pressing Ctrl-Shift. Word will copy the formatting to the selected text.

USING THE PASTE SPECIAL COMMAND

A nifty new feature in Word for Windows is the *Paste Special* command which you can use instead of the standard Paste command. Paste Special offers several advantages over ordinary pasting.

When you are performing a move or copy operation, you can use Paste Special to copy or move text *without* the character formatting. To do this, use the following procedure:

1. Select the block you want to copy or move.

2. Transfer the selection to the Clipboard using Cut or Copy.

3. Place the cursor at the desired target location.

4. Choose **Edit/Paste Special**. Word will display the dialog box illustrated in Figure 5.5.

5. Select the **Unformatted Text** item from the **Data Type:** list and click the **Paste** button.

The contents of the Clipboard will be inserted with the format of the character preceding the insertion point.

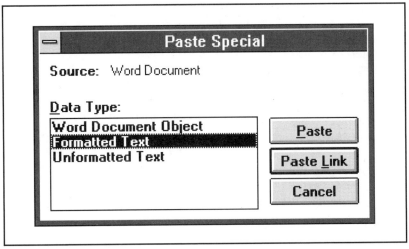

Figure 5.5: The Paste Special dialog box

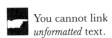 If you choose the **Formatted Text** item in the Data Type list and then click the **Paste** button, the Paste Special command has the same effect as the standard Paste command.

When copying, you can use Paste Special to *link* the copy to the original selection. To create a link, use the following procedure:

1. Select the block you want to copy.

2. Transfer it to the Clipboard using Copy.

3. Place the cursor at the desired target location.

4. Choose **Edit/Paste Special.** Word will display the dialog box illustrated back in Figure 5.5.

5. Select the **Formatted Text** item in the **Data Type:** list.

6. Click the **Paste Link** button. Word will insert the linked block.

You cannot link *unformatted* text.

Initially, the effect of the paste link operation will seem the same as that of a standard Paste operation. However, if you later change the original selection, you can quickly update the copy, using the following procedure:

You can update *all* linked data in a document by selecting the entire document (press **Ctrl-5**) and then pressing **F9.**

1. Place the cursor anywhere in the copy you inserted in step 6 above.

2. Press **F9.**

The copy will be updated to match the current version of the source, both in content and formatting.

You can use this procedure to establish links within a single Word document or even between separate Word documents. Linking data is useful when you have a block that appears in several places in one or more documents. This way, you can create a single master version of the data and insert linked copies in all other places you want it to appear. Then if you want to modify the data, you need edit only the master version and update the linked copies using **F9**.

You already saw how to create a linked copy within a single document—using the drag-and-drop mouse technique—in the section "Moving and Copying without Using the Clipboard."

Searching and Replacing

CHAPTER 6

THIS CHAPTER DESCRIBES THE *FIND* AND *REPLACE* commands. These two commands are great time-savers, especially when you are working with a document longer than a few pages. The Find command finds all occurrences of a specified text string or formatting in a document. The Replace command searches for text and formatting and replaces them with alternative text and formatting.

SEARCHING

With the Find command, you can look for occurrences of specified text, formatting, or a combination of text and formatting within your document.

To find text or formatting:

1. Place the cursor where you want to begin the search.
2. Choose **Edit/Find**; Word will display the Find dialog box.
3. Enter the text you want to find in the **Find Next:** box.
4. Remove any formatting criteria by clicking the **Clear** button.
5. Specify any formatting you want to find.
6. Select the **Up** or **Down** option to specify the search direction.
7. If desired, select the **Whole Word Only** option, the **Match Case Option**, or both.
8. Click the **Find Next** button to begin the search. Word will highlight the first occurrence it finds; continue clicking this button to find additional occurrences.

SEARCHING FOR TEXT

Selecting a block of text prior to issuing the Find command does *not* confine the search to the selection.

Methods for copying text into the Clipboard are discussed in Chapter 5.

When searching for text, you normally issue the **Edit/Find** command and type the sequence of characters directly into the **Find What:** box (Figure 6.1). You can also paste the contents of the Clipboard into this box by pressing **Ctrl-V**. If you have previously issued the Find or Replace command, the Find What box will contain the information you entered. If you type in new search text the new characters will *replace* the existing ones, unless you press an arrow key or click within the text. The maximum number of characters you can type into the Find What box is 255.

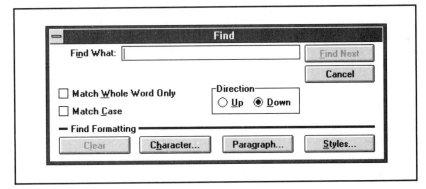

Figure 6.1: The Find dialog box

As mentioned in Chapter 3, you enter a soft return (*newline*) character into your document by pressing Shift-Enter. This causes a line break within a paragraph, and is normally invisible.

When entering text into the Find box, you can specify special characters by entering the appropriate code. The codes are listed in Table 6.1. For example, ^n represents a newline character. Accordingly, the expression

    Casper^n

would match the word **Casper** only where this word comes immediately before a new line.

The string ^w matches any amount of *white space*. White space consists of one or more space or tab characters. This option is useful if a

Table 6.1: Special Character Codes

TO SPECIFY	TYPE
Annotation reference mark*	^5
Beginning of a field**	^19
Caret character (^)	^^
Column break	^14
End of a field**	^21
Footnote reference*	^2
Graphic	^1
Newline character	^n
Nonbreaking hyphen	^ ~
Nonbreaking space	^s
Optional hyphen	^-
Paragraph mark	^p
Question mark	^?
Section mark, page break mark	^d
Tab character	^t
White space*	^w
Character whose ANSI code is *nnn*	^*nnn*
Any single character*	?
Exact text matched***	^m
Clipboard contents***	^c

*   Find What only
**   Code must be visible
*** Replace With only

variable amount of space may fall between two words you want to find. For example, the expression

Friendly^wGhost

would match

Friendly Ghost

or

Friendly   Ghost

A question mark (?) embedded in a search expression represents *any single character*. For example, the expression

a?e

would match Abe, ace, age, ale, and so on. If you want to include an actual question mark as part of the expression, you must precede it with a caret (^), as in the expression

say what^?

However, if no other characters are included in the search expression, ? is equivalent to ^?.

Once you have specified the desired text, you have the option of limiting the search by choosing the **Match Whole Word Only** option, the **Match Case** option, or both.

The **Match Whole Word Only** option causes Word to ignore matches with any text string that is *part* of a word. For example, if you type cat into the Find What box, Word will find cat but not caterpillar or concatenation.

The **Match Case** option causes Word to ignore matches with any text that varies from the specified search text in case. For example, if you type cat into the Find What box, Word will find cat but not Cat or CAT.

To begin the search, choose the **Up** or **Down** option and click **Find Next** or press Enter. Word will search from the insertion point toward the end of the document (if you have chosen the **Down** option) or the beginning (if you have chosen the **Up** option).

If you haven't started the beginning, when you reach the end of the document, Word will display the message

> **Word has reached the end of the document. Do you want to continue searching at the beginning?**

You now have the option of searching the entire document or terminating the search. A similar message appears if you are searching **Up**.

If Word searches the entire document but does not find a match, it displays the message

> **Search text is not found.**

If Word finds a match, it highlights the text, leaving the Find dialog box on the screen. If you want to search for other occurrences, click **Find Next** or press Enter.

If you want to remove the Find dialog box, click Cancel or press **Esc**. You can then make any necessary changes. You can resume the search by pressing **Shift-F4**. This command does not display the Find dialog box, though. Instead it uses the information you have already entered and highlights the next occurrence. You can continue to use **Shift-F4** to find all remaining occurrences in your document.

If you have issued the **Go To** command (described in Chapter 4) since issuing the **Find** command, **Shift-F4** will repeat the Go To command rather than the Find command.

SEARCHING FOR FORMATTING

You can use the Find command to search for occurrences of specific formatting within your document. *Formatting* refers to the printed appearance of the document, and is covered in detail in Part III. When you assign formatting to individual characters, you specify font, size, enhancements such as italics, and so on. When you assign formatting to entire paragraphs, you specify alignment, indents, and so on.

In both the character and paragraph dialog boxes, there are sample boxes that show your selections.

You can search for both text and formatting by following the instructions given later in this section. Alternatively, you can search for formatting only.

When you specify formatting in the Find dialog box, Word saves these settings. Therefore, you should click the **Clear** button to remove them when you start a new search.

You can search for the following types of formatting:

- Character formatting
- Paragraph formatting
- A format style

When you choose one of the formatting buttons, Word lists all possible options below the Find What box. To remove all formatting specifications, click **Clear**.

Word will then search for the specified text in any format.

When you have specified the formatting you wish to search for, click **Find Next** and proceed as described previously in the chapter.

Specifying Character Formatting

To add character formatting to your search criterion, click the **Character** button.

Word will open a dialog box identical in content to that displayed by **Format/Character**, which you will learn more about in Chapter 16.

Initially, all the check boxes in the **Find Character** dialog box are filled with gray. If you leave a box gray, its character feature will be ignored in the search. For example, if you check the **Italic** box but leave the **Bold** box gray

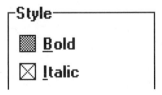

Word will find bold, italic characters and non-bold, italic characters. However, if you double-click so the check box is blank, Word will search for only those characters that do not have the corresponding feature. For example, if you check the Italic box, and double-click the Bold box,

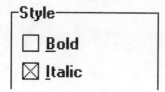

Word will search for only non-bold, italic characters.

If you leave any of the other fields blank, the formatting will be ignored in the search.

When you have finished specifying formatting features, click OK or press Enter. Then click **Find Next** to begin the search.

Another way to specify formatting criteria is by issuing the keyboard command for the feature. These commands are given in Chapter 16. When you press the key combination, a description of the feature will be added to the line below the Find What box. For example, if you press the command for bold text, **Ctrl-B**, bold will be added to the search specification.

Find What: `auspicious`

Format: Bold

Specifying Paragraph Formatting

Adding paragraph formatting to your search criteria is quite similar to adding character formatting. To add paragraph formatting, click the **Paragraph** button.

Word will open a dialog box identical in content to that displayed by **Format/Paragraph**, which you will learn more about in Chapter 15.

When you have finished specifying the formatting, click OK or press Enter. Then click **Find Next** to begin the search.

Another way to specify formatting criteria is by issuing the keyboard command for the feature. These commands are given in Chapter 15. When you press the key combination, a description of the feature will be added to the line below the Find What box. For example, if you press **Ctrl-E** and **Ctrl-2**, Word will search for text that has been assigned the centered and double-spaced format features.

Fi̲nd What: | serendipitous| |

Format: Centered, Line Spacing 2 li

If you specify *only* paragraph formatting (no text, character formatting, or style), Word will highlight the first paragraph with the specified formatting. Even if several adjoining paragraphs have the specified formatting, Word will select only the first one. (If you then click **Find Next** or press **Shift-F4**, Word will highlight the next paragraph).

Specifying a Style

To search for a specific style, click the Styles button.

Word will display a dialog box containing a list of defined styles for the current document. Select a style from the list and click OK or press Enter.

If your search criterion consists of *only* a style specification, Word will highlight the first paragraph that has been assigned the style. If you combine a style specification with text and formatting, Word will highlight the first block that has the specified text and formatting *and* is within a paragraph with the specified style.

REPLACING

To replace text or formatting:

1. Choose **Edit/Replace**. Word will display the Replace dialog box.

2. Enter the text you want to find into the **Find What:** box.

3. Remove any previous formatting by clicking **Clear** and specify the formatting features you want to find, as described earlier.

4. Enter the replacement text into the **Replace With:** box.

5. Remove any previous formatting by clicking **Clear** and specify the formatting features you want to apply to the replacement text.

6. If desired, select **Whole Word Only**, **Match Case**, or both.

7. Click **Find Next** to have Word highlight the first matching occurrence. Then click **Replace** to replace it, or **Find Next** to let it stand.

8. Alternatively, click **Replace All** to replace all occurrences without confirmation.

REPLACING TEXT

If you have already used the Find or Replace command, the **Find What:** box will contain the text you entered. If you have already used the Replace command, the **Replace With:** box will also contain text. You can accept this information or enter new text.

You can enter text into the **Find What:** and **Replace With:** boxes the same way you enter text in the Find dialog box, explained previously in the chapter. Again, you can either type or paste in the text. The Replace dialog box is shown in Figure 6.2.

To specify special characters, you can use the codes listed in Table 6.1. However, you cannot use the codes ?, ^w, ^2 or ^5 in the Replace With box.

There are two additional codes you can enter into the Replace With box. First, ^m represents the exact text that was matched.

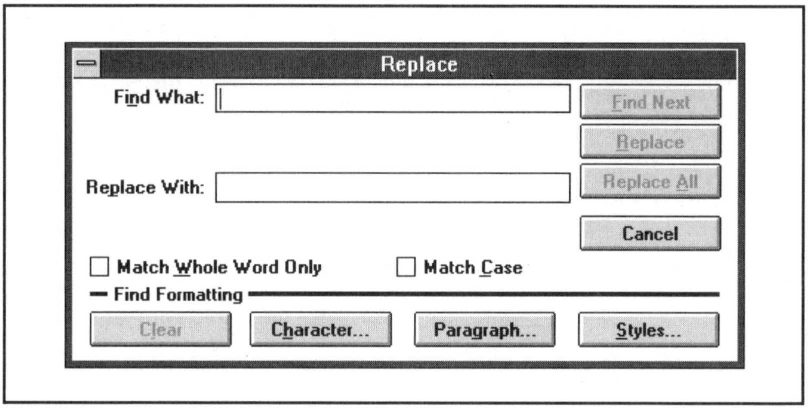

Figure 6.2: The Replace dialog box

For example, if you type

>   Chapter ?

into the Find What box, and

>   "^m"

into the Replace With box, Word will replace all occurrences of

>   Chapter 1

with

>   "Chapter 1"

and all occurrences of

>   Chapter 2

with

>   "Chapter 2"

and so on, effectively placing quotation marks around all chapter titles.

The other special code is ^c, which represents the current contents of the Clipboard. You can enter this code by itself, or in conjunction with other text. Try this example. Type the short document shown in Figure 6.3.

Recent studies have shown that pets make wonderful companions to the elderly. Whereas human nurses often make septuagenarians feel helpless, pets can give them a sense of independence and freedom. Many elderly persons who keep pets are living longer and enjoying life more. Many pets make few demands upon their owners and remain loyal and loving.

Figure 6.3: The sample document

Copy the following expression to the Clipboard:

   dogs, cats, birds, alligators

Then issue the **Edit/Replace** command and enter the following word into the Find What box:

   pets

and the following expression into the Replace With box:

   ^c, etc.

Click **Replace All** and Word will replace every occurrence of the word pets in the document with

   dogs, cats, birds, alligators, etc.

Although you can usually paste the contents of the Clipboard directly into the Replace With box using ^c has two important advantages:

- The number of characters you can enter in the Replace With box is limited to 255. The number of characters you can copy from the Clipboard is unlimited. This can be very useful for legal applications.

- You cannot enter a graphic directly into the Replace With box. However, you *can* place a graphic in the Clipboard and enter the ^c code into the Replace With box to paste it into your document.

You can limit the search and replace operation by choosing the **Match Whole Word Only** option, the **Match Case** option, or both.

The **Match Whole Word** option governs the way the Replace command searches for text; it causes Word to ignore matches with any text that is *part* of a word. This process is analagous to that of the Find command, described earlier.

The **Match Case** option affects both the way Word searches for text and the way it replaces text. If you do *not* choose this option, Word ignores the case of all letters when searching for text. When replacing text, it matches the existing capitalization style. For example, if you enter tabby in the Find What box and Manx in the Replace With box, Word will replace tabby with manx, Tabby with Manx, and TABBY with MANX.

If, however, you choose the **Match Case** option, Word searches only for text that matches the case of the text string in the Find What box. It replaces text exactly as it appears in the Replace With box. For example, if you enter tabby in the Find What box and Manx in the Replace With box, Word will replace tabby with Manx and ignore Tabby and TABBY.

Use **Replace All** with caution: it replaces *all* occurrences without confirmation.

You can click the **Replace All** button to have Word immediately replace *all* occurrences of text or formatting from the cursor to the end of the document. When the operation is finished, the Replace dialog box remains open; you can either begin a new replacement operation or click the **Close** button.

You can use **Replace All** to change only those occurrences of text or formatting within a *highlighted* section.

Alternatively, you can replace occurrences one by one by clicking **Find Next**. Word will highlight the first occurrence of the search text and pause, still displaying the Replace dialog box. You now have a choice; you can do any of the following:

- Click **Replace** to replace the highlighted text and continue with the search.

- Click **Find Next** to search for the next occurrence *without* replacing the highlighted text.

- Click **Replace All** to replace *all* remaining occurrences without confirmation.

- Click **Close** (or **Cancel**, if no replacements have yet been made) to stop the replace operation and close the dialog box.

Each time you click **Replace** or **Find Next**, Word highlights the next occurrence, and you again have the options listed above. When Word cannot find additional occurrences, it displays the message

Search text is not found.

You can then specify a new replace operation or click **Close** (or **Cancel**) to remove the dialog box and return to the document window.

You can undo a replacement operation if you issue **Edit/Undo** immediately. If you have clicked **Replace**, Undo will reverse only that single replacement. However, if you clicked **Replace All**, Undo will reverse all the replacements.

REPLACING FORMATTING

When performing a replace operation, you can add formatting features to either your search specification or your replacement specification.

To search for formatting, place the insertion point in the **Find What:** text box and then click **Character**, **Paragraph**, or **Styles**. The corresponding dialog box will appear, and you can specify the formatting. These dialog boxes work the same way as those displayed by the Find command; for instructions, see the previous section, "Searching for Formatting." You can also add formatting criterion to the search by pressing keyboard commands (as explained previously for the Find command). Each feature you specify—using either a dialog box or a keyboard command—is added to a format description below the Find What box.

When you begin a new replace operation, click **Clear** to remove any formatting specifications assigned during a previous replace.

Fi<u>n</u>d What: | fortuitous |

Format: Underline, Centered

To assign one or more formatting features to the replacement specification, move the insertion point to the **Replace With:** box and proceed as described above. Word will add any format features you specify to a description below the Replace With box. Then, when Word replaces text, it will assign the specified formatting to the new text.

By combining text and formatting specifications in the Find What and Replace With boxes in various ways, you can perform several operations at once and save a lot of time. Table 6.2 summarizes the different results you can obtain.

Leaving the **Replace With:** box empty instructs Word to *erase* all instances of text that match what you specified in the **Find What:** box.

Table 6.2: Possibilities with the Replace Command

TO DO THIS	SPECIFY IN THE FIND WHAT BOX	SPECIFY IN THE REPLACE WITH BOX
Replace text but leave formatting intact	Text, formatting, or both	Text
Add formatting to text	Text	Formatting
Replace formatting	Formatting, or text and formatting	Formatting
Replace text and add formatting	Text	Text and formatting
Replace text and add formatting	Formatting, or text and formatting	Text and formatting
Erase text and formatting	Text, formatting, or both	Nothing (leave blank)

For example, the first item in the table shows how to replace a block of text while leaving the formatting intact: specify text, formatting, or a combination of the two in the Find What box, and specify text only in the Replace With box.

The third item shows how you can replace one or more formatting features throughout a document. For example, if you wanted to change all italic text to underlined text, without affecting the text itself, you would do the following:

1. Place the insertion point in the **Find What:** box.

2. Erase any text in the Find What box and remove any previous formatting criteria by clicking the **Clear** button.

3. Press **Ctrl-I** to specify *italic*.

4. Move the insertion point to the **Replace With:** box.

5. Erase any text in the Replace With box and click **Clear** to remove any formatting.

6. Press **Ctrl-U** to specify *underlined* characters. A dialog box will appear, as shown in Figure 6.4.

7. Begin the search by clicking **Find Next** or **Replace All**, as described above.

Fi**n**d What:	
Format:	Italic
Replace With:		
Format:	Underline

Figure 6.4: Changing italic text to underlined text

Polishing Your Writing

CHAPTER **7** _____

THIS CHAPTER DESCRIBES THREE IMPORTANT tools Word for Windows provides to help you proof your documents: the *spell checker*, the *thesaurus*, and the *grammar checker*. You can use the spell checker to check your spelling, even verifying the spelling of words as you create a document. Using the thesaurus, you can find synonyms for words, as well as antonyms and related terms. This can help you add variety to your writing. The grammar checker analyzes the grammar and style of your sentences. It displays possible grammatical errors or stylistic weaknesses, suggesting ways to correct your errors or improve your style. It also reports on the overall readability of the document. The final section of the chapter describes how to use any of these tools to proof text written in a foreign language.

When you install Word, you can exclude the proofing tools. If you have not included a particular tool, it will not appear on the **Tools** menu. You can run the Word **Setup** program again, though, to install any of the proofing tools.

CHECKING YOUR SPELLING ___

To check your spelling:

1. Place the insertion point where you would like to start the spell check, or select a block of text to check.

2. Choose **Tools/Spelling** or click the **Spelling button** on the Toolbar to start checking the document.

3. Alternatively, you can press **F7** to check just the word at the insertion point.

4. Whenever the spelling utility encounters a word it cannot find in its dictionary, it highlights the word and displays the Spelling dialog box. Word suggests a replacement word in the **Change To:** box; you can

accept this word, type another into the box, or select a word from the **Suggestions:** box.

5. Click the **Change** button to replace the current word with the word in the **Change To:** box. (**Change All** replaces all occurrences.)

6. Click **Ignore** to leave the current occurrence unchanged. (**Ignore All** prevents Word from flagging the word again.)

7. Click the **Add** button to leave the word unchanged and add it to a custom dictionary.

8. Click **Undo Last** to undo your previous replacement.

9. Click **Cancel** to terminate the spell check.

10. Click **Options** to customize the criteria that govern the way the speller checks your document.

To check *hidden* text, it must be visible (see Chapter 16). In *outline view,* you must display any text you want to spell check (see Chapter 24).

The grammar checker, described later in the chapter, can help you spot word usage errors, such as using **their** instead of **there**, that the spell checker wouldn't catch.

You can use the Word Spelling command to confirm the spelling of a single word, a group of words, or all the words in a document. The spell checker looks up words in one or more internal dictionaries. If it finds the word in a dictionary, it assumes it is spelled correctly; if it does not find the word, it flags it as a possible misspelling, leaving you to judge whether it is wrong.

The spell checker, however, is not infallible. The following are two important limitations:

- All words that are not contained in an internal dictionary are flagged, even if they are actually spelled correctly. Word's dictionaries may not contain proper names, unusual words, or technical terms that you use. You can gradually minimize this problem by building a custom dictionary.

- The spell checker will not flag correctly spelled words that are used inappropriately. For example, it will not flag the word **their** used instead of **there**.

Although the spell checker does not replace careful proofing, it can catch many mistakes and is a valuable complement to your own checks. In addition to flagging misspellings, the spell checker will signal repeated words, words with unusual capitalization (such as **bAt**), and words in which the first letter should be capitalized (for example, american).

USING THE SPELL CHECKER

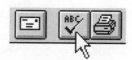 For information on checking the spelling of foreign words, see the final section in the chapter, "Proofing Foreign Language Text."

To check your spelling, place the cursor where you want the check to begin. When you issue the Spelling command, Word will check all words to the end of the document. However, if you select one or more words, Word will check only the selected text.

Next, choose **Tools/Spelling** or click the **Spelling button** on the Toolbar.

Word will immediately begin the spell check. Each time the program finds a word that is not in its dictionary, it highlights the word and displays the Spelling dialog box, which is illustrated in Figure 7.1. At the top of the Spelling dialog box, the questionable word is displayed in the **Not in Dictionary:** box.

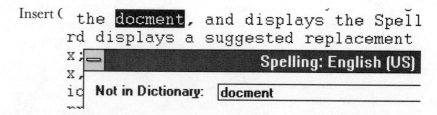

The Suggestions box might list one or more correctly spelled words that resemble the questionable word, and one of these words will be displayed in the **Change To:** box (Word's best guess). If Word cannot come up with any alternate spellings, it copies the unknown word into the Change To box so you can correct it.

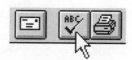 If you interrupt a spell check, you may not have corrected all instances of a misspelled word, *even* if you clicked **Change All** when the word was initially flagged by the spell checker.

When the Spelling dialog box is displayed, you can do one of the following:

- Click **Ignore** to leave the unknown word unchanged and continue the spell check. (If the same word is encountered later, Word will flag it again.)

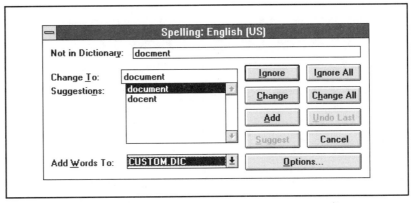

Figure 7.1: The Spelling dialog box

- Click **Ignore All** to leave the word unchanged and to ignore any further occurrences of it.

- Click **Change** to replace the word in the document with the word in the Change To box and continue the spell check.

- Click **Change All** to replace *all* occurrences of the unknown document word with the word in the Change To box. Word will continue the spell check and, if it encounters the same unknown word again, will replace it without prompting you.

- Click **Add** to add the word to the custom dictionary, leave it unchanged in the document, and continue the spell check. The word will be added into the custom dictionary that is selected in the **Add Words To:** list. It will not be flagged again during the spell-check session, nor during any future spell check that uses the same custom dictionary. Custom dictionaries are discussed later in the chapter (in the section "Setting Spelling Options").

- Click **Cancel** to leave the word unchanged and terminate the spell check. Any corrections you have already made will remain, but you must save the document to retain the changes.

Before clicking **Change** or **Change All**, you can type a new replacement word in the Change To box. When you click **Change**, Word will check the spelling of the new word before making the replacement and notify you if it cannot find the word in its dictionary. Rather than typing a new word, you can select one of the words in the **Suggestions:** list; click on a word, and it will be copied into the **Change To:** box. Alternatively, you can simply double-click any word in the Suggestions box; Word will immediately perform the replacement and continue the spell check.

When you type a new word into the Change To box, you can click **Suggest,** and a list of similar, correctly spelled words will appear. You can even include the special characters **?** or ***** within the word to indicate the general pattern of the words you want listed. These characters are known as *wildcards*; the **?** character represents any single character, and the ***** character represents any number of characters. For example, if you enter

    a?e

in the Change To box and click **Suggest,** Word will list

    ace
    age
    ale
    ape

and so on. And if you enter

    king*

Word will list

    king
    kingly
    king's

and so on.

In addition to flagging words not in its dictionary, the Word speller also displays the Spelling box if it encounters a word that is repeated (such as the the). The repeated word will be displayed at the top of the dialog box and labeled **Repeated Word,** rather than **Not in Dictionary.**

The Suggest feature, in conjunction with the **?** wildcard character, can be used as a powerful tool for solving crossword puzzles!

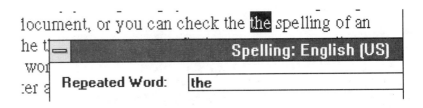

You can erase a misspelled word by clearing the Change To box and clicking **Delete** or **Delete All.**

In this case, the Change To box will be empty, and **Change** and **Change All** will be relabeled **Delete** and **Delete All.** Click **Delete** and the repeated word will be erased. **Delete All** is analogous to **Change All.**

The speller also flags words with nonstandard capitalization, such as bAt. In this case, the box displaying the word is labeled **Capitalization.** Proceed as with a misspelling.

USING THE SPELLING KEY (F7)

You can use the Spelling Key, **F7,** as a shortcut to check the spelling of a single word. When you press F7, Word will check the word that is nearest to the cursor. If it does not recognize the word, the Spelling dialog box will appear, as described in the previous section. Whether it recognizes the word or not, Word then allows you to quit the spell check or continue checking the rest of the document.

If you actually *select* one or more words, pressing F7 has the same effect as issuing the **Tools/Spelling** command or clicking the **Spelling button** on the Toolbar. Word will first check the text in the selection and then display a message box giving you the option of quitting or checking the rest of the document.

You can continue to work on your document even when the Spelling dialog box is on the screen. (Most Word dialog boxes must be closed before you can resume work.) To resume working on your document, simply click within the document or press **Ctrl-Tab.** To return to the Spelling dialog box, click the **Start** button or press **F7.** You can move the Spelling box to anywhere on the screen by dragging its title bar.

CUSTOMIZING THE SPELLING OPTIONS

You can customize the spelling options in one of two ways. First, if the Spelling dialog box is displayed, you can click the **Options** button.

Second, you can choose the **Tools/Options** command and select the **Spelling** icon in the **Category:** list.

Whichever method you use, Word will display the options illustrated in Figure 7.2. Any options you set will remain in effect until you explicitly change them.

You can select one or both of the options within the box labeled **Ignore** to have the speller ignore certain words. If you select the **Words in UPPERCASE** option, Word will ignore words that consist entirely of uppercase letters or numbers (such as **DNA** and **RS232**). If you select the Words with Numbers option, Word will ignore all words that contain numbers (such as **r2d2**). Neither of these options is selected when you first install Word.

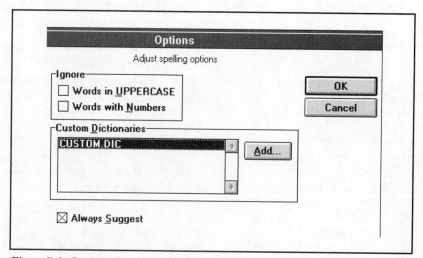

Figure 7.2: Options for the Spelling command

Whether or not you have selected the **Words with Numbers** option, Word automatically ignores all words that consist of numbers together with a single letter, such as **221B**.

Working with Custom Dictionaries

For special applications, you can create supplemental dictionaries. These dictionaries appear on the Custom Dictionaries list. Initially, this list contains only a single dictionary, but you will see how to add dictionaries to the list. When Word performs a spell check, it *always* consults its main dictionary. By selecting dictionaries from the Custom Dictionaries list, you can have Word consult them. The advantage is that the spell checker will not flag a word contained in one of these dictionaries.

When you first install Word, only CUSTOM.DIC is included within the Custom Dictionaries list. It is also selected in the list, which means it is consulted during spell checks. At first, CUSTOM.DIC is empty; however, you add to it each time you click the **Add** button, as explained earlier. You can add proper names, technical terms, and any words you use regularly that are not in Word's main dictionary. As you build CUSTOM.DIC, spell checks will become more efficient, since Word will stop flagging words you have added.

You can add additional custom dictionaries, for special applications.

By using several custom dictionaries, you can increase the efficiency and accuracy of your spell checks. For example, if you write about both computers and psychiatry, you could use one custom dictionary for computer articles (called *COMPUTER.DIC*) and for psychiatry articles (called *PSYCH.DIC*). You could store the general terms you use in all types of documents in CUSTOM.DIC. While writing on computers, you could select CUSTOM.DIC and COMPUTER.DIC. While writing on psychiatry, you could select CUSTOM.DIC and PSYCH.DIC. In this manner, the spell checker would need to search only the supplemental dictionary with words relevant to your topic.

To add a dictionary, click the **Add** button in the **Custom Dictionaries:** box.

For information on how to format text so that it is always ignored by the spell checker, see the final section in the chapter, "Proofing Foreign Language Text."

The main dictionary and the custom dictionaries are normally stored in the same directory as your Word program files (usually **\WINWORD**).

Word will display the following text box:

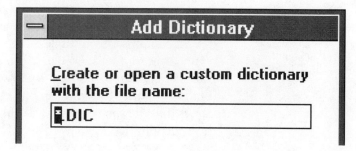

Delete the * character and type a valid file name (1 to 8 characters) in front of the .DIC extension, as in the following example:

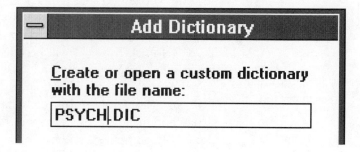

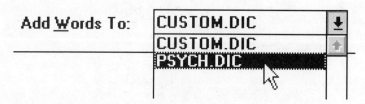
Only the dictionaries that are selected (that is, highlighted) in the Custom Dictionaries list will be actually used for spell checks.

You can add any number of dictionaries to the Custom Dictionaries list. To select a custom dictionary, either click on it with the mouse or move to it using the arrow keys and press the Spacebar. You can select up to four custom dictionaries.

Initially, each dictionary you add to the Custom Dictionaries list will be empty. You add words to a dictionary by selecting it in the **Add Words To:** list,

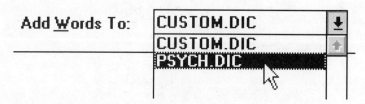

and then clicking the **Add** button.

Finally, selecting the **Always Suggest** option in the Options dialog box instructs the spell checker to automatically display alternate

You can quickly add many words to a custom dictionary by creating a document containing just those words and then running a spell check, clicking the **Add** button with each word.

spellings whenever it encounters an unknown word. These words appear in the **Suggestions:** list in the Spelling dialog box. This option is initially selected; if you disable it, you must click the **Suggest** button when you want a list of alternative spellings.

Undoing a Spell Check

When you are running a spell check, you can click the **Undo Last** button

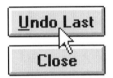

at any time to display your most recent correction. You will then have the opportunity to revise your correction. You can continue clicking **Undo Last** button to revise up to five corrections.

You can also undo *all* the corrections made during a spell check by choosing **Edit/Undo,** pressing **Ctrl-Z,** or clicking the **Undo button** in the Toolbar. You must, however, issue the undo command *immediately* after finishing the spell check.

Creating an Exclude Dictionary

As you have seen, the spell checker will not flag any word contained within its main dictionary. You might, however, want Word to flag a word even if it is correctly spelled. For example, if you are writing a book called *The Compleat Woodworker*, you might want to use the quaint spelling **compleat** throughout your manuscript, having the speller flag only occurrences of the conventional spelling **complete**.

While you cannot remove a word from the main dictionary, you can create an *exclude* dictionary, a document that lists words that you want flagged, even if they are in the main dictionary. To create an exclude dictionary, perform the following steps:

1. Create a new Word document.

2. Enter all words you want the spell checker to flag, one word per line.

3. Save the document in the same directory as the main dictionary (usually, **\WINWORD**). Assign it the same name as the main dictionary, but with the **.EXC** extension. If you are using the standard American English dictionary, name the exclude dictionary **SP_AM.EXC**.

FINDING SYNONYMS WITH THE THESAURUS

To find a synonym for a word:

1. Place the cursor within or immediately after the desired word.

2. Choose **Tools/Thesaurus** or press **Shift-F7.** Word will display the Thesaurus dialog box listing meanings and synonyms for your chosen word.

3. Select the appropriate meaning from the **Meanings:** list box. A list of appropriate synonyms will appear in the **Synonyms:** list box.

4. If Word cannot find synonyms for the word, it will display an alphabetical list of similarly spelled words; if one of them is correct, select it and click the **Look Up** button.

5. Select the desired synonym from the **Synonyms:** list.

6. Click the **Replace** button to replace the word in your document with the selected synonym.

7. If you don't find a synonym you like, click the **Cancel** button to remove the dialog box without altering your document.

You can use the thesaurus to look up synonyms for words in your documents, thereby lending variety and precision to your writing style. To call up the Thesaurus, choose **Tools/Thesaurus** or press

Shift-F7. Word will display the dialog box illustrated in Figure 7.3. This box was opened with the cursor immediately following the word pretty.

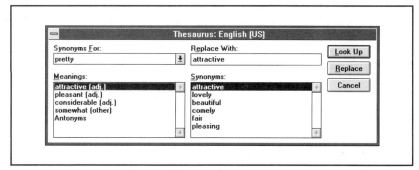

Figure 7.3: The Thesaurus dialog box

When Word displays the Thesaurus dialog box, it attempts to place it on the screen as far away as possible from the word in your document. If the dialog box covers some portion of the window you want to see, you can move it on the screen.

The Synonyms box initially contains the word from your document. Since many words have multiple meanings, the list of synonyms depends upon which meaning you intend. Therefore, the thesaurus displays each possible meaning in the **Meanings:** list. First select the correct meaning from this list by clicking the meaning or by moving the highlight to it with an arrow key. For example, if the word you had in your document were brief, the following meanings would be listed:

When you select a meaning, a collection of synonyms will appear in the **Synonyms:** list. For example, if you were to select summary (noun) in the Meanings box, the following synonyms would appear:

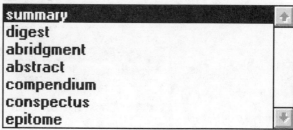

Select the desired synonym and click **Replace.** The dialog box will vanish and the selected synonym will replace the original word. In the above example, if you chose the word abstract from the Synonyms box, Word would erase the word brief in your document and replace it with the word abstract. Alternatively, you could click Cancel to remove the dialog box without changing the original word.

If Word can't find any synonyms for the word in your document, it will display a list of similarly spelled words for which it does have synonyms. They will appear in a list box labeled **Alphabetical List:,** which will replace the Meanings list box. If you see the correct word within this list (you may have misspelled the original word), select it and click **Look Up.** The selected word will replace the original word in the **Synonyms For:** box; you can continue as described above.

FINDING ANTONYMS AND RELATED WORDS

An antonym is a word with the *opposite* meaning.

When you look up a word in the thesaurus, in addition to synonyms, you might see the following items in the **Meanings:** list:

Antonyms
Related Words

If you select Antonyms, a list of antonyms for the word will appear in the adjoining list box (which will now be labeled **Antonyms:** rather than **Synonyms:**). Similarly, if you select Related Words, the thesaurus will display a list of words with meanings that are related to the word in your document. For example, if the word is **replace**, Word will display **place** as a related word.

If desired, you can replace the word in your document with an antonym or related word by highlighting the word and clicking **Replace.**

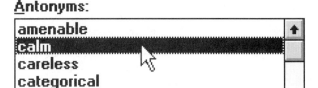

EXPLORING OTHER WORDS

To see a list of synonyms for a word in the **Synonyms:** box, simply double-click the word.

When the Thesaurus dialog box is open, you can obtain synonyms for any word in the **Synonyms:** list box. Simply select the word and click **Look Up.** Alternatively, you can type a word directly into the **Replace With:** box and then click **Look Up.** The word you selected or typed will be copied to the **Synonyms For:** box and a list of meanings will appear in the **Meanings:** box. Select the desired meaning, and a list of synonyms will appear in the Synonyms box. You can then replace the word in your document or obtain synonyms for another word.

Each time you click **Look Up** to obtain synonyms for a particular word, that word is copied to the Synonyms For box. Previous words from the Synonyms For box are not lost, however; they are added to the list below the box. If you then want to find synonyms for one of these words, select it from this list.

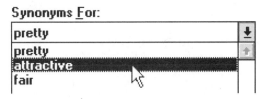

CHECKING YOUR GRAMMAR AND WRITING STYLE

To check your grammar and writing style:

1. Place the cursor where you would like to start checking grammar. Alternatively, you can select a block of text and confine the check to the selection.

2. Choose **Tools/Grammar.** When the grammar checker discovers an error, it displays the Grammar dialog box. This box shows the offending sentence, explains the problem, and suggests possible corrections.

3. If Word displays corrections in the **Suggestions:** list box, you can select one and click **Change** to effect the change in your document.

4. If Word does not list any corrections, you can switch to your document to make edits by clicking in the text or pressing **Ctrl-Tab.** To return to the Grammar dialog box, click the **Start** button, or choose **Tools/Grammar.**

5. To skip the current error and continue the check, click **Ignore, Next Sentence** (to start with the next sentence), or **Ignore Rule** (to skip any further occurrences of the same error).

6. If you want an explanation of the current error, click **Explain.**

7. If you want to stop the grammar check, click **Cancel.**

8. If you want to customize the criteria that governs the way Word checks your grammar, click **Options.**

The Grammar command is a new feature in Word. It checks both grammar and writing style, even generating a report on the readability of the document.

The Grammar command checks your document from the insertion point to the end of the document, or, if you have selected a block of text, just within that selection.

Once you have positioned the cursor or selected the desired text, choose **Tools/Grammar.** Word will begin checking your document; you can interrupt the process at any time by pressing **Esc**.

Each time the grammar checker encounters a possible grammatical error or stylistic weakness, it highlights the offending sentence and displays the Grammar dialog box, as shown in Figure 7.4.

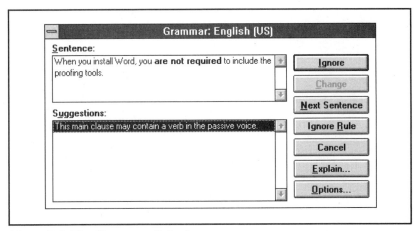

Figure 7.4: The Grammar dialog box

At the top of this dialog box (in the box labeled **Sentence:**), Word displays the entire sentence, highlighting the questionable word or phrase. (You can scroll this box, if necessary, to see the entire sentence).

In the lower portion of the Grammar dialog box is the **Suggestions:** list. This either briefly describes the problem (as shown in Figure 7.4) or suggests actual corrections. If the Suggestions box contains corrections, you can select one and click **Change** to have Word implement it in your document (or simply double-click the correction).

If the Suggestions box contains only a description of the problem, but offers no corrections, the **Change** button will be disabled. You can manually change the sentence, though either by clicking in the document or pressing **Ctrl-Tab.** To resume the grammar check, click the **Start** button in the Grammar dialog box or choose **Tools/Grammar**.

If you want to ignore an error but continue the grammar check, you can do one of the following:

- Click the **Ignore** button to leave the present error unchanged but flag any other errors in the same sentence.

- Click the **Next Sentence** button to leave the present error unchanged and skip any other errors in the same sentence.

- Click the **Ignore Rule** button to leave the present error unchanged and skip any further infractions of the same rule.

For example, if Word flags a sentence containing a passive verb, you can click **Ignore Rule** to instruct Word to skip over any additional passive verbs.

If you click **Explain,** Word will specify the rule of grammar or style that was violated and suggests possible corrections. Press **Esc** or double-click the control box in the upper-left corner of the box to remove it.

If you click **Cancel,** Word will terminate the grammar check but will *not* reverse changes already implemented. To reverse all changes made during the session, select **Edit/Undo** immediately.

When Word checks your grammar, it also checks your spelling. If it encounters a word not in its dictionary, it displays the Spelling dialog box. Complete instructions for using the spell checker are given earlier in the section "Checking Your Spelling."

> If you choose **Edit/Undo,** press **Ctrl-Z,** or click the **Undo button** on the Toolbar *immediately* after completing a grammar check, Word will reverse *all* changes you made during the grammar-checking session.

READABILITY STATISTICS

When Word finishes the grammar check, it displays a box containing statistics on the readability of your document. This box is illustrated in Figure 7.5. The first part of the box displays word count, character count, and so on. The section part supplies several averages, such as the number of sentences per paragraph. The final part gives an indication of the overall readability of your document; these indicators are briefly explained in Table 7.1. You might be interested to know that the statistics displayed in Figure 7.5 are based upon the text for the chapter you are now reading (before final editing).

SETTING GRAMMAR CHECKING OPTIONS

You can set a variety of options to govern the way the Grammar command checks your document. If a grammar check is in progress and the Grammar dialog box is displayed, you can set these options

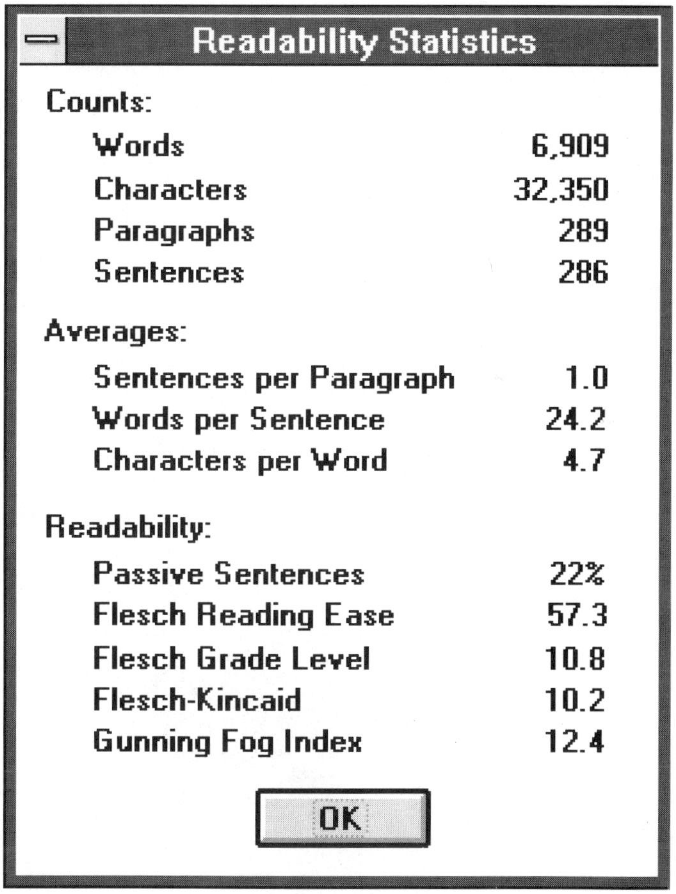

Readability Statistics

Counts:

Words	6,909
Characters	32,350
Paragraphs	289
Sentences	286

Averages:

Sentences per Paragraph	1.0
Words per Sentence	24.2
Characters per Word	4.7

Readability:

Passive Sentences	22%
Flesch Reading Ease	57.3
Flesch Grade Level	10.8
Flesch-Kincaid	10.2
Gunning Fog Index	12.4

OK

Figure 7.5: The Readability Statistics box

Table 7.1: Readability Indicators

INDICATOR	MEANING
Passive Sentences	Percentage of sentences containing verbs in the passive voice.
Flesch Reading Ease	An index ranging from 0 to 100, based upon the average number of words per sentence and of syllables per word. The higher the number, the greater the readability. The value for standard text is approximately 60–70, which corresponds to a *Flesch Grade Level* of 7–8.
Flesch Grade Level	An index based upon the same criteria as the *Flesch Reading Ease,* but expressed as a school grade level. Standard writing has a value of 7–8, which means that it can be understood by a person who has completed 7–8 years of education.
Flesch-Kincaid	Another indicator that expresses readability in terms of a school grade level.
Gunning Fog Index	An indicator based upon sentence length and the percentage of words that contain more than one syllable. A higher value indicates a more complicated writing style.

by clicking the **Options** button in the lower-right corner of the dialog box. If not, you can set the options by choosing **Tools/Options,** and then selecting the **Grammar** icon in the **Category:** list.

Word will display the Options dialog box, illustrated in Figure 7.6.

```
┌─────────────────────────────────────────────────────────────┐
│  ┌───────────────────────────────────────────────────────┐  │
│  │                      Options                          │  │
│  │              Adjust grammar checking options          │  │
│  │  ┌─Use Grammar and Style Rules─┐                      │  │
│  │  │  ○ Strictly (All Rules)     │      ┌──────────┐    │  │
│  │  │  ◉ For Business Writing      │      │    OK    │    │  │
│  │  │  ○ For Casual Writing        │      ├──────────┤    │  │
│  │  └─────────────────────────────┘      │  Cancel  │    │  │
│  │       ┌────────────────────────┐      └──────────┘    │  │
│  │       │  Customize Settings...  │                      │  │
│  │       └────────────────────────┘                      │  │
│  │     ☒ Show Readability Statistics after Proofing      │  │
│  └───────────────────────────────────────────────────────┘  │
└─────────────────────────────────────────────────────────────┘
```

Figure 7.6: The Grammar Options dialog box

If you remove the check from **Show Readability Statistics after Proofing,** the grammar checker will not display the statistics described in the previous section. You can set the overall strictness of the grammar check by selecting one of the options in the **Use Grammar and Style Rules** area. If you choose **Strictly (All Rules),** Word will enforce all grammar and style rules. If you choose **For Business Writing,** Word will not enforce all rules, applying instead a set of rules more appropriate for business writing. This option is selected when you first install Word. If you select **For Casual Writing,** Word will enforce even fewer rules, using criteria appropriate to informal writing.

Choosing one of these three options may be all you need to do to achieve the desired level of grammar checking. However, you can fine tune the grammar checker by selecting the exact set of rules that you want it to enforce. To do this, first check an option in the **Use Grammar and Style Rules** area, and then click the **Customize Settings** button. Word will open the Customize Grammar Settings dialog box, shown in Figure 7.7.

These are the grammar and style rules enforced for the general level you have chosen. The enforced rules are checked. You can add or remove check marks at your discretion. Use the scroll bars, if necessary, to scroll through these lists. To add or remove a check mark, click on the rule or move the selection (a dotted rectangle) to the rule

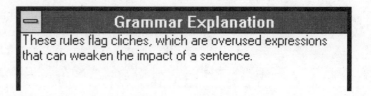

Figure 7.7: The Customize Grammar Settings dialog box

with the arrow keys and press the Spacebar. You can click the **Explain** button to obtain a brief explanation of any selected rule.

> **Grammar Explanation**
> These rules flag cliches, which are overused expressions that can weaken the impact of a sentence.

You can also control how strictly Word enforces certain rules by choosing options within the **Catch** area at the bottom of the Customize Grammar Settings dialog box. By choosing an option in the **Split Infinitives:** box, you can specify how many words may be placed between **to** and an infinitive verb before the grammar checker flags an error. For example, if you choose the **By More than One Word** option, the phrase

    to boldly go

would be acceptable, but the phrase

    to very boldly go

would cause the grammar checker to flag an error.

Similarly, you can choose an option in the **Consecutive Nouns:** box to specify how many contiguous nouns will trigger an error. The **Prepositional Phrases:** box controls how many adjoining prepositional phrases will trigger an error.

Click the **Reset All** button to restore the default set of rules for the selected level of grammar checking. When you have finished specifying rules, click OK to return to the Options dialog box. When you click OK in the Options dialog box, your changes will be saved and applied until you explicitly change them.

PROOFING FOREIGN LANGUAGE TEXT

For more information on proofing multi-language documents, see the *Microsoft Word User's Guide* and the documentation accompanying your foreign-language proofing files.

You can use any of the proofing tools discussed in this chapter with a document containing more than one language. To do this, follow these general steps:

1. Obtain and install the appropriate *proofing files* for the language or languages you are using. These files are not included in the Word package; they must be obtained separately from Microsoft.

2. Format any foreign language text in your document by selecting the text, choosing **Format/Language,** and highlighting the appropriate language in the list. See Chapter 16 for information on applying language formatting, as well as other character-formatting features.

3. Run any of the proofing tools as described in this chapter. It will automatically use the appropriate file when proofing text formatted for a particular foreign language.

When you are formatting text using **Format/Language,** you can also choose the **No Proofing** option.

M̲ark Selected Text As:

(no proofing)
Brazilian Portuguese

The proofing tools will ignore any text to which you apply this formatting feature. You might want to apply this feature to tables of technical terms, excerpts from programming languages, or other elements in your documents not suitable for normal proofing.

8

Using Tables

CHAPTER **8**

THE TABLE FEATURE ALLOWS YOU TO ARRANGE text in an array of rows and columns. The feature is quite flexible, and makes it easy to organize data. In this chapter, you will learn how to create, edit, and format tables. You will also learn how to perform calculations on numeric data contained in tables—or elsewhere in a document. Finally, you will learn how to *sort* document text both inside and outside of a table.

CREATING A TABLE

To create a table:

1. Place the insertion point at the position in your document where you want to insert the table.
2. Choose **Table/Insert Table**.
3. Enter the desired number of rows and columns, and the column width, and click OK.
4. Alternatively, you can create a table by placing the mouse pointer on the **Table button** in the Toolbar, pressing the button, and dragging the highlight to indicate the number of rows and columns you want.

The Tab key is discussed in Chapters 3 and 15. Chapter 15 explains how to set indents and other paragraph formatting features.

If the Table feature were not available, you would have to arrange tabular data using the Tab key, together with appropriate paragraph formatting. Figure 8.1 illustrates two simple tabulations of text within a Word document. The first was created simply by using tab characters; the second was generated by using tab characters and setting the paragraph indents. The table in Figure 8.2, however, would be quite difficult to create with these methods. As you will see, however, it can easily be produced using the Table feature.

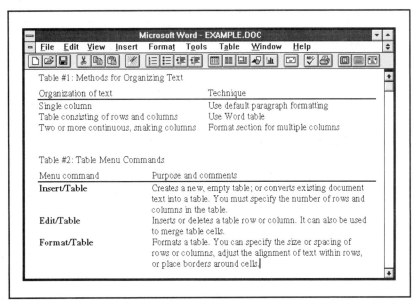

Figure 8.1: Two simple tables created by using tab characters and by adjusting paragraph indents

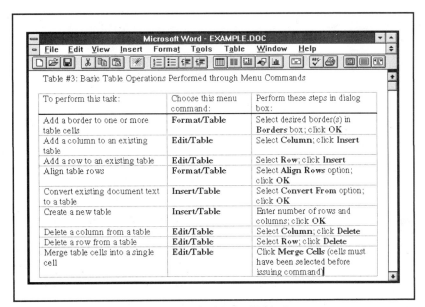

Figure 8.2: A complex table created with the Table feature

When you create a table in Word, you begin with a framework, which is a collection of separate *cells* or boxes arranged in rows and columns. You then insert text or graphics into each cell.

To create a new, empty table, first place the insertion point at the position in your document where you would like the table, and then choose the **Table/Insert Table** menu command. Word will display the dialog box illustrated in Figure 8.3.

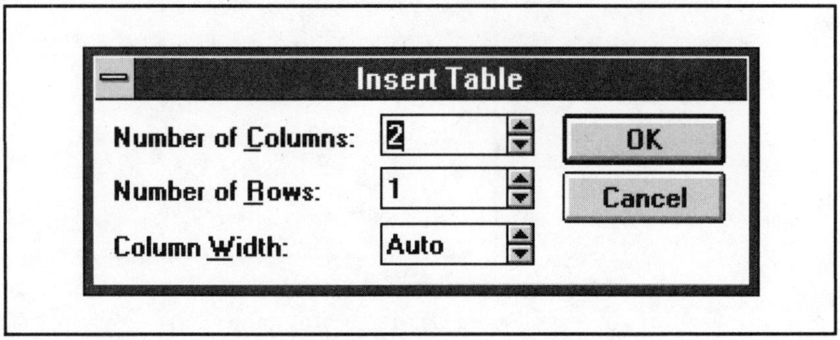

The commands listed on the Table menu *change* according to the position of the insertion point or the current selection. Therefore, you may not see a menu command mentioned in this chapter until you perform the initial steps in the procedure being described.

Figure 8.3: The Insert Table dialog box

Enter the number of columns you want into the **Number of Columns:** field, and the number of rows into the **Number of Rows:** field. If you'd rather, you can click the up or down arrow at the right end of the text box to automatically increase or decrease the amount displayed in the box, instead of typing in a value.

Word initially suggests 2 columns and 1 row. However, if you are not sure how many rows you will need, you can simply accept the suggested value of 1; as you will see, it is easy to add new rows as you enter text into the table. Also, you can later adjust the number of rows or columns in a table you have already created, using **Insert Cells**, **Insert Rows**, or **Insert Columns** from the Table menu. These commands are discussed in the section "Editing a Table."

If you want to arrange text in two or more continuous snaking columns, like those appearing in a newspaper, you must use *document formatting* commands (presented in Chapter 13) rather than the Table feature.

When creating a table, you can also specify the **Column Width**. The default value that Word suggests is *Auto*. The Auto value causes Word to automatically calculate the column width by evenly dividing the total distance between the left and right page margins. For

Page margins are discussed in Chapters 13 and 15.

example, if the total width of the text between the margins is 6 inches, and if you insert a table with three columns, the width of each column will be 2 inches. (The actual usable width is slightly less, since Word normally leaves space between table columns. You will see how to adjust the amount of space between columns in the section "Formatting a Table.")

Alternatively, you can specify a numeric column width value. For example, if you enter 1 inch into the Column Width field, and if you specify 2 columns, the table will have a total width of 2 inches, and each of the columns will be 1 inch wide. Thus, when you first create a new table, the columns in the table are always equally wide. In the section "Using the Table Formatting Options," you will see how to adjust the width of each column individually, so that you can give the columns different widths.

Finally, click the OK button to insert the table framework into your document and return to the editing window.

When you return to the editing window, the insertion point will be within the first cell of the new table. So that you can see the boundaries of the table cells, Word displays *grid lines* around each cell. To see these lines, however, the **Table/Gridlines** menu option must be selected (as it is when you first install Word).

Displaying grid lines makes it easier to work with a table. These lines are shown on the screen, but do *not* appear on printed copies of the document.

CREATING A TABLE GRAPHICALLY

Word also provides a graphical method for inserting a new table. First, click and hold the **Table button** on the Toolbar.

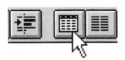

Word displays a graphic representation of a table under the Toolbar button. While holding down the button, drag the highlight over the cells you want to include in your table. When the table has the desired configuration, release the button; Word will instantly insert a table with the selected number of rows and colums at the position of the insertion point. For example, to insert a table with 2 rows and 3 columns, drag the highlight until you obtain the following pattern

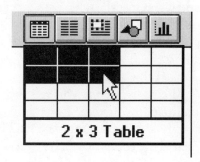

and then release the mouse button. When you use this method, Word automatically assigns the Auto column width value.

To cancel the operation, move the mouse pointer either above or to the left of the grid, and release the button:

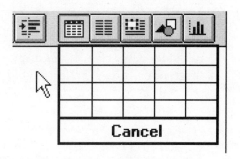

ENTERING TEXT INTO A TABLE

To enter text into a table:

1. Place the insertion point within the desired cell by clicking in it, and type as if you were creating a normal paragraph. Word confines the text to the cell, and automatically inserts line breaks and increases the row height as necessary.

2. You can create separate paragraphs *within* a table cell by pressing Enter.

3. Move the insertion point to enter text in other cells.

You can also insert a graphic into a table cell—see Chapter 9. You cannot, however, insert another table into a table (in other words, tables cannot be nested).

The maximum height for a single cell is one document page.

As mentioned, when you insert a new table, the insertion point is initially placed at the beginning of the *first* cell (that is, the cell in the upper left corner of the table). You can place the insertion point within any cell in the table by clicking anywhere within the boundaries of the cell. You can also quickly move the insertion point from cell to cell in an empty table by using the arrow keys, as outlined in the following section.

Once the insertion point is within the desired cell, you can enter text as if you were creating a normal paragraph. As usual, simply continue typing without pressing the Enter key at the edge of the column; Word will automatically insert line breaks as needed.

Notice that as you type, all text is kept within the boundaries of the cell. If additional space is needed to accommodate the text, Word automatically increases the *height* of the cells in the current row; it does not expand the *width* of the cell unless you direct it to do so. Word normally makes a row just high enough to accommodate the tallest cell in the row (that is, the cell containing text with the greatest vertical dimension); the cells in any given row always have the same height. As you will see in the section "Using the Table Formatting Options," you can specify a minimum or absolute row height.

NAVIGATING THROUGH A TABLE

FAST TRACK

To move the insertion point through a table, use one of the following methods:

- Place the insertion point at any character position by clicking on the position.
- Use the arrow keys to move character by character.
- Press **Tab** to move to the **next** cell, or **Shift-Tab** to move to the *prior* cell. (If you press Tab in the last cell, another row is added.)
- Use any of the other keystrokes listed in Table 8.1.

You can place the insertion point at any character position within a table simply by clicking the desired position.

You can move through a table in any direction—character by character—by using the **arrow keys**. When the insertion point reaches the last character in a cell, it moves to the next cell; when it reaches the boundary of the table, it moves outside of the table.

You can also move from cell to cell by pressing Tab or Shift-Tab. Wherever the insertion point is within a cell, pressing **Tab** moves it to the *next* cell and selects any text occurring within it. Specifically, it moves the insertion point to the cell to the immediate right; if it is already at the end of the row, it moves it to the leftmost cell in the row below. In a similar manner, **Shift-Tab** moves the insertion point to the *previous* cell, selecting any text it contains.

If you press Tab when the insertion point (or selection) is in the *last* cell of the table (that is, the rightmost cell in the bottom row), Word automatically inserts a new empty row at the end of the table and places the insertion point in the first cell of this row. The new bottom row is given the same number of cells and the same cell widths as the row above it.

Since it is therefore so easy to add new rows to the end of a table, when you create a new table you really only need to specify the full number of columns. You can simply add rows as needed when you are entering information into the table.

Table 8.1 summarizes the keystrokes discussed in this section, as well as several other keystrokes for quickly moving the insertion point within a table.

To enter an actual tab character while you are in a table, you must press **Ctrl-Tab**.

Table 8.1: Keystrokes for Navigating through a Table

PRESS THIS KEY	TO MOVE TO
↑, ↓, ←, or →	Next character position
Tab	Next cell; if in last cell of table, adds a new row
Shift-Tab	Previous cell
Alt-Home	First cell in current row
Alt-End	Last cell in current row
Alt-PgUp	Top cell in current column
Alt-PgDn	Bottom cell in current column

PARAGRAPHS WITHIN A TABLE

 The end-of-cell mark may also appear as a shining sun or other distinctive symbol depending on your screen font.

Text within a single table cell consists of one or more complete paragraphs. If you make paragraph marks visible (by choosing **Tools/ Options**, selecting the **View** button in the **Category:** list, and selecting the **Paragraph Marks** option), you will see that a special character, a square # symbol known as an *end-of-cell mark,* replaces the paragraph symbol that would otherwise appear at the end of each cell. For example, Figure 8.4 illustrates a table with paragraph marks enabled. The first two cells each consist of a single paragraph, with end-of-cell marks at the end of each one. The last cell, however, consists of two paragraphs, since the Enter key was pressed immediately following the word Cells.

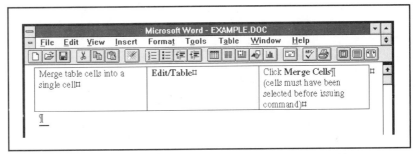

Figure 8.4: A table with paragraph (and end-of-cell) marks enabled

In Figure 8.4 notice also that the same mark appears at the end of each row, just beyond the right boundary of the table. Because in this case the mark serves to indicate the end of a row, it is known as an *end-of-row mark.*

As usual, you can press **Shift-Enter** while typing text into a table cell to insert a line break without forming a new paragraph.

CONVERTING TEXT TO A TABLE

FAST TRACK

To convert text to a table:

1. To indicate how you want the text placed into cells, divide the text by using a **paragraph mark** to start a new row, and a **tab** or **comma** to separate columns.

2. Select the text.

3. Issue the **Table/Convert Text to Table** menu command.

In addition to inserting a new, empty table, you can also select a block of existing document text and have Word *convert* this text to a table. As long as the text is arranged with "rows" on separate lines and "columns" separated consistently by either tabs or commas, Word will automatically create a table of the appropriate size and insert the text into the table cells.

To convert text to a table, you must prepare the text with the appropriate characters that will divide the text into smaller units, each of which is to be inserted into a separate table cell. Figure 8.5 illustrates three blocks of text ready to be converted to tables. The first block of three lines uses paragraph marks to delimit text that is to go into three rows, and the second and third use tabs and commas, respectively, to delimit text that is to go into three columns.

After arranging a block of text for conversion, select the block and then **Table/Convert Text to Table**. Figure 8.6 illustrates the three

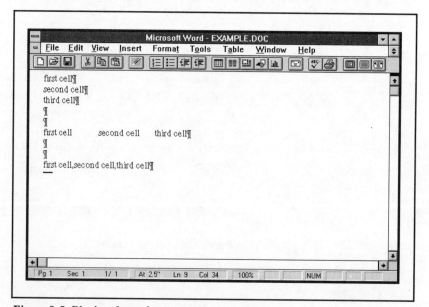

Figure 8.5: Blocks of text for conversion to tables

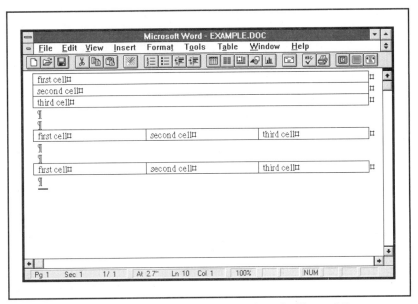

Figure 8.6: Tables generated from the blocks of text in Figure 8.5

blocks from Figure 8.5 after they have been converted to tables, with the number of rows and columns automatically calculated by Word.

If your block of text included both tabs and commas, Word will display a dialog box asking you which delimiting character you want to use.

CONVERTING A TABLE TO TEXT

To convert a table into regular text:

1. Select the row or rows in the table that you want to convert (you must select *all* the cells in each row).

2. Choose **Table/Convert Table to Text**. Word will display a dialog box.

3. Choose the **Paragraph Marks**, **Tabs**, or **Commas** option to indicate how you want the contents of separate cells to be separated.

When you convert a table to normal text, Word removes the table framework, but preserves the text or graphics contained in the cells. The text or graphics appear in your document, separated by paragraph marks, tabs, or commas (you specify which).

See the section "Selecting within a Table" for information on efficiently selecting all or portions of a table.

The first step is to select the table row or rows that you want to convert. You must select one or more entire rows. Next, select **Table/Convert Table to Text** and choose one of the following three items within the dialog box that Word displays: Paragraph Marks, Tabs, or Commas. If you choose **Paragraph Marks**, Word will insert the contents of each cell as a separate paragraph in your document (that is, each on top of the next, not across from it as it was in its table row). This is useful for "spilling" long table entries into a single list. If you choose **Tabs**, Word will separate the contents of each cell within a given row with a tab character, and will separate each row with a paragraph mark. Thus, the original row and column appearance of the table will be maintained when it is converted to text. If you choose **Commas**, Word will separate the contents of each cell with a comma (thus, you lose the visual spacing you had within the table row), and each row with a paragraph mark.

EDITING A TABLE

To edit a table:

- Insert cells by selecting a block of existing cells the size and shape of the cells you want to insert, and choosing **Table/Insert Cells** (or **Rows** or **Columns**).

- Delete cells by selecting the cells you want to remove and choosing **Table/Delete Cells** (or **Rows** or **Columns**).

- Combine a group of two or more cells into a single cell by selecting the cells and selecting **Table/Merge Cells**.

- Divide a merged cell into its constituent cells by selecting the cell and using **Table/Split Cells**.

- Divide a table into two tables (with a paragraph mark between) by placing the insertion point where you want the division and choosing **Table/Split Table** or pressing **Ctrl-Shift-Enter**.

■ Delete, move, or copy cell contents using the standard block editing operations discussed in Chapter 5.

In this section, you will learn how to insert or delete cells within an existing table. You will also learn how to merge individual cells, and how to divide a table into two parts. Finally, you will learn how to delete text within one or more cells and how to copy or move text from one part of a table to another.

INSERTING OR DELETING CELLS

You already saw how to insert an entire row of cells at the end of a table by pressing the Tab key while the insertion point is in the last cell. In this section, you will learn how to insert or delete entire rows or columns anywhere in the table, and how to insert or delete arbitrary *blocks* of cells. To perform these operations, however, you must first learn how to select one or more cells within a table.

Selecting within a Table

With the keyboard, you can select one or more characters or graphics within a cell, one or more entire cells, or even create a selection that includes both a table and text outside of the table.

As explained in Chapter 5, you can use either **Shift** in conjunction with an arrow key, or **F8** and then an arrow key. When selecting within a table, however, there are several unique features:

Remember that to unmark a selection, you simply click on the text, press an arrow key, or press any other key that normally moves the insertion point (such as PgUp).

- While pressing Shift, or after pressing F8, you can use any of the Alt-key combinations listed in Table 8.1 to rapidly extend the selection.

- You can select the *entire table* by pressing **Alt-5** (5 on the numeric keypad—but be sure NumLock is *on*).

- You can extend the selection one character at a time only while the selection remains within a single cell; as soon as the selection is extended into a neighboring cell, pressing the arrow key again selects *all* characters in *both* adjoining cells. Each time you again press the arrow key, another entire adjoining cell is selected, until the entire row or column is selected. Pressing the arrow key again at this point selects the following *entire* row or column.

- There is no column selection mode while in a table—pressing Ctrl-Shift-F8 has the same effect as pressing F8.

You can also use **Select Row**, **Select Column**, and **Select Table** from the Table menu to select entire portions of a table.

With the mouse, you can select text or graphics within a table using the mouse techniques described in Chapter 5; however, there are several unique considerations when selecting within a table:

- You can extend the selection one character at a time only while the selection remains within a single cell; as soon as the selection is dragged into an adjoining cell, both entire cells are selected.

- There is no column selection mode within a table—pressing the right mouse button does nothing.

- In addition to the usual selection bar to the left of the table, each cell has its *own* selection bar in the leftmost portion of the cell. In this area, the mouse pointer becomes an arrow pointing up and to the right.

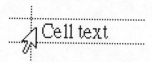

- To select an *entire cell,* click in the cell's selection bar.

- To select an *entire row,* double-click in any selection bar within the row. (You can also select the entire row by single-clicking in the selection bar to the left of the table, next to the desired row.)

- Each column has a selection area at the top of the column. In this area, the mouse pointer becomes a downward-pointing arrow.

- To select an *entire column,* click in the column selection area above the desired column. (You can also select an entire column by clicking with the *right mouse button* anywhere within the column.)

Inserting or Deleting Entire Rows or Columns

To *insert* new rows into a table, first select the desired number of rows (including the end-of-row marks) and choose **Table/Select Row**. Then choose **Table/Insert Rows**. The same number of new, empty rows will be inserted *above* the selected rows, with the same number of cells and the same cell widths.

To *delete* rows, select the (entire) rows and choose. **Table/Delete Rows**. Any rows remaining below will move up to fill in the gap. Note that deleting a row or column with **Table/Delete Rows** or **Table/Delete Columns** removes all of the cells in the row or column, together with all of the text contained in the cells. In contrast, selecting a row or column and pressing **Del** removes the content of the cells, but leaves the empty cells in the table.

As with inserting rows, you insert a new column by selecting an entire column in the table, and then choosing **Table/Insert Columns**. The new column will be inserted to the *left* of the selected column, and will have the same number of cells and the same cell widths as the column to its right.

To insert a new column to the *right* of the table, select the entire column of end-of-row marks:

before issuing the Insert Columns command. (In this case, the new column will be given the same cell widths as the column to its *left*.)

Word will not display the **Insert Rows** or **Delete Rows** commands on the Table menu until an *entire* row has been selected—including the end-of-row mark, whether the mark is visible or not.

Once you have selected an entire single row or column, you can easily extend the selection to its neighbor by pressing **Shift** and an arrow key, or by clicking in the neighboring row or column while pressing Shift.

Moving Blocks of Cells within a Table

In addition to inserting or deleting entire table rows or columns, you can also insert or delete more arbitrary blocks within an existing table.

To insert an empty block of cells, first indicate the shape of the block you want to insert by selecting a block of existing cells, as shown in Figure 8.7, then select **Table/Insert Cells**. Word will then display the Insert Cells dialog box (shown in Figure 8.8) so you can specify how to rearrange the table to accommodate the new cells.

Figure 8.9 illustrates the different results of choosing **Shift Cells Right** and **Shift Cells Down** when inserting cells into the table first seen in Figure 8.7. Notice that Word additionally fills in empty cells at the bottom of all the other columns when moving cells vertically, to make them all the same height.

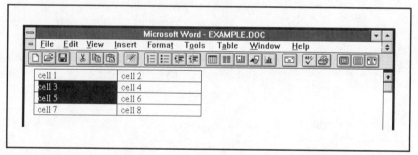

Figure 8.7: A table with a selected block of cells

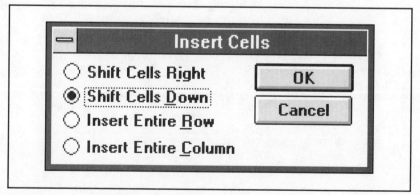

Figure 8.8: The Insert Cells dialog box

As you can see in the Insert Cells dialog box, you can also insert an entire row or column by placing the insertion point anywhere within an existing row or column and selecting **Table/Insert Cells**. You can then choose the **Insert Entire Row** or **Insert Entire Column** option in the dialog box. Unlike the methods described in the previous section, you do not need to select an entire row or column prior to issuing the menu command.

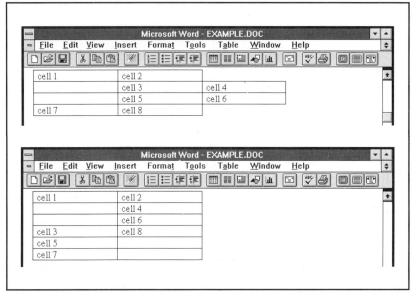

Figure 8.9: Top: The result of Insert Cells Right. Bottom: The result of Insert Cells Down.

In a similar fashion, you can delete an arbitrary block of one or more table cells. First, select the block you want to remove (as shown in Figure 8.7). Then choose **Table/Delete Cells**. Word will display the Delete Cells dialog box (Figure 8.10). Select either the **Shift Cells Left** or the **Shift Cells Up** option to tell Word which way to shift the existing table cells to fill the gap left by the deletion. Figure 8.11 illustrates the different effects of deleting the block of cells selected in Figure 8.7 with the Shift Cells Left and the Shift Cells Up options.

MERGING AND SPLITTING CELLS

You can merge two or more adjacent cells within the same row to form a single cell. First, select the cells you want to combine, then choose **Table/Merge Cells**.

You cannot merge cells that are within the same column, since all cells within a given row must be the same height.

For example, you might want to merge all of the cells within the first row of a table, so that you can place a centered title in a single

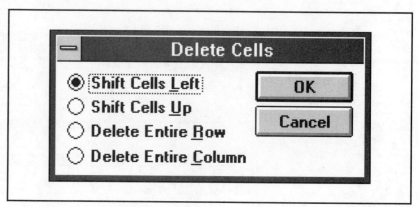

Figure 8.10: The Delete Cells dialog box

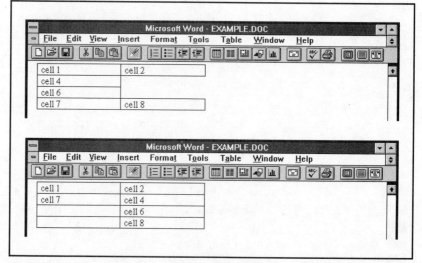

Figure 8.11: Top: The result of deleting the cells selected in Figure 8.7 with Shift Cells Left. Bottom: The result of deleting the cells selected in Figure 8.7 with Shift Cells Down.

wide cell across the top. The following steps would accomplish this task:

1. Double-click within the selection bar of any cell in the first row. This selects all cells within the first row.

2. Choose **Table/Merge Cells**. The top row will become a single cell.

3. Place the insertion point at the upper left corner of the single top-row cell, and type the desired title.

4. To center the title, choose **Format/Paragraph** and select **Centered** within the **Alignment:** list box.

5. Delete any unnecessary paragraph markers within the cell containing the title. (When Word merges cells, it inserts into the combined cell a separate paragraph for each cell that was merged; accordingly, the new cell contains more vertical space than the cells that were merged.)

When you select a cell that was previously combined, Word remembers the number of cells that were merged to create the combined cell, and it replaces **Merge Cells** on the Table menu with **Split Cells**.

After you have merged a group of cells, you can later use **Table/ Split Cells** to split the single resulting cell back into the same number of cells that were used to create it. You cannot split a cell unless the cell was created by merging cells.

DIVIDING TABLES

You can split a table between any rows in order to insert standard text by placing the insertion point (or selecting) within a row and choosing **Table/Split Table** or pressing **Ctrl-Shift-Enter**. (If the insertion point is within the top row, this command simply inserts a normal paragraph above the table.)

Note that you can recombine a table that has been split by simply deleting the paragraph mark (whether visible or invisible) that lies between them. In general, you can merge separate tables be deleting any paragraph marks that separate them.

Hard page breaks are discussed in Chapter 3.

You can also split a table by pressing **Ctrl-Enter** to insert a hard page break immediately above the row containing the insertion point (or selection).

DELETING, MOVING, AND COPYING TEXT WITHIN A TABLE

You can delete, copy, or move a block of text or graphics that is entirely *within* a cell of a table using the standard techniques explained in Chapter 5.

You can also use many of the standard techniques given in Chapter 5 to move or copy a block consisting of one or more entire table cells. However, when moving or copying such a block, the following special rules apply:

- You cannot use **F2** to move or copy a block that includes one or more entire cells. If you attempt to do so, Word will display the message

  Not a valid selection

- If you select one or more *entire table cells* and press **Del**, Word will delete the contents of the cells but will leave the empty cells within the table framework. If, however, the table selection includes one or more characters *outside* of the table, pressing Del will remove both the contents *and* the selected cells.

- If the selection encompasses all or part of a table *and* one or more characters outside of the table, the Cut or Copy command will transfer both the characters and the selected cells with their contents to the Clipboard. In this case, you cannot paste the Clipboard contents into a table.

- If you select a block of cells consisting of one or more *entire rows or columns* and then choose **Edit/Cut**, the table cells and their contents will be completely removed from the table and placed in the Clipboard. You can then paste this data from the Clipboard to the left cell of another row or the top cell of another column to reinsert the cells and their contents. Remember that to select an entire row, the end-of-row mark (whether visible or invisible) must be included in the selection.

- In contrast, if you select *less than* an entire row or column, Edit/Cut erases only the *contents* of the cells, leaving the cells themselves empty but intact in the table framework. Also, Edit/Cut and Edit/Copy will transfer only the cell contents to the Clipboard.

- If you then paste this data into a new location in a table, the data will *overwrite* the contents of the existing cells at the new location; it will *not* insert additional cells. (If you paste the data into a document *outside* of a table, Word will create a new table framework to contain the pasted cell contents.)

To illustrate the difference between two of these techniques, try this exercise in moving a column of cells from one position to another within a table:

1. Select an entire column and choose **Edit/Cut** or press **Ctrl-X**. All cells in the selected column, as well as their contents, will be removed from the table and placed in the Clipboard.

2. Place the insertion point in any cell *but* a top one and select **Edit/Paste Columns** or press **Ctrl-V**. Word will simply overwrite the contents of the cells in the target column.

3. Place the insertion point within the *top* cell of a column and again select **Edit/Paste Columns** or press **Ctrl-V**. The Clipboard's cells with their contents will be inserted as a new column to the left of the column containing the insertion point.

USING THE TABLE FORMATTING OPTIONS

To format a table:

- Adjust the width of one or more table cells by selecting the cells, selecting **Table/Column Width**, and entering the desired width into the **Width of Column:** box.

- Adjust the spacing between cells by selecting one or more table rows, choosing **Table/Column Width**, and entering the spacing into the **Space Between Cols:** box.

- Assign a row indent by selecting one or more table rows, choosing **Table/Row Height**, and entering into the **Indent From Left:** box either a positive value (to move the rows right) or a negative value (to move the rows left).

- Set the height of one or more rows by selecting the rows, choosing **Table/Row Height**, and setting the desired values in the **Height of Row:** box and the **At:** box.

- Adjust the horizontal alignment of one or more rows by selecting the rows, choosing **Table/Row Height**, and choosing the **Left**, **Center**, or **Right** option.

- Place borders around cells by selecting the cells and choosing **Format/Border**.

You can format any of the characters or paragraphs within a table using the standard formatting commands discussed in Chapters 15 and 16. Simply select text or graphics within one or more table cells, and apply the appropriate formatting command. This section covers formatting features that are unique to tables, as well as a few standard features that exhibit special properties when applied to tables. The following features are discussed:

- The column width

- The space between columns

- The amount the rows are indented

- The row height

- The alignment of rows

- Borders placed around cells

Setting the Column Width

See Appendix C for information on specifying various units of measurement when entering values into dialog boxes.

You can adjust the width of one or more cells in a table. First, select the cells you want to adjust (if you want to change the width of a single cell, you can simply place the insertion point within this cell). Next, choose **Table/Column Width**; Word will display the Column Width dialog box, illustrated in Figure 8.12. Enter the desired width into the **Width of Column:** box and click the OK button. Word will set the width of all selected cells to the specified value.

As you saw, you must specify an initial column width when creating a table through the **Table/Insert Table** command; this width applies uniformly to all cells in the table. The Column Width dialog

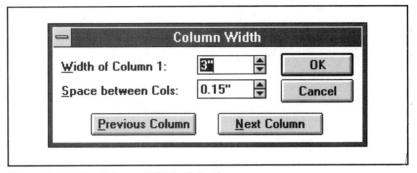

Figure 8.12: The Column Width dialog box

box, however, allows you to specify the width of individual cells or groups of cells. Also, the Table/Insert Table command allows you to enter a column width value of **Auto**, so that Word *automatically* calculates the initial column width; when using the Column Width dialog box, however, you must enter a specific numeric value (Auto is not accepted as a valid measurement).

If you are assigning the *same* width to cells in several adjoining columns, it is easiest simply to select all of the cells in advance, and then issue the **Table/Insert Cells** command. If you want to assign *different* width values to cells in adjoining columns, you can use the following procedure:

1. Select the desired cell or cells in the first column.

2. Choose **Table/Column Width**.

3. Enter the desired width for the first column's cells into the **Width of Column:** box.

4. Click the **Next Column** button to apply the specified width to the cell's first column, and then move to the corresponding cells in the next column to the right.

5. Repeat steps 3 and 4 for all remaining columns you want to adjust.

6. After you have formatted the cells in all columns, click OK.

You can also use the mouse to adjust the width of *all* cells in a given column, using the following procedure:

1. Place the mouse pointer over one of the vertical gridlines of the table. The pointer will assume the following shape:

2. Press the mouse button and drag the gridline to the left or right to adjust the width of the column (the one to the left of the gridline). Notice that as you drag the gridline, any cells to the right are also moved over to make room or take up the space. (If you drag the leftmost gridline, you will simply indent the entire table.)

3. Alternatively, press **Shift** while you drag the gridline. In this case, any cells to right of the gridline remain stationary.

As you will discover in Chapter 15, you can also use the *ruler* to rapidly adjust the width of one or more cells in a table.

Setting the Column Spacing

Unlike setting the column *width* as described in the previous section, adjusting the column *spacing* does not change the width of the cells or the overall width of the table as indicated by the gridlines. Column spacing refers to the space Word maintains between the left and right edges of the cell and the cell's contents. It therefore changes the amount of horizontal space available for text in each cell.

1. Select one or more cells in each row you want to adjust. Setting the column spacing always affects *all* cells in a given row.

2. Choose the Table/Column Width menu command. Word will display the Column Width dialog box, illustrated in Figure 8.15.

3. Enter the desired column spacing value into the **Space Between Cols:** box (the default value is 0.15''), and click OK.

Setting the Row Indent

The row indent is the amount of space between the left page margin and the beginning of the first cell in the row. By default, the indent is 0, meaning that the first cell is aligned evenly with the left margin. If you assign a positive value, the cells are moved right, toward the center of the page. If you assign a negative value, the cells are moved left, out into the margin area. Figure 8.13 illustrates positive and negative row indents.

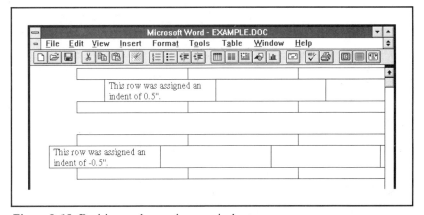

Figure 8.13: Positive and negative row indents

To set the row indent, as well as the row height and alignment (discussed in the next two sections), first select the row or rows (you may select one or more cells in each row), and then **Table/Row Height**. Word will display the Row Height dialog box, illustrated in Figure 8.14.

To indent the selected rows enter the amount of the indent into the **Indent From Left:** box, and click the OK button.

You can also set the indent of all rows in a table by dragging the leftmost table gridline with the mouse. Drag to the right to create a positive indent, or to the left to create a negative indent.

As explained in Chapter 15, you can also use the *ruler* to set the indent of one or more rows.

Setting the Row Height

While the Row Height dialog box (Figure 8.14) is open, you can also adjust the height of all the cells in the selected row or rows

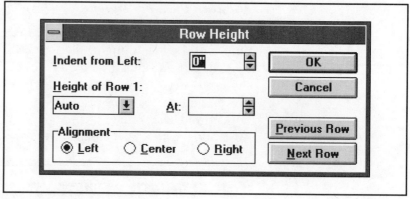

Figure 8.14: The Row Height dialog box

(remember that the cells in a given row always have the same height). First, you need to select one of the three items in the **Height of Row:** list box:

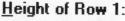

See Appendix C for information on entering measurement values.

If you choose **Auto** (the default), Word will make the row just high enough to accommodate the tallest text or graphics contained in the row. If you choose **At Least** or **Exactly**, then you must also enter a numeric value into the **At:** box (the default value is 1 line).

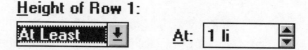

If you choose the At Least item, then Word will use the value in the At box as the minimum row height; if, however, the cell contents do not fit within this height, the height will be increased just enough to accommodate the contents. If you choose the Exactly item, then Word will make the row the height specified in the At box *regardless of whether the contents fit.* In this case, though the text or graphics entered into cells within the row may not be entirely visible, you can later make the contents visible by selecting Table/Row Height again to increase the cell height.

Setting the Row Alignment

Row alignment affects the horizontal position of a table row with respect to the page margins. Setting the alignment by setting the Alignment option shifts the horizontal position of the *entire selected row or rows*. (In contrast, you can set the alignment of *paragraphs within specific cells* by using the ruler or the **Format/Paragraph** command, as discussed in Chapter 15.)

You can pick one of three alignment styles from the **Alignment** area of the Row Height dialog box:

Remember that when you create a table through the Table/Insert Table command, it fills the entire space between the left and right page margins by default. In this case, changing the row alignment style will have almost no effect. However, if you create a table with a column width other than Auto, or if you later change the width of one or more columns, you may want to specify the row alignment.

Placing Borders around Cells

Do not confuse table *borders* with table *gridlines*. Gridlines are optionally displayed on the screen to mark the edges of the cells so that it is easier to work with the table; they do not appear on the printed copy of the document. Borders, however, are lines that appear both on the screen and on the printed copy. Borders are placed directly on top of the edges marked by gridlines.

The options for borders are quite flexible. You can choose from a variety of line styles, and you can place borders on any combination of the cell edges that are marked with gridlines.

Borders are added by selecting one or more table cells and choosing **Format/Border**. The method for placing borders around table cells is almost identical to the method for adding borders to paragraphs of text, and is discussed in Chapter 16 ("Paragraph Formatting").

CALCULATING AND SORTING

Using Word, you can perform calculations on numeric data contained within a document. You can also sort text within a specified document area. Calculating and sorting can be performed on data either within tables, or in any other part of a document. These operations are included in this chapter, however, because they are especially useful when working with tables.

CALCULATING

To perform a calculation:

1. Enter the numbers and operators into a table or other position within a document.
2. Select the numbers and operators.
3. Choose **Tools/Calculate**.
4. Alternatively, you can perform a calculation by entering an equals sign, followed by an arithmetic expression, into a field.

You can perform a calculation on numeric data within a document either by selecting the data and issuing the Tools/Calculate command, or by using a field.

Calculating with a Selection

To perform a calculation, first enter the appropriate numbers and *mathematical operators* (such as + , − , and so on) into your table or document. Then, select this data using either normal or column selection mode and issue the **Tools/Calculate** command. Word will evaluate the numbers and operators starting from the beginning of the selection and proceeding character by character to the end of the selection. Characters that are neither numbers nor operators are simply ignored. The result of the calculation is placed in the Clipboard and displayed in the status bar; it can then be pasted into any document location.

Table 8.2 lists the mathematical operators that are recognized by the Calculate command.

In general, you should place an operator between every two numbers. There are two exceptions to this rule:

- If there is no operator in front of a number, Word will *add* the number to the result. This makes totaling columns fast and easy.

- You should place the percentage operator (%) *after* a number.

Table 8.2: Operators You Can Use in a Calculation (in Order of Precedence)

OPERATOR	DESCRIPTION
^	Exponentiation (raising a number to a power)
%	Percentage
*	Multiplication
/	Division
+ (or no operator)	Addition
–	Subtraction

Also, although the Calculate command normally ignores characters that are neither numbers nor operators, you should not include an exclamation mark in your expression. It may cause the calculation to fail (Word will display the **Syntax Error** message in the status bar).

When you combine more than one operator in a single expression, you may have to specify the order in which the operations are to be performed. For example, you might think that Word would evaluate the expression

3 + 5 / 2

by adding 5 to 3 and then dividing the result by 2, arriving at a final result of 4. Word, however, always performs division *before* addition. Therefore, it would first divide 5 by 2, and then add the result to 3,

Placing parentheses around *a single number* causes Word to treat the number as negative. Similarly, Word displays a negative result in the status bar by enclosing the number in parentheses.

obtaining a final value of 5.5. You can change the normal order of precedence by grouping the appropriate numbers and operators with *parentheses*. To force Word to perform the addition first, you can use parentheses as follows:

$$(3 + 5) / 2$$

In this case, Word treats the $3 + 5$ as a single unit to be evaluated first, and then divided by 2. The final result would be 4.

The operators in Table 8.2 are listed in the order in which Word performs the corresponding operations. Specifically, Word first performs any exponentiation (raising a number to a power) or percentage (that is, dividing the number preceding the % by 100). It then performs any multiplication or division (moving from left to right). Finally, it performs any addition or subtraction (also moving from left to right).

Also, if you place a dollar sign ($) in front of any number in the selection, Word will format the final result as a monetary amount.

Figure 8.15 illustrates a simple table. To obtain the total in the last row, the right column was selected, the Tools/Calculate command was issued, and the result was pasted into the bottom right cell.

Schedule C, Part II: Business Expenses	
Advertising	1,245
Depreciation	897
Insurance	593
Legal services	1,576
Rent	10,472
Travel	2,571
Meals and Entertainment	14,782
Total	32,136

Figure 8.15: A column totaled by using Tools/Calculate

Calculating with a Field

You can use an *expression* field to perform a calculation within your document. The advantage of using a field rather than the Tools/Calculate command is that if you change the numbers in any of the cells, or if you insert new cells, the sum in the bottom row will reflect the change whenever you perform the very simple step of updating the field.

The following simplified steps illustrate how to use the expression field to perform a calculation. (For complete information on how to use this field, see the Fields topic in the *Microsoft Word for Windows Technical Reference.*)

1. Place the insertion point where you would like to insert the result of the calculation.

2. Issue the **Insert Field** command by pressing **Ctrl-F9**. Word will insert the following special brace characters:

   {}

   and will place the insertion point between them.

3. Now type an equals sign inside the brace characters, followed by the *expression* consisting of a combination of numbers and operators conforming to the rules outlined in the previous section. For example,

   { = \$231.79 * 6.25%}

4. While the insertion point is still between the brace characters, press **F9** to "update" the field. Word will instantly replace the brace characters and the expression they contain with the *results* of the expression.

The example field just given would be replaced with the following:

\$14.4869

In addition to operators recognized by the Tools/Calculate command (described in the previous section), you can use the following elements in an expression field:

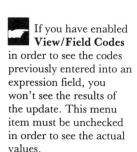
If you have enabled **View/Field Codes** in order to see the codes previously entered into an expression field, you won't see the results of the update. This menu item must be unchecked in order to see the actual values.

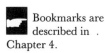
Bookmarks are described in . Chapter 4.

- *Bookmark names.* The bookmark must have been assigned to a block of text containing a number or numeric expression conforming to the rules given in the previous section.

CH. 8

- *References to table cells.* You can specify a row and column in the current table by the expression

    {RmCn}

    where *m* is the number of the row and *n* is the number of the column. You can express a *range* of cells as follows:

    {RaCx:RbCy}

    where *a* and *b* are the starting and ending rows, and *x* and *y* are the starting and ending columns. (References to cells can be used for functions, such as the SUM function.)

If you have included fields in your document, you should always choose the **Update Fields** option when you go to make a printed copy (using **File/Print**), so that the values printed are as up to date as possible.

As an example, consider the table illustrated in Figure 8.15. Rather than selecting the right column and issuing the Tools/ Calculate command, you could include the following expression in the lower right cell:

{ = SUM({R2C2:R5C2})}

(Remember that you do *not* type the brace characters. Rather, they are inserted by Word when you press **Ctrl-F9**.) When you update this field (by pressing **F9**), the field will be replaced by its result.

SORTING

Tools/Sorting lets you sort groups of paragraphs, rows in a table, or the contents of a single column in the document. When performing a sort, you can also choose among several options that affect the *way* the items are sorted:

- The *type* of sort key used to sort the items (alphanumeric, numeric, or date)

- Sensitivity to *case* (uppercase, lowercase) when sorting

- The *position* of the sort key (that is, you can sort using a specific *field*)

- The sorting *order* (ascending or descending)

Specifying the Items to Sort

Before issuing the Tools/Sorting command, you must select the collection of items you want Word to sort. Each of these items is known as a *sort record*. The following are the different types of sort records you can select:

- Entire paragraphs. (These can be paragraphs of numeric data, of course, but you might find a situation where you want to sort text paragraphs—for instance, paragraphs you have set up as a glossary.)

- Entire rows in a table

- The lines of text, or rows of a table, within a single column

When performing a sort, Word rearranges the relative positions of the sort records, which are treated as single units; Word does not perform any sorting within them.

To sort a group of entire paragraphs (that is, to use paragraphs as the sort records), perform the following steps:

1. Select the paragraphs you want to sort.

2. Select **Tools/Sorting**. Word will display the dialog box illustrated in Figure 8.16.

If you do not make a selection prior to issuing the Tools/Sorting command, Word automatically selects the entire document, and sorts the document paragraphs.

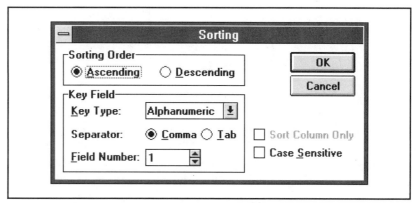

Figure 8.16: The Sorting dialog box

3. Choose the desired sort options, as described in the following sections.

4. Click the OK button.

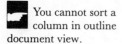 You can undo a sort by issuing the Edit/ Undo command immediately after the sort operation.

If you are in outline view (described in Chapter 24), and if your selection begins with a heading, Word uses entire headings as the sort records, and it sorts only the heading level that is at the beginning of the selection. Each heading is treated as a unit, and is moved with all of its subheadings and subtext. If it encounters a higher-level heading later in the selection, it stops the sort at this point, without including the higher level.

To sort rows in a Word table, simply select one or more *entire rows,* and then follow steps 2 through 4 described above. As you will see in subsequent sections, by selecting only one or more columns of the desired rows, you can confine the sort to selected columns, or you can specify an alternative sort key.

You can sort a single column of items, either outside or inside of a Word table. When you perform a column sort, only the text *within* the selected column is rearranged; text outside of the selection is left unaltered.

You cannot sort a column in outline document view.

To sort a column outside of a table, select the desired text using a column selection mode. When you open the Sorting dialog box, you must choose the **Sort Column Only** option. When sorting within a column, each *line* is treated as a separate sort record, even if the lines belong to the same paragraph. Figure 8.17 illustrates a column of text before and after sorting.

Sorting Key Types

When performing a sort, you can specify the type of data that is being sorted. Specifically, you can specify the type of data contained in the *sort key*: the portion of the sort record used to make the comparisons between the different sort records. Normally, Word uses the first 65 characters of the sort record as the key; however, in the section "Sorting by Field," you will see how to use a different portion of the sort record as a key.

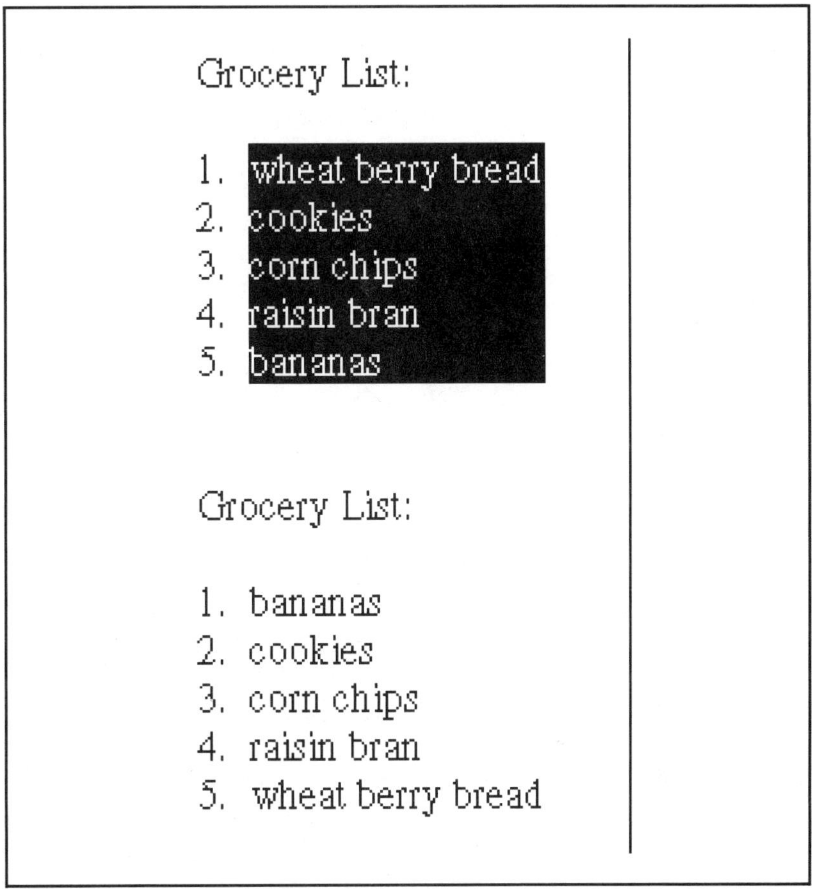

Grocery List:

1. wheat berry bread
2. cookies
3. corn chips
4. raisin bran
5. bananas

Grocery List:

1. bananas
2. cookies
3. corn chips
4. raisin bran
5. wheat berry bread

Figure 8.17: Sorting a column of text

To specify the sort key type, choose one of the options from the **Key Type:** box within the Sorting dialog box:

- Alphanumeric
- Numeric
- Date

Alphanumeric sorts the records according to a special sorting table containing symbols, numbers, and letters. (The table itself is listed in Appendix C of the *Microsoft Word for Windows User's Reference.*) In this

When comparing sort keys, Word ignores quotation marks, spaces, tabs, and diacritical marks.

table, punctuation marks precede numbers, numbers precede letters, and, for each letter, the uppercase letter precedes the lowercase letter. (In the next section you will see how to cause Word to ignore the case of letters when sorting.)

Numeric sorts according to the *numeric value* of the sort keys. To determine the numeric value of a given key, Word evaluates all numbers and mathematical operators it finds within the key, according to the rules used by the **Tools/Calculate** command (presented in the section "Calculating with a Selection"). Thus, for example, the character 9 would come before 10. As with the Tools/Calculate command, nonnumeric characters are ignored.

Date sorts according to date, of course, and each sort record must contain a date. Word will sort the records chronologically according to these dates, ignoring all characters not in date format.

Case Sensitivity

The **Case Sensitive** option in the Sorting dialog box is available only when you have chosen the Alphanumeric sort key type. If you choose this option, the uppercase version of a letter will precede the lowercase version of the same letter. If this option is off, the case of all letters will be ignored.

The following lists illustrate a column of items sorted with and then without the Case Sensitive option enabled.

> **Case Sensitive:**
>
> Acme
>
> Actress
>
> ace
>
> actor
>
> **Not Case Sensitive:**
>
> ace
>
> Acme
>
> actor
>
> Actress

Sorting by Field

Don't confuse a *sort field* with an *expression field,* which was explained previously in the chapter (in the section "Calculating with a Field").

As you saw previously, the sort key is the portion of the sort record used to make the comparisons between the different records. Normally, Word uses the first 65 characters of the sort record as the sort key. You can, however, have Word use a *specific portion* of the sort record, known as a *field*, as the sort key. The manner for specifying a field depends upon whether the sort is being performed outside or inside of a table.

Figure 8.18 illustrates sorting on a specified field in a record that is not part of a table. It shows a sequence of lists before (top figure) and after (bottom figure) sorting the lists using *the second field* in each record as the sort key. To create this example, the following values were specified in the Sorting dialog box:

Separator: ◉ **Comma** ◯ **Tab**

Field Number: 2

Within a table, Word considers each cell in a row to be a separate field. Therefore, when you perform a sort within a table, the **Separator:** item is not available in the Sorting dialog box. You need only

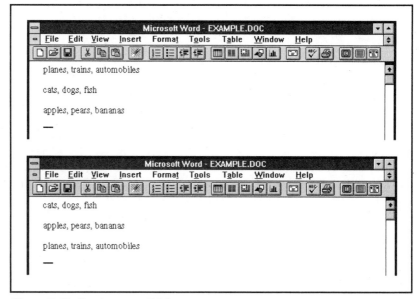

Figure 8.18: Sorting on a field

enter a number into the **Field Number:** box to indicate the number of the cell to be used for the sort key. Cells in the sort record are counted as though they are numbered starting with 1 at the beginning of the selection. Therefore, if you selected columns 4 through 9 as your sort record, you could use column 5 as the sort key by specifying a Field Number of 2.

Sorting Orders

Finally, you can specify the sorting order by choosing either the **Ascending** or **Descending** option within the **Sorting Order** area of the Sorting dialog box.

Ascending arranges records in an alphanumeric sort in alphabetical order, records in a numeric sort from smaller to larger, and records in a date sort from past to present to future.

Descending arranges records in an alphanumeric sort in reverse alphabetical order, records in a numeric sort from larger to smaller, and records in a date sort from future to present to past.

9

Incorporating Graphics

CHAPTER 9

IN THIS CHAPTER, YOU WILL LEARN HOW TO ADD variety to your Word documents by including graphic images or *pictures*. Unlike characters, pictures can consist of any shape or pattern. You can design pictures yourself or import them from a variety of sources. Once a picture is inserted in a document, you can freely adjust its position, size, and proportions.

You cannot create pictures in Word itself; rather, you must use the Microsoft Draw utility (included with Word) or another Windows application. You can even *import* graphic images from disk. For example, a picture might be derived from a freehand sketch produced in Microsoft Draw or Windows Paintbrush, from a chart generated in a spreadsheet application (such as Excel), or from a scanned image.

Because Word is extrememly flexible in terms of page layout, you can smoothly integrate pictures and text in your documents. Figure 9.1 illustrates a full printed page that includes a picture.

INSERTING PICTURES

To insert a picture into your document, use one of the following methods:

- Copy a graphic image from a drawing program or other Windows application to the Clipboard and choose **Edit/ Paste** to paste the image into your Word document.

- To *import* a picture from a disk file, place the cursor where you want the image to appear, choose **Insert/ Picture**, and specify the name of the graphics file.

- To create a picture using Microsoft Draw, place the insertion point where you want the image, choose **Insert/Object**, and select the **Microsoft Drawing** item

I created this page to illustrate how you can combine both text and graphics within a Word document. First, I designed the picture using Paintbrush, a Windows drawing program. When I judged that the sketch was about as good as it was going to get, I selected the rectangular area of the drawing that I wanted to use, and copied it into the Clipboard by choosing the Paintbrush **Edit/Copy** command.

Next, I switched into Word, opened a new document, and inserted the picture at the beginning of the document using the **Edit/Paste** menu command. I decided *not* to change the size of the picture (by cropping) or the proportions of the picture (by scaling).

I then specified the exact position on the page where I wanted the picture to be placed, by performing the following steps:

1.   I selected the picture by clicking it.

2.   I clicked the Frame button on the Toolbar, and clicked the Yes button when Word asked if I wanted to switch into Page Layout view.

Since the picture was initially placed in the position where I wanted it, I did not have to drag it in Page Layout view. Placing the picture in a frame not only caused Word to position it at a specific location on the page, but it also caused Word to flow text around the picture. (The picture is contained in its own paragraph. If it were not placed in a frame, it would be treated as a normal paragraph; that is, it would occupy the entire column width and the text in the following paragraph would be placed *beneath* it.)

While the picture was still selected, I assigned it a border by choosing the **Format/Border** menu command, and then selecting the desired line style in the Line area of the Border Picture dialog box.

I then typed in the document text. Before printing the document, I entered the Print Preview document view (using the **File/Print Preview** menu command) to check the final page layout.

Figure 9.1: A picture integrated into a document

(or click the **Draw button** on the Toolbar). The Draw program will be activated; you can then create a picture, which will be embedded in your document.

CH. 9

PASTING A PICTURE FROM THE CLIPBOARD

To print a document containing pictures, you must install a Windows printer driver that can print graphics. The actual amount of graphic detail that will be printed depends upon your printer's resolution (the maximum number of dots-per-inch it can print). See Chapter 17 for more information on printing.

You can store a graphic image from another Windows program in the Clipboard and then insert the image as a picture into a Word document. The source for the image could be a simple drawing program such as Windows Paintbrush or a full-featured illustration program such as CorelDRAW or Micrografx Designer.

The following are basic steps for transferring graphics from another Windows program to a Word document:

1. While running the other Windows application, copy the desired graphic image into the Clipboard.

2. Switch to Word for Windows and place the cursor where you want the picture to appear. Once the graphic is contained in the Clipboard, you can exit the source program before switching to Word.

3. Choose **Edit/Paste** or press **Ctrl-V**. The graphic image in the Clipboard will be inserted into the document.

If a picture you have inserted is not completely visible, make sure that the Line Spacing value is set to **Auto** (see Chapter 15).

Word treats a picture as if it were a single character. Thus, a picture can be either a stand-alone paragraph or part of a paragraph already containing text. Figure 9.2 illustrates a picture that has been inserted at the beginning of a line of text.

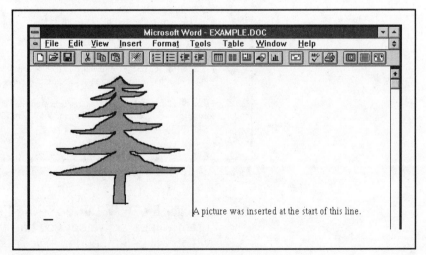

Figure 9.2: A picture at the beginning of a line

The maximum-size picture you can insert is one 22 inches on a side. If a picture is larger than the document window, you may have to use the scroll bars to see each part. If the picture is larger than the paper you plan to print it on, the appearance of the printed copy is unpredictable. Later in the chapter, you will see how to adjust the size and proportions of a picture in Word.

As you scroll through a document, Word must redraw a picture each time it comes into view. Redrawing is time-consuming and can slow scrolling considerably. You can fix this problem by choosing **Tools/Options**, selecting the **View** icon in the **Category:** list, and checking **Picture Placeholders**. Then, Word will display *placeholders* only for each picture (empty boxes), rather than drawing the actual image. You might want to disable the **Pictures** option while you are entering text, and then enable it to examine the final printed appearance of your document. Pictures are also displayed as blank boxes in *draft document* view, described in Chapter 4.

INSERTING A PICTURE FROM A DISK FILE

You can import pictures into Word from disk files of graphic images. For each *format* you want to import, however, you must have the appropriate *graphic filter*. A graphic filter is a conversion file that allows Word to import a specific type of graphic data. When you run the Word for Windows **Setup** program (described in Appendix A), you can install the filters provided with the Word program. If you did not originally install all available filters, re-run **Setup** and follow the instructions.

You can view a list of the filters that are installed by following these steps:

1. Choose **Tools/Options** and select the **Win.ini** icon from the **Category:** list.

2. Choose the **MS Graphic Import Filters** option from the **Application:** list. Word will display a complete list of the installed filters in the **Startup Options:** list box.

Displaying the list of filters tells you exactly which types of graphic files you can import. For example, if the list contains the item **PC Paintbrush(.PCX)**, then you know you can import graphics files with the .PCX extension (created by PC Paintbrush among others).

To import a picture from a disk file, first place the cursor where you want to insert the picture. Then choose **Insert/Picture**. Word will display the dialog box illustrated in Figure 9.3.

The techniques are the same as those used for **File/Open**, for finding and choosing the files described in Chapter 3. In addition, if you select a file in the **File Name:** list and click **Preview**, Word will display a reduced image of the graphic in the **Preview Picture** box.

Choose the **Link to File** option

Link to File

if you want to be able to update the picture in the document whenever the original image is altered. See the next section for instructions on updating a linked picture.

Word includes a set of files in Windows Metafile Format (with the .WMF extension). These files are normally placed within the **CLIPART** directory of your Word for Windows directory (usually **\WINWORD**). They contain a variety of useful clip-art images you can incorporate into your documents.

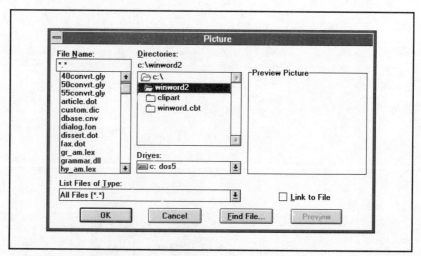

Figure 9.3: The Insert/Picture dialog box

When you are ready to open the selected file, click OK or press Enter. Word will insert the graphic image into your document, and you can manipulate it just as if you had pasted it from the Clipboard.

Updating a Linked Picture

You can update a linked image in your document by following these steps:

1. Make any desired changes to the image in the application that originally created the image.

2. Save the altered graphics file to disk.

3. Open the document you imported the picture to.

4. Choose **Edit/Links**. Word will display the Links dialog box.

5. Select the picture you want to update in the Links list box. Pictures are identified by the name of their original files.

6. Click **Update Now** and close the dialog box by clicking OK. Word will update the picture.

INSERTING A MICROSOFT DRAW OBJECT

The current version of Word for Windows includes a drawing program called *Microsoft Draw*. This program cannot be run as an independent Windows application; it can be run only within Word. This section examines two important uses of Microsoft Draw: to create and insert graphic images into Word documents, and to edit graphic images that have been pasted or imported from other programs. For complete information on using Draw, invoke the program's online help or see the manual *Microsoft Draw for Windows*, included with the Word for Windows package.

To create a picture in Draw and insert it into your document, perform the following steps:

1. Place the cursor where you would like the picture to appear.

2. Choose **Insert/Object**. Word will display the Object dialog box. Choose the **Microsoft Drawing** item in the list box and

click OK. As an alternative, you can simply click the **Draw button** on the Toolbar.

You can import into Draw any of the .WMF clip art files included with Word. These files are normally found in the **CLIPART** directory of your Word for Windows directory (usually **WINWORD**).

3. Word will activate Draw. Use the program's tools and commands to create a drawing or import a drawing from a disk file by choosing **File/Import Picture**.

4. When you have finished drawing, choose **File/Exit and Return**. Click **Yes** when Draw asks if you want to update your document. Draw will terminate and the drawing you have created will be inserted into your Word document.

Once the Draw picture has been inserted into the document, you can manipulate it like any other graphic. If you later want to change the picture, simply double-click on it. The Draw program will become active and the picture will appear in the Draw window. When you have finished editing the picture, choose **File/Exit and Return** click **Yes** to update the drawing.

A picture inserted as describe in this section is called an *embedded object*. The data for an embedded object is stored as part of the Word document. Word maintains a connection, though, between the object and the program that created it. If you double-click on the object, the original program will run so you can edit it. Word includes several other programs for creating embedded objects. Using these programs, as well as the general topic of embedding objects, is discussed in Chapter 27.

You can use Draw to edit any pictures in your document. To edit a picture, simply double-click on it. The Draw program window will open, displaying the picture. You can now use Draw to edit the picture; when you are done, choose **File/Exit and Return** and click **Yes** to update the picture. When you edit a picture using Draw, it is converted into an Draw embedded object.

FORMATTING A PICTURE

To format a picture:

1. Select the picture by clicking on it.

2. *Crop* the picture by pressing **Shift** and dragging one of the eight sizing handles that surround a picture when it is selected.

3. *Scale* the picture by dragging one of the sizing handles, without pressing **Shift**. Alternatively, you can crop or scale the picture by choosing **Format/Picture** and entering the desired dimensions.

4. To place a border around the picture, choose **Format/ Border** and select the desired line style.

5. To delete, move, or copy a picture, use the standard editing commands discussed in Chapter 5.

6. To manually position the picture, choose **Insert/Frame**, or click the **Frame button** on the Toolbar. When Word switches into Page Layout view, drag the picture to the desired position on the page.

Since you must *select* a picture before you can format it, a brief discussion on selecting a picture is in order.

SELECTING A PICTURE

Remember that Word treats a picture as if it were a single character. You can therefore select a picture using any of the basic methods for selecting characters that were described in Chapter 5. Several unique features apply when selecting a picture:

- You can select a picture by clicking anywhere in it.

- If you select a picture and any adjoining text, the entire selection is highlighted, as shown in Figure 9.4.

- If you select only a picture, Word places a border around the picture rather than highlighting it. Within this border are eight small squares known as *sizing handles*, which are used for cropping or scaling the picture (see Figure 9.5). When a picture is selected, the mouse pointer becomes an arrow rather than the usual I-beam. You can deselect the picture and restore the I-beam by clicking anywhere outside the picture.

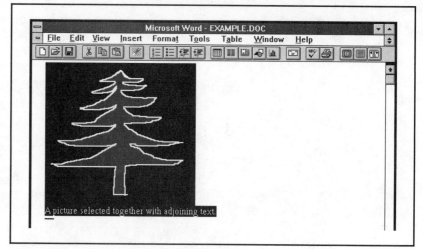

Figure 9.4: A selection including both a picture and text

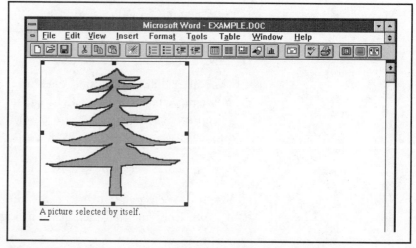

Figure 9.5: A selection including only a picture, with sizing handles

CROPPING OR SCALING A PICTURE

Word always saves the graphic data for an entire picture. If you eliminate a portion of the image by cropping, you can later restore this portion by cropping the picture back to its original size.

Once a picture has been inserted into a document, you can use Word to *crop* or *scale* it. To crop a picture is to change its overall dimensions without changing the size of the image contained within the picture. When you reduce the original picture size by cropping, you usually lose some portion of the image (like using scissors to cut a photograph). Figure 9.6 illustrates the effect of cropping. The first picture shows the original size. The second has been reduced by cropping. (Borders were added to these pictures to show their dimensions.)

Figure 9.6: Cropping a picture

To *scale* a picture is to change the overall dimensions of both the picture and its image. When you scale a picture, you don't lose any of the original image. The first picture in Figure 9.7 shows the original image size. The second and third pictures have been reduced and enlarged by scaling. Keeping the same vertical to horizontal ratio is called *proportional* scaling.

You can crop or scale a picture either with the mouse or with **Format/Picture**.

Figure 9.7: Scaling a picture

Cropping and Scaling with the Mouse

To *crop* a picture with the mouse, select it by clicking anywhere inside the picture (do not include any adjoining text.) Word will place a frame around the picture that contains eight square sizing handles, as shown back in Figure 9.5. To crop the picture, hold down **Shift** and drag the appropriate handle toward the center of the picture (the mouse pointer will change to a double arrow when placed over a handle). A center handle moves only its associated side:

A corner handle moves both attached sides simultaneously, maintaining the original proportions of the picture:

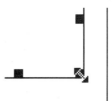

Since Word always saves graphic data for an entire picture, you can restore a cropped portion by holding down **Shift** and dragging the side in the opposite direction.

To *scale* a picture with the mouse, simply drag the appropriate sizing handle without holding down Shift. When scaling a picture, it makes no difference which side you drag; the resulting size, position, and content of the picture will be the same.

While you are cropping a picture, Word displays the distance you have moved the side in the status bar.

Cropping: 0.32" Right   0.25" Bottom

These measurements refer to the actual size of the picture and are given in the current default unit of measurement.

When you are scaling a picture, Word displays the size of the picture as a percentage of the original size.

Scaling: 97% High   116% Wide

Cropping and Scaling with Format/Picture

You can also crop or scale a picture using the **Format/Picture** command. This has advantages over the mouse method under the following circumstances:

- You want to specify an exact measurement.

- You want to reverse all cropping and scaling that has been applied to a picture.

The first step is to select the picture as before (do not include text in the selection). Next, choose **Format/Picture**. Word will display the dialog box shown in Figure 9.8. Notice that the original size of the picture appears at the bottom of the dialog box.

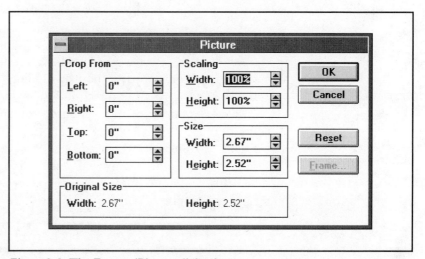

Figure 9.8: The Format/Picture dialog box

To *crop* the picture, you direct Word to move one or more of the four sides of the picture. In the appropriate box in the **Crop From** area, enter the distance you want to move the side from its original position.

For example, to crop ¼″ off the right side of the picture, enter **0.25** into the **Right:** box.

Since Word always saves the graphic data for the entire picture, you can restore a cropped portion by having Word move the side away from the center.

To *scale* the selected picture, enter a value into one or both of the boxes in the **Scaling** area. To scale the picture vertically, enter the new vertical dimension into the **Height:** box. To scale the picture horizontally, enter the new horizontal dimension into the **Width:** box. The dimensions are measured as percentages.

For example, to scale the picture so that it is 50 percent taller than its original height, but only 90 percent as wide, enter the following values:

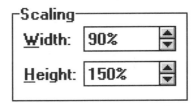

You can set the actual dimensions of the picture (rather than specifying a change from the original size), by entering the desired values into the **Size** area.

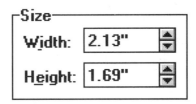

If you alter the values in the **Width:** or **Height:** box in the **Size** area, Word adjusts the size of the picture by *scaling* it rather than cropping it.

Finally, you can restore the picture to its original size by clicking **Reset**.

To close the dialog box and have Word apply the specified dimensions, click OK.

PLACING A BORDER AROUND A PICTURE

To place a border around a picture, select the picture (do not select any adjoining text) and choose **Format/Border**. Word will display the

Border Picture dialog box. Select the desired line style by clicking one of the samples in the **Line** box

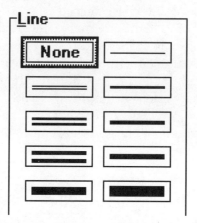

and click OK. The Border Picture dialog box allows you to place lines individually on each side of the picture; full details are given in Chapter 15.

DELETING, MOVING, OR COPYING A PICTURE

Since Word treats a picture as a single character, you can delete, move, or copy it using the block-editing techniques discussed in Chapter 5. To execute one of these operations, select the picture alone or in conjunction with adjoining characters.

POSITIONING A PICTURE

You cannot delete a picture by backspacing over it. Word merely beeps if you press the Backspace key when the cursor is immediately after a picture.

Normally, when you print a document, pictures are printed where you have placed them. The position of a picture may even change as you insert or delete text. This section presents a simplified procedure for placing a picture in a *specific* position on the page. For complete details on positioning text or pictures, see Chapter 15.

After you have inserted a picture, you can assign it a specific position by following these steps:

1. Select the picture. You can select the picture alone or with adjoining text (perhaps a title).

2. Choose **Insert/Frame** or click the **Frame button** on the Toolbar.

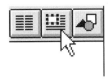

Insert/Frame places the picture (and any text that was also selected) within a *frame*.

3. If you are not in Page Layout view, Word will now ask you if you want to switch to Page Layout view. Click **Yes**.

4. Once in Page Layout view, place the mouse pointer on the picture (it will become a cross with four arrows) and drag it to any position on the page (even outside of the text margins).

The picture will now print at the assigned position on the page. Normal (unpositioned) text and graphics will *flow around* the picture. If you return to normal document view, the picture will not appear in the actual position where it will print; however, Word will place a small square to the left of the picture to indicate that it has been positioned.

The document illustrated in Figure 9.1 contains a picture that was assigned a specific position on the page using the method just described.

In addition to using a frame, there are several other ways to adjust the position of a picture.

First, since a picture is treated as a single character, you can use **Format/Character** to assign it a superscript or subscript value. The following is the basic procedure:

1. Select the picture.

2. Choose **Format/Character**. Word will display a dialog box.

3. In the **Super/subscript:** list box, select either **Superscript** (to raise the picture), or **Subscript** (to lower it).

4. Enter an amount into the **By:** box (to the right of the Super/subscript list). Unless you specify another unit, the number you enter will be assumed to be in points (the default is **3** points).

Second, you can use standard paragraph-formatting commands to adjust the position of a picture. For example, you can have Word align the picture in the center of a column, or you can have it add space above or below the paragraph containing the picture. For a thorough description of paragraph-formatting commands, see Chapter 15.

10

Adding Headers, Footers, and Footnotes

CHAPTER *10*

IN THIS CHAPTER, YOU WILL LEARN TWO IMPORTANT ways you can use Word to automate your work. First, you will learn how to create headers and footers—page numbers and/or other identifying text printed at the top or bottom of the pages of a document or document section. Second, you will learn how to add footnotes to your documents, and have Word automatically keep them in the correct order and print them in the appropriate locations.

WORKING WITH HEADERS AND FOOTERS

To add a header or footer to the current document section:

1. Choose **Insert/Page Numbers** to add a simple page number at the top or bottom of each page.

2. Choose **Header/Footer** from the **View** menu to add a header and/or a footer containing text or other information. Word will display the Header/Footer dialog box.

Headers and footers typically contain such information as the page number, the document or section title, and the author's name. As you will see, you can also easily add the time or date when you print the document. You can create either a header or footer that consists of a page number only, or a full header or footer that can contain text—and graphics—in addition to the page number.

You can specify a different header or footer for each section of your document. (Sections are discussed in Chapter 14.) If you want all sections to have the same header or footer, you can simply assign the header or footer to the first section; Word will automatically copy it to all remaining sections. Of course, if you have *not* divided your document into sections, the header or footer you specify will be printed throughout the entire document.

CREATING A SIMPLE PAGE-NUMBER HEADER OR FOOTER

If you want a header or footer that consists of the page number only, you can save time by choosing **Page Numbers** from the **Insert** menu rather than **Header/Footer** from the **View** menu.

The Insert/Page Numbers command displays the Page Numbers dialog box, which is illustrated in Figure 10.1. You can now specify the position of the number on the page. First, choose either the Top of Page option if you want to create a header, or the Bottom of Page option if you want to create a footer. Then choose either the Left, Center, or Right option in the Alignment area to specify the alignment of the number between the left and right margins. Clicking the OK button creates the header or footer and removes the dialog box. To *see* the page number at the specified position on each page, however, you must print the document or activate the Page Layout or Print Preview document view (explained in Chapter 17).

If you have previously added a header or footer, **Insert/ Page Numbers** will *replace* it. In this case, Word will ask you whether you want to replace the existing header or footer.

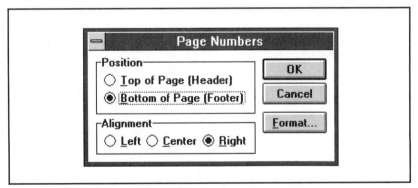

Figure 10.1: The Page Numbers dialog box from the Insert menu

A header or footer you create with the Insert/Page Numbers command has the following default characteristics:

- The header or footer consists of a page number only; no other text is included.

- The page numbers are Arabic numerals (2, 3, 4, and so on).

- The first page in the document is assigned number 1, the second page number 2, and so on throughout the entire document.

- Numbering does *not* start over again for each document section.

- No number is printed on the first document page. The first number printed is 2, on the second page.

You can change any of these defaults using the methods described later in the chapter.

CREATING AND FORMATTING COMPLETE HEADERS OR FOOTERS

To enter a full header or footer for the current document section, choose **Header/Footer** from the **View** menu. Word will display the dialog box shown in Figure 10.2.

You must tell Word the type of header or footer you want to create by selecting an item from the Header/Footer list box. Unless you have previously issued the View/Header/Footer command, this list contains initially only two items: Header and Footer. As you will see later, additional items may be added to the list as you choose various options within the dialog box.

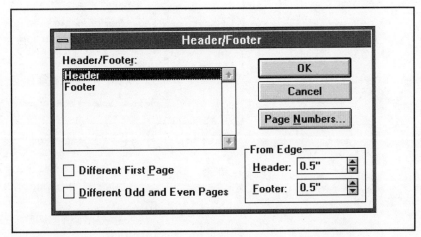

Figure 10.2: The Header/Footer dialog box from the View menu

To create a standard header or footer that is the same on all document pages, you simply choose the Header or the Footer option, and click the OK button. Word splits the window horizontally into two divisions, which are known as *panes*. (See Chapter 26 for complete information on managing split windows.) Figure 10.3 illustrates a window just after clicking the OK button; it shows the document pane and the newly opened header/footer pane below it.

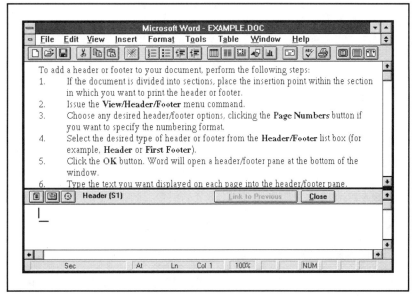

Figure 10.3: A window split into a document pane and a header/footer pane

Notice that at the top of the header/footer pane, Word displays the type of header or footer that is being edited (in this case, simply *Header*), followed by the number of the current document section (in this case, *S1*—indicating the first section). The icons and buttons displayed at the top of the pane are described later.

Word places the insertion point within the header/footer pane so that you can immediately start entering the text for the header or footer. Note that you do *not* have to finish entering this text and close the header/footer pane to resume editing the document; rather, you can leave the header/footer pane open and simply move the insertion point back to the document pane. You can later return to the header/ footer pane to further edit the header or footer text. To switch between panes, simply click in the desired pane or press **F6**. You can

If you are in the normal or outline document view, Word does not display headers or footers at their designated positions on the pages of the document; they are visible only within the header/footer window pane. The headers or footers *will* be displayed at their appropriate positions on the printed copy of the document, as well as in the Page Layout and Print Preview modes. See Chapter 17 for a summary of all of the document views provided by Word.

also adjust the size of the header/footer pane by dragging the *split bar* in the desired direction.

If you have previously entered a header or footer—even if it was just to enter page numbers through the Insert/Page Numbers command—the text will appear in the header/footer pane and you can now edit it.

If you issue the View/Header/Footer command while in the Page Layout mode, Word will simply place you at the position of the header or footer displayed within the document window, rather than opening a separate window pane.

You can insert one or more of the following items of information anywhere within the header or footer text:

- Page number
- Date when the document is printed
- Time when the document is printed

The first step is to place the insertion point at the position where you want to insert the item of information. You can then use either the mouse or the keyboard to select the type of information you want. To insert the page number with the mouse, click the first icon at the top of the header/footer pane:

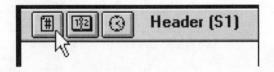

To insert the date, click the second icon. To insert the time, click the third icon.

You can also insert any of these items with the keyboard while you are in the header/footer pane by pressing **Shift-F10** and then one of the following keys:

KEY	ITEM
p	Page number
d	Date
t	Time

If you entered the page number into a header or footer through the **Insert/Page Numbers** command, the page number may not be visible within the header or footer text in the header/footer pane. To make it visible, select the entire header or footer in the pane and press **F9**.

When you insert a page number, the number that Word displays in the header/footer pane has no particular significance; the correct page number, however, will be displayed on each page when you print the document, or when you preview the document in the Page Layout or Print Preview view. Furthermore, when you insert the date or time, Word displays the *current* date or the *current* time; however, when you print the document, it replaces these with the date or time *when the document is printed*. To see the actual number, date, or time, as illustrated in this chapter, make sure that the View/Field Codes menu item is *not* selected. Figure 10.4 illustrates a header containing the page number, date, and time.

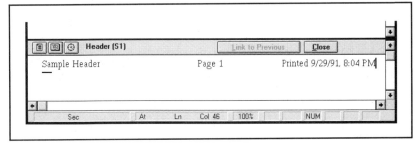

Figure 10.4: A header containing the page number, date, and time

When you insert the page number, date, or time, you are actually inserting a *field*. You can use fields to insert other information into a header or footer, such as the document title or author's name. For information on fields, see the Word *User's Reference* and *Technical Reference*.

Linking Headers or Footers to Sections

The information in this section applies only if you have divided your document into sections.

Initially, the headers or footers within all sections of a document are *linked*. This means that a header or footer you assign to a given section is automatically copied to all of the *following* sections in the document. For example, if a document consists of three sections, and you enter a header for section 1, sections 2 and 3 will automatically be assigned the same header. Furthermore, if you *change* the header for section 1, the headers for sections 2 and 3 will also be changed.

However, as soon as you change or add header or footer text for a section other than section 1, Word removes the link with the previous section. If, in the example just given, you change the header text for section 2, it will not affect section 1. Similarly, any changes to the header for section 1 will no longer affect section 2.

You can restore the link between a header in a given section and that belonging to the previous section by clicking the **Link to Previous** button at the top of the header/footer pane:

or by pressing **Shift-F10** and then **L**. This will cause Word to replace the header or footer for the current section with that belonging to the previous section. Before doing so, however, it will display the message

> **Do you want to delete this header/footer and link to the header/footer in the previous section?**

Formatting Headers or Footers

Headers are automatically assigned the **header** style and footers the **footer** style. You can change the default formatting used for all headers and footers in one or more documents by redefining this style, as described in Chapter 20.

Do *not* assign the **Keep with Next** paragraph formatting feature to a header or footer (discussed in Chapter 15).

You also can apply either character or paragraph formatting to the text for a header or footer in the same way you would format text within the body of a document. The following are some examples of formatting features that you might want to assign a header or footer (these features are discussed in Chapters 15 and 16):

- Boldface characters

- Centered paragraph alignment

- A border above or below the text

You might also want to adjust the tab stops within a header or footer. Initially, a header or footer has only two tab stops, one in the center of the page and one at the right margin.

Adjusting the Position of Headers and Footers

When you first enter a header or footer through the View/Header/ Footer command, Word initially positions a header 0.5 inches from the top of each page, or a footer 0.5 inches from the bottom of each page. Once you have added a header or footer, you can adjust either its horizontal position or its vertical position on the page. To adjust the horizontal position, you can use appropriate paragraph formatting commands, which are described in Chapter 15. For example, you could assign the header or footer a negative left or right indent to move it out into the left or right margin of the page. Also, you could assign the centered alignment style to center a header or footer between the right and left margins.

Print Preview is described in detail in Chapter 17.

You can easily adjust the vertical position of a header or footer by switching into the Print Preview mode and using the methods described in Chapter 17 to drag a header or footer to the desired vertical position within the margin area.

Finally, you can place a header or footer at any position on the page by placing it inside a *frame* (through the **Insert/Frame** command or the **Frame button** on the Toolbar), as explained in Chapter 15.

Closing the Header/Footer Pane

You can close the header/footer pane at any time by clicking the Close button at the top of the pane or by pressing **Shift-F10** and then pressing **C**. You can also close it by dragging the split bar all the way to the top or the bottom of the window.

Word saves all text you have entered into the header/footer pane, and you can resume entering or editing this text later by reissuing the View/Header/Footer menu command.

If you want to enter a different type of header or footer, or if you want to enter a header or footer for another document section, you do *not* need to close the header/footer pane. Rather, you can simply re-issue the View/Header/Footer command; the pane for the new header or footer will overlie the existing pane.

SETTING HEADER AND FOOTER OPTIONS

Before clicking the OK button to begin entering the text for the header or footer, you can specify one or more of the following options in the Header/Footer dialog box:

- Different First Page
- Different Odd and Even Pages
- Distance From Edge
- Page Number Format

Different First Page

Choosing **Different First Page** allows you to create a separate header or footer for the first page of the current section, or to eliminate the header or footer from the first page, as is traditionally done for title pages. When you choose this option, the following two items are added to the **Header/Footer:** list box:

    First Header
    First Footer

You must open the Header/Footer dialog box (by selecting Header/Footer from the View menu) for *each* type of header or footer you want on your document. Once in the dialog box, you must select the appropriate item from the **Header/Footer:** list box before clicking OK.

To eliminate or enter different text for the header or footer on the first page of the section, you must select the First Header or First Footer item before clicking the OK button. Use the resulting header/footer pane to enter the special header or footer for the first page. If you don't enter text for a first-page header or footer at this point, Word will leave the header or footer on this page blank.

Different Odd and Even Pages

If you have also selected the **Different First Page** option, the list box will contain the First Header and First Footer items. In this case, choosing one of the Even or Odd items from the list box will affect pages *other* than the first page.

If you select the **Different Odd and Even Pages** option, you can enter separate headers or footers for odd and even pages. This feature would be useful, for example, if you wanted the page number always printed on the *outside* edge of pages intended to be printed on both sides and bound into a booklet. (In other words, if you wanted the page number printed on the left side of even pages, but on the right side of odd pages.)

When you select this option, Word *replaces* the Header and Footer items in the Header/Footer list box with the following:

    Even Header
    Even Footer

Odd Header
Odd Footer

As you have seen, you can enter or edit the text for only one of these at a time. You must issue the View/Header/Footer command separately for each type of header you want to enter.

Distance from Edge

If you place a header or footer closer than 0.5 inches from the top or bottom edge of the page, some laser printers may not be able to print it.

You can specify the distance between a header and the top of the page, or between a footer and the bottom of the page, by entering the desired values into the **From Edge** area of the Header/Footer dialog box. By default, both distances are 0.5 inches. If you place the header or footer within the area of the page normally occupied by the text, Word will *move* the text so that the header or footer and the text do not overlap. In other words, the top or bottom margin is automatically increased. You can also easily adjust the position of headers or footers by placing them in frames (see Chapter 15), or by moving them in Print Preview mode.

Page Number Format

Headers or footers commonly contain page numbers; you already saw how to insert a page number into the header or footer text. Using the Page Number Format dialog box, you can set the following two features of page numbers:

- The type of numbers displayed (for example, Arabic or roman)

- The starting page number

To display the Page Number Format dialog box, either click the **Page Numbers** button in the *Header/Footer* dialog box (opened by the View/Header/Footer command), or click the **Format** button in the *Page Numbers* dialog box (opened by the Insert/Page Numbers command). The Page Number Format dialog box is illustrated in Figure 10.5.

To specify the type of numbers used for numbering pages, choose an item from the **Number Format:** list. You can choose Arabic, or upper or lowercase alphabetic or roman characters; the choices are illustrated in Figure 10.6. By default, Word uses Arabic numerals.

You can specify the starting page number by choosing one of the options in the **Page Numbering** area.

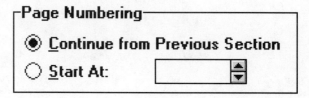

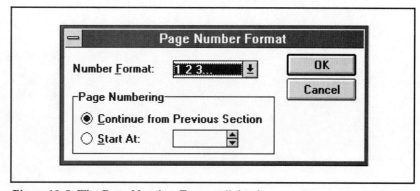

Figure 10.5: The Page Number Format dialog box

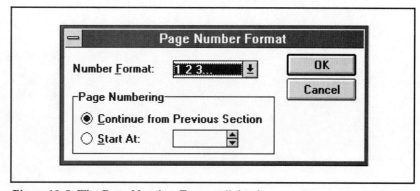

Figure 10.6: The Number Format list box

If you choose the **Continue from Previous Section** option (the default), Word will start with a number that is 1 greater than the number of the last page of the previous section. If there is no previous section, Word will start numbering with 1.

If you choose the **Start At:** option, Word will start numbering the beginning of the current section (that is, the section containing the insertion point) with the number you enter into the text box to the right of this option. If, for example, the insertion point is in the second document section, and you enter *100* into the Start At box, Word will start numbering the pages 100, 101, and so on when it reaches the second section.

Once the document has been paginated (or if automatic pagination is enabled), the page number that would be printed in a header or footer for the current page is displayed within the status bar, following the **Pg** display.

Changing Options for Existing Headers or Footers

You normally set all required options before entering the text for a header or footer. You might, however, decide to change one or more options after entering the text. In this case, it may not be obvious exactly how Word processes the existing text. Table 10.1 summarizes the effects of changing the Different First Page option or the Different Odd and Even Pages option after you have entered header or footer text.

Table 10.1: Results of Changing Options after Entering Header or Footer Text

CHANGE IN OPTION	EFFECT
Turn *on* Different First Page option	Header or footer on first page of section is left blank
Turn *off* Different First Page option	Text for header or footer on first page of section is discarded
Turn *on* Different Odd and Even Pages option	Existing header or footer text is copied to both odd and even headers or footers
Turn *off* Different Odd and Even Pages option	Text from *odd* header or footer is used for *both* odd *and* even pages.

USING FOOTNOTES IN YOUR DOCUMENT

To insert a footnote:

1. Place the insertion point at the position where you want the footnote reference and choose **Insert/Footnote**.

2. In the Footnote dialog box, select either **Auto-Numbered Footnote** or **Custom Footnote Mark** and enter the desired footnote reference into the text box.

3. Click the OK button. Word will open a footnotes window pane.

4. Enter the desired footnote text following the matching reference mark in the footnotes pane.

Word greatly simplifies the task of adding footnotes to your documents. It automatically numbers the references (if desired) and prints the footnote text in the correct order and at the appropriate positions within the document.

Later in the chapter, you will learn how to specify the type of separator used to divide the footnotes from the document text.

Figure 10.7 illustrates the three basic components of a footnote: the footnote reference, the footnote text, and the footnote separator (the line separating the footnote from the document text).

This sentence contains a footnote reference.[1]

---
[1]This is the footnote text.

Figure 10.7: A footnote reference and the corresponding text

The footnote reference usually consists of a superscript number that is assigned by Word; these references are automatically kept in numeric order. If you'd rather, you can specify another reference mark, such as an asterisk.

The footnote text begins with the same mark used for the reference. Word normally prints the text for each footnote at the bottom of the page on which the reference occurs. Alternatively, however, footnotes can be placed at the end of the section or at the end of the document.

In this section, you will learn how to insert a footnote reference and type in the corresponding footnote text. You will then learn how to delete, move, or copy a footnote. You will also learn how to specify the separator used to divide the footnote text from the document text (by default, Word uses a simple line). Finally, you will learn how to designate the position of the footnote text within the document, and the numbering scheme used for automatically numbered footnote references.

INSERTING A FOOTNOTE

To insert a footnote reference, place the insertion point at the desired position in your document, and choose **Insert/Footnote**. Word will display the dialog box shown in Figure 10.8.

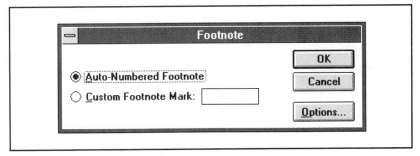

Figure 10.8: The Footnote dialog box

Once the dialog box is displayed, you first specify the type of footnote reference mark you want, and then click the OK button to begin entering the footnote text.

Specifying the Footnote Reference

You can either select the Auto-Numbered Footnote option, or select the Custom Footnote Mark option and then enter any desired reference symbol into the text box.

You can change the *formatting* of footnote references. For example, you could assign a different font, character size, position, or other feature (see Chapters 15 and 20).

The **Auto-Numbered Footnote** option, which is selected by default, causes Word to use a number as a reference mark; this number is normally formatted as a small superscript character. Usually, the first footnote reference in the document is assigned number 1, the second footnote reference is assigned number 2, and so on. If you insert a footnote reference before an existing reference, Word automatically renumbers the references to keep them in correct numerical order. Later in this chapter, you will learn how to specify a starting number other than 1 (in the section "Specifying the Footnote Position and Numbering Scheme").

You can enter both automatically numbered footnote reference marks *and* reference marks specified in the Footnote Reference Mark box into the same document.

Alternatively, you can have Word use a specific footnote reference mark by selecting the **Custom Footnote Mark** option and typing the desired character or characters into the box. You might, for example, enter an asterisk.

◉ **Custom Footnote Mark:** [*]

You can also insert characters that do not appear on the keyboard—by pressing **Alt** and typing the character's ASCII code using the numeric the numeric keypad, as described in the section "Entering Special Symbols" in Chapter 3.

If you type a *number* into the Custom Footnote Mark box, Word will use this number as a footnote reference and it will *not* renumber it automatically. Specifically, it will not change the number to keep it in sequence with surrounding numbers, and the number will not affect the numbering of any nearby automatically numbered references.

Typing the Footnote Text

When you have specified the type of footnote reference and you are ready to begin entering the footnote text, click the OK button in the Footnote dialog box or press Enter. Word will split the window into a document pane and a footnote pane, and will insert the specified footnote reference into *both,* as illustrated in Figure 10.9. The insertion point is automatically positioned immediately to the right of the reference in the footnote pane so that you can begin typing the footnote text.

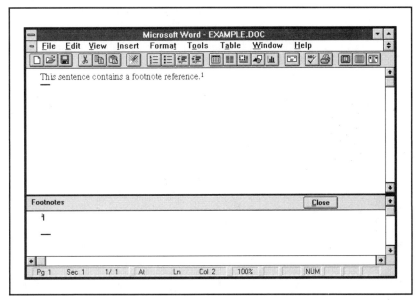

Figure 10.9: The footnote reference immediately appears in both the document pane and the footnote pane

You can format footnote text as you wish, using the same methods you would use to format other text, as explained in Chapters 15 and 16. (As you will see in Chapter 20, footnote references are initially assigned the *"footnote reference" style,* and footnote text the *"footnote text" style.*)

You can use the **Go To** command (discussed in Chapter 4) to move the insertion point to a specific footnote reference in your document. First, press **F5** or choose **Edit/Go To**, then, at the prompt, type **f** followed by the number of the footnote. The Go To command counts all footnote references from the beginning of the document, ignoring the actual numbers (if any) contained in the reference marks.

To move the insertion point back and forth between the two panes, click within the desired pane or press **F6**. To adjust the size of the footnote pane, drag the split bar up or down.

Document views are summarized in Chapter 17.

Remember that when you are in the normal, or outline document view, Word does not display footnotes within the document; rather, they are displayed only within the footnote pane. Footnotes *will* appear in their appropriate positions on the page on the final printed copy, as well as in Page Layout and Print Preview views. In fact, if the Page Layout view is active when you issue the Insert/Footnote command, Word simply places the insertion point at the position on the page where the footnote text will be printed. Thus, in this view you can edit a footnote without having to go to a footnote pane to do it.

EDITING A FOOTNOTE

Once Word has opened the footnote pane, you can edit any of the footnotes that have been entered for the current document. You can scroll through the footnotes and position the insertion point using the same methods employed within a normal document window. Notice that when you place the insertion point within the text for a particular footnote, the document pane automatically scrolls, if necessary, to reveal the corresponding footnote reference in the document. Likewise, when you place the insertion point within a line containing a footnote reference in the document, the footnote pane automatically scrolls, if necessary, to reveal the corresponding footnote text.

You can *close* the footnote window at any time using one of the following three methods:

- Drag the **split bar** all the way to the top or bottom of the window.
- Double-click a **footnote reference** within the footnote pane.
- Choose the **View/Footnotes** command. Choosing this item will remove the checkmark from it and will disable the option.

You can also *open* the footnote pane at any time using one of the following three methods:

- Hold down the **Shift** key while dragging the **split bar** down to the desired position.
- Double-click any **footnote reference** within the document.
- Choose the **View/Footnotes** command. Choosing this item will add a checkmark in front of it, and will enable the option.

DELETING, MOVING, OR COPYING A FOOTNOTE

You can delete, move, or copy a footnote reference together with its associated text by performing a single operation on the footnote reference.

To delete both a footnote reference and the corresponding footnote text, you must *select* the footnote reference in the document and press **Del**; you cannot delete them by positioning the *insertion point* and using Del or Backspace.

If you move a footnote reference within the document using one of the standard moving techniques (presented in Chapter 5), Word will move both the reference and its associated text. If the footnote has an automatically numbered reference, Word will also renumber the footnotes appropriately.

Finally, you can copy a footnote by copying the footnote reference using one of the standard copying and pasting methods (again, see Chapter 5). Word will insert the copied footnote reference at the target position, and will insert a copy of the footnote text at the corresponding position within the footnote area. Again, Word will maintain correct numbering if Auto-Numbered Footnote was selected for the original footnote.

SPECIFYING FOOTNOTE SEPARATORS

You can specify the characters that Word uses to separate the footnote text from the document text on each page where footnotes are printed. You can also specify the message that Word prints whenever footnotes are continued on the next page.

To specify one of these items, select **Insert/Footnote** and then click the **Options** button within the Footnote dialog box. Word will then open the Footnote Options dialog box, illustrated in Figure 10.10.

Once the Footnote Options dialog box has been opened, click one of the three buttons within the **Footnote Separators** area:

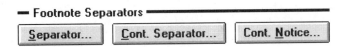

Whichever button you choose, Word will open a separate pane. As usual, you can move the insertion point between panes by clicking

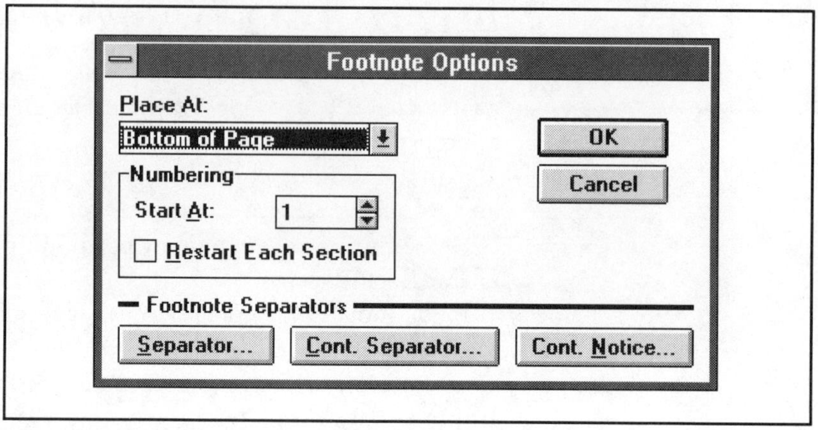

Figure 10.10: The Footnote Options dialog box

within the desired pane, or by pressing **F6**. You can adjust the size of the separator pane by dragging the split bar, and you can close the pane using one of the following methods:

- Click the **Close** button.

- Press **Shift-F10** and then **C**.

- Drag the **split bar** all the way to the top or bottom of the window.

If you click the **Separator** button, the pane will contain the current separator used to divide the document text from the footnotes at the bottom of the page. By default, this separator is a single line extending approximately a third of the way across the text column (as illustrated in Figure 10.7). You can replace this separator with one or more other characters, or you can add characters to it. Notice that Word treats the separator line as a single character; you can therefore delete or copy it in its entirety, but you cannot change its length.

If you click the **Cont. Separator** button, you can edit the separator Word uses to divide the document text from footnotes *that have been continued from the previous page*. Normally, all footnote text is printed at the bottom of the page on which the reference occurs. Occasionally, however, there is insufficient room on this page; in this case, Word will continue the footnotes on one or more following pages. By default, the continuation separator is a line extending across the

Continuation separators and notices are not used if you place footnotes at the end of each section or at the end of the document.

entire text column. This line is also treated as a single character; you can replace it or add characters to it.

If you click the **Cont. Notice** button, you can type in the message you want Word to display at the bottom of the page when footnotes are continued on the *next* page. The default is no message. However, you might want to enter a message, such as

Footnotes continued on next page...

just in case Word has to divide a footnote between pages. The message will be displayed only when Word must break for a new page in the middle of a footnote. It does not display the continuation message if the page break falls *between* footnotes.

While any one of these three footnote separator panes is open, you can restore the original separator or message defaults by clicking the **Reset** button, or by pressing **Shift-F10** and then **R**.

SPECIFYING THE FOOTNOTE POSITION AND NUMBERING SCHEME

In the Footnote Options dialog box (see Figure 10.10), you can specify the *position* of footnotes within the document and the *numbering scheme* used for automatically numbered footnote references. You open this box by choosing the **Insert/Footnote** menu command and then clicking the **Options** button in the Footnote dialog box.

Specifying the Footnote Position

You can tell Word where to place the footnotes within your document by choosing the appropriate item from the **Place At:** list box

Place At:

End of Section
Bottom of Page
Beneath Text
End of Document

within the Footnote Options dialog box.

Bottom of Page is the default option. It causes Word to print the footnote text at the bottom of the page containing the footnote reference. With this option, the footnote text is always printed at the lowest possible position within the text area of the page. Therefore, if there is not enough text on the page to fill the area above the footnotes, Word will leave a gap between the document text and the footnote text. This situation is illustrated in Figure 10.11.

The **Beneath Text** option also causes Word to print the footnote text at the bottom of the page containing the footnote reference. With this option, however, the footnote text is printed immediately below the text on the page. For pages with sufficient text to fill the entire available space, the effect appears no different from that produced by the Bottom of Page option. However, if there is too little document text on a page to fill the available space, the Beneath Text option prevents Word from leaving a gap between the document text and the footnote text. Figure 10.12 illustrates the same page shown in Figure 10.11, but with the Beneath Text option chosen.

The **End of Section** option causes Word to place all the footnotes for a section at the end of that section.

You can also have Word move the footnote texts for one section to the end of the *next* section by *disabling* footnote text for a specific section, as follows:

1. Make sure you are in normal or Layout View, then place the insertion point within the section whose footnotes you want to appear after the following section.

2. Choose **Format/Section Layout**. Word will display a dialog box.

3. Check the **Suppress Footnotes** option.

Finally, you can select the **End of Document** option to have Word place all footnote text at the end of the document. Such footnotes are sometimes called *end notes*.

Specifying the Numbering Scheme

As you saw previously in the chapter, Word automatically maintains the correct sequence of all footnotes that were inserted with the

Chapter 10: Adding Headers, Footers, and Footnotes

In this chapter, you will learn two important ways you can use Word to automate your work. First, you will learn how to create headers and footers; a header is text that is printed at the top of each page of a document, and a footer is text that is printed at the bottom of each page. Second, you will learn how to add footnotes to your documents, and have Word automatically keep them in the correct order and print them in the appropriate locations.[1]

Working With Headers And Footers

Once you have entered a header or footer, Word will automatically print it on each page of the document. You can enter either a header or a footer, or both. Headers and footers typically contain such information as the page number, the title, and the author's name. As you will see, with Word you can also easily add the time or date when you print the document.[2]

When you create a header or a footer, it is applied to the current document section. A section is a division of a document that can be assigned certain formatting values, such as a specific number of columns. (In Chapter 14, you will see how to divide a document into sections, and how to format each section.) If you have divided your document into sections, you can specify a different header or footer for each section. If you have not divided your document into sections, the header or footer you specify will be printed throughout the entire document.[3]

---

[1]This is the first footnote on the page.
[2]This is the second footnote on the page.
[3]This is the third footnote on the page.

Figure 10.11: A page illustrating the Bottom of Page footnote placement option

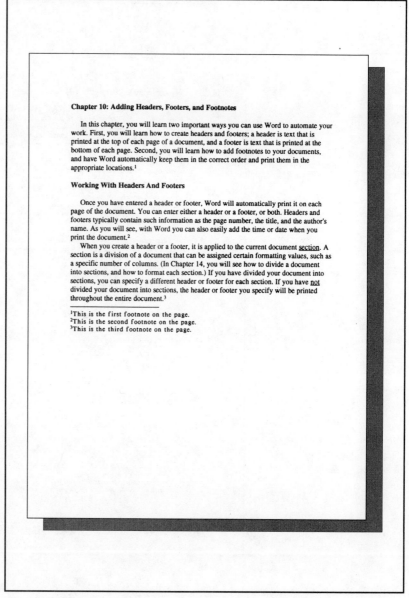

Chapter 10: Adding Headers, Footers, and Footnotes

In this chapter, you will learn two important ways you can use Word to automate your work. First, you will learn how to create headers and footers; a header is text that is printed at the top of each page of a document, and a footer is text that is printed at the bottom of each page. Second, you will learn how to add footnotes to your documents, and have Word automatically keep them in the correct order and print them in the appropriate locations.[1]

Working With Headers And Footers

Once you have entered a header or footer, Word will automatically print it on each page of the document. You can enter either a header or a footer, or both. Headers and footers typically contain such information as the page number, the title, and the author's name. As you will see, with Word you can also easily add the time or date when you print the document.[2]

When you create a header or a footer, it is applied to the current document section. A section is a division of a document that can be assigned certain formatting values, such as a specific number of columns. (In Chapter 14, you will see how to divide a document into sections, and how to format each section.) If you have divided your document into sections, you can specify a different header or footer for each section. If you have not divided your document into sections, the header or footer you specify will be printed throughout the entire document.[3]

[1]This is the first footnote on the page.
[2]This is the second footnote on the page.
[3]This is the third footnote on the page.

Figure 10.12: A page illustrating the Beneath Text footnote placement option

Auto-Numbered Footnote option. Word normally starts numbering these footnotes with 1, but you can change this starting number in the **Start At:** box in the **Numbers** area of the Footnote Options dialog box:

```
┌Numbering──────────────────┐
│                           │
│  Start At:      ┌───┬──┐   │
│                 │ 1 │▲▼│   │
│                 └───┴──┘   │
│  ☐ Restart Each Section    │
│                           │
└───────────────────────────┘
```

By default, Word usually numbers footnotes in a single continuous sequence throughout the document. You can, however, have Word restart the numbering at the beginning of each section by checking the **Restart Each Section** option. Note, however, that the numbering *in each section* will start at the number displayed in the Starting At box; so make sure it says **1**.

11

Creating Indexes
and Tables of Contents

CHAPTER *11* _____

IN THIS CHAPTER, YOU WILL LEARN HOW TO HAVE
Word automatically create indexes, tables of contents, and other
tables of items for your documents.

An *index* is a list of important words and topics contained in a document, together with the page number or numbers on which each
word or topic is found. Rather than manually going through a finished document and typing each item into an index, you can have
Word automatically compile an index from entries you insert while
you are writing the document. Not only does Word's indexing feature save you the time required to type and format an index, but also
you can have Word automatically update the index whenever any of
the page breaks in the document change position.

In this chapter, the general term *table of contents* is used to refer to all
types of lists created using the table of contents feature. You can use
Word to automatically create lists of all the heads in a document—the
traditional table of contents—as well as lists of all the figures, tables,
photographs, or illustrations.

CREATING INDEXES

Using the Word indexing feature consists of two main steps:

1. Specifying each item that is to be included in the index by
   inserting *an index entry* directly into the document text at the
   point where the word or topic is discussed.

2. Inserting *the index itself*. When you insert an index, Word generates an index based upon the entries that you inserted.

INSERTING INDEX ENTRIES

To insert a simple index entry:

1. Place the insertion point following the text you want to index.
2. Choose **Insert/Index Entry**.
3. Type the entry you want to appear in the index, and click OK.

If a topic may span more than a single page, the best way to insert an index entry is to use a *bookmark* to specify a range. See the section "Using Options in the Index Entry Dialog Box," later in the chapter.

For each item you want Word to include in the index, you must insert an index entry into the document text. For example, to index the topic *watering* in a book on house plants, you might place the insertion point after the following sentence:

> Thus, the importance of regular watering cannot be overemphasized.

You would then choose **Insert/Index Entry** to display the Index Entry dialog box, shown in Figure 11.1.

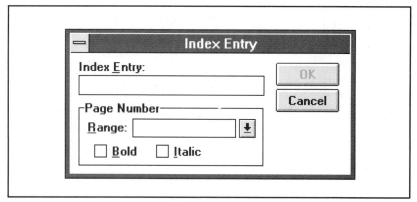

Figure 11.1: The Index Entry dialog box

Type the description you want to appear in the index into the Index Entry box, as in the following example:

If you cannot see the index entry, choose **Tools/Options**, select the **View icon** in the **Category:** box, and check the **Hidden Text** option in the **Nonprint-ing Characters** area. Hidden text is discussed later in this section.

When you click the OK button, Word will insert the entry into the document at the insertion point. In the example just given, the index entry would be placed at the end of the sentence and would look like this on the screen:

Thus, the importance of regular watering cannot be overemphasized.{XE "watering"}

The meaning of the various parts of this entry will be described shortly.

If the example index entry were located on page 12 of the document, Word would include the following item in the index when you compiled the index as described later in the chapter:

watering, 12

In this example, since the topic (watering) is *included* in the line you want indexed, you could save typing by *selecting* the topic within the line:

1. *Select* the word or the description of the topic within the docu-ment text, as in the following example:

Thus, the importance of regular watering cannot be overemphasized.

2. Choose **Insert/Index Entry**. Notice that the selected text already appears in the Index Entry box within the Index Entry dialog box.

3. Click the OK button or press Enter.

You can select (or enter) up to 253 characters. However, if the current selection contains more than 64 characters, the Index Entry box will show only the first 64.

Note that with this alternative method, Word places the index entry immediately after the word *watering* rather than at the end of the sentence. See the section "Using Options in the Index Entry Dialog Box" later in the chapter for a discussion on the problem of choosing the best location for each index entry.

Every time you insert the same index entry for two or more occur-rences, Word will combine these entries into a single item in the index. For instance, if you inserted the example entry on pages 12 *and* 25, the resulting index item would be as follows:

watering, 12,25

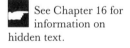 Unlike most fields, the field code for an index entry is visible even if **View/Field Codes** is *not* enabled. It can still be hidden, however, by disabling **Hidden Text**. To do so, choose **Tools/ Options**, select the **View** icon in the **Category:** list, and disable the **Hidden Text** option (in the **Non-printing Characters** area).

See Chapter 16 for information on hidden text.

The text that is inserted into your document when you issue the Insert/Index Entry command is a particular type of field called an *index entry field,* which has the following appearance in your document:

{XE."watering"}

A field is an *instruction* embedded in a document telling Word to insert an item or perform an action. It is *not* part of the normal text that is printed.

The { and } braces surrounding the field indicate the field's *boundaries.* You cannot enter these characters directly using the keyboard; rather, you must insert them into your document through an appropriate command, such as **Insert/Index Entry** or **Ctrl-F9.** (You can, however, type or edit text *between* the braces.) The letters **XE** tell Word that the field is an index entry. The quotation marks enclose the exact text that is to appear in the resulting index item.

Once you have inserted an index entry through the Insert/Index Entry command, you do not need to reissue this command if you want to alter the text for the index item. Rather, you can simply edit the characters inside the quotation marks using standard editing methods.

Notice that the entire index entry field is underlined with a dotted line. This marking indicates that the characters are formatted as *hidden text.* You can make the hidden text visible on the screen by selecting the **Hidden Text** item within the Options dialog box. (You can also *print* hidden text by selecting the Hidden Text item in the Print Options dialog box at the time you print the document—see Chapter 17.) Because index entries are formatted as hidden text, you should observe the following guidelines while working with a document containing index entries:

- Enable the display of hidden text while entering text into your document, so you can see where index entries have been inserted and so you can edit the entries if desired.

- Disable the display of hidden text when previewing the printed appearance of the document and making final formatting changes.

- Disable the printing of hidden text when you print the document, so that the index entries are not printed.

To delete, move, or copy the index entry, make sure that you select the entire field before performing the operation.

Note finally that you can delete, move, or copy part of an index entry field that has been inserted into your document, using the standard operations presented in Chapter 5. Since, however, an index entry is a field, you will notice when performing these operations that you must place the insertion point in front of the index entry and press **Shift-right arrow**, or place it after the index entry and press **Shift-left arrow**, to select the entire index entry with a single keystroke. If, however, you place the insertion point inside the index entry field, you can select one or more individual characters.

Specifying Multiple-Level Index Items

Index items can contain two or more levels. For example, the following index items are displayed on two levels:

```
bugs
    eliminating, 24
    identifying, 20
    on orchids, 115
```

To insert an actual colon character into the text for an index item—without creating an additional level—type \: (that is, a backslash immediately in front of the colon).

To create an index item that consists of two or more levels, simply insert a colon (:) into the entry text to separate each level. For example, to create the first of the example index items shown above, you would type the following text into the Index Entry box:

```
bugs:eliminating
```

Identifying Topics That May Continue from Page to Page

To insert an index entry that will indicate the range of pages covered by a topic:

1. First, identify the extent of the topic you want indexed, by selecting the entire block and identifying it by means of a *bookmark*. Thus, select it, press **Ctrl-Shift-F5**, and type a bookmark name at the status-line prompt.

2. Now that you have precisely identified the full extent of the topic, create an index entry for it:

    a. Place the insertion point anywhere within the topic block.

FAST TRACK

> b. Choose **Insert/Index Entry**.
> c. In the **Index Entry:** box, type the index entry.
> d. In the **Range:** box, select the bookmark name you specified in step 1, and click OK.

As explained in the section "Go To a Bookmark" in Chapter 4, a bookmark is a label you can assign to a position in a document or to a block of text.

If you have topics that run to any length at all, there is always a chance that they may start on one page and stop on another. In such cases, the index will normally identify only the last page, because that is normally the place where you would have placed the index entry for that topic. To have Word display the range of pages that a topic falls on, you must identify the entire occurrence of that topic as an index entry. You do this by identifying the topic block as a *bookmark,* and then including the name of the bookmark in the index entry. The steps for doing this are outlined in the Fast Track above.

If you follow the steps listed for an index entry you have named *watering* and identified with a bookmark named *w,* the index entry field should look like this:

```
{XE "watering" \r "w"}
```

Although defining and specifying a bookmark adds extra work to inserting an index entry, it is the safest general method to use. If you specify a bookmark and the corresponding text ends up on only a single page, then Word will display only a single page number. But if it ends up on more than one page, you will already have the possibility covered.

Using Switches to Specify Index Entry Options

While the Index Entry dialog box is open, you can also select the **Bold** option, the **Italic** option, or both. Bold causes Word to use bold text for the number in the index, and Italic causes Word to use italic text for the number.

You can also specify one or more additional options that affect the way Word processes an index entry by using *switches.* A switch is a backslash (\) followed by a letter and possibly some text; it is inserted directly into the index entry field. For example, the switch **\b** that is a part of the following index entry would cause Word to use boldface letters for the page number in the index entry (it has the same effect as choosing the **Bold** option within the Index Entry dialog box):

{XE."fertilizers".\b}

Table 11.1 lists the switches you can include in an index entry field. Notice that except for \t, each of the switches in Table 11.1 produces the same effect as an option within the Index Entry dialog box. (These options were explained in the previous section.)

Table 11.1: Switches You Can Use in an Index Entry Field

SWITCH	EFFECT
\b	Specifies bold page number (same as Bold option in Insert/Index Entry dialog box).
\i	Specifies italic page number (same as Italic option in Insert/Index Entry dialog box).
\r *bookmark*	Prints the range of page numbers that contain the specified bookmark (same as Range option in Insert/Index Entry dialog box).
\t *"text"*	Prints text rather than a page number (must enclose the text in quote characters if it includes any spaces).

Use the following general procedure to specify an index entry option with a switch:

1. Place the insertion point at the position where you would like to insert the index entry, and select **Insert/Index Entry**.

2. Type the text for the index entry into the **Index Entry:** box in the dialog box. Do *not,* however, include the switch or any of the text that follows the switch.

3. Click the OK button. Word will insert the index entry field in the document.

4. Type the switch and any following text directly into the field. You can include more than one switch in a single index entry field.

The *text* you enter into the Index Entry box will show up between quotation marks in the actual field. Because switches must *follow* the closing quote mark, you must type them in *after* you have inserted the index entry field into the document.

You can use the \t switch to create cross-references. Specifically, you can create an index item that refers to another item rather than including the page number(s). To use this switch, type the following four items into the index entry field immediately after the entry text (in the order given): a space, the \t switch, another space, and the text for the cross-reference. If the text for the cross-reference itself contains spaces, the entire text must be enclosed in quotes. For example, you would enter the following index entry field

{XE "moisture" \t "see watering"}

to generate this item in the index:

    moisture, see watering

INSERTING THE INDEX

To insert an index:

1. Place the insertion point at the desired position in the document and choose **Insert/Index**.
2. Select the desired options and click OK.
3. To update an index, place the insertion within the index and press **F9**.

The different options you can choose are discussed in the next section, "Using Options in the Index Dialog Box."

If **View/Field Codes** is enabled, you will see the field code **{INDEX}** rather than the index itself.

Once you have completed writing your document and have inserted index entries at every point you want indexed, you can have Word compile the index from these entries and insert it into the document. Use the following steps for creating an index:

1. Place the insertion point at the position in the document where you want the index. Although you would normally place an index near the end of a document, Word allows you to insert it at any location.

2. Select **Insert/Index**. Word will display the dialog box shown in Figure 11.2.

3. Choose the desired options, and click OK.

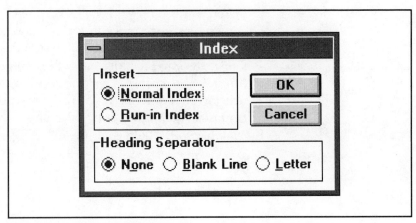

Figure 11.2: The Index dialog box

Word will insert an up-to-date index based on the index entries it finds in the document. When Word creates an index, it automatically paginates the document as described in Chapter 17.

If you later delete, add, or change one or more index entries, or make any editing or formatting changes to the document that may change the position of page breaks, you must *update* the index. To update the index, place the insertion point anywhere within the index and press **F9**. Alternatively, you can update an index by choosing the **Update Fields** option when printing the document (see Chapter 17).

You can delete, move, or copy an entire index using the standard operations presented in Chapter 5. Like an index entry, the index itself is actually a *field.* Therefore, when performing these operations, you will notice that

- You must *select* the index field in order to delete it; you cannot simply use Del or Backspace from the insertion point.

- You must place the insertion point in front of the index and press **Shift-right arrow**, or place it after the index and press **Shift-left arrow**, to select the *entire* index with a single keystroke.

Using Options in the Index Dialog Box

While the Index dialog box is open, you can choose one or more options that affect the appearance of the index. First, within the Insert

Although you can freely edit text within a compiled index, your editing changes will be lost if the index is subsequently updated.

To delete, move, or copy the index, make sure that you select the *entire* field before performing the operation.

box you can choose either the Normal Index option or the Run-in Index option. These options determine the way Word formats multiple-level index items.

Normal Index, the default option, causes Word to start each index subitem on a new line, and to indent each subitem. For example, the following index item contains three levels and was created with the Normal Index option:

> plants
>   carnivorous
>   feeding, 78

The **Run-in Index** option causes Word to place all subitems within the same paragraph. Word will automatically separate the first two subitems with a colon and the remaining items with semicolons, rather than separating them all with line breaks. If the index item shown in the example just given had been created with the Run-in Index option, it would be formatted as follows:

> plants: carnivorous; feeding, 78

You can also choose one of the three options in the **Heading Separator** area:

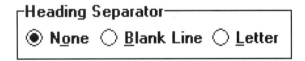

These options specify how Word divides the index items for each letter of the alphabet (that is, how it divides the items starting with the letter *a* from those starting with the letter *b,* and so on).

The default option is **None,** which leaves no separator or lines between groups of index items. The following is a portion of an index formatted with the None option:

> African violet, 214
> Amaranthus, 267, 315
> Aphids, 38
> Avocado, 239–241

Creating multiple-level index items is discussed in its own section earlier in the chapter.

Banana, 189, 218
Begonia, 146–148

The **Blank Line** option would cause Word to leave a blank line between sections, e.g, between *Avocado* and *Banana* in the list above, and the **Letter** option would cause Word to label each section with the appropriate letter, e.g. the letter *A* on a line by itself before the first "A" entry, the letter *B* on a line by itself before the first "B" entry, and so on.

Using Switches to Specify Index Options

You can use switches to specify several options that affect the way Word compiles an index.

When you use switches for compiling an index, it is easier to manually enter the entire field contents using the Insert Field key (**Ctrl-F9**), rather than using the **Index** from the Insert menu. Use the following general method to specify an option with a switch when you create an index:

1. Place the insertion point where you want the index.

2. Press **Ctrl-F9** (the Insert Field key) to insert an empty field at the position of the insertion point.

3. Type the following items into the field (in the order given): the word **index**, a space, and one or more switches together with any accompanying text (the text for each switch should follow that particular switch). For example, the following field would create an index containing only those entries beginning with the letters **a** through **g**:

{index \p A-G}

4. When you have completed typing in the contents of the field, press **F9** while the insertion point is still within the field. Word will compile the index, and replace the field with the actual index.

The switches used for specifying index options are different from those used for specifying index entry options.

You could also enter an index field by using the Insert/Field menu command. See the topic *Fields* in the *Microsoft Word User's Guide* or the *Microsoft Word for Windows Technical Reference*.

You can include more than one switch in a single index field.

 If the **Field Codes** command on the View menu is checked, you will see only the field code for the index rather than the index itself. Select the command again to see the index.

5. If you need to edit the field contents, you can temporarily remove the index and restore the field by pressing **Shift-F9** while the insertion point is within the index. When you have completed editing the field, press F9 again to recompile and display the latest version of the index.

Table 11.2 lists the most important switches you can use within an index field.

Table 11.2: Switches You Can Include in an Index Field

SWITCH	EFFECT
\b *bookmark*	Compiles index using only entries found in the block of text labeled by the specified bookmark.
\e *characters*	Specifies separator between description and page number in index item (default is a comma followed by a space). If you use a tab character, be sure to enclose it in quotes.
\g *characters*	Specifies separator between the two page numbers in a range (default is a hyphen; for example, **23-28**).
\h *characters*	Specifies characters to be used as headings for each group of index items beginning with a given letter. (See Table 11.3.)
\l *characters*	Specifies characters to be used to separate individual numbers in a list of page numbers for an index item.
\p *letter-letter*	Includes only index items beginning with letters in the range specified.
\r	Does not separate index subitems with line breaks (same as the Run-in Index option in Insert/Index dialog box).

characters denotes one or more characters; if it includes any space or tab characters, you must enclose all of the characters in quotes.

The **\b** (*bookmark*) switch allows you to compile an index for a selected *portion* of a document. Simply assign a bookmark to the portion of the document you want to index, then type the bookmark name following the \b switch in the index field. (The method for assigning bookmarks is discussed in Chapter 4 in the section "Go To a Bookmark.")

The **\h** switch permits you specify the characters, if any, to be used as *headings* for each group of index items that begin with the same letter. This switch permits a finer level of control over the index headings than the options within the Index dialog box described earlier. Table 11.3 describes the effects of specifying different characters with this switch.

Finally, the **\p** switch allows you to generate *partial* indexes. With this switch, Word will compile an index that contains only those entries that begin with the letters within the specified range of the alphabet.

Table 11.3: Effects of Specifying Various Character Combinations with the \h Switch

CHARACTERS USED WITH \h	EFFECT
Any single letter	Headings will be consecutive letters starting with *A*.
Several letters	Headings will match the *number* of letters given; for example, whether you specify **xxx, abc,** or **xyz** headings would be **AAA, BBB, CCC,** and so on.
Nonalphabetic characters(s)	These character(s) will be printed literally in headings; for example, specifying ***x*** would result in the headings ***A*, *B*, *C*,** and so on.
Blank space (that is, " ")	Inserts a blank line between each group of index items (the same as Blank Line option in Insert/Index dialog box).
No character (that is, "")	No headings (the same as None option in Insert/Index dialog box).

See Chapter 26 for information on creating a single index for an entire group of documents.

Note that compiling a large index can cause your computer to run out of memory. Microsoft recommends that if the index contains over 4,000 entries, you should compile it a portion at a time. Simply specify the different portions of the index in separate fields using the \p switch, placing these fields next to each other in the document. For example, the following fields would create a complete index in two sections:

$$\{index \text{ } \backslash p \text{ } A\text{-}M\}\{index \text{ } \backslash p \text{ } N\text{-}Z\}$$

After inserting index fields for separate portions of the index, select *all* of them and press F9 to convert them into the separate index section. Word will insert a blank line between each section when it compiles the index; if necessary you can manually delete these blank lines.

CREATING TABLES OF CONTENTS

The process for creating a table of contents is similar to that for creating an index. Like an index, a table of contents is created in two basic steps:

If you have entered outline headings into your document, you can use them instead of entries to generate a table of contents. See Chapter 24.

1. You specify each item that is to be included in the table of contents by inserting a *table of contents entry* directly into the document text at the position of the item you want listed.

2. You insert the table of contents itself. Word will automatically compile the table either from table of contents entries or from outline headings.

In this section, you will learn how to insert table of contents entries, and how to generate a table of contents from these entries.

INSERTING TABLE OF CONTENTS ENTRIES

To insert a table of contents entry:

1. Place the insertion point after the item you want to have referenced.
2. Press **Ctrl-F9**.

3. Type the following between the brace characters: **tc**, a space, quotes, the text to appear in the table of contents, and quotes again.

A *table of contents entry* tells Word the text that is to appear in the table of contents item, as well as the page number that should be displayed for this item.

Like index entries, table of contents entries are *fields*. Since Word does not provide a menu command specifically for inserting table of contents entries, you must insert them using one of the general methods for inserting fields.

> You can also use **Insert/Field** to insert a table of contents entry field. See the Word *User's Reference* or *Technical Reference* for instructions.

The following procedure is a convenient method for creating a single, general table of contents or a table of other items such as illustrations. Later in the chapter, you will see how to specify entries when you are including more than one table within a document.

1. Place the insertion point immediately after the item that you want to have referenced in the table of contents. For example, you might place it after a heading or the title for a section.

II. Fertilizer|

2. Press **Ctrl-F9** to insert an empty field.

II. Fertilizer{|}

> If the table of contents field disappears as soon as you type **tc**, choose **Tools/Options**, select the **View** button in the **Category:** list, and enable the **Hidden Text** item.

3. Type the following items into the field: the letters **tc**, a space, quotes, the exact text you want to appear in the table of contents, and quotes again.

II. Fertilizer{tc "Fertilizer"|}

If the heading in the example above occurred on page 12, the entry just shown would generate the following item in the table when you compile the table of contents:

Fertilizer 12

Like index entries, table of contents entries are automatically formatted as hidden text. You should therefore observe the guidelines for working with hidden text (listed in the section "Inserting Index Entries").

Once you have inserted a table of contents entry, you can delete, move, or copy it in the same manner as an index entry field, as described previously in the section "Inserting Index Entries."

Using Switches to Specify Table of Contents Entry Options

There are two switches to specify options when inserting table of contents entries. To specify a switch, simply type it into the *tc* field following the entry text.

First, use the \l switch to specify the *level* of the table of contents item. The level of an item is indicated by its indentation. A level-1 item is flush with the left margin, a level-2 item is indented one tab stop, a level-3 item is indented two tab stops, and so on. Simply type the number of the desired level one space after the \l switch. You can specify levels 1 through 9; if you do not specify a level, the item will automatically be formatted at level-1.

For example, if the following two table of contents entries were inserted on pages 12 and 13:

{tc "Carnivourous Plants"}

{tc "Venus Fly Traps (Dionaea muscipula)" \l 2}

the following entries would be created in the table of contents:

Carnivorous Plants 12
Venus Fly Traps (Dionaea muscipula) 13

If you do *not* include the \f flag, or if you include the switch but do not specify a letter, Word automatically assigns the letter **C** (for *Contents*) to the entry you are inserting.

Use the \f switch to specify a particular table if you are including more than one table of contents in your document. For example, you might want to include both a general table of contents and a table of illustrations. Following the \f switch, type a single letter (any letter you want to use) to identify the particular table in which you want to include the item. You must use a different letter for each table of contents. For example, you could use *C* for contents, *I* for Illustrations, *P* for the names of plays being reviewed in the document, etc. (Later in the chapter, you will see how to assign these letters to to the separate tables.)

For example, if you wanted to generate a general table of contents and a table of illustrations, you could label all entries for the general table with the letter **C**:

{tc "Planting" \f C}

and all entries for the table of illustrations with **I**:

{tc "A Hyacinth growing upside down in water" \f I}

INSERTING THE TABLE OF CONTENTS

To insert a single general table of contents:

1. Place the insertion point at the desired position.
2. Choose **Insert/Table of Contents**.
3. Select the **Use Table Entry Fields** option, and click OK.
4. To update the table of contents, place the insertion point anywhere within the existing table, and press **F9**.

Once you have completed entering all of the table of contents entries, you can insert the table of contents itself at any position in your document. (If you are including more than one table of contents in your document, you must manually enter the table field as described in the section following this one.) When you follow the instructions in the "Fast Track" above, Word will compile the table of contents entries and insert the resulting table of contents at the position of the insertion point.

You can edit text within an actual compiled table of contents. However, your editing changes will be overwritten if you subsequently update the table.

If you later delete, add, or change any table of contents entries, or make *any* editing or formatting change to the document that alters the position of page breaks, you must update the table of contents. To do this, place the insertion point anywhere within the table of contents— or select it—and then press **F9**. Alternatively, you can choose the **Update Fields** option when *printing* the document.

You can delete, move, or copy a table of contents in the same manner as an index, as described in the section "Inserting the Index" earlier in this chapter.

Using Switches to Specify Table of Contents Options

Word provides several switches to control the way it compiles a table of contents. If you want to specify a switch when compiling a table of contents, you should manually enter the field using **Ctrl-F9** (the Insert Field key) rather than using the **Table of Contents** from the Insert menu. Use the following general method:

1. Place the insertion point where you want the table of contents.

2. Press **Ctrl-F9** (the Insert Field key) to insert an empty field at the position of the insertion point.

3. Type the following items into the field in the order listed: the word **toc**, a space, one or more switches, and any accompanying text (the text for each switch should follow that particular switch).

4. When you have completed typing the contents of the field, press **F9** while the insertion point is still within the field. Word will compile the table of contents, which will replace the field within the document.

If you need to edit the field, you can temporarily remove the actual table of contents and restore the field by pressing **Shift-F9** while the insertion point is within the table of contents. When you have completed editing the field, press **F9** again to display the latest version of the table of contents.

Table 11.4 lists the most important switches you can use within a table of contents field.

The **\b** (*bookmark*) switch allows you to compile a table of contents for a *portion* of a document. Simply assign a bookmark to the portion of the document for which you want to create a table, and enter the name of the bookmark following the \b switch. (The method for assigning bookmarks was presented in Chapter 4, in the section "Go To a Bookmark.")

Table 11.4: Some Useful Switches You Can Use within a Table of Contents

SWITCH	EFFECT
\b *bookmark*	Compiles table of contents using only entries found in the block of text labeled by the specific bookmark.
\f *character*	Compiles table of contents using entries identified by the specified *character.*
\o *level1–level2*	Compiles table from outline headings with levels within the range specified (see Chapter 24).

In order to compile a table of contents from table of contents entries, you *must* include the \f flag in the field. Otherwise, Word will compile a table from outline headings.

To compile a table of contents from general contents entries only— that is, from entries that are labeled with the character **C** or not labeled at all—include the \f flag alone:

{TOC \f}

You already saw (in the section "Using Switches to Specify Table of Contents Entry Options") how to label table of contents entries.

To compile a table of contents using only entries that are labeled with a specific letter, include this letter after the \f flag. For example, the following field would compile a table of contents from all table of contents entries that you had identified with the letter **I**:

{toc \f I}

Part

III

Formatting and Printing

In this part of the book you will learn how to control the overall *appearance* of a document, from the margins and layout on the page to the specific typefaces and sizes of text characters, and you will learn how to output the final version of the document on your printer. Specifically, you will learn how to format each level of a document, how to preview the look of the document before printing, how to print the document, and how to generate form letters. As you will see, Word takes full advantage of the graphics interface provided by Microsoft Windows, and provides many of the features offered by dedicated desktop publishing programs.

12

An Overview of Formatting and Printing

WORD FOR WINDOWS IS DESIGNED TO GIVE YOU A high degree of control over the printed appearance of your documents. This control is provided through a wide variety of *formatting* commands, which are applied to various levels of the document, ranging from individual characters to the entire document. Using these commands, you can precisely control the style and position of each element on the pages of your document.

Working with this large and sophisticated set of commands, however, can be confusing. It may not be clear where to start and what steps to take, and it can be difficult to find the exact command required to format a particular document element. Before Part III plunges into the many details of formatting, this chapter is provided to assist you in two ways.

First, to help you get started, it provides an overview of the basic steps required to format and print a document. Second, to help you find the appropriate formatting commands, it provides a table of each of the important document elements, showing the menu command used to format the element and the chapter where that command is discussed.

Note that this part of the book—and the overview in this chapter— focuses on formatting the document *text* at various levels. Word also provides commands for formatting special document elements; see Chapter 8 for additional considerations for formatting Word tables, and Chapter 9 for formatting pictures.

THE BASIC STEPS AND SEQUENCE

The very first step in effectively formatting your document is entering the content as a collection of text paragraphs. Once you have entered the basic document content, as described in Parts I and II, you are ready to adjust the printed appearance of the document and to generate the final printed copy. The following are the basic steps for formatting and printing your document:

Chapter 13 covers
document formatting.

Chapter 14 covers
section formatting.

Chapter 15 covers paragraph formatting.

Chapter 16 covers
character formatting.

Chapter 17 covers
hyphenation, document views, and printing.

1. Apply *document formatting* commands. Using these commands, you can set features such as the placement of footnotes and the default spacing of tab stops.

2. Apply *section formatting commands*. These commands set features such as the number of text columns, the page size, and the margins. As you will see, a document consists of one or more sections, each of which can be assigned a different set of section formatting features.

3. Apply *paragraph formatting commands*. These set features such as the alignment on the page, indentations, the line spacing, and many other characteristics.

4. Apply *character formatting commands*. These set features such as the font, the character size, and the presence of enhancements such as italics.

5. If desired, perform *automatic hyphenation*. This must be done after you have completed editing and formatting the document so that all line breaks are at their final positions.

6. *Preview the printed appearance* of the document and perform any required formatting adjustments by entering the Print Preview or Page Layout document view, or zoom the document view to any degree of magnification.

7. Perform automatic hyphenation again if you are hyphenating the document, and if changes made in step 6 affected the positions of one or more line breaks.

8. Set the printing options and print the document.

You may not need to perform all of these steps, and you may not want to perform them in the order given, for several reasons. First, as you saw in Chapter 3, when you create a new document, it is based upon a document template that specifies a set of default formatting features. You do not need to issue a formatting command unless you want to *change* a default feature. For example, you may want to accept all of the default document and section formatting features. In this case, you do not need to perform steps 1 and 2 above.

Second, you may want to issue formatting commands while you are still entering text and graphics into the document. For example, while typing in the document text you might want to choose the italic character enhancement, enter the text that is to appear in italics, and then turn off the italic enhancement to resume entering normal characters.

Third, although you do not always *need* to apply the formatting commands in the order listed—steps 1 through 4 *can* be performed in any order, there is an advantage to following this order. Notice that according to the list, the document is formatted starting with the highest level (the entire document) and proceeds toward the lowest level (characters). To specify certain document features, you *must* follow this order. For example, to have Word display line numbers, you must first specify a section formatting option to enable line numbering for the entire section; only then can you turn line numbering off for one or more paragraphs through the appropriate paragraph formatting feature.

Finally, as you become a more experienced Word user and begin using advanced features such as document templates and style definitions, you may follow a very different series of steps when preparing a document.

FINDING THE CORRECT FORMATTING COMMAND

The formatting commands discussed in Chapter 13 always affect the entire document. The commands presented in Chapter 14 can be applied to individual sections of a document (they affect the entire document if they are assigned to all sections in the document, or if the document consists of only a single section). Those discussed in Chapter 15 affect paragraphs, and those in Chapter 16 affect individual characters.

When you want to format a specific document element, the particular category of the command you need to use may not be obvious. For example, if you want to set the number of text columns, is this a feature that is only applied to an entire document, or to a document section, or to an individual paragraph? Table 12.1 is presented to help you resolve these questions; it will help you rapidly find the menu command used to format an individual feature, and the chapter in which this command is discussed.

Table 12.1: Key to Formatting Commands

DOCUMENT FORMATTING		
ELEMENT	**MENU COMMAND**	**CHAPTER**
Footnotes: position within document (bottom of page, beneath text, end of section, end of document)	Insert/Footnote	10
Footnotes: starting number	Insert/Footnote	10
Footnotes: restarting each section	Insert/Footnote	10
Footnotes: separator & continuation character, and continuation notice	Insert/Footnote	10
Tab stops: default spacing	Format/Tabs	13
Template attached to document	File/Template	13
Widow/orphan control	Tools/Options (select Print category icon)	13
SECTION FORMATTING		
ELEMENT	**MENU COMMAND**	**CHAPTER**
Columns of text: number of	Format/Columns	14
Columns of text: space between	Format/Columns	14

Table 12.1: Key to Formatting Commands (continued)

SECTION FORMATTING		
ELEMENT	**MENU COMMAND**	**CHAPTER**
Columns of text: line between	Format/Columns	14
Footnotes: enable printing at end of section	Format/Section Layout	14
Header and footer formatting	Insert/Page Numbers, or View/Header/Footer	10
Line numbering: enable	Format/Section Layout	14
Line numbering: starting number	Format/Section Layout	14
Line numbering: restart position (restart on each page, section, or number continuously throughout document)	Format/Section Layout	14
Line numbering: increment value (that is, count by 1, by 2, by 3, and so on)	Format/Section Layout	14
Line numbering: distance between numbers and text	Format/Section Layout	14
Margins: enable mirrored margins (Facing Pages)	Format/Page Setup	14
Margins: top, bottom, left, right, inside, or outside	Format/Page Setup	14
Page: orientation (landscape or portrait)	Format/Page Setup	14

Table 12.1: Key to Formatting Commands (continued)

SECTION FORMATTING		
ELEMENT	**MENU COMMAND**	**CHAPTER**
Page: width & height (& choose predefined paper size)	Format/Page Setup	14
Paper source (first page, other pages)	Format/Page Setup	14
Section: starting position (on same page, on new page, etc.)	Format/Section Layout	14
Section: vertical alignment (with top, center, or justified)	Format/Section Layout	14

PARAGRAPH FORMATTING		
ELEMENT	**MENU COMMAND**	**CHAPTER**
Alignment: left, centered, right, or justified	Format/Paragraph	15
Border: position of lines, line style, and color	Format/Border	15
Indent: left, right, or first line	Format/Paragraph	15
Line numbering: suppress	Format/Paragraph	15
Page break before paragraph	Format/Paragraph	15
Paragraph: keep together on page	Format/Paragraph	15
Paragraph: keep together with next paragraph	Format/Paragraph	15

Table 12.1: Key to Formatting Commands (continued)

PARAGRAPH FORMATTING		
ELEMENT	**MENU COMMAND**	**CHAPTER**
Position of paragraph	Insert/Frame and Format/Frame	15
Shading of paragraph	Format/Border	15
Space before or after paragraph	Format/Paragraph	15
Space between lines in paragraph	Format/Paragraph	15
Style of paragraph	Format/Style	20
Tab stops: position and type	Format/Tabs	15

CHARACTER FORMATTING		
ELEMENT	**MENU COMMAND**	**CHAPTER**
Color	Format/Character	16
Enhancements: bold, italic, strikethrough, hidden, small caps, all caps, or underline	Format/Character	16
Font (Tms Rmn, Courier, and so on)	Format/Character	16
Language (or omit proofing)	Format/Language	7 and 16
Position: normal, superscript, or subscript	Format/Character	16

Table 12.1: Key to Formatting Commands (continued)

CHARACTER FORMATTING		
ELEMENT	**MENU COMMAND**	**CHAPTER**
Size in points	Format/Character	16
Spacing: normal, expanded, or condensed	Format/Character	16

The ruler is covered in Chapter 15, and the ribbon is discussed in Chapters 15 and 16.

As you will see in the following chapters, you can issue the paragraph and character formatting commands using the keyboard as well as through the menu commands listed in Table 12.1. You will also see that you can apply many paragraph and character formatting features using the *ribbon* or the *ruler*, which are collections of icons you can optionally display at the top of the window. Finally, you will learn how to apply certain formatting commands using the Word Toolbar.

FEATURES FORMATTED AT SEVERAL LEVELS

If a single feature is formatted at more than one document level, you should format it first at the highest level and then proceed toward the lowest level. You do this in order to anticipate exceptions. An example of such a feature is line numbering. You must *first* enable line number for one or more entire sections using the Format/Section Layout command. You can *then* turn line numbering off for one or more selected paragraphs by issuing the Format/Paragraph command, and choosing the Suppress option.

Footnotes are another example of a feature formatted at more than one level. As you saw in Chapter 10, you determine where footnotes are placed within your document through the Insert/Footnote command; setting the footnote placement affects the entire document. If you choose the End of Section option, footnote text will be placed at the end of each section. You can then, however, suppress footnotes within one or more specific sections through the Format/Section

Layout command (in this case, the footnote text will be moved to the end of the next section for which footnotes are enabled).

Tab positions are also set at several document levels. First, you can set the default tab spacing for the entire document using the Format/ Tabs command. You can then adjust the position and type of tab stops for one or more individual paragraphs through the Format/ Paragraph or Format/Tabs command.

13

Formatting Documents

CHAPTER *13*

IN THIS CHAPTER, YOU WILL LEARN HOW TO CHOOSE formatting options that affect the entire document. Under previous versions of Word, these options were all set through a single menu command (Format/Document). In the latest version, this command has been eliminated, and document formatting options are set through a variety of other menu commands. You will learn how to set the following formatting options:

- Template attached to the document
- Default spacing of tab stops
- Footnote formatting
- Widow and orphan control

You will also learn how to override the document formatting settings for one or more individual sections or paragraphs.

CHANGING THE DOCUMENT TEMPLATE

To change the template attached to the document:

- Choose **File/Template**.
- Select the desired template in the **Attach Document To:** list, and click OK.

As you have seen, when creating a new document within Word, you specify a document *template*, which is the basic framework upon which the document is built. Chapter 19 discusses document templates, and the other chapters in Part IV (Chapters 20 through 23) explain each of the features that can be assigned to a document template.

The Description box displays the contents of the **Title** field of the document's *document summary information*. If the Title field is blank, no description will appear.

You can also *change* the template associated with a document at any time, by choosing the **File/Template** command. Word will display the Template dialog box, illustrated in Figure 13.1. Select the name of the desired template from the **Attach Document To:** list. Notice that as you select each one, a description of the template (if available) appears in the Description box. When you have selected the desired template, click the OK button.

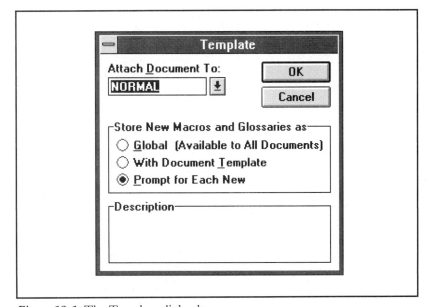

Figure 13.1: The Template dialog box

The Template dialog box also allows you to set the way that Word saves any new *glossary entries* or *macros*; this feature will be discussed in Chapters 21 and 22.

Attaching a new template to a document does *not* change any text, pictures, formatting, or styles belonging to the template. It can change only the glossary entries or the macros, or the keyboard, menu, or Toolbar assignments. All of these elements are discussed in Part IV of the book.

SETTING THE DEFAULT TAB STOPS

To set the default tab stop spacing:

- Choose **Format/Tabs**.
- Enter the desired measurement into the **Default Tab Stops:** box and click OK.

As you have seen, each time you press the Tab key while typing in document text, Word aligns the insertion point at the next tab stop. Word automatically assigns a series of tab stops to all new paragraphs you enter into a document. The *default tab stops* value is the distance between these tab stops. For example, if this measurement is 0.5″, the first tab stop will be 0.5″ from the left margin, the second tab stop 1.0″ from the left margin, and so on until the right margin is reached.

The initial default tab stops value is 0.5″. To change this value, issue the **Format/Tabs** command. When Word displays the Tabs dialog box, and enter the desired measurement into the **Default Tab Stops:** box

In Chapter 15, you will learn how to adjust the positions and types of tab stops for one or more paragraphs. The tab stops you set for specific paragraphs will override the default stops.

Default Tab Stops: 0.5″

All of the values entered into the Tab dialog box, except the Default Tab Stops, *apply only to the selected paragraph or paragraphs*, and are therefore discussed in Chapter 15.

FORMATTING FOOTNOTES

To set the footnote formatting features:

- Choose **Insert/Footnote**.
- Click the **Options** button.
- Enter the desired values into the Footnote Options dialog box.

The formatting features of footnotes also affect the entire document. As explained in Chapter 10, you can set the following footnote formatting features by choosing the **Insert/Footnote** command and then clicking the **Options** button:

- The footnote position (bottom of page, beneath text, end of section, or end of document)

- The starting footnote number

- Whether footnote numbering restarts with each document section

- The characters used to separate the footnote text from the normal document text.

- The separating character used for footnotes that have been continued on another page, as well as the message displayed when a footnote is continued.

These features are described in Chapter 10.

CONTROLLING WIDOWS AND ORPHANS

To turn the widow and orphan control option on or off:

- Choose **Tools/Options**.
- Select the **Print icon** in the **Category:** list.
- Check or uncheck the **Widow/Orphan Control** option.

If a paragraph has three lines or less, the **Widow/Orphan Control** option will have no effect.

When the **Widow/Orphan Control** feature is enabled, Word will adjust the page breaks in the document so that a single line of a paragraph is never separated from the rest of the paragraph by a page break. Specifically, Word will perform the following two actions:

- If the last line of a paragraph is about to be printed alone at the top of a new page (a *widow*), Word will move the previous line to the new page, so that this page will contain the last *two* lines of the paragraph.

- If the first line of a paragraph is about to be printed alone at the bottom of a page (an *orphan*), Word will move this line to the next page, so that the entire paragraph will be printed on the next page.

To enable or disable this feature, choose the **Tools/Options** command, select the **Print icon** in the **Category:** list

and check or uncheck the **Widow/Orphan Control** option.

When Word is installed, this option is initially enabled.

When the Widow/Orphan Control option is activated, the number of lines on each page can vary slightly. Therefore, if each page must have exactly the same number of lines (for example, certain legal documents), you should disable the option.

OVERRIDING DOCUMENT FORMATTING

Although the options discussed in this chapter apply to the entire document, you can override or modify some of them for one or more sections or paragraphs. Specifically, you can override the following formatting settings:

- Default tab stops
- Footnote placement
- Widow/orphan control

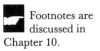
Footnotes are
discussed in
Chapter 10.

Chapter 15 explains how to add or remove tab stops for one or more paragraphs. You can set the position and style of each tab stop.

If you have chosen the **End of Section** option through the **Insert/Footnote** command (to place footnote text at the end of each document section), you can override this option for one or more sections by suppressing footnotes through the **Format/Section Setup** command. If you disable footnote text for a given section, Word places it at the end of the next section for which footnote text is enabled.

Also, if you turn off the **Widow/Orphan Control** option through the **Tools/Options** command (**Print** category), you can apply a similar option—**Keep Lines Together**—for one or more individual paragraphs. You set the Keep Lines Together option through the **Format/Paragraph** dialog box, which is explained in Chapter 15. Unlike the Widow/Orphan Control option, Keep Lines Together causes Word to always keep the *entire* paragraph together on a single page.

Formatting Sections

CHAPTER *14* _____

IN THE PREVIOUS CHAPTER, YOU LEARNED HOW TO
format an entire document. In this chapter, you will learn how to format *sections*. A section is a division of a document that can be assigned
separate formatting features.

First you will learn how to *create* separate sections in your documents. Then you will learn how to *format* specific sections.

DIVIDING A DOCUMENT INTO SECTIONS

To divide a document into sections:

1. Place the cursor where you want a division.
2. Choose **Insert/Break**.
3. Select the type of section break you want from the **Section Break** area of the dialog box and click OK.
4. Repeat steps 1 through 3 at any other places you want section breaks.

When you create a new document, it consists of a single section.
You can, however, divide a document into two or more sections to
vary the section formatting from one part to another. For example,
you could arrange the text in a single column throughout one section
of the document and two columns throughout another. (You could
even vary the number of columns displayed on a single page.)

To create a new section within a document, you must insert a *section break* (similar to a page break). The first section break divides the
document into two sections; all text before belongs to *section 1* and all
text after belongs to *section 2*. If you insert a second section break, the

document will consist of three sections, and so on. Figure 14.1 illustrates a document that has three sections.

To insert a section break:

You cannot insert a section break while you are in *Outline* view.

1. Place the insertion point where you want the break.

2. Issue **Insert/Break**. Word will display the Break dialog box, shown in Figure 14.2.

3. Choose one of the four types of section break from the **Section Break** area. The option you choose will determine where Word will start printing the new section in relation to the previous one.

4. Click OK.

If you select the **Next Page** option, Word will start the section on a new page.

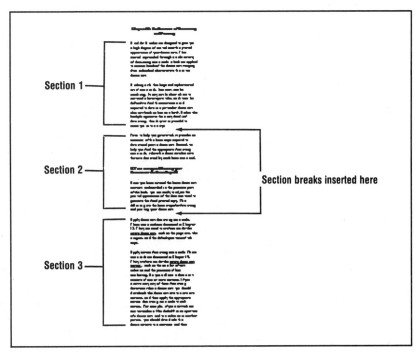

Figure 14.1: A document consisting of three sections

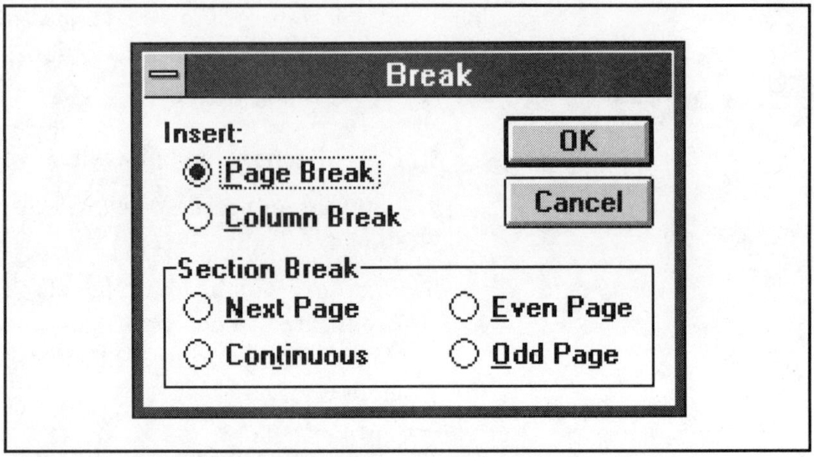

Figure 14.2: The Break dialog box

As you saw in Chapter 10, Word numbers pages continuously, ignoring section breaks; however, you can force Word to start numbering a section with a specified line number.

If you select the **Even Page** option, Word will start printing the new section on the next even-numbered page. If you select **Odd Page**, Word will start printing it on the next odd-numbered page. Note that the Even Page and Odd Page options may result in a blank page in your document.

Here's an example of when you might want to choose the **Odd Page** option: You are writing a document that contains a title page in front of each chapter. The title pages have a different page layouts than the chapters, so you place each in a separate document section. You will want each title page and chapter to start on an odd-numbered page. Choose the **Odd Page** option when inserting section breaks.

Finally, if you select the **Continuous** option, Word will start printing the new section with no page break. Choose this option if you want different section formats to appear on the same page. For example, you could create a page that has a single column at the top and two columns of text at the bottom.

Regardless of the option you choose when inserting a page break, you can later change the position with **Format/Section Layout**.

Word marks the position of a page break by displaying a double dotted line extending across the text column. The mark will not appear on the printed document copy.

When you apply section formatting, it is a good practice to first divide the document into sections and then apply the formatting. Some commands require it. They fall under the following sections:

- "Formatting the Section Layout"
- "Formatting Headers and Footers"

Other formatting commands, however, do not require you to insert section breaks before choosing the command. These are found in the following sections:

- "Formatting Columns"
- "Formatting the Page Setup"

GOING TO A SECTION

To quickly move the insertion point to a specific document section:

1. Choose **Edit/Go To** or press **F5**.
2. At the prompt, type **s** followed immediately by the section number, and press Enter.

Once you have divided a document into sections, you can move the insertion point to a particular section using the **Go To** command. Remember that sections are numbered beginning with 1. To go to a specific section, issue **Edit/Go To** or press **F5**; at the prompt, type **s** followed immediately by the section number, and press Enter. For example, to go to the third section, type the following at the prompt:

s3

Also, as you saw in Chapter 4, you can go to a particular line or page within a section. For example, to go to the top of the second page in the third section, type the following at the **Go To** command prompt:

s3p2

FORMATTING THE LAYOUT OF A SECTION

 If you select more than one section when working with **Format/Section Layout**, the formatting will be applied to all selected sections.

To format a section of your document, first place the cursor in the desired section. Choose **Format/Section Layout**. Word will display the Section Layout dialog box, illustrated in Figure 14.3.

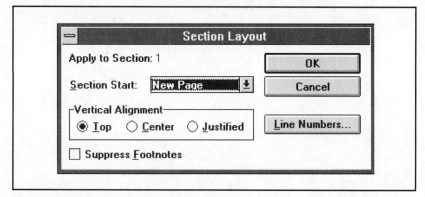

Figure 14.3: The Section Layout dialog box

To format the layout of the selected section or sections:

1. Choose **Format/Section Layout**. Word will display the Section Layout dialog box.

2. To specify where the section starts, select one of the options in the **Section Start:** list.

3. To adjust the vertical alignment of the text on each page of the section, choose one of the options in the **Vertical Alignment** box.

4. To move footnotes to the end of the next section, check the **Suppress Footnotes** option.

5. To enable and format line numbering within the section, click the **Line Numbers** button. Enter the desired values into the Line Numbers dialog box.

Throughout this chapter, the term *current section* refers to the section or sections containing the insertion point or selection at the time you issue a formatting command. Any formatting options you choose are applied to the current section.

The options in the Line Numbers dialog box allow you to specify the following:

- The section starting point
- The vertical alignment of text
- Line numbering
- The location of footnotes

Notice that each text box within the Section Layout dialog box displays the current setting. You do not need to enter a value unless you want to change a current setting. To remove the dialog box and apply your changes, click OK. To remove the dialog box without applying changes, click Cancel.

SPECIFYING WHERE THE SECTION STARTS

You can specify the starting position of the current section by selecting one of the options from the **Section Start:** pull-down list in the Section Layout dialog box.

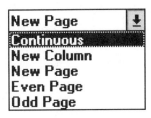

The starting option you choose here will override the one chosen when you created the new section. The Section Start box also has an option not found in the Break dialog box, called **New Column**. The other options in the list are equivalent to the those provided by **Insert/ Break**.

Formatting text in multiple columns and inserting column breaks are discussed later in the chapter, in the section "Formatting Columns."

The **New Column** option instructs Word to start printing the current section at the top of a new text column. This option assumes that the previous section and the current section have the same number of columns; if they don't, Word starts printing the current section at the beginning of a new page. Figure 14.4 illustrates a section that has been assigned the **New Column** starting option.

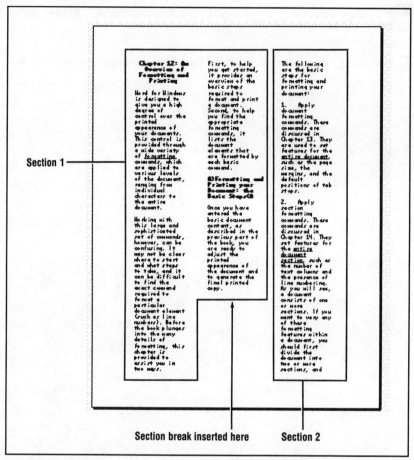

Figure 14.4: A section that starts with the New Column option

Insert/Break does not offer an equivalent to the **New Column** option. Therefore, to insert a section that starts on a new column, you must issue Insert/Break and temporarily choose some other starting position option (such as **Next Page**). Then issue **Format/Section Layout** and specify the **New Column** option.

SPECIFYING THE VERTICAL ALIGNMENT

You specify the vertical alignment of each page by choosing one of the options in the **Vertical Alignment** area of the Section Layout dialog box. For these options to have any effect, the selected paragraphs must be preceded and followed by section breaks. You have three options:

Top
Center
Justified

If you assign **Center** or **Justified** alignment to a section, the specified alignment will appear on the printed copy and in *Print Preview* view. It will not show in *Normal* or *Page Layout* views.

If a given page already contains the maximum number of lines, the vertical alignment option will have no effect.

The **Top** option (which is the default) aligns the text with the top margin. Figure 14.5 illustrates a page formatted with the **Top** vertical alignment option.

The **Center** option aligns text on the page between the top and bottom margins. Figure 14.6 illustrates the same section shown in Figure 14.5, formatted with the **Center** option.

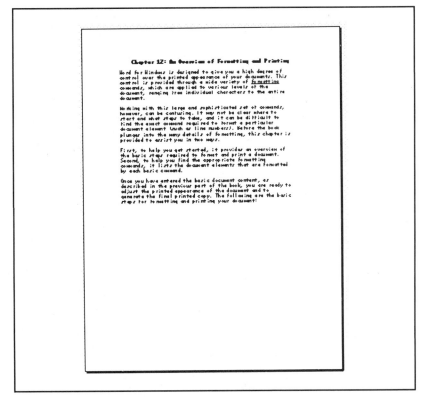

Figure 14.5: A page illustrating the Top vertical alignment option

The **Justified** option adds space evenly *between* each paragraph. It does not alter the line spacing within paragraphs. Figure 14.7 illustrates the same page shown in the previous figures, formatted with the **Justified** option.

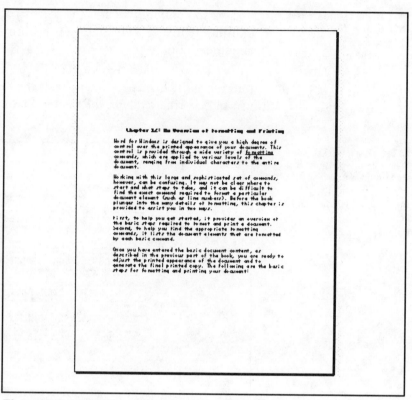

Figure 14.6: A page illustrating the Center vertical alignment option

A Practical Exercise in Alignment

As an example of setting the vertical alignment of a section, you could center the text contained on a title page both vertically and horizontally, using the following steps (these steps assume that you have already typed in the title text):

1. If the title page is not at the beginning of the document, place the insertion point immediately in front of it and insert a section break by choosing **Insert/Break**. Select the **Next Page**, **Even Page**, or **Odd Page** option and click OK.

2. Place the insertion point at the end of the title page and insert another section break, using the method described in step 1. The title page is now contained in its own section.

If you want to align the text on a page using a pattern not provided by these three options, you can use **Insert/Frame** and **Format/Frame**, described in Chapter 15. These commands allow you to place paragraphs almost anywhere on the page.

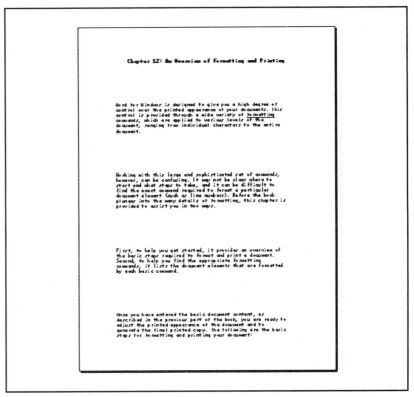

Figure 14.7: A page illustrating the Justified vertical alignment option

3. Place the insertion point anywhere within the title page and choose **Format/Section Layout**. Select the **Center** option in the **Vertical Alignment** area of the dialog box and click OK. The title page text will now be centered vertically.

4. Select all paragraphs on the title page and press **Ctrl-C** to center the text horizontally.

Note that the vertical alignment will not appear until you print the document or examine it in *Print Preview* view.

NUMBERING LINES

To have Word automatically display numbers next to the lines in the current section, click the **Line Numbers** button within the Section

Line numbers are displayed only in *Print Preview* and on the final printed page.

Layout dialog box. Word will then open the Line Numbers dialog box, which is illustrated in Figure 14.8. To enable line numbering, check the **Add Line Numbering** option.

If you vertically justify the current section with **Format/ Section Layout**, you may see extra blank space between the line numbers.

When you have enabled line numbering for a section, Word displays consecutive numbers to the left of the text lines. Blank lines inserted by pressing Enter are numbered along with lines that contain text. Blank lines created by adding space before or after a paragraph, though, are *not* numbered. Figure 14.9 illustrates the beginning of a document section containing line numbers.

The Line Numbers dialog box also allows you to control the way Word numbers the lines in the current section.

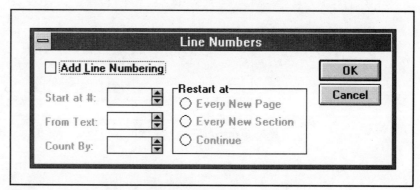

Figure 14.8: The Line Numbers dialog box

```
1   This document section contains line numbers. By choosing the Line Numbering option
2   within the Line Numbers area of the Format/Section dialog box, you can have Word
3   display numbers in front of the lines of the current section. Other options within the
4   Line Numbers area allow you to specify the starting line number, the distance between
5   the line numbers and the text, which lines you want Word to number, and where you
6   want Word to restart the numbering.
```

Figure 14.9: A portion of a printed document displaying line numbers

The **Start At #:** box specifies the starting line number. By default, the starting number is 1. If you would like Word to start numbering with another number, you can enter a positive integer into the Start At # box.

The **From Text:** box specifies the distance between the right edge of the line numbers and the left text margin. The default value is **Auto**, which sets a distance of 0.25" for text arranged in a single column or 0.13" for text in multiple columns. If you want Word to use a different distance, enter the desired measurement into this box. (Entering **0** has the same effect as **Auto**.)

The **Count By:** box specifies *which* lines to number. Word will number only lines that are multiples of the number entered into this box. The default value is **1**, which numbers every line. If you enter **2**, Word will number every other line. For example, if the starting number in the Start At # box is **1** and you enter **2** in the Count By box, Word will number lines 2, 4, 6, 8, and so on. Similarly, if you enter **3** into the Count By box, Word will number lines 3, 6, 9, and so on.

Every New Page restarts line numbering on every page with the number entered into the Start At # box.

Every New Section starts numbering the current section with the number entered into the Start At # box.

If you select the **Continue** option, Word will continue the numbering from the previous section ignoring the value entered into the Start At # box. If you apply this to the first section of a document, Word will begin numbering with the number specified in the Start At # box.

You can select only *one* of the following options: **Every New Page**, **Every New Section**, or **Continue**.

SUPPRESSING FOOTNOTES

As you saw in Chapter 10, you can have Word move footnote text from the end of its current section to the end of the next section for which footnotes are enabled. To move the footnote text, simply check the **Suppress Footnotes** option

The **Suppress Footnotes** option is not available if you have not placed footnotes at the end of the section with **Insert/Footnote**.

in the Section Layout dialog box.

FORMATTING COLUMNS

To break text into two or more columns:

1. Choose **Format/Columns**. Word will display the Columns dialog box.

2. Enter the desired number of columns into the **Number of Columns:** box and the space you want Word to leave between columns into the **Space Between:** box.

3. If you want Word to print a vertical line between columns, check the **Line Between** option.

4. Select an option from the **Apply To:** box (explained in Table 14.1) to specify the portion of the document in which you want to change the column arrangement and click OK. As an alternative method, you can quickly change the number of columns within the selected section by using the **Text Columns button** on the Toolbar.

5. To force a column break, place the insertion point where you want to break the column and press **Ctrl-Shift-Enter**.

Do not confuse the snaking columns of text created with **Format/Columns** with the rows and columns of cells created using tables, as described in Chapter 8.

Normally, document text is arranged in a single column on each page. You can, however, have Word arrange text in two or more columns. To arrange the text into multiple columns, choose **Format/Columns**. Word will display the Columns dialog box, illustrated in Figure 14.10.

The type of columns created with **Format/Columns** are known as *snaking* columns, like those in a newspaper. Text flows from the bottom of one column to the top of the next, left to right. Figure 14.11 illustrates the flow of text on a page with three columns.

To break text into snaking columns, first enter the desired number of columns into the **Number of Columns:** box (the default is 1). The maximum number of columns you can have depends upon the size and layout of the page; the resulting text width of each column must be at least 0.5″. If you enter a number of columns that would result in narrower text, Word will issue a warning.

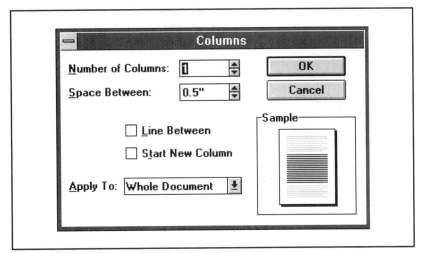

Figure 14.10: The Columns dialog box

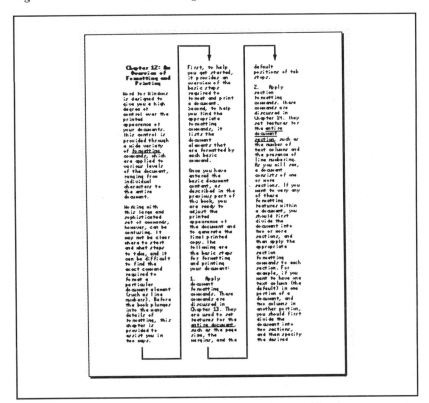

Figure 14.11: Snaking columns created with the Format/Section command

A vertical line between columns created with the **Line Between** option appears only on the printed copy or in *Print Preview* view.

The **Space Between:** box specifies the space between each column. The default value is 0.5″. If you want a different amount of space, enter the desired measurement into this box.

Line Between prints a vertical line between each column. The lines will all be as long as the longest text column on the page.

As you specify options in the Columns dialog box, Word illustrates the layout of the resulting columns in the Sample box.

Unlike the other commands you have seen in the chapter, **Format/Columns** allows you to apply formatting before breaking the document into section. You choose options from the **Apply To:** list which are summarized in Table 14.1.

If Word automatically inserts a section break it will start the new section without generating a new column or page. (If the number of columns in the new section differs from the number in the previous section, Word will begin a new column on the same page).

If, however, you select **Start New Column** in the Columns dialog box,

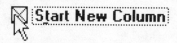

Word *will* start the new section within a new column. (If the number of columns in the new section differs from the number in the previous section, Word will begin the new column on the *next* page.)

The columns displayed on the screen will approximate actual printed widths. However, in *Normal* view, *Outline* view, and *Draft* view, only a one column is shown at a time. In *Page Layout* and *Print Preview* views, however, the columns are shown side by side, as they will appear on the final printed copy.

Table 14.1: Results of Apply To Options

APPLY TO OPTION	RESULT
Whole Document	Format applied to the entire document; no section breaks inserted.
This Point Forward	Option available only if there is no selection; section break inserted at position of insertion point; format applied to section or sections following the insertion point.
Selected Text	Option available only if text is selected; section breaks are inserted before and after selection; format applied to only the selected text.
This Section	Option available only if the document consists of more than one section and there is no selection; format applied to only the section containing the insertion point; no section breaks inserted.
Selected Sections	Option available only if the document consists of more than one section and text is selected; format applied to the section or sections containing the selections; no section breaks inserted.

USING THE TEXT COLUMNS BUTTON ON THE TOOLBAR

With the latest version of Word, you can rapidly change the number of columns within the selected section or sections by using the **Text Columns button** on the Toolbar. The technique is as follows:

1. Place the cursor where you want to alter the number of columns. If you want to change more than one section, select all desired sections.

2. Click and hold the **Text Columns button** on the Toolbar.

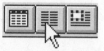

A graphical representation of text columns will drop below the button.

3. While holding down the mouse button, highlight the desired number of columns and release the button. The following choice would create two text columns:

The button method does *not* automatically insert section breaks. (you must manually insert any necessary section breaks *before* using the **Text Columns button**).

4. While still holding down the left button, you can cancel the column formatting by moving the pointer to the left of the grid and releasing the button.

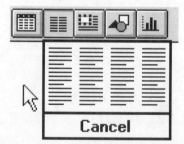

A Practical Exercise in Column Arrangement

Word allows you to vary the column arrangement on a single page. For example, to display a single column of text at the top of a page, two columns in the center, and one column again at the bottom, follow these steps (this technique assumes that the text on the page is currently formatted in a single column):

Using this method, you do *not* need to insert section breaks before issuing the formatting command.

1. Select the block of text in the center of the page that you want to arrange in two columns.

2. Choose **Format/Columns**.

3. Enter **2** into the **Number of Columns:** box.

4. If you want to change the default space between columns (0.5"), enter the desired value into the **Space Between:** box.

5. If you want a vertical line printed between the two columns, check the **Line Between** option.

6. Make sure that the **Start New Column** option is not checked (otherwise, the selected text will be placed on a separate page).

7. In the **Apply To:** box, select the **Selected Text** item.

8. Click OK.

Word will arrange the selected text into two columns, automatically inserting section breaks before and after them. The selected text will also remain on the same page as the single-column text immediately before and after it. The resulting page is illustrated in Figure 14.12.

INSERTING COLUMN BREAKS

As Word arranges text into columns, it automatically breaks the columns when they reach the limits of the margins. This process is analogous to the way Word automatically places text on a new page when it reaches the end of the current page.

You can force Word to start a new column by manually inserting a column break. As with a hard page break (described in Chapter 3), Word will always begin a new column where you have inserted a column break. To insert a column break, place the cursor where you want the break and then choose **Insert/Break**. Select **Column Break** and click OK. Alternatively, you can insert a column break by simply pressing **Ctrl-Shift-Enter**. A column break is displayed on the screen

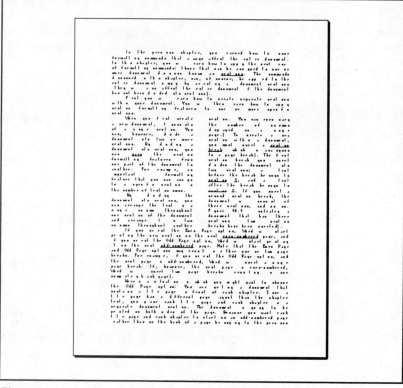

Figure 14.12: A single page containing both one column and two columns of text

as a single dotted line. Figure 14.13 illustrates a column break that has been manually inserted before the end of the second column.

FORMATTING THE PAGE SETUP

To format the page layout within one or more selections, or within the entire document:

1. Choose **Format/Page Setup**. Word will display the Page Setup dialog box.

2. To set the margins, select the **Margins** option at the top of the Page Setup dialog box and enter the desired measurements.

3. To set the size and orientation of the page, choose the **Size and Orientation** option, select the desired options and enter the appropriate measurements.

4. To specify which paper bin to use for which section, choose the **Paper Source** option.

5. Select an option from the **Apply To:** box (explained back in Table 14.1) to specify the portion of the document where you want to change the page setup.

6. Click the **Use as Default** button if you want Word to use your settings as the defaults when creating new documents based upon the same template.

7. When you have finished making all desired settings, click OK to apply your settings and remove the dialog box.

Format/Page Setup displays the Page Setup dialog box. The first step is to select one of the three options at the top of the dialog box

⦿ Margins ○ Size and Orientation ○ Paper Source

to let Word know which set of attributes you want to set. As soon as you select one of these options, Word will display an associated group of items in the Page Setup dialog box.

As you change settings in the dialog box, Word will display a visual representation of the current settings in the **Sample** box.

If you click the **Use as Default...** button, Word will save all of the settings in the Page Setup dialog box. Then, the settings will be assigned to any new documents based on the same document template.

While the Page Setup box is open, you can select one of the options at the top of the box, make changes, then select another option,

○ Margins ⦿ Size and Orientation ○ Paper Source

You can apply page formatting automatically by choosing an option from the **Apply To:** list box. The options in this list are analogous to those in the **Apply To:** list in the Format/ Columns dialog box. For an explanation of each option, see Table 14.1.

make more changes, and so on. When you have made all desired modifications, click OK (or Cancel to remove the dialog box without changing the document).

Figure 14.13: A manually inserted column break in column 2

SETTING MARGINS

You can override the margins for one or more specific paragraphs by setting paragraph *indents*, as explained in Chapter 15.

A *margin* is the distance between the document text and the edge of the paper. You can specify document margins by choosing the **Margins** option at the top of the Page Setup dialog box and then entering the desired values. When you have selected the **Margins** option, the dialog box will appear as shown in Figure 14.14.

The way that Word sets the margins depends upon whether you choose the **Facing Pages** option.

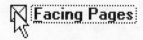

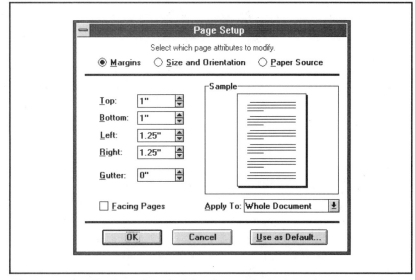

Figure 14.14: The Page Setup dialog box with the Margins option selected and the Facing Pages option turned off

Setting Margins without the Facing Pages Option

If you are designing a document that is to be printed on only one side of the paper, do not select the **Facing Pages** option. When this option is not selected, you can set the top, bottom, left, and right margins, as well as the *gutter,* which will be explained later. If the **Facing Pages** option is not selected, the text boxes for setting the margins will appear as shown in Figure 14.14.

The **Top:**, **Bottom:**, **Left:**, and **Right:** boxes display the current margin settings. If you want to change a setting, enter the desired measurement into the appropriate box, or use the arrows at the edge of the boxes to adjust the values. Figure 14.15 illustrates the four page margins, as well as the page width and height.

You can also specify a gutter margin by entering the desired value into the **Gutter:** box. When the **Facing Pages** option is off, the *gutter margin* is an additional space that is added to the left margin of each page.

The purpose of a gutter margin is to allow room for binding the printed document. Figure 14.16 illustrates the same document shown in Figure 14.15 after specifying a 0.5″ gutter margin.

If you enter a negative value into the **Top:** or **Bottom:** box, Word will set the margin as if the number were positive; however, Word will not adjust the margin if a header or footer is too large to fit within the margin area (rather, the text and header or footer will overlap).

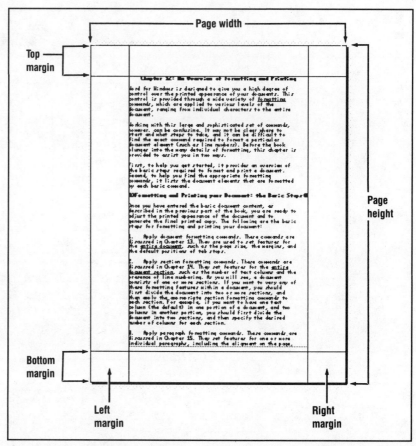

Figure 14.15: The top, bottom, left, and right document margins (Facing Pages not selected)

Setting Margins with the Facing Pages Option

If you are creating a document that is to be printed on both sides of the paper, choose the **Facing Pages** option so that the left and right margins on facing pages will be mirror images of each other. When you select this option, the Page Setup dialog box will appear as shown in Figure 14.17.

Notice that the **Left:** box is replaced with the **Inside:** box and the **Right:** box is replaced with the **Outside:** box.

Specifying a gutter margin does not change the value displayed in the **Left:** box; rather, when Word calculates the left margin, it adds the values in the **Left:** and **Gutter:** boxes.

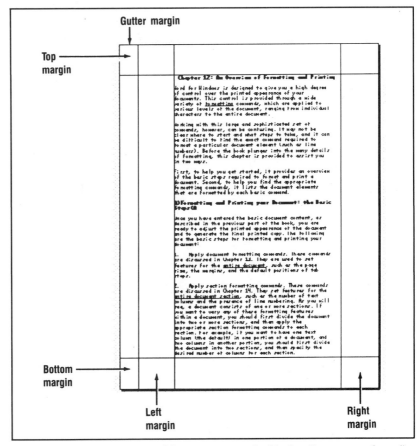

Figure 14.16: A document with a gutter margin (Facing Pages not selected)

The value entered into the **Inside:** box specifies the left margin on odd-numbered (right or *recto*) pages and the right margin on even-numbered (left or *verso*) pages. If the printed document pages are bound in a book, this margin will always be on the inside near the binding.

Likewise, the value entered into the **Outside:** box specifies the right margin on odd-numbered pages and the left margin on even-numbered pages. When the pages are bound, this margin will always be on the outside away from the binding.

The **Top:**, **Bottom:**, **Inside:**, and **Outside:** boxes contain the current margin settings. If you want to change a setting, enter the

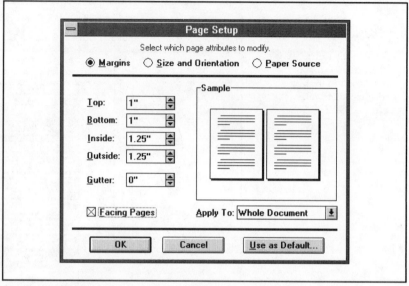

Figure 14.17: The Page Setup dialog box with the Margins option and the Facing Pages option selected

desired measurement into the appropriate box. Figure 14.18 illustrates two facing pages belonging to a document that has been assigned an inside margin of 1.75″ and an outside margin of 0.75″.

You can specify a gutter margin by entering the desired value into the **Gutter:** box. When **Facing Pages** is selected, the gutter margin is an additional space added to the inside margin on all pages. Specifying a gutter margin does not change the value displayed in the **Inside:** box; rather, when Word calculates the inside margin, it adds the values in the **Inside:** and **Gutter:** boxes. Figure 14.19 illustrates the document shown in Figure 14.18 with a 0.5″ gutter margin.

SETTING THE PAGE SIZE AND ORIENTATION

You can specify the page size and orientation by choosing the **Size and Orientation** option at the top of the Page Setup dialog box and then entering the desired values. When you have selected the **Size and Orientation** option, the dialog box will appear as shown in Figure 14.20.

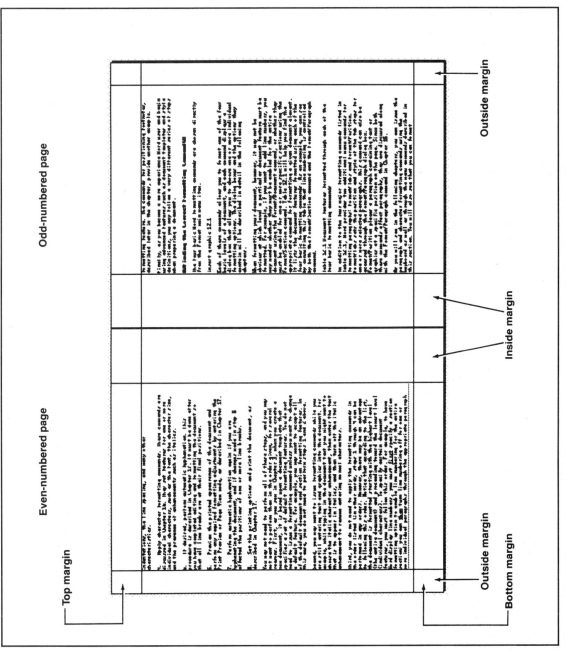

Figure 14.18: The top, bottom, inside, and outside page margins (Facing Pages selected)

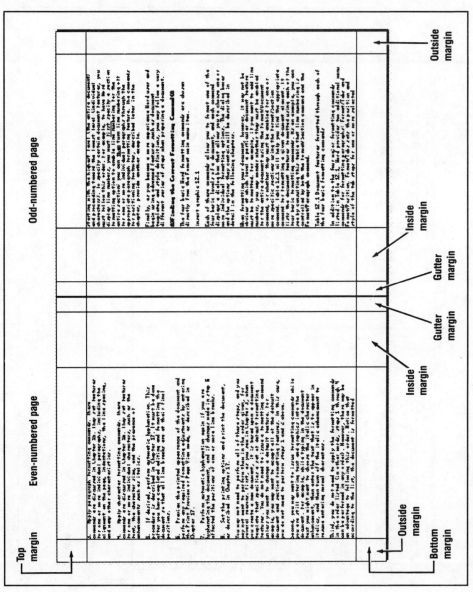

Figure 14.19: A document with a gutter margin (Facing Pages selected)

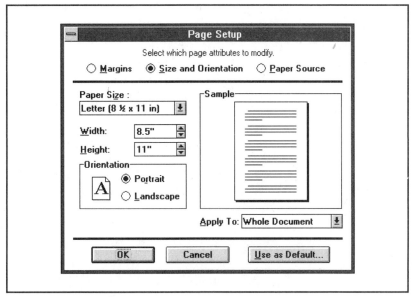

Figure 14.20: The Page Setup dialog box with the Size and Orientation options selected

The *page size* is the physical size of the paper on which you are going to print your document. To set the page size, simply select one of the paper sizes within the **Paper Size:** list box. This box lists the standard paper sizes that are supported by the current default Windows printer. Notice that when you select one of these sizes, the width and height automatically change to the **Width:** and **Height:** text boxes. If you want Word to use a page size other than one of the standard paper sizes in the list, enter the desired width and height into the **Width:** and **Height:** boxes.

You can also specify the paper orientation by choosing either the **Portrait** or **Landscape** option in the **Orientation** area. The **Portrait** option (the default) prints the document from top to bottom on the page

Unlike previous versions of Word, the current version allows you to specify different paper orientations for different parts of a single document.

The **Landscape** option prints the document sideways on the page

Landscape orientation is convenient for printing extra-wide tables, graphs, or other objects.

SETTING THE PAPER SOURCE

The specific items that appear in the **First Page:** and **Other Pages:** list boxes depends on your printer.

Finally, if your printer has more than one paper tray, you can have Word use different paper sources for selected portions of your document. To do this, first choose the **Paper Source** option at the top of the Page Setup dialog box. The dialog box shown in Figure 14.21 will appear. Then, in the **First Page:** list box, select the paper source you want Word to use for the first page of the selected section. Finally, in the **Other Pages:** list, choose the paper source you want Word to use for the remaining pages.

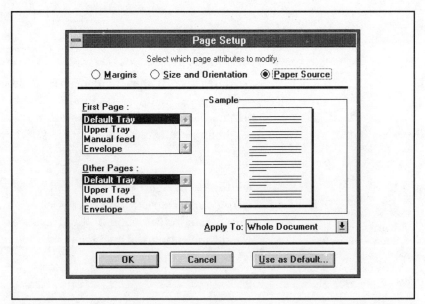

Figure 14.21: The Page Setup dialog box with the Paper Source option selected

For example, if you printer has two bins, you might place your letterhead stationary in one bin and blank stock in the other. You could then have Word print the first page of a letter or report on letterhead, and the remaining pages on blank stock.

15

Formatting Paragraphs

CHAPTER *15*

IN THIS CHAPTER, YOU WILL LEARN HOW TO ASSIGN formatting features to specific paragraphs within your document. The chapter begins by defining what is meant by *paragraph,* and describing how to divide a document into separate paragraphs. You will then learn the three basic methods for applying paragraph formatting: the **Format/ Paragraph** menu command, the ruler and ribbon, and the keyboard. You will also discover how to place a paragraph containing text or graphics at a specific position on the page. Finally, you will learn how to draw a border around a paragraph containing text or graphics and how to add shading to a paragraph.

CREATING AND SELECTING PARAGRAPHS

To work with paragraphs:

- To insert a new paragraph, press Enter.
- To make paragraph marks visible, choose **Tools/ Options**, select the **View** icon in the **Category:** list, and check the **Paragraph Marks** option.
- To move or copy paragraph formatting, you can move or copy the paragraph mark at the end of the paragraph.

A new Word document consists of a single paragraph. As you saw in Chapter 3, whenever you press the Enter key, you add a new paragraph to the document. Paragraphs are separated by means of *paragraph marks.* A paragraph mark is a special character that is normally invisible. You can, however, make paragraph marks visible (as ¶ characters) by choosing the **Tools/Options** command, selecting the **View** icon in the **Category:** list, and checking the **Paragraph Marks** option (this option is initially turned off).

A single paragraph consists of all characters and pictures that come *after* the preceding paragraph mark (or after the beginning of the document, if there is no preceding mark) *up to and including* the following paragraph mark. Thus, Figure 15.1 illustrates a document that consists of *three* paragraphs. Notice that the second paragraph consists of only the paragraph mark itself—it was inserted to create a blank line between the two paragraphs that contain text. (Later in the chapter, you will learn how to have Word automatically insert a blank line between paragraphs without inserting an extra paragraph.)

The first paragraph in a new document is initially assigned a set of *default* paragraph formatting features. The default settings this chapter refers to are those initially set by Microsoft. You can accept the default

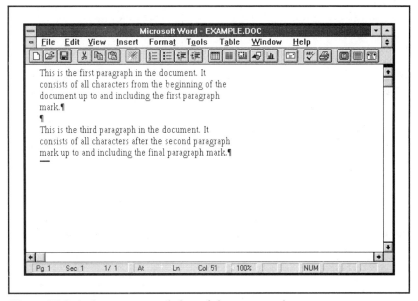

Figure 15.1: A document consisting of *three* paragraphs

formatting features, or you can change one or more of them for specified paragraphs, as described in this chapter, and they will remain the default for any new paragraph. (In Part IV, you will learn how to *modify* the default settings that are automatically assigned to new documents. If you have already performed such a modification, your defaults may not be the same as those mentioned in this chapter.)

When you insert a paragraph by pressing Enter, the new paragraph normally gains all of the paragraph formatting features (default or assigned) possessed by the paragraph that contained the insertion point when you pressed Enter. (In Chapter 20, however, you will see an exception to this rule.)

Conceptually, the paragraph formatting is contained in the paragraph mark at the end of the paragraph. If you have made paragraph marks visible through the **Paragraph Marks** option, you can easily delete, copy, or move a paragraph mark like any other character. (You can also perform these operations if paragraph marks are *not* visible, although it is more difficult.) If you delete a paragraph mark, you will remove the formatting from the associated paragraph, and the paragraph text becomes part of the following paragraph. (You cannot, however, delete the last paragraph mark in the document, nor can you backspace over a paragraph mark if the paragraphs before and after the mark have different formats.)

See the end of Chapter 5 ("Copying Formatting") for instructions on using the mouse to copy paragraph formatting.

If you move or copy a paragraph mark, the text preceding the point where you insert the mark becomes part of a new paragraph, which acquires the formatting contained in the mark. Copying a paragraph mark thus provides a method for copying a set of paragraph formatting features within a document or between documents.

Before applying paragraph formatting using any of the methods described in this chapter (the menu commands, the ruler, or the keyboard), you must indicate the paragraph or paragraphs that you want to format. To format a single paragraph, you can select all or part of this paragraph, or simply place the insertion point anywhere within the paragraph. To format several paragraphs, select all or part of the desired paragraphs. The selection must include at least one character within the first and last paragraphs in the group of paragraphs you want to format (this character can be the paragraph symbol).

USING THE
FORMAT/PARAGRAPH COMMAND

To format one or more paragraphs:

1. Select the paragraph or paragraphs.

2. Select **Format/Paragraph**. Word will display the **Paragraph** dialog box.

3. In the **Paragraph** dialog box, specify the desired alignment, indentation, pagination, and spacing.

   a. Check the Suppress option to eliminate line numbering from the selected paragraphs (if line numbering has been enabled for the current document section).

   b. To format custom tab stops for the selected paragraphs, click the Tabs button. Specify the position and style of one or more tab stops in the Tabs dialog box (you can also open this dialog box by choosing the Format/Tabs menu command).

   c. To quickly change the indenting of the selected paragraphs, click the Indent or Unindent button on the Toolbar.

   d. To rapidly convert the selected paragraphs into a numbered or bulleted list, click the Bulleted List or Numbered List button on the Toolbar.

The most flexible and complete method for formatting the selected paragraph or paragraphs is to choose the **Format/Paragraph** command. In response to this command, Word displays the Paragraph dialog box, which is illustrated in Figure 15.2.

The Paragraph dialog box displays the current paragraph formatting settings. You need enter only those values that you want to *change* from their current setting. Through this dialog box, you can control the following basic formatting features:

- The paragraph indents
- The paragraph alignment

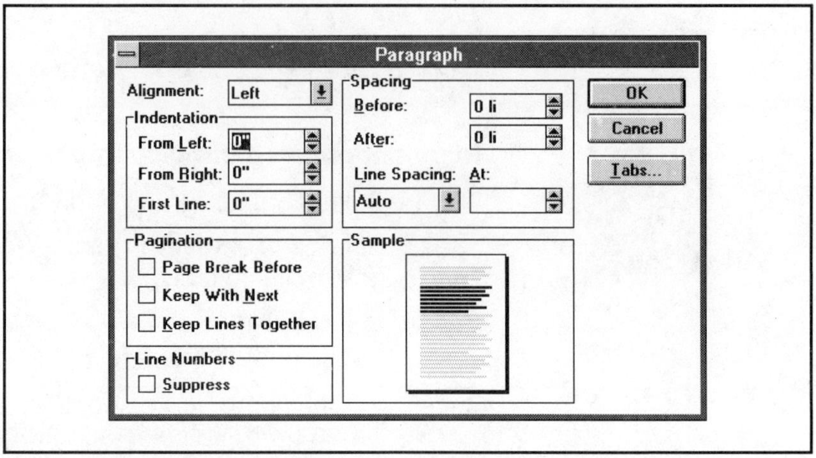

Figure 15.2: The Paragraph dialog box

- The spacing between paragraphs, and the spacing between lines within a paragraph

- The position of page breaks

- Numbering of the paragraph lines

- Tab stops (set through the Tabs dialog box)

Appendix C summarizes the measurements used in Word.

Word can use various units of measurement in its dialog boxes: lines, inches, centimeters, points, or picas. Most options in this chapter use lines or inches as the default unit of measurement.

Note that Word illustrates the formatting features that are currently selected by drawing a graphic representation of the resulting paragraph in the **Sample** box. As you make various changes in the dialog box, the illustration is instantly updated.

SETTING THE INDENTS

In Chapter 14, you learned how to set the four document margins through the Page Setup dialog box. The margins are the default distances between the text and the edges of the page, and they are used throughout the entire section or document. In this discussion, you will learn how to adjust the distances between the text and the left and right edges of the page for one or more entire paragraphs by setting the left and right paragraph *indents.* An indent is the distance between the edge of the paragraph and the margin.

The indents are set in the **Indentation** area of the Paragraph dialog box. By default, the left and right paragraph indents are 0. In other words, a paragraph initially aligns with the document margins. To set the left indent, enter into the **From Left:** box the distance you want to move the left edge of the paragraph away from the left margin. A positive measurement will move it toward the center of the page, and a negative measurement will move it toward the left edge of the page.

Similarly, you can enter into the **From Right:** box the distance you want to move the right edge of the paragraph away from the right margin. A positive measurement will move it toward the center of the page, and a negative measurement will move it toward the right edge of the page.

The position and width of the paragraph text depends upon the page width, the document margins, and the paragraph indents. Figure 15.3 illustrates both positive and negative paragraph indents in relation to the page width and document margins.

You can also indent the first line relative to the rest of the paragraph by entering a measurement into the **First Line:** box. A positive value moves the beginning of the first line to the right, and a negative value moves it to the left. If, for example, you enter **0.5** into the **From Left** box, and **0.25** into the **First Line** box, the first line will be assigned a total left indent of 0.75″ and the remaining lines will be assigned a left indent of 0.5″. As another example, if you enter **0** into the **From Left** box (or leave it blank) and **−0.5** into the **First Line** box, the first line will project ¹/₂″ into the left margin, and the remaining lines in the paragraph will have *no* indent.

Figure 15.4 illustrates two paragraphs for which the first line indent has been adjusted. Both paragraphs have been assigned a From Left indent of 0. The first paragraph has a First Line indent of 0.5, and the second paragraph has a First Line indent of −0.5.

Setting Indents for Multiple-Column Text

The discussion on indents given so far has assumed that the paragraph text is arranged in a single column. You can also assign paragraph indents to text formatted in two or more columns. With multicolumn text, an indent is the distance between the edge of the text and *a column*

If you assign a negative indent, the paragraph extends *into* the margin; a negative indent acts like a margin release on a typewriter.

Formatting text in multiple columns is discussed in Chapter 14.

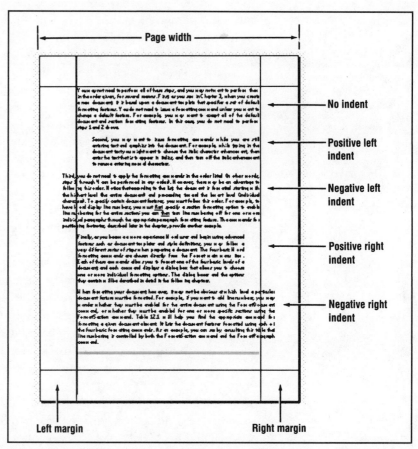

Figure 15.3: Positive and negative paragraph indents

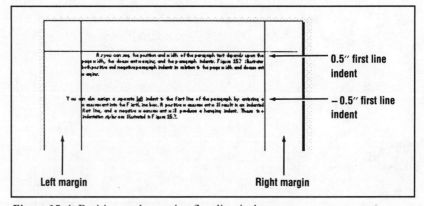

Figure 15.4: Positive and negative first line indents

The left boundary of the leftmost column is at the position of the left document margin, and the right boundary of the right-most column is at the position of the right document margin.

See Chapter 8 for information on tables.

boundary. The column boundaries are the edges of the columns of text; the positions of the boundaries are assigned when you specify the column formatting.

If you assign a positive indent, the edge of the text in the column is moved toward the center of the column. If you assign a negative indent, the edge of the text is moved away from the center of the column. Figure 15.5 illustrates text arranged in two columns; the figure shows the column boundaries and several types of indents.

Note that you can also assign indents to a paragraph of text within a table. In this case, the indent moves the text away from the edges of the *cell.* You should not attempt to assign a negative indent to a paragraph in a table, since this can make a portion of the text disappear.

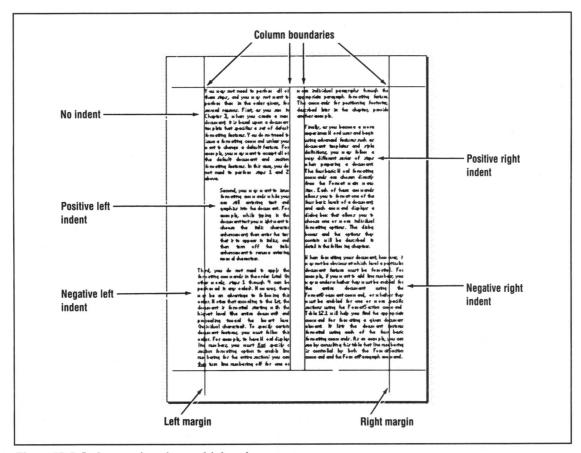

Figure 15.5: Indents assigned to multiple-column text

Setting Indents Using the Toolbar

You can also quickly indent a selected paragraph or paragraphs (or the paragraph containing the insertion point) to the next tab stop by clicking the **Indent button** on the Toolbar:

Each time you click this button, the indent will be increased by another tab stop. To *reduce* the indent by one tab stop, click the **Unindent button**:

You can also convert the selected paragraph or paragraphs to a numbered list by clicking the **Numbered List button**:

Word will automatically insert consecutive numbers in front of the paragraphs, and will also assign a *hanging* indent to each paragraph (that is, all lines except the first will be indented). If some or all of the selected paragraphs have already been numbered by means of the **Numbered List** button, clicking this button will *renumber* the paragraphs.

Alternatively, you can convert the selected paragraphs into a bulleted list, by clicking the **Bulleted List button**:

This button will place a bullet symbol in front of each paragraph and apply a hanging indent.

Setting Indents Using Tools/Bullets and Numbering

An alternative method of converting selected paragraphs into a numbered or bulleted list allows you to adjust the format that Word uses for numbered and bulleted lists, by choosing the **Tools/Bullets and Numbering** menu command. When you choose this command, Word will display the Bullets and Numbering dialog box. To apply a numbered list, or change the numbering format used for lists, select the **Numbered List** option at the top of the dialog box.

When you have selected this option, the Bullets and Numbering dialog box will appear as shown in Figure 15.6.

Choose an option from the **Format:** list box in the **Number** area to specify the numbering style (Arabic, roman, or alphabetic). To choose the character Word uses to separate the number from the following text, select an item from the **Separator:** list, or type one or more characters into the box (the characters cannot be numbers

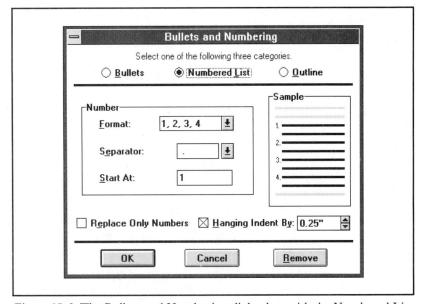

Figure 15.6: The Bullets and Numbering dialog box with the Numbered List option selected

or letters). You can also specify the starting number (that is, the number used for the first paragraph in the selection), by entering an integer value into the **Start At:** box.

If you are *renumbering* paragraphs, and you check the **Replace Only Numbers** options, Word will update existing numbers within the block you have selected, but will not add numbers to any paragraphs that are not already numbered. Finally, you can disable hanging indents by removing the check from the **Hanging Indent** option. If hanging indents are enabled, you can change the indent distance in the **Hanging Indent By:** box:

⊠ **H**anging Indent B**y**: | 0.25" | ▲▼

After you have specified any options you want to change, click OK to save the options and apply numbering to the selected paragraphs. Click **Cancel** to discard the options and leave the document unchanged. Click **Remove** to save the options but remove the dialog box *without* applying numbering.

To change the format used for *bulleted lists,* select the **Bullets** option at the top of the Bullets and Numbering dialog box.

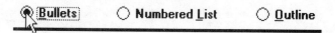

When you have selected this option, the dialog box will appear as shown in Figure 15.7.

To choose the bullet character that will be placed in front of each paragraph, select one of the symbols in the **Bullet Character** area (just click on the symbol). If you click the **New Bullet** button, Word will open a dialog box that allows you to choose *any* character from any available font; this dialog box works exactly like the one explained in the section ''Entering Symbols'' in Chapter 3. You can also change the size of the selected bullet by entering the desired height into the dialog box's **Point Size:** box.

The remainder of the items in the Bullets and Numbering dialog box work as just explained for numbered lists.

See Chapter 24 for an explanation of the options available if you select the **Outline** option at the top of the Bullets and Numbering dialog box.

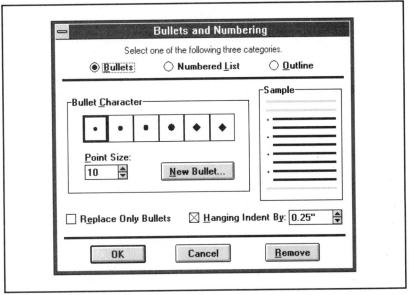

Figure 15.7: The Bullets and Numbering dialog box with the Bullets option
selected

SETTING THE ALIGNMENT

In the previous section, you saw how to adjust the horizontal limits
of a column of text by setting paragraph indents. In this section, you
will learn how to specify the horizontal alignment of the paragraph
text *within* the paragraph indents. To specify the paragraph alignment, select one of the options within the **Alignment:** list box of the
Paragraph dialog box (see Figure 15.2).

Remember that the
first line may have a
different left indent than
the remaining lines of the
paragraph.

Left (the default) causes Word to align the left end of each line of
the paragraph with the left indent, leaving the right edge of the paragraph *ragged* (that is, uneven).

Centered centers each line of the paragraph between the left and
right indents. With this option, both the left and right edges of the
paragraph are ragged.

Right aligns each line with the right indent. With this option, the
left edge of the paragraph is ragged.

Word does not attempt to justify the *last* line of the paragraph; it is simply left-aligned.

The **Justified** option causes Word to align the left ends of the lines with the left indent and the right ends with the right indent. With this option, neither the left nor the right edge of the paragraph is ragged. Word achieves the justified alignment by adding space as necessary between words. You can minimize the amount of space Word must add between words by hyphenating the paragraph, as described in Chapter 17.

Figure 15.8 illustrates each of the four paragraph alignment styles applied to the same paragraph.

> The horizontal position and length of each line within a paragraph is a function of four main factors: the document page width, the document margins (or column boundaries if the text is arranged in two or more columns), the paragraph indents, and the paragraph justification.
>
> The horizontal position and length of each line within a paragraph is a function of four main factors: the document page width, the document margins (or column boundaries if the text is arranged in two or more columns), the paragraph indents, and the paragraph justification.
>
> The horizontal position and length of each line within a paragraph is a function of four main factors: the document page width, the document margins (or column boundaries if the text is arranged in two or more columns), the paragraph indents, and the paragraph justification.
>
> The horizontal position and length of each line within a paragraph is a function of four main factors: the document page width, the document margins (or column boundaries if the text is arranged in two or more columns), the paragraph indents, and the paragraph justification.

Figure 15.8: The four paragraph alignment styles

SETTING THE SPACING

You can set the amount of vertical space Word places between lines and paragraphs by entering the desired measurements into the **Spacing** area of the Paragraph dialog box.

To add additional space *before* the paragraph, enter the desired amount of space into the **Before:** box. The default value is 0; by entering a nonzero measurement, you can have Word insert additional

If you have added a border above the paragraph (as described at the end of the chapter), the additional space is inserted *above* the border.

When specifying measurements in the **Spacing** area, the default unit is the *line;* the standard abbreviation for this unit is **li**. One li is equivalent to ¹/₁₆″, or 12 points. Word will assume this unit if you do not enter a unit after the number you type. See Appendix C for more information on entering measurements.

space between the current paragraph and the preceding paragraph. For example, if you enter **1.5** or **1.5 li**, Word will add ³/₃₂″ (18 points) of vertical space.

In a similar fashion, you can add additional space *after* the current paragraph by entering a measurement into the **After:** box. If you have added a *border* below the paragraph (as described at the end of the chapter), the additional space is inserted below the border.

You can specify the line spacing *within* the paragraph by selecting an option from the **Line Spacing:** list:

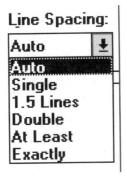

The default option is **Auto**; this value causes Word to use for each line the minimum amount of vertical space necessary to accommodate the tallest character on that line. (As you will see in Chapter 16, you can assign characters different heights.)

Choosing **Single**, **1.5 Lines**, or **Double** will produce line spacings of 1 li (¹/₁₆″), 1.5 li (³/₃₂″), or 2 li (¹/₈″). Note that these three options indicate *specific* heights; technically, because Word defines 1 li to be equal to 12 points, they produce single, 1-¹/₂, or double spacing only if the characters are 12 points high. (Also, these options create *minimum* line heights; if one or more characters in a line is higher than the value, the line height will be increased just enough to accommodate the tallest character.)

If you choose the **At Least** or **Exactly** option, you must then enter a measurement into the **At:** text box. The At Least option causes Word to treat this measurement as a minimum line height; if one or more characters are too tall to fit within the space, Word will automatically increase the line height to accommodate the tallest character.

The Exactly option causes Word to treat the measurement you enter as an *absolute* line spacing. If a character on a line is too tall to fit within this space, Word does *not* adjust the space; rather, it simply allows the characters to overlap the line above on the printed copy. (On the screen, the characters appear cut off at the top.)

CONTROLLING PAGE BREAKS

The Paragraph dialog box (see Figure 15.2) provides three options that control the position of page breaks with respect to the paragraph.

The **Keep Lines Together** option prevents Word from inserting a page break anywhere within the paragraph. If the paragraph does not fit completely on the current page, Word will move the entire paragraph to the next page.

The **Keep With Next** option forces Word to print the paragraph on the same page as the beginning of the following paragraph. In other words, it will not insert a page break *between* a paragraph assigned this feature and the following paragraph (rather, Word will move the first paragraph to the next page). As an example, you could format a paragraph containing a heading with this option so that Word does not insert a line break between the heading and the body of text that follows it.

Hard page breaks are discussed in Chapter 3 (in the section Creating Text Breaks).

Finally, the **Page Break Before** option causes Word to insert a hard page break immediately before the paragraph. You can select this option to make sure that the paragraph is printed at the top of a page (this feature is also useful for headings).

Note that in addition to assigning the three options discussed in this section to one or more individual paragraphs, you can also assign the **Widow/Orphan Control** option to all paragraphs in the document, by selecting the **Tools/Options** menu command and then select the **Print** icon in the **Category:** list). As you saw in Chapter 13, the Widow/Orphan Control option prevents Word from inserting a page break between the first or last line of a paragraph and the remainder of the paragraph.

SUPPRESSING LINE NUMBERING

As discussed in Chapter 14, if you have enabled line numbering for a document section, you can prevent Word from numbering a selected paragraph within this section by checking the **Suppress** option within the **Line Numbers** area of the Paragraph dialog box.

SETTING TAB STOPS

If you are creating tables of text or graphics, it is generally much easier to use the Table feature discussed in Chapter 8, rather than using tab characters.

As you saw in Chapter 3, pressing the Tab key causes Word to move the insertion point to the next tab stop. When you press the Tab key, Word inserts a tab character. If you have selected the **Tabs** or **All** option within the Options dialog box (choose the **Tools/Options** menu command and select the **View** icon from the **Category:** list), all tab characters in the document will be displayed as arrows pointing to the right. If neither of these options is selected, tab characters will invisible. On the screen and on the printed copy of the document, a tab character creates just enough white space to align the following text at the position of the next tab stop.

Each paragraph is assigned its own set of tab stops (the tab stops can vary from one paragraph to another). A given tab stop can be placed at any horizontal position on the page, and can be assigned one of several alignment styles and *leader character* styles (these styles will be explained later). Initially, a paragraph is assigned the default tab stops that have been defined for the entire document. As discussed Chapter 13, the original default tab stops are placed 0.5″ apart. They are left-aligned and have no leader character.

In this section, you will learn how to define *custom tab stops* to replace the default tab stops for one or more paragraphs. When you define a custom tab stop, Word automatically removes all default tab stops to the left of the custom stop.

As described in Chapter 13, you can set the default tab stop for the entire document by entering a value into the **Default Tab Stops:** box of the Tabs dialog box.

To define custom tab stops for the selected paragraph or paragraphs, click the **Tabs** button within the Paragraph dialog box. Word will apply the formatting features specified in the Paragraph dialog box and then display the Tabs dialog box, illustrated in Figure 15.9. (Alternatively, if the Paragraph dialog box is not currently open, you can open the Tabs dialog box immediately by choosing the **Format/ Tabs** menu command.)

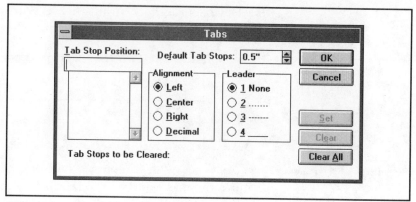

Figure 15.9: The Tabs dialog box

Once the Tabs dialog box is open, you can define a new custom tab stop, remove or modify an existing custom tab stop, or remove all custom tab stops. You can define, remove, or modify an entire series of custom tab stops while the dialog box remains displayed, using the methods described in this section.

Defining a New Custom Tab Stop

To define a new custom tab stop, first enter the position of the tab stop into the **Tab Stop Position:** box. The numeric value you enter into this box specifies the distance between the left margin and the tab stop. You can place the tab stop either inside or outside of the document margins. If you enter a negative measurement, the tab will be placed the specified distance to the left of the left margin.

To specify the tab alignment style, choose one of the options within the **Alignment** area: **Left**, **Center**, **Right**, or **Decimal**.

Left is the default. With this style, the text you type immediately after inserting the tab character appears to the right of the tab stop.

If you choose the **Center** style, the text you type immediately after inserting the tab character will extend equally in the left and right directions (in other words, this text is automatically centered on the tab stop). The text will stop extending in the left direction, however, if it is about to overlap an existing character.

Assigning the **Right** alignment style causes the text you type after inserting the tab character to appear to the left of the tab stop. The text

To use the **Decimal** style, the period character must be surrounded by numeric characters; otherwise, Word will continue moving characters to the left and will not center the period.

will stop extending in the left direction, however, if it is about to overlap an existing character; it will then extend in the right direction.

Finally, if you assign the **Decimal** alignment style to a tab stop, the text you type immediately after inserting the tab character extends to the left (until encountering an existing character); however, once you type a decimal point (that is, a period), the text begins extending to the right. The result is that the decimal point is positioned at the tab stop. If you enter a column of numbers centered on the same decimal tab stop, the decimal points within the numbers will be aligned vertically.

Figure 15.10 illustrates the four tab stop alignment styles.

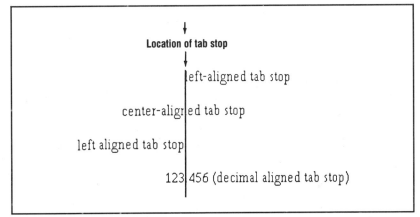

Figure 15.10: The four alignment styles of tab stops

You can also add a *leader* to a custom tab stop. A leader is a series of characters that Word automatically inserts between the position where you press the Tab key and the text that you enter after pressing Tab (in other words, the leader fills the white space created by the tab character). The leader is specified through the **Leader** area of the Tabs dialog box.

By default, **1 None** is selected. To add a leader, select one of the other three options. The second, third, and fourth options cause Word to use periods, hyphens, or underline characters, respectively, as the leader character. The following line illustrates the second leader style:

Total number of birds 27

In this line, the tab stop immediately in front of the **27** was assigned the second leader style. The Tab key was pressed after typing the word **birds**.

When you have finished defining the tab stop, click the **Set** button to add the tab stop to the paragraph (or just click OK if you are making no further changes). Clicking the Set button does *not* remove the dialog box. Rather, Word leaves the dialog box open so that you can format additional tab stops, and adds the measurement for the tab you defined to the **Tab Stop Position:** list box. All tab stops you have defined will be added to the paragraph when you remove the dialog box by clicking OK. You can define up to 50 tab stops.

Removing or Modifying a Custom Tab Stop

To remove or modify a custom tab stop, first select the measurement for this tab stop from the **Tab Stop Position:** list box.

Tab Stop Position:

4.5"
1.75"
2.25"
3"
4.5"

As soon as you select the measurement from the list box, Word copies it to the **Tab Stop Position:** text box above the list.

To remove the custom tab stop at the measurement currently contained in the **Tab Stop Position:** box, click the **Clear** button in the Tabs dialog box. Clicking the **Clear** button does *not* remove the dialog box and immediately clear the indicated tab stop. Rather, the dialog box remains open so that you can continue to perform tab operations, and Word displays the tab stop measurement following the **Tab Stops to be Cleared:** label at the bottom of the dialog box. If you delete additional tab stops, their measurements will be added to this list.

Tab Stops to be Cleared: 1.75″, 3″, 4.5″

When you remove the dialog box by clicking the OK button, all tab stops in the list will actually be removed. If, however, you remove the dialog box by clicking the **Cancel** button, none of the indicated tabs will be cleared.

As mentioned, when you add a custom tab stop Word automatically removes all default tab stops to its left. If you later delete a custom tab stop, Word restores these default tab stops.

You can instruct Word to remove *all* custom tab stops you have added to the paragraph by clicking the **Clear All** button within the Tabs dialog box. Word will then display **All** following the **Tab Stops to be Cleared:** label at the bottom of the dialog box. When you click the OK button to remove the dialog box, all custom tab stops will be removed and all default tab stops will be restored.

To modify the alignment or leader for the tab stop currently displayed in the **Tab Stop Position:** box, simply select the desired options from the **Alignment** or **Leader** areas of the dialog box, and then click the **Set** button (or just click the OK button if you are making no further changes). The changes will be implemented when you remove the dialog box by clicking OK.

USING THE RULER AND RIBBON

The ruler and ribbon are collections of list boxes, buttons, and other icons that you can use with the mouse to directly apply paragraph formatting features to the selected paragraph or paragraphs. To display the ruler (or hide it, if it is already displayed), choose the **View/Ruler** menu option. To display (or hide) the ribbon, choose the **View/Ribbon** menu option. A Word window with both the ruler and the ribbon displayed is illustrated on the inside front cover of the book.

Using the ruler and ribbon, you can apply the following paragraph formatting features:

- Paragraph indents
- Paragraph alignment
- Style assigned to the paragraph
- Custom tab stops

Each of these paragraph formatting features was explained previously in this chapter, in the section "Using the Format/Paragraph Command." Refer to this prior section for information on the *effect* of each feature. The following sections focus on the methods for *applying* the features using the ruler and ribbon.

The ribbon also contains several tools for applying *character* formatting features. These will be discussed in Chapter 16. Additionally, you can use the ruler to set the following two features, which are not *paragraph* formatting features:

- Document margins and inner column boundaries

- Column widths in tables

You will learn about margin ruler view in the section "Using the Ruler to Set Document Margins and Inner Column Boundaries," and you will learn about column view in the section "Using the Ruler to Set Column Widths in Tables."

The ruler can be in one of three different views: paragraph view, margin view, or column view. (Column view is available only when the selection is within a table). You can switch from view to view by clicking the icon at the left end of the ruler.

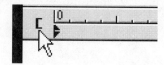

(The icon changes to indicate the *next* ruler view that will be displayed when you click it.)

To apply paragraph formatting features, the ruler should be in paragraph view, which is illustrated in Figure 15.11. In this view, the 0 on the numeric scale is even with the left margin and a series of arrows below the scale indicate the current positions and styles of the tab stops. If the ruler is not in paragraph view, click the icon at the left end of the ruler once (or twice, if necessary) to switch it into paragraph view.

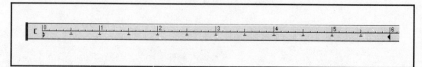

Figure 15.11: The ruler in paragraph view

SETTING THE INDENTS

You can set a paragraph *indent* by dragging the appropriate triangular icon to the desired position. To set the *right* indent, drag the triangular icon at the right end of the ruler scale.

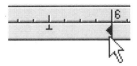

You can drag this icon to the left to create a positive right indent, or to the right to create a negative right indent.

To set the *left* indent, drag the two stacked triangular icons at the left end of the ruler. You must place the pointer on the lower triangle to drag both of these icons simultaneously.

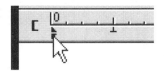

To set the *left indent for the first line only,* drag the *upper* triangular icon.

Notice that the upper icon moves independently of the lower one.

You can also adjust the left indent of all lines in the paragraph *except the first line,* by dragging only the lower icon. To drag the lower icon alone, press **Shift** while you are dragging it.

To set a negative left indent, you must drag the upper, lower, or both left indent icons to the left while holding the Shift key. (Actually, you have to Shift-drag a little to the right before you can continue to the left. Word will then extend the ruler scale to the left of the margin.)

Setting the indents with the ruler has the same effect as setting the indents through the **Indentation** area of the Paragraph dialog box.

SETTING THE ALIGNMENT

You can set the paragraph alignment by clicking one of the four alignment buttons on the ribbon.

These buttons generate, in order, a left-aligned, centered, right-aligned, and justified paragraph indent, as explained earlier in the chapter (in the section "Setting the Alignment").

ASSIGNING THE STYLE

See Chapter 20 for information on styles and on assigning or defining a style using the ribbon.

You can assign a style to the selected paragraph or paragraphs by typing the name of the style into the box at the left of the ribbon or by selecting a style name from the associated pull-down list. See Figure 15.12.

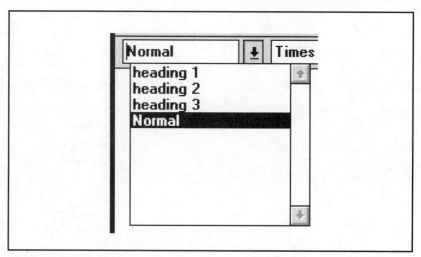

Figure 15.12: The paragraph style list on the ribbon

SETTING TAB STOPS

Tab stops were explained previously in the chapter, in the section "Setting Tab Stops."

When the ruler is in paragraph view, the scale contains a mark for each tab stop, as shown in Figure 15.11. You can use the ruler, in conjunction with the ribbon, to add or remove one or more custom tab stops for the selected paragraph or paragraphs. To define a custom tab stop, perform the following two steps:

1. Click one of the following four buttons on the ribbon to choose the alignment style for the tab stop:

These buttons create, in order, a left-aligned, a center-aligned, a right-aligned, and a decimal-aligned tab stop, as explained earlier in the chapter (in the section "Defining a New Custom Tab Stop").

2. Click the position on the ruler scale where you want to place the tab stop. Word will place a marker on the scale indicating the new custom tab stop

(in this case, a centered tab), and will remove any default tab stops to its left.

If you want to assign a *leader character* to a custom tab stop, you will have to use the Tab dialog box, as described previously in the chapter.

To remove a custom tab stop, simply drag the marker for the stop either above or below the ruler scale.

USING THE RULER TO SET DOCUMENT MARGINS AND INNER COLUMN BOUNDARIES

In addition to the paragraph formatting features described so far, you can also use the ruler to set the document margins and inner column boundaries. The term *document margins* refers to the left and right document margins explained in Chapter 13, where you saw how to set them using **Format/Page Setup**. The term *inner column boundaries* applies only to text formatted in two or more columns, and it refers to the inner edges of the text columns. The column boundaries are normally set when you specify the number of columns and column spacing using **Format/Columns**, as described in Chapter 14. The document margins and inner column boundaries are illustrated in Figure 15.13.

To set the document margins or inner column boundaries, the ruler must be in *margin view*. In this view, the **0** on the ruler scale is aligned with the left edge of the page, and Word displays a **[** or **]** bracket at the position of each margin or inner column boundary.

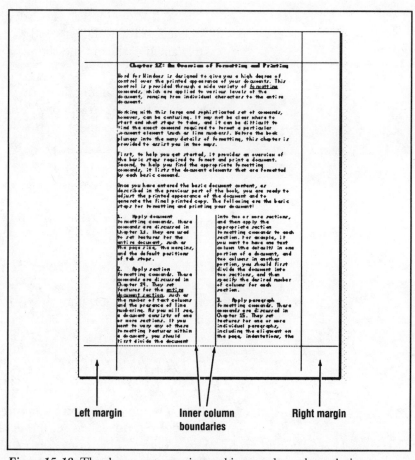

Figure 15.13: The document margins and inner column boundaries

Figure 15.14 illustrates the ruler in margin view. In this figure, the selected text was arranged in two columns; notice that the left and right margins as well as the two inner column boundaries are marked with brackets.

To switch the ruler into margin view, click the ruler view icon once or twice until the ruler appears as shown in Figure 15.14. You can adjust the left or right margin by simply dragging the appropriate bracket on the ruler.

If you have selected the **Facing Pages** option through the **Format/ Page Setup** menu command, moving the left bracket sets the *inside*

The **Facing Pages** option is discussed in Chapter 13.

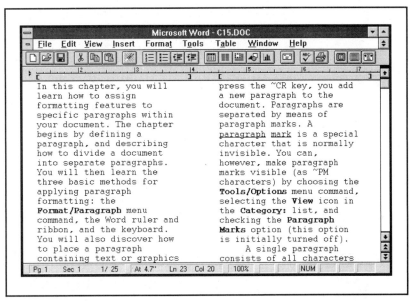

Figure 15.14: The ruler in margin view

margin on all pages in the document, and moving the right bracket sets the *outside* margin on all pages.

To set the inner column boundaries, drag any one of the brackets marking an inner column edge.

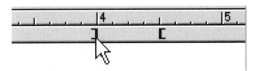

When text is divided into multiple snaking columns, each of the columns is given the same width, and the spacing between the columns is kept equal.

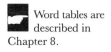

Whichever of these brackets you move, Word will automatically move all of the other inner brackets in order to give all columns the same width and spacing.

USING THE RULER TO SET COLUMN WIDTHS IN TABLES

Word tables are described in Chapter 8.

You can also use the ruler to adjust the width of one or more columns within a table. First, place the insertion point anywhere within the table (or select all or part of the table). Then, click the icon at the left end of the ruler once or twice to switch into *column view.* In column view, the positions of edges of the table columns are indicated with T-shaped markers.

To adjust the position of a cell edge, simply drag the **T** icon that is above the edge to the desired position. Notice that as you drag an edge, any cells to the right are also moved. If you drag the leftmost gridline, you will simply indent the entire table. If, however, you press **Shift** while you drag an edge, any cells to the right remain stationary.

USING THE KEYBOARD

To format paragraphs using the keyboard:

1. Select the paragraph or paragraphs.
2. Press **Shift-Ctrl-F10**.
3. Issue any of the keystrokes listed in Table 15.1 to directly apply the desired paragraph formatting.

You can use the keyboard to format a paragraph by means of the Paragraph dialog box or the ruler. The keyboard commands described in this section are applied directly, without the need to open a dialog box or display the ruler.

Using a keyboard formatting command can be more efficient than using the Format/Paragraph command or the ruler. It may be worth the effort to learn some of the more commonly used ones. The keyboard commands are described in Table 15.1.

Notice that for each command, Table 15.2 describes the equivalent method using the Format/Paragraph menu command. Each formatting feature listed in the table is described earlier in this chapter, in the section "Using the Format/Paragraph Command."

The **Ctrl-Q** keyboard command is especially useful. With this single keystroke, you can restore all of the paragraph formatting features of the selected paragraph to the default values defined by the paragraph's *style.* (Styles are discussed in Chapter 20.)

Table 15.1: Keyboard Commands for Formatting Paragraphs

FORMATTING FEATURE	FORMAT/PARAGRAPH DIALOG BOX METHOD	KEYSTROKE
Centered paragraph alignment	Choose **Alignment:**, **Centered** option	Ctrl-E
Indent: decrease left indent to previous tab stop (first line keeps its same offset)	Enter appropriate value into **Indentation, From Left**: box	Ctrl-M
Reduce hanging indent: decrease left indent to previous tab stop; adjust first-line offset to keep first line at its current position	Enter appropriate values into **Indentation, From Left**: and **Indentation, First Line**: boxes	Ctrl-G
Indent: increase left indent to next tab stop (first line keeps its same offset)	Enter appropriate value into **Indentation, From Left**: box	Ctrl-N
Increase hanging indent: increase left indent to next tab stop; adjust first-line offset to keep first line at its current position	Enter appropriate values into **Indentation, From Left**: and **Indentation, First Line**: boxes	Ctrl-T
Justified paragraph alignment	Choose **Alignment:**, **Justified** option	Ctrl-J
Left paragraph alignment	Choose **Alignment:**, **Left** option	Ctrl-L
Apply **Normal** style	Choose **Format/Style** menu command and choose **Normal**	Alt-Shift-5 (5 on keypad with NumLock off)

Table 15.1: Keyboard Commands for Formatting Paragraphs (continued)

FORMATTING FEATURE	FORMAT/PARAGRAPH DIALOG BOX METHOD	KEYSTROKE
Reset all features to defaults defined by style	Set each option in dialog box back to default	Ctrl-Q
Right paragraph alignment	Choose **Alignment:**, **Right** option	Ctrl-R
Spacing: add 1 line of space before paragraph	Enter **1** into **Spacing, Before:** box	Ctrl-O (the letter "O")
Spacing: apply double (24-point) line spacing	Enter **2** into **Spacing, Line:** box	Ctrl-2
Spacing: apply 1.5-line spacing (18 points)	Enter **1.5** into **Spacing, Line:** box	Ctrl-5
Spacing: apply single line spacing (12 points)	Enter **1** into **Spacing, Line:** box	Ctrl-1
Spacing: remove 1 line of space before paragraph	Enter **0** into **Spacing, Before:** box	Ctrl-0 (zero)
Style: apply a new style	Choose **Format/Style** menu command	Ctrl-S, then type style name and press Enter

POSITIONING PARAGRAPHS

To place a block of text or graphics at a specific position on the page:

1. Select the block of text or graphics.

2. Issue the **Insert/Frame** menu command, or click the **Frame button** on the Toolbar to apply a *frame* to the selected block.

3. If you are not already in Page Layout view, click the **Yes** button when Word asks you if you want to switch to this view.

4. Select the frame (if it is not already selected) by clicking near one of its edges.

5. Move the selected block to the desired position on the page by dragging the frame with the mouse.

6. Change the size of the frame, if desired, by dragging one of the sizing handles that are displayed when the frame is selected.

7. If necessary, choose **Format/Frame** while the frame is still selected to make fine adjustments in the position of the frame, or to select options that affect how the block of text or graphics in the frame is displayed.

So far in this chapter, you have seen how to adjust the position of a paragraph relative to the document margins and the surrounding paragraphs (by setting the indents, the alignment, and the space before and after the paragraph). In this section, you will learn how to place a block of one or more paragraphs containing text or graphics at *any* specific position on the printed page. As you will see, when you position such a block of text or graphics, you can also adjust the shape of the block, and Word will automatically flow the adjoining text around it.

To perform the procedure described here, make sure you select at least one character or picture before choosing the **Insert/Frame** menu item.

First, select the block of text or graphics you want to position. You can select one or more entire paragraphs, or a portion of a single paragraph. Next, issue the **Insert/Frame** menu command, or click the **Frame button** on the Toolbar.

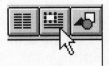

If you are not already in Page Layout view, Word will ask if you want to switch to this view. Click the **Yes** button. Word will insert the block into a *frame* and will switch to Page Layout view.

When Word switches to Page Layout view, the block you selected will be surrounded by a border marking the edges of the frame. You can then perform normal block-editing operations on the text or graphics within the border. You can also move or change the size of the frame.

To move the frame, place the pointer near one of the edges; notice that the pointer turns into two double-arrows:

Page Layout view allows you to edit the document *and* to see each element on the page at the position where it will actually be printed. See Chapter 17 for details on this document view.

> This text is in a frame.

Now press the mouse button, drag the frame to the desired position on the page, and release the button. You can place the frame at any position on the page, even outside of the page margins. If you place the frame at a position already occupied by text, Word automatically moves the text out of the way.

To change the size or shape of the frame, first click near one of the borders to *select* it. When a frame is selected, Word places eight sizing handles on its edges.

> This text is in a frame.

You can drag any of these handles to change the size of the frame. As you do so, Word automatically rearranges the text within the frame, if necessary, so that it fits within the new shape. (Word will not let you make the frame too small to hold the block of text or graphics contained within it.)

Do not confuse *border* and *frame.* A border is a line drawn around one or more paragraphs. A frame is a property assigned to one or more paragraphs that allows you to position them.

Word initially assigns a single-line border to the frame. You can remove this border, or change the line style, by selecting the frame (click near an edge), and then choosing **Format/Border**, described in the next section. If you remove the border, the edges of the frame will not be visible; however, you will still see the sizing handles when the frame is selected.

You can adjust the precise position of a frame, and set other options, by selecting the frame and choosing **Format/Frame**; Word will display the Frame dialog box, which is illustrated in Figure 15.15.

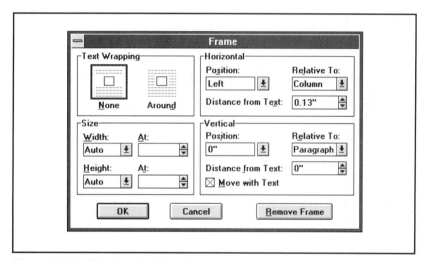

Figure 15.15: The Frame dialog box

In general, it is easier to specify the *size* and *position* of the frame by dragging the appropriate objects within Page Layout view, as just described. The Frame dialog box, however, contains several useful options. First, you can control the way Word arranges adjoining text around the frame, by choosing an option in the **Text Wrapping** area. If you select the **None** option, adjoining text will be placed above and below the frame, but not to its left or right. If you select the **Around** option, Word will arrange the adjoining text on *all* sides of the frame (provided there is room for text on a particular side).

Also, by entering a value into the **Distance from Text:** box in either the **Horizontal** or **Vertical** area of the dialog box, you can adjust the horizontal or vertical space that Word leaves between the frame and the surrounding text.

Finally, if you click the **Remove** button, Word will remove the frame from the paragraph(s) and/or graphics that are contained within it. The paragraphs will then become part of the normal document text. Note that removing the frame will *not* remove any border that has been assigned to the paragraphs; to remove the border, you must use the **Format/Border** menu command, as described in the next section.

 If you select a frame and press the **Del** key, both the frame *and the paragraphs contained within it* are removed.

ADDING BORDERS AND SHADING

To apply borders or shading to a document element:

1. Select one or more paragraphs or table cells, or select a single picture.

2. Choose **Format/Border**; Word will display the Border dialog box.

3. To apply a box border, choose a style in the **Preset** area, and select a line style and color in the **Line** area.

4. To create a custom border style, select one or more edges in the **Border** area. To select a single edge, click on it; to select several edges, click the edges while holding down the **Ctrl** key. Then select a line style and color in the **Line** area.

5. To adjust the distance between a border and the text or graphics within it, enter the desired value into the **From Text:** box.

6. To apply shading to paragraphs or table cells, click the **Shading** button, and choose the desired shade of gray or color.

7. When you have finished your border and shading specification, click the OK button within the Border dialog box.

The latest version of Word now provides a simple, uniform method for applying borders or shading to a variety of document elements. You can use the **Format/Border** menu command to place (or remove) borders around—or shading within—any of the following document elements:

- One or more paragraphs (including paragraphs in a frame, as discussed in the previous section)

- A picture (no shading)

- One or more cells within a table

The first step in applying a border or adding shading is to select the desired portion of your document. To apply a border or shading to one or more paragraphs, simply select them, using any of the methods described in Chapter 3. The paragraphs can be a part of the normal document text, or they can be inside a frame (for positioning) as described in the previous section.

To assign a border to a picture, simply select the picture itself by clicking on the picture (do *not* include adjoining text in the selection; including text would apply the border to the entire *paragraph* containing the picture rather than adding the border to the picture itself). Note that you cannot add shading to a picture.

To assign a border to one or more cells in a table, select the *entire* cells. If you want to put a border around a single cell, you can simply place the insertion point within the cell. If, however, you select one or more characters within a cell, without selecting the entire cell, Word will assign the border or shading to the *paragraph within the cell*, rather than assigning it to the cell itself.

Once you have selected the desired portion of your document, choose the **Format/Border** menu command. Word will display the Border dialog box, which is illustrated in Figure 15.16. The title displayed in this dialog box depends upon the type of document element you have selected, and will be one of the following:

Border Paragraphs
Border Picture
Border Cells

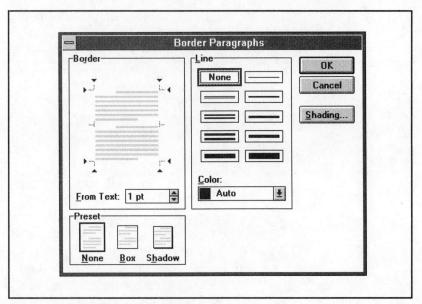

Figure 15.16: The Border dialog box

If you want to place the selection within a simple box, you can simply click one of the options within the **Preset** area, choose the desired line style and color from the **Line** area, and then click OK. If, however, you want to apply borders to only some of the edges of the selection, or if you want to use different line styles for different edges, you must format the edges individually. To choose a line style (or remove the line) for a particular edge, select it by clicking the graphic representation of the edge within the **Border** area. When you select a particular edge, Word places an arrow at either end:

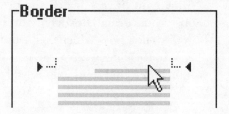

Once you have selected an edge, you can choose a line style or color from the Line area. To select another edge, click on that edge and choose the desired line style. (Selecting another edge will remove the selection from the currently selected edge or edges; to *add* an edge to an existing selection, press **Ctrl** while clicking on the new edge.)

You can also adjust the amount of space Word leaves between the border and the text or graphics inside the border, by entering a value into the **From Text:** box.

When you are satisfied with the border pattern shown in the Border area, click the OK button to remove the dialog box and apply the border.

APPLYING SHADING

While the Border dialog box is open, you can also click the **Shading** button to apply shading to the selection in your document (unless you have selected a picture; pictures cannot be shaded). Word will open the Shading dialog box, shown in Figure 15.17.

Once you have opened this dialog box, the easiest way to specify the shading you want is to choose the desired shade of gray from the

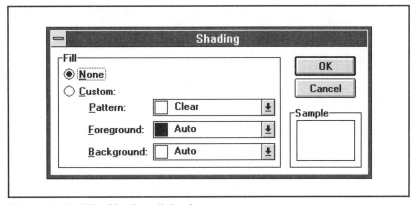

Figure 15.17: The Shading dialog box

Pattern: list box:

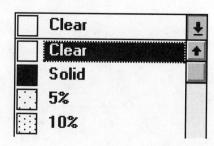

Word will apply the selected monochrome shading to the selected portion of your document.

Alternatively, you can choose foreground and background colors from the **Foreground:** and **Background:** list boxes. Depending on the type of printer you use the selection will have the colors you specified (on a color printer) or will be assigned shades of gray corresponding to the selected colors (on a monochrome printer).

As you select various options in the Shading dialog box, Word displays a sample of your selection within the **Sample** area.

16

Formatting Characters

CHAPTER *16*

IN THIS FINAL CHAPTER ON FORMATTING, YOU WILL learn how to apply formatting to individual characters. Character formatting controls the appearance of characters both on the screen and on the final printed copy of the document.

The chapter first explains how to select characters prior to formatting and how to adjust the appearance of character formatting features on the screen. It then describes the three basic methods for applying character formatting: **Format/Character**, the *ribbon,* and the keyboard commands. You should read the section on **Format/ Character** even if you are primarily interested in the ribbon or keyboard methods, since this section includes more thorough explanations of the formatting features.

As you read through the chapter, keep in mind that you do not need to issue a formatting command unless you want to *change* the default formatting for one or more characters. The default character formatting depends upon the *style* currently assigned to the paragraph containing the characters.

SELECTING CHARACTERS

To assign character formatting to one or more characters in your document, you must first select the characters. If the document does *not* contain a selection when you assign character formatting, the features you choose will be applied to characters you type at the insertion point.

For example, if you select a block of text and then assign the Bold character enhancement, the selected characters will become bold. If, however, you assign the Bold character enhancement without selecting any characters, you will see no immediate change. But any characters you type at the insertion point will be bold.

In general, when you type characters, they are assigned the formatting of the character immediately before the insertion point, in

Prior to formatting, you can select a block of characters using the normal selection mode or the column selection mode, as explained in Chapter 5.

addition to any formatting you assign. There is one exception: If the insertion point is immediately in front of the first character of a paragraph, any characters you type will assume the formatting of that first character plus any assigned formatting.

VIEWING CHARACTER FORMATTING

To see all characters exactly as they will print:

1. Choose **Tools/Options**.
2. Select the **View** icon from the **Category:** list.
3. Check the **Line Breaks and Fonts as Printed** option.

The **Line Breaks and Fonts as Printed** option also inserts line breaks at the actual positions where they will print.

Your printer may not be able to print all character formats. For example, a printer can typically print only a limited number of character fonts and sizes. It also may not be able to print certain character enhancements, such as italics.

If you select the **Line Breaks and Fonts as Printed** option, Word will display on the screen only those character formats that your printer can actually print. To turn on this option, choose **Tools/Options** and then select the **View** item in the **Category:** list. Consider, for example, formatting a group of characters as italic when the **Line Breaks and Fonts as Printed** option is selected. If your printer can print italics, then the characters will be displayed on the screen in italic. If, however, the printer cannot generate italic characters, then the characters will appear on the screen in nonitalic type. Even if italics do not appear on the screen, this formatting feature is nevertheless assigned to the characters; if you later turn off **Line Breaks and Fonts as Printed** or change to a printer that can generate italics, the characters will be converted to italics on the screen.

If **Line Breaks and Fonts as Printed** is not selected, then the characters will appear in italics regardless of the printer's capabilities.

The following sections will note the effect of the current printer selection and the **Line Breaks and Fonts as Printed** option on the appearance of specific formatting features.

USING THE FORMAT/CHARACTER COMMAND

To format one or more characters:

1. Select the characters.
2. Choose **Format/Character**.
3. Specify the font, size in points, style, color, vertical position (super/subscript), and spacing of the characters.
4. Click the OK button.

When you choose **Format/Character**, Word will display the Character dialog box, which is shown in Figure 16.1.

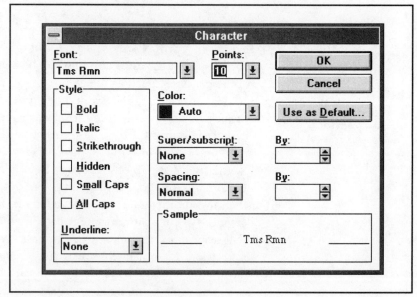

Figure 16.1: The Character dialog box

Through this dialog box, you can specify the following character formats:

- The font
- The size
- The color
- The style
- The vertical position of characters (superscript or subscript)
- The spacing

For each of these features, the Character dialog box displays the value currently assigned to the selection or insertion point. Note, however, that if the current selection includes characters with contradictory formatting (for example, two different character sizes), then the area specifying the feature will be left blank or will be filled with gray shading. In any case, you need enter a value only if you want to change the current setting.

If you click **Use as Default**, Word will assign the character formatting features currently entered into the Character dialog box to the **Normal** style. The format will be applied to characters in paragraphs that have been assigned the **Normal** style, both in the current document and in any documents you create based upon the same template. See Chapter 19 for an explanation of templates and Chapter 20 for a discussion on styles.

Clicking the OK button removes the dialog box and applies the formatting features you have selected. Clicking Cancel removes the dialog box without applying the specified formatting.

CHOOSING THE FONT

Fonts specify the general shape or style of characters. A specific font is identified by a name, such as **Tms Rmn** or **Courier**. The **Font:** box in the Character dialog box contains the name of the font currently assigned to the selection or insertion point. Note, however, that if the selection contains more than one character font, the Font box will be empty.

To assign a specific font, choose the name of the desired font from the Font pull-down list (shown in Figure 16.2). This list displays the names of fonts that can be printed on your printer. The list that appears on your system will probably be different from that shown here. Figure 16.3 illustrates the printed appearance of several different fonts.

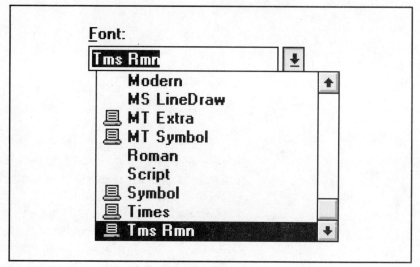

Figure 16.2: The Font: pull-down list

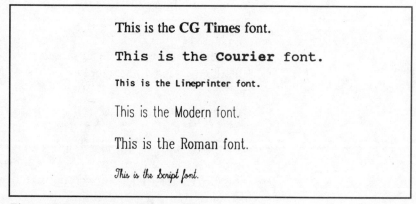

Figure 16.3: A printout of several fonts

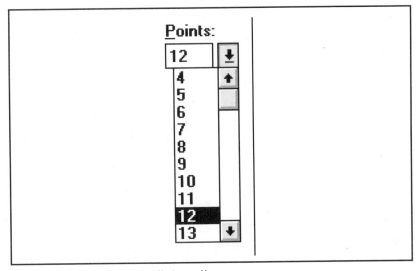

To see a list of the fonts that can be displayed on the screen, choose the **Fonts** icon in the Windows Control Panel.

If you want to use a Windows font that is not included in the list, type its name into the **Font:** box. If **Line Breaks and Fonts as Printed** is not selected, then Word will display the specified font on the screen even if the current printer cannot produce it. When Word prints the document, it will use a printer font that is similar in appearance to the specified font. If you later change the printer to one that can generate the specified font, it will be printed.

SETTING THE CHARACTER SIZE

The character *size* is displayed in the **Points:** box. The number in this box is the height of the character in points. If the current selection contains more than one character size, the Points box will be empty.

If you want to specify a different size, choose the desired number of points from the Points pull-down list (see Figure 16.4). This list displays a set of suggested character sizes that your printer can print, using the font currently specified in the **Font:** box. To obtain an accurate list of sizes, select the font *before* selecting the size.

Figure 16.4: The Points: pull-down list

Figure 16.5 illustrates the printed appearance of a given font printed in several different sizes. Notice that as the character height changes, the width also changes, so that the characters maintain the same proportions.

This is 8 points.

This is 10 points.

This is 12 points.

This is 16 points.

This is 20 points.

Figure 16.5: Characters in several sizes

Alternatively, you can type a character size not listed directly into the Points box. When Word prints the document, if the printer cannot print the specified size, the nearest available size will be used. If **Line Breaks and Fonts as Printed** is enabled, Word will display the nearest available size on the screen, rather than the exact size you entered.

SPECIFYING THE CHARACTER COLOR

The current character color is displayed in the **Color:** box in the Character dialog box. If the selection contains more than one color, this box will be empty. To specify a particular color, choose a color from the pull-down list illustrated in Figure 16.6.

The value Auto uses the color that is currently assigned to **Window Text** in the Windows environment (this color is set by running the Windows Control Panel program, choosing the **Colors** icon, and assigning a color to the **Window Text** screen element).

If your printer (or plotter) can print colors, the selected characters will be printed in the specified color; otherwise, the color assigned to

See your Windows manual for information on setting the Window Text color through the Control Panel.

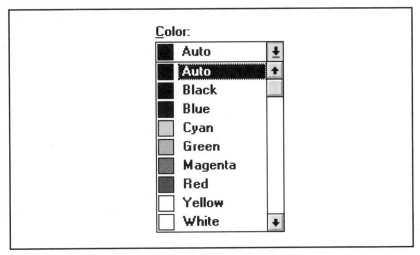

Figure 16.6: The Color: pull-down list

the characters will be ignored. If you have a color monitor, the characters will be displayed on the screen in the designated color, even if you have chosen **Line Breaks and Fonts as Printed** and your printer cannot print colors.

CHOOSING THE CHARACTER STYLE

You can assign a variety of character enhancements to emphasize the selected text. The following enhancements are available:

- Bold
- Italic
- Strikethrough
- Hidden
- Small Caps
- All Caps
- Single Underline
- Words Only Underline
- Double Underline

An enhancement currently assigned to the selected text has an **X** in the box next to it,

⊠ **Italic**

except for the current underline style, which is displayed in the **Underline:** box.

Underline:

None	▼

If, however, an enhancement is assigned to only a *portion* of the selected text, the box is shaded rather than being marked with an **X**, and the **Underline:** box is empty.

If an enhancement is not currently enabled (the box is empty), or is enabled for only a portion of the selected text (the box is shaded), you can enable it for all of the selected text by clicking the box. If an enhancement is currently enabled (the box has an **X**), you can turn it off by clicking the box. You can apply a specific underlining style to the entire selection by choosing an item from the pull-down list.

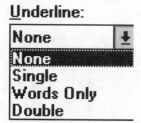

In general, you can combine enhancements; for example, you can assign both **Bold** and **Italic** to the same text. However, you can choose only a single underline style (**None, Single, Words Only,** or **Double**) or cap style.

Figure 16.7 illustrates various character enhancements assigned to characters of the same font (**Times**).

If you have selected **Line Breaks and Fonts as Printed**, Word will display on the screen only those enhancements that the selected printer can create.

Times characters with no character enhancements.

Times characters with the Bold enhancement.

Times characters with the Italic enhancement.

Times characters with the Bold and Italic enhancements.

~~Times characters with the Strikethrough enhancement.~~

TIMES CHARACTERS WITH THE SMALL CAPS ENHANCEMENT.

TIMES CHARACTERS WITH THE ALL CAPS ENHANCEMENT.

Times characters with the Single Underline enhancement.

Times characters with the Words Only Underline enhancement.

Times characters with the Double Underline enhancement.

Figure 16.7: Selected character enhancements

If you assign the Hidden enhancement, the selected characters will exhibit the following features:

- If the **Hidden Text** view option is enabled (choose **Tools/ Options** and select the **View** icon in the **Category:** box), the characters will be displayed on the screen with a dotted underline.

```
This is a line of hidden text.
```

- If **Hidden Text** is disabled (click the **Options** button in the Print dialog box, or choose **Tools/Options**, and select the **Print** category), the characters will not be visible on the screen.

- If the **Hidden Text** printing option is enabled, hidden text will be printed.

ADJUSTING THE VERTICAL POSITION OF CHARACTERS

You can adjust the vertical placement of the selected characters by choosing one of the options from the **Super/subscript:** list box.

None
Superscript
Subscript

The **None** option leaves the text in its standard vertical position. **Superscript** raises the characters above the baseline and decreases the character size. **Subscript** lowers the characters below the baseline and decreases the size. If you select **Superscript** or **Subscript**, you can enter the amount the characters should be raised or lowered by entering a measurement into the adjacent **By:** box. The default measurement is **3** points. You can enter a value between **0** and **63.5** points, in 0.5-point increments.

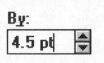

ALTERING THE CHARACTER SPACING

You can adjust the amount of space *between* characters on the printed copy by choosing one of the options from the **Spacing:** list.

Normal
Expanded
Condensed

If you select **Normal**, Word will neither increase nor decrease the standard amount of space printed between each character. If you select **Expanded**, Word will increase the amount of space between characters; this space is added to the right side of each character. If you select **Condensed**, Word will subtract space from the right side of each character.

If you have selected **Expanded** or **Condensed**, you can specify the amount of space to be added or subtracted by entering the number of points into the adjoining **By:** box. For **Expanded**, the default amount is **3** points; you can enter a measurement between **0** and **14** points, in

0.25-point increments. For **Condensed**, the default amount is **1.75** points; you can enter a measurement between **0** and **1.75** points in 0.25-point increments.

You can adjust the space between characters to add emphasis to a block of text; for example, you might want to emphasize a title by formatting it as expanded text. You can also adjust the spacing to improve the appearance of characters that don't fit well together, such as an italic character placed next to a *roman* or normal character.

USING THE RIBBON

To use the Word ribbon:

1. Display or hide the ribbon by choosing **View/Ribbon**.
2. Select the character or characters you want to format.
3. Use the list boxes to select the desired font and character size.
4. Use the enhancement buttons to apply or remove the bold, italic, or underline enhancement.
5. Click the ¶ button at the right end of the ribbon to enable/disable the display of all nonprinting characters.

You can apply many of the character formats using the *ribbon* in conjunction with the mouse. The ribbon is a set of list boxes and buttons that you can optionally display at the top of the window. It contains formatting options for both paragraphs and characters; using the ribbon for formatting paragraphs is explained in Chapter 15.

To display (or hide) the ribbon, choose **View/Ribbon**. Figure 16.8 illustrates a window with the ribbon displayed at the top.

Using the ribbon, you can apply the following character formats:

- The font
- The size
- Bold, italic, and single underline
- Show nonprinting characters

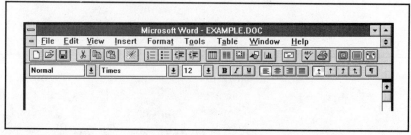

Figure 16.8: The ribbon

You can use the second list from the left

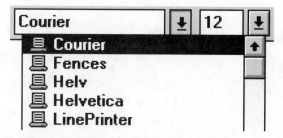

to specify the font, and the third box from the left

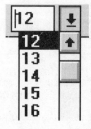

to choose the character size. These boxes work the same way as the
Font: and **Points:** boxes in the Character dialog box, covered earlier.

To the right of the list boxes, the ribbon contains three buttons for
selecting character enhancement:

These buttons allow you to apply bold, italic, and single underline. If
a given enhancement is already assigned to the current selection or
insertion point, the corresponding button will appear pressed. If the

enhancement is assigned to only a *portion* of the current selection, the button will be reverse lighted. For example, the following ribbon buttons indicate that *all* characters in the selection are bold, *some* of the characters are italic, and *none* of the characters are underlined:

If a feature is not assigned to the selection or to only a portion of the selection, you can assign it to the entire selection by clicking the button. If a feature is already assigned to the entire selection, you can remove it from the entire selection by clicking the button.

Clicking the button on the far right of the ribbon

hides or displays all nonprinting characters, such as tabs, spaces, and paragraph marks. (Clicking this button is the same as choosing **Tools/ Options**, selecting the **View** Category, and checking the **All** option.)

USING THE KEYBOARD

To format characters using the keyboard:

1. Select the character or characters you want to format.
2. Apply any of the keystrokes described in Table 16.1.

In addition to using **Format/Character** or the ribbon, you can directly apply many character formats using keyboard commands. The keyboard commands for formatting characters are also listed in Table 16.1.

Note that when you issue the following two keyboard commands, you must type a valid value at the prompt:

- **Ctrl-F** (font)
- **Ctrl-P** (size)

Each formatting feature is described in the section "Using the Format/Character Command."

Table 16.1: Keyboard Commands for Formatting Characters

CHARACTER FORMATTING FEATURE	KEYSTROKE
All capital letters†	Ctrl-A
Boldface†	Ctrl-B
Font	Ctrl-F, then type font name at prompt
Hidden text†	Ctrl-H
Italics†	Ctrl-I
Nonprinting characters, display or hide	Ctrl-Shift-Asterisk (not the asterisk on the numeric keypad)
Reset to defaults	Ctrl-Spacebar
Size of characters	Ctrl-P, then enter size at prompt
Increase character size	Ctrl-F2
Decrease character size	Ctrl-Shift-F2
Small Caps†	Ctrl-K
Subscript (3 points), apply or remove	Ctrl- = (Ctrl-equal sign)
Superscript (3 points), apply or remove	Ctrl-Shift- = (Ctrl-Shift-equal sign)
Underline†	Ctrl-U
Double underline†	Ctrl-D
Word underline†	Ctrl-W

† Key combination acts as a toggle, either applying or removing the format.

Unlike using the Character dialog box, when using either of these commands, you do not have the benefit of a pull-down list of choices; rather, you have to type an allowable value at the prompt at the bottom of the window. If the ribbon is displayed when you issue **Ctrl-F** or **Ctrl-P**, Word will move the insertion point to the appropriate box within the ribbon rather than displaying a prompt. You can pull down the list associated with a box by typing Alt-down-arrow.

Note also that **Ctrl-Spacebar** eliminates any formatting you have applied. This command restores the default character formatting as defined by the style assigned to the paragraphs containing the selected characters.

17

Previewing and Printing Your Documents

CHAPTER *17*

IN THIS CHAPTER, YOU WILL LEARN HOW TO preview your documents before printing them, how to make final formatting adjustments, how to set printer options, and how to print your documents. You will also learn how to print envelopes. The chapter begins with a discussion of automatic hyphenation, because it should be performed immediately before previewing a document.

PERFORMING AUTOMATIC HYPHENATION

To hyphenate the text in your document:

1. Select the lines you want to hyphenate, or place the cursor where you want to begin hyphenation.
2. Choose **Tools/Hyphenation**. Word will display the Hyphenation dialog box.
3. Select the **Confirm** option in the Hyphenation dialog box if you want to verify each hyphenation before Word performs it.
4. Click OK. Select the **Confirm** option to check each hyphenation and have control over the position of the hyphen.

In this section, you will learn how to have Word automatically hyphenate words within all or part of your document. To *hyphenate* a word means to break the word with a hyphen so part of the word can be moved up to the end of the previous line.

If a paragraph is left-aligned, hyphenating the appropriate words can lessen the raggedness of the right edge of the paragraph. If the paragraph is justified, hyphenating can reduce the amount of space between words.

Before learning how to perform automatic hyphenation, you should understand the different types of hyphens that can be entered into a Word document. Table 17.1 lists the different types of hyphen characters, showing the appearance of each character and the keystroke used to enter it.

Table 17.1: The Different Types of Hyphens

HYPHEN NAME	APPEARANCE	KEYSTROKE
Regular	-	- (hyphen key)
Em dash	—	Alt-0151 (type on numeric keypad with Num Lock on)
En dash	–	Alt-0150 (type on numeric keypad with Num Lock on)
Nonbreaking	-	Ctrl-Shift-hyphen

Regular hyphens, *em* dashes, and *en* dashes always remain visible on the screen and on the printed document. If you have inserted one of these characters into a word and the word falls near the end of a line, Word will break the word at the location of the hyphen or dash.

If you do *not* want to break the word at the position of the hyphen, you can use a nonbreaking hyphen rather than a regular hyphen. If **Optional Hyphens** is enabled, a nonbreaking hyphen is displayed on the screen as a long dash; otherwise, it appears as a normal hyphen character. **Optional Hyphens** does not affect the way the hyphen is printed.

An optional hyphen will behave differently under varying circumstances:

- If the word falls within a line, the optional hyphen will not print.
- If the word falls near the end of a line, the word will break and the optional hyphen will print.

To display all hyphens, choose **Tools/Options** and select **View** in the **Category:** list box. Then check the **Optional Hyphens** box. Enabling the **All** option will have the same effect on the way Word displays hyphens.

• If you select **Optional Hyphens**, the optional hyphen will be displayed on the screen as a *logical not* character

but will not print.

• If you turn off **Optional Hyphens**, the optional hyphen will be displayed on the screen only when it occurs at the end of a line.

When you perform automatic hyphenation, Word inserts optional hyphens at the appropriate positions within words to help fill out lines.

To decide when it is appropriate to hyphenate, consider the following guidelines:

> *If you edit or format text after hyphenating, you may lose the benefits of the hyphenation.*

• You should hyphenate *after* entering all document text and after performing basic formatting. Automatic hyphenation inserts optional hyphens only where line breaks can occur. If you change the content or format of the text, hyphenate again to insert optional hyphens in new positions.

• You should hyphenate *before* previewing the printed appearance of your document (as described later in the chapter), since hyphenation can change the positions of line and page breaks and alter the page layout.

• If you adjust formatting while previewing your document, hyphenate the altered text again.

To automatically hyphenate a portion of your document, select the text you want to hyphenate. If there is no selection, Word will hyphenate from the cursor to the end of the document.

> *If **Hyphenation** is not on the **Tools** menu, it has not been installed. To install it, run **Setup** and specify the hyphenation feature.*

Next, choose **Tools/Hyphenation**. Word will display the Hyphenation dialog box, which is illustrated in Figure 17.1. Before beginning automatic hyphenation, you can customize the options that govern the way Word performs the hyphenation.

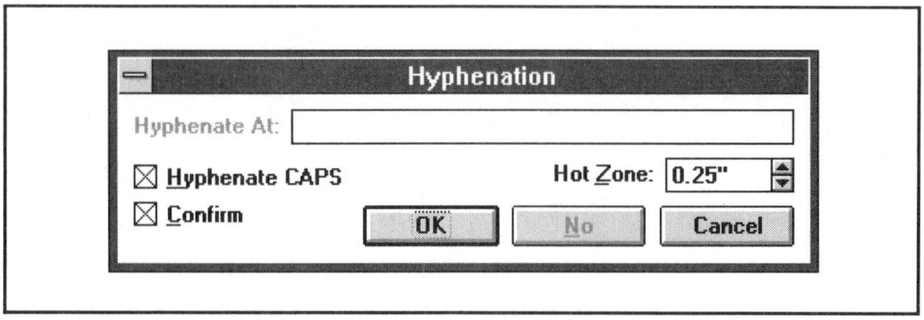

Figure 17.1: The Hyphenation dialog box

First, if you select the **Hyphenate CAPS** option, Word will hyphenate words that consist entirely of capital letters.

If you choose the **Confirm** option Word will allow you to review each proposed hyphenation.

You can specify the hyphenation *hot zone* by entering a measurement into the **Hot Zone:** box. The hot zone is the amount of empty space that Word must find at the end of a line before it attempts to hyphenate the first word on the next line. For example, if the hot zone is set to **0.5″**, whenever there is at least 0.5″ of free space between the last character on the line and the right indent, Word will hyphenate (if possible) the first word on the following line. The default hot-zone value is **0.25″**. In general, if you specify a small value, Word will attempt to hyphenate more words, resulting in a more even right margin (or in justified text, less space between words). If you specify a large value, Word will attempt to hyphenate fewer words resulting in fewer single syllables at the ends of lines.

When you have set the desired options and are ready to begin, click OK. Word will automatically switch into Page Layout view (explained later in this chapter) so all line breaks will appear on the screen where they will occur on the printed page.

If you have not selected the **Confirm** option, Word will remove the dialog box and begin hyphenating, displaying the percentage completed. If you want to cancel hyphenation before it is finished, press **Esc**; Word will stop hyphenating, but will *not* remove any of the hyphens already inserted. You can remove all hyphens, though, by issuing the Undo command.

If you want to remove the dialog box without doing any hyphenation, click Cancel.

If you have selected **Confirm**, Word will begin hyphenating, allowing you to review each proposed hyphenation by displaying it in the **Hyphenate At:** box.

Hyphenate <u>A</u>t: | for‸mat-ting |

The words appear divided into syllables, the position of the proposed hyphen marked by a flashing insertion point. You now have the following choices:

> Before clicking **Yes** or **No** to resume hyphenation, you can change any of the options in the Hyphenation dialog box.

- You can have Word insert an optional hyphen at the proposed location by clicking **Yes**.

- You can have Word insert an optional hyphen at another position by moving the insertion point and then clicking **Yes**. To move the insertion point, press the left-arrow or right-arrow key or click the desired position. Notice that the word also contains a dotted vertical line, indicating the position of the right indent; Word cannot break the word after this point. The optional hyphen will be inserted anyway. Then if the text is later rearranged, the word can be broken at this position.

> The **Yes** button replaces the **OK** button once hyphenation has started.

- You can omit hyphenating the current word and move on to the next by clicking **No**.

- You can cancel hyphenation by clicking Cancel. Clicking this button stops hyphenation, but does not remove any hyphens that have already been inserted.

If you issue Undo immediately after performing an automatic hyphenation, Word will remove *all* hyphens. To issue the Undo command, choose **Edit/Undo Hyphenation** or press **Ctrl-Z**.

PREVIEWING YOUR DOCUMENT

You will probably want to enter the bulk of the document text while you are in Normal or Draft view, since scrolling and other commands operate more efficiently in these modes than in Page Layout view. When you are creating the document, you might want to activate Page Layout occasionally to gain a more accurate picture of the printed appearance of the document while still editing. Immediately before printing the document, activate Print Preview to see the overall layout of each page and make final formatting adjustments.

To preview the printed appearance of your document, use one or more of the following methods:

- To see your document exactly as it will print and to continue editing the document, choose **View/Page Layout** to switch into the *Page Layout* view.

- To see a reduced representation of one or two entire document pages, without being able to edit them, choose **File/Print Preview** to switch into the *Print Preview* view.

- To zoom in or zoom out on your document and continue editing the document, choose **View/Zoom** or click one of the **Zoom buttons** on the Toolbar. You can use the zoom feature while you are in any document view except Print Preview.

You can enable *Draft* view while in *Normal* view or Outline view (if you are in Page Layout or Print Preview view, Word will automatically switch to Normal view before enabling Draft view). Draft view was described in Chapter 4.

View/Draft toggles Draft view on and off. To switch out of Normal, Outline, or Page Layout view, you must choose another **View** menu option: **Normal**, **Outline**, or **Page Layout**.

You can preview the printed appearance of your document using Page Layout, Print Preview, or **View/Zoom**. As you saw in Chapter 2, a document view is a particular way of looking at and working with a document. Table 17.2 summarizes the five basic document views provided by Word. By the end of this chapter, you will have learned about all except *Outline* view, which is described in Chapter 24.

Note that when you are in Normal view, you can see a more accurate representation of the printed appearance of the document by selecting the **Line Breaks and Fonts as Printed** option (to enable this option, choose **Tools/Options** and select the **View** category). This option displays all character formatting exactly as it will be printed. Also, Word will insert line breaks where they will occur on the printed page.

PAGE LAYOUT VIEW

To switch into Page Layout view, choose **View/Page Layout**. Page Layout view provides a way of viewing and working with your document that is intermediate between Normal view and Print Preview.

Table 17.2: The Five Document Views

DOCUMENT VIEW	CHARACTERISTICS
Normal View	Default editing view. Displays as printed: character and paragraph formatting, line and page breaks, tab-stop alignment, and pictures. Does *not* display as printed: headers, footers, footnote text, line numbering, multiple columns, and positioned objects. Provides all editing and formatting commands (intermediate speed).
Outline View	Shows the organization of a document, and allows you to quickly rearrange the document content (see Chapter 24).
Draft View	Displays all text using the system font, in a single character size. All character enhancements are displayed as underlined text. Displays pictures as empty frames. Provides all editing and formatting commands (fast). Draft view can be enabled while Normal or Outline view is active; if you try to enable it from Page Layout or Print Preview view, Word will first switch to Normal view.
Page Layout View	Displays all features (except line numbering) exactly as they are printed. Text is displayed full size; thus, you can usually view only a portion of a page. Provides all editing and formatting commands (slow).
Print Preview	Displays one or two entire pages exactly as they will be printed. Text is reduced in size. Provides no editing or formatting ability, but allows you to move margins, headers, footers, page breaks, and paragraphs in frames (positioned paragraphs).

Page Layout shares the following features with Normal view:

- You can normally see only a *portion* of the printed page at a given time (unless you use zoom); however, each character is fully legible.

- You can type text and perform normal editing and formatting tasks. Use the same techniques that have been described in this book for Normal view.

Page Layout view shares the following characteristics with Print Preview:

Page Layout view does *not* display line numbering. Line numbering appears only in Print Preview and on the printed copy.

- You can see the boundaries of each page.

- Multiple snaking columns are displayed side-by-side, as they will be printed.

- Headers, footers, and footnotes appear in their assigned positions.

- Positioned paragraphs (that is, paragraphs placed within *frames*) appear in their assigned positions on the page.

Word automatically activates Page Layout view while performing certain commands, such as **Tools/Hyphenation** and **Insert/Frame**.

While you are in Page Layout view, you can use two special techniques to navigate through the document:

- If the text is arranged in two or more columns, you can move the cursor from column to column by pressing **Alt-down-arrow** or **Alt-up-arrow**.

- You can go immediately to the previous page by clicking the double up-arrow at the bottom of the vertical scroll bar.

• You can scroll to the next page by clicking the double down-arrow at the bottom of the vertical scroll bar.

PRINT PREVIEW

 To see the entire page while you are in Print Preview, maximize the Word window by clicking the up-arrow icon in the upper-right corner of the window.

To activate Print Preview, choose the **File/Print Preview**. The Print Preview screen is illustrated in Figure 17.2. As you can see, Print Preview shows you a reduced view of entire pages. Click the **Two Pages** or **One Page** button at the top of the window depending upon how many pages you want to see.

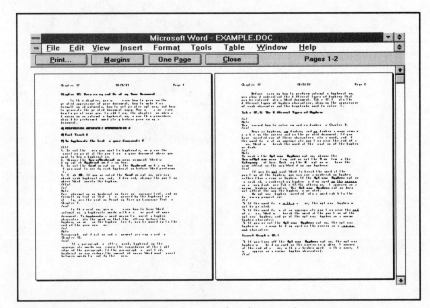

Figure 17.2: The Print Preview screen showing two document pages

Although the text is normally *greeked* (too small to be legible), Print Preview provides a good overall view of the layout of each page of the document. Using Print Preview to examine page layout before printing can save you time, paper, and effort.

While in Print Preview, you can scroll through the document using the vertical scroll bar or by pressing **PgDn** and **PgUp**. Word displays the current page number or numbers to the right of the buttons at the top of the window.

In Print Preview, you can adjust the position on the page of any of the following objects:

- Page margins
- Headers and footers
- Page breaks

To move one or more of these objects, first click the **Margins** button. Word will draw a line indicating each margin and a box around headers, footers, or page breaks. If you are viewing two pages, Word will display these boundary lines in only one page. You can move the lines to the other page by clicking anywhere on it. Clicking the **Margins** button again removes the lines and boxes.

Once boundary lines are displayed, you can adjust a document margin using the following steps:

1. Move the mouse pointer to the black square on the line that marks the margin you want to move.

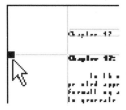

The mouse pointer will become a cross.

2. Drag the margin to the desired new position. That is, press and hold the left mouse button and move the line to the new position and then release the button.

While in Print Preview, many menu and keyboard commands are unavailable.

In Print Preview, you cannot move an object to a different page.

While you are moving an object in Print Preview, Word displays the current coordinates of the object at the top of the window.

3. To have Word draw the margin in its new position, click the Print Preview window anywhere outside of the page.

Since the margin position is an aspect of section formatting, adjusting a margin on one page automatically changes it on all other pages that are in the same document section.

While boundary lines are displayed, you can also move headers, footers, and page breaks. To move one of these objects, use the following steps:

1. Place the mouse pointer within the box surrounding the object you want to move. The arrow pointer will turn into a cross.

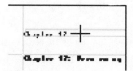

2. Drag the object to the desired new location on the page. To drag a header or footer inside of a margin, hold down **Shift** while dragging it.

3. Click the Print Preview window anywhere outside of the page to have Word display the object in its new position.

Note that you can move the header or footer only in the vertical direction. Since headers and footers are features assigned to a document section, moving a header or footer on one page automatically moves it on all pages in the same section.

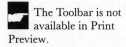
The Toolbar is not available in Print Preview.

In Print Preview, you can print the document by clicking the **Print** button near the upper-left corner of the window, by choosing **File/Print** or by simply pressing **P**. Word does *not* immediately start printing the document; rather, it opens the Print dialog box, described in the next section. You can terminate Print Preview by using one of the following methods:

• Click Cancel or Close or press **Esc** to activate whatever document view was active before you switched into Print Preview (the Cancel button becomes the Close button if you make a change to the document in Print Preview). You can also choose **File/Print Preview** or the **Close** item on the document control menu to restore the former document view.

- Choose the desired document view from the **View** menu by choosing **Outline**, **Page Layout**, or **Draft** (which will automatically switch you to *Normal* view).

ZOOMING THE DOCUMENT VIEW

In addition to opting for one of the document views discussed in this chapter, you can also magnify the document with the *zoom* feature. The zoom feature zooms in or zooms out on the text and graphics in the window.

The purpose of the zoom feature is to make it easier to view certain types of documents. For example, if a document contains small character sizes, zooming in (that is, magnifying the size of text and graphics) can make it easier to see and work with the smaller type sizes. As another example, if the document page is wide (perhaps because you have set Landscape orientation), zooming out can allow you to see the entire page width without scrolling. Also, you may simply want to be able to see more text within the program window.

You can change the magnification using **View/Zoom** when you are in any document view except Print Preview.

To zoom in or out, choose **View/Zoom**. Word will display the Zoom dialog box, shown in Figure 17.3. To specify the level of magnification, choose one of the options within the **Magnification** area. Initially, the **100%** option is selected, which corresponds to the standard view. Choose a magnification over 100% to zoom in, or one under 100% to zoom out. If you do not see the exact value you want, select the **Custom** option and enter the desired percentage value into the adjoining box (you can enter a value ranging from **25%** to **200%**).

Unlike the Print Preview, a zoomed view permits you to fully edit the document.

Alternatively, you can click the **Page Width** or **Whole Page** button. The Page Width button sets the magnification so that you can see the entire width of the text on the page, without scrolling horizontally (the actual magnification produced by clicking this button depends upon the width of the text. Clicking Whole Page sets the magnification so that you can see the entire page. When you have chosen the desired magnification, click OK.

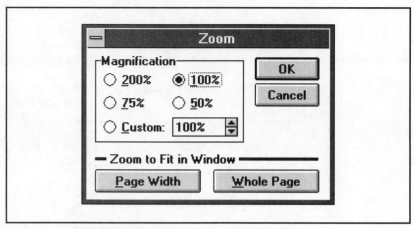

Figure 17.3: The Zoom dialog box

If you are in Page Layout view and have clicked the **Page Width** or **Whole Page** button in the Zoom dialog box (or the corresponding button on the Toolbar), Word will *maintain* the full width or full page view even if you change the size of the program window.

You can also quickly change the magnification using the Toolbar. Click the **Zoom Whole Page button**

to switch to Page Layout view and see the entire page (as if you clicked Whole Page in the Zoom dialog box).

Click the **Zoom Page Width** button

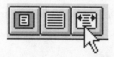

to see the entire text width (as if you had clicked Page Width in the Zoom dialog box).

Finally, click the **Zoom 100 Percent** button

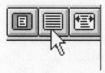

to switch to Normal view and standard 100% magnification.

SETTING UP YOUR PRINTER

To prepare your printer for printing a document:

1. Choose **File/Print Setup**. Word will display the Print Setup dialog box.

2. If you have more than one printer installed, select the printer you want to use in the Print Setup box.

3. If you want to change the settings for the selected printer, click the **Setup** button, and make any desired changes in the Setup dialog box that is displayed for the particular printer. Click OK to accept the changes and return to the Print Setup dialog box.

4. Click OK in the Print Setup dialog box.

You can run the Windows Control Panel from within Word by choosing the **Run** command from the Word control menu (in the upper left corner of the Word window), selecting the **Control Panel** option, and clicking the OK button.

For information on using the Control Panel, see the *Microsoft Windows User's Guide*.

Before you can print with Word, you must install a printer in Windows and choose the desired printer options. If you install more than one printer, you must specify which printer is to receive output from Windows programs (known as the Windows *default* printer). Normally, you perform these steps when you install Windows. However, you can later install additional printers, change printer settings, or select a new default printer, using the Windows Control Panel (select the **Printers** icon).

You can also select the default printer (if you have installed more than one printer), and adjust the options for any installed printer, through **File/Print Setup**. You can issue this command at any time. Note, however, that changing the default printer or altering the printer setup can change the appearance of your document. For example, it can alter the available fonts and character enhancements, and the position of line and page breaks. Ideally, therefore, you should install and set up the desired printer *before* entering and formatting document text. If you later change the printer setup, make sure that the page layout and other document features are correct before printing the document. To examine these features, use the Page Layout view and Print Preview.

When you choose **File/Print Setup**, Word displays the Print Setup dialog box, illustrated in Figure 17.4. The **Printer:** list box contains a list of printers that have been installed in the Windows environment. The description of each printer includes the name of the computer *port* that the printer connects to (such as **LPT1** or **LPT2**, or **None** if it is not connected to any port or is designated as *inactive*).

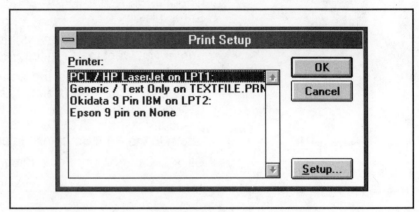

Figure 17.4: The Print Setup dialog box

If the default printer is not attached to a port, or if no printer is designated as the default, you cannot switch into Print Preview mode or print the document.

The name of the default printer is highlighted. If you want to change the default printer so that you can direct Word output to another printer, select the desired printer from this list by clicking it. Note, however, that you *cannot* print to a printer that is not attached to a port (that is, if the printer description is followed by the expression **on None**); you must set up the printer and designate it as active in the Windows Control Panel.

To change one or more options for the default printer, click the **Setup** button. The appearance of the printer setup dialog box that Word displays depends upon the specific printer. For example, if the default printer is an **HP LaserJet II**, Word displays the dialog box shown in Figure 17.5.

The following are options commonly found in a printer's setup dialog box:

- The graphics *resolution,* which is the amount of detail that is printed, measured in *dpi* (dots per inch). This option will be available if your printer can print graphics at more than one resolution.

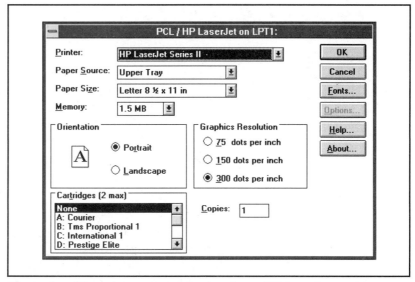

Figure 17.5: The printer setup dialog box for an HP LaserJet II printer

- The names of any font cartridges that have been installed (it is important to specify these so that Word can access the fonts).

- The *orientation* of the paper: portrait or landscape, as explained in Chapter 14. Note that regardless of your setting in the printer's setup dialog box, Word will override it according to the value entered into the Page Setup dialog box. (If you specify the paper source, this setting will likewise be overridden by the option chosen in the Page Setup dialog box.)

Word will not warn you if the print and page setup orientations don't match.

The printer options you set through **File/Print Setup** remain in effect until you explicitly change them through this command or through the Windows Control Panel. These options govern printing from Word as well as other Windows applications. In contrast, the printer options you set through the File/Print dialog box affect the printing of documents only within Word.

PRINTING YOUR DOCUMENT

To print your document:

1. Choose **File/Print**.
2. Specify the number of copies you want to print.
3. Set any other desired print options (clicking the **Setup** button to access options not displayed in the Print dialog box).
4. Click OK to begin printing.

When you are finally ready to print your document, choose **File/Print**. Word will display the dialog box illustrated in Figure 17.6. At the top of the dialog box, Word displays the name of the default printer, and the port to which it is connected.

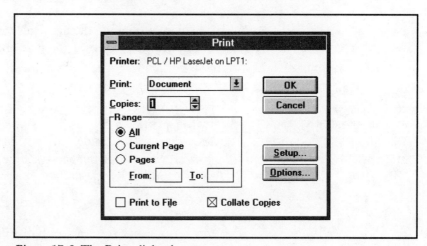

Figure 17.6: The Print dialog box

First make sure that Document is selected in the **Print:** box so that Word will print the document. You can print other items, such as the document summary information or annotations, by selecting the appropriate item from the pull-down list attached to the Print box.

Enter the number of copies you want to print into the **Copies:** box (the default is 1). If you print more than one copy, the way Word organizes the copies depends upon whether you have selected the **Collate Copies** option at the bottom of the dialog box. If this option is enabled, Word will first print all of the pages of the first copy of the document, then all of the pages of the second copy, and so on. If the **Collate** option is not selected, Word will print all copies of the first page, then all copies of the second page, and so on.

The portion of the document that is to be printed is specified through the options in the **Range** area of the dialog box:

All
Current Page
Pages: From...To

If you choose **All** (the default), Word will print the entire document. If you choose **Current Page**, Word will print only the page containing the cursor. If you select text prior to issuing **File/Print**, **Current Page** will be replaced with **Selection**, which will print only the selected text. If you choose **Pages**, Word will print a range of pages within your document. Enter the first page in the desired range into the **From:** box and the last page into the **To:** box.

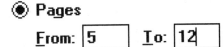

Before using **Print to File**, install the drive for the printer you ultimately want to print on.

If you select the **Print to File** option, Word will send the printer output to a disk file rather than to the printer itself. This allows you to print on a printer not connected to your computer. Before printing, it will prompt you for the file name; be sure to choose a name for the file that does not already exist. The output will be stored in this file in a format suitable for the current default printer; you can later print the file by simply copying the contents of the file to the printer (for example, by using **File/Copy** in the Windows File Manager).

If you click the **Setup** button, Word will open the Print Setup dialog box, to allow you to set up the printer before printing. This is the same dialog box that is displayed through **File/Print Setup**.

To choose additional printing options, click **Options**. Word will open the Options dialog box, which is illustrated in Figure 17.7. You can also set these options by choosing **Tools/Options** and selecting the **Print** icon in the **Category:** list. The effect of each of these additional options is summarized in Table 17.3.

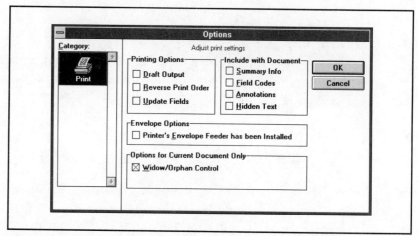

Figure 17.7: The Options dialog box

Note that Word *saves* your settings for the **Print to File** and **Collate Copies** options, as well as any options you set through the print Options dialog box. It will continue to use each option for all future print jobs, until you explicitly change the option (the **Widow/Orphan Control** option, however, will affect only the current document).

When you have chosen all desired options and are ready to begin printing, click OK. Word will display a message box indicating that it is printing the document. You can stop printing by pressing **Esc** or clicking Cancel.

Clicking Cancel while Word is printing a document will probably not stop the printer immediately, since many pages of output may have already been sent to the Windows Print Manager and to the printer's buffer.

USING THE PRINT BUTTON

Rather than choosing **File/Print**, you can print you document immediately by clicking the **Print button** on the Toolbar.

Table 17.3: Additional Print Options

PRINT OPTION	EFFECT
Draft Output	Eliminates character formatting when printing, and prints pictures as empty boxes (all enhancements, such as italics, are shown as underline). This option increases printing speed when formatting and graphics are not required.
Reverse Print Order	Prints document pages from last to first. This option is helpful for printers that stack pages in reverse order (such as some early laserprinter models).
Update Fields	Updates all fields before printing the document. Fields are instructions embedded within a document.*
Summary Info	Prints a document summary on a separate page following the document itself.
Field Codes	Prints the codes for any fields contained in the document (that is, the special { } characters and the text within them), rather than printing the results of the fields.*
Annotations	Prints any annotations starting on a separate page following the document.
Hidden Text	Prints any hidden text in the document. Note that this can change the positions of line and page breaks.
Printer's Envelope Feeder has been Installed	Word will use the printer's envelope feed when printing envelopes by means of **Tools/Create Envelope** or the **Envelope button** on the Toolbar.
Window/Orphan Control	Word will not insert a page break between a single line at the beginning or end of a paragraph and the remainder of the paragraph.

* For information on fields, see the Word *User's Reference* or *Technical Reference* under the topic Fields.

If you click this button, Word will start printing the current document immediately. Rather than displaying the Print dialog box, it will use all default print settings; namely, it will print a single copy of the entire document, using the current settings for other options.

PRINTING ENVELOPES

To print an envelope for a letter you are writing:

1. Write the letter.
2. Choose **Tools/Envelope** or click the **Envelope button** on the Toolbar.
3. If necessary, correct the recipient's address displayed in the **Addressed To:** box.
4. If necessary, edit the return address. Choose **Omit Return Address** if you are using a preprinted envelope.
5. To print the envelope, click the **Print Envelope** button.
6. To insert the envelope text at the beginning of the document, so that it will automatically print when you print the letter, click **Add to Document**.

If you are writing a letter in Word, you can have Word print the corresponding envelope, or have it add the text for the envelope directly to your document.

After you have written the letter, choose **Tools/Create Envelope** or click the **Envelope button** on the Toolbar.

Word will display the Create Envelope dialog box, shown in Figure 17.8. The recipient's address is entered into the **Addressed To:** box. Word will attempt to locate the recipient's address within you document, displaying any text it finds in this box; if the address is not correct, you can edit it or enter a new one.

Figure 17.8: The Create Envelope dialog box

The first time you print an envelope, enter the desired return address into the **Return Address:** box. Word will remember this address, and will use it for printing all subsequent envelopes unless you later change it. If you do not want Word to print a return address (perhaps you are using preprinted envelopes), select **Omit Return Address**.

Make sure that the size of the envelope you are printing is selected in the **Envelope Size:** list box; if it is not, select the appropriate size.

When you are ready to print the envelope, click the **Print Envelope** button. If you have selected **Printer's Envelope Feeder has been Installed** in the Print Options dialog box, Word will automatically use the printer's envelope feeder. Otherwise, Word will prompt you to manually insert an envelope.

If you click **Add to Document**, Word will insert the text for the envelope in a separate section at the beginning of your document, assigning this section all appropriate page layout settings for printing an envelope. The envelope will then be printed—together with the body of your letter—each time you print the document.

The **Envelope Feeder has been Installed** option can be set by issuing **Tools/ Options**, and then selecting the **Print** category or by clicking the **Setup** button in the Print dialog box.

18

Printing Form Letters

CHAPTER **18**

THE *PRINT MERGE* FACILITY WILL AUTOMATICALLY
print multiple copies of a document, customizing each copy according to your instructions. You can use this facility to create form letters, mailing labels, and other applications that require different
copies of similar documents.

When you use the print merge command, Word combines a *main
document*, a template file that is the same for every printed copy, with a
data document, which contains the text that is unique to each copy. In
this chapter, you will learn how to create the main and data documents, and how to print customized copies with the print merge
command.

CREATING PRINT-MERGE DOCUMENTS

To create the documents for a print merge:

1. Create a new document, or open an existing one, to
   serve as the main print-merge document.

2. Choose **Print/Merge** and click the **Attach Data File**
   button in the Print Merge Setup dialog box.

3. Click the **Create Data File** button within the Attach Data
   File dialog box.

4. For each field of variable information in your print-
   merge document, enter a name into the **Field Name:**
   box and click the **Add** button in the Create Data File dialog box.

5. Click OK in the Create Data File dialog box. Word will
   now display the Save As dialog box.

6. In the Save As dialog box, choose a name and location
   for the data document and click OK. Word will save and
   open the newly created data document.

7. Enter into the data document the information for each record you want to print, then save the document.

8. Return to the main document opened in step 1 by choosing the document name from the **Window** menu. Type in the *constant* text.

9. To insert a field of *variable* text, click the **Insert Merge Field** button at the top of the main document window, choose a field name from the Insert Merge Field dialog box, and click OK.

ATTACHING A DATA DOCUMENT

Before typing text into a new main document—or editing text in an existing document—attach a print-merge data document. The data document contains the text (or graphics) that varies from copy to copy. When you attach a data document to a main document, Word can help you complete the main document. To attach a data document, choose **File/Print Merge**. Word will display the Print Merge Setup dialog box, illustrated in Figure 18.1.

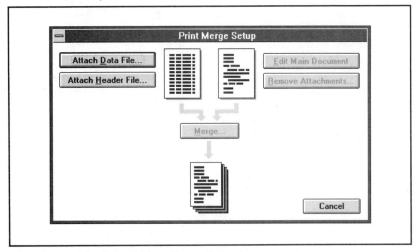

Figure 18.1: The Print Merge Setup dialog box

Next, click the **Attach Data File** button in the Print Merge Setup dialog box.

Word will now open the Attach Data File dialog box. Since you are creating a new data document rather than opening an existing one, click the **Create Data File** button in this dialog box.

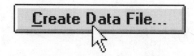

Word will then open the Create Data File dialog box, shown in Figure 18.2, which helps you create the print-merge data document.

You must now devise names for each field of variable information. For each field, enter the desired name into the **Field Name:** box

A field name may consist of a combination of up to twenty letters, numbers, or underscore characters. The first character, however, must be a letter.

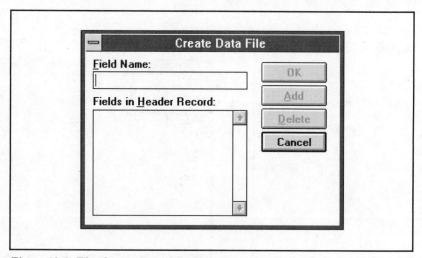

Figure 18.2: The Create Data File dialog box

within the Create Data File dialog box

Field Name:

and click the **Add** button (or press Enter). Each field name you add is inserted into the **Fields in Header Record:** list box.

For example, if you are creating a form letter to send to business customers, you might want one field for the customer's name, another for the item purchased, and another for the date of purchase. In this case, you might enter the following field names:

Fields in Header Record:

| customer |
| item |
| date |

Once you have entered a name for every field of variable information, click the OK button in the Create Data File dialog box. Word will then display the familiar Save As dialog box; choose a file name and directory location for the data document. When you click OK, Word will save the data document to disk and automatically open the data document so you can add information to it.

When Word opens the data document, you will see that it has created a table, with one column for each field you named in the Create Data File dialog box. For instance, if you had entered the field names shown in the previous example, the document would appear as shown in Figure 18.3.

> You can delete a field name by selecting it in the **Fields in Header Record:** list and clicking **Delete**.

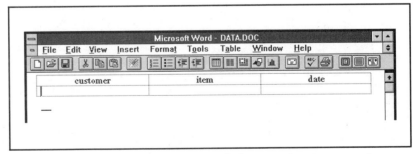

Figure 18.3: An example data document before entering the merge data

Remember that when the insertion point is in the last cell of a table, you can press the Tab key to create another row at the bottom of the table.

You can now enter the information for each *record*. A record is the data used for a single copy of the merge document (for example, the data used to print a single letter or mailing label). Enter the data for each record in a separate row of the table. Figure 18.4 illustrates the same data document shown in Figure 18.3, after data for three records has been entered.

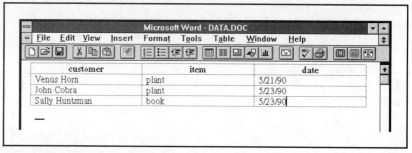

Figure 18.4: The example data document of Figure 18.3, after entering three records

If you prefer, you can enter the information into the data document later (as long as you do it before printing the copies!). You have already performed the most important tasks for this stage of the process: attaching a data document to the main document, and assigning names to each merge record.

You can later attach a *different* data document to the main document by opening the main document, choosing **File/Print Merge**, and repeating the procedure just described.

When you have finished working with the data document, save it to preserve any changes you have made and then switch back to the main document by choosing its name from the **Window** menu or by pressing **Ctrl-F6**—repeatedly if necessary— until it appears. When you switch to the main document, you will notice that a new toolbar has appeared at the top of the document window. This toolbar, illustrated in Figure 18.5, is the *print-merge toolbar*. It is designed to assist you in completing the main print-merge document.

Figure 18.5: The print-merge toolbar

You can remove the link between the main document and the print-merge document by choosing **File/Print Merge** when the main document is open and clicking the **Remove Attachments** button. The main document will then become a standard Word document, and the print-merge toolbar will vanish.

Rather than defining the field names at the beginning of the data document, you can define them in a separate header file. See the *Microsoft Word User's Guide* for information on attaching header files.

You can also insert one of a variety of special instructions into your main document by selecting an item from the **Word Fields:** list box in the Insert Merge Field dialog box. These instructions can be used to prompt for data during printing and insert text conditionally, among other things. See the *Microsoft Word User's Guide* for more information.

Notice also that the name of the data document is displayed at the right end of the print-merge toolbar. When you attach a data document to the main document, Word forms a permanent link between the two. Whenever you reopen the main document, the print-merge toolbar will again appear. Although these documents are linked, you can open, edit, and close them individually, just like standard Word documents.

COMPLETING THE MAIN DOCUMENT

Once you have attached the data document, you are ready to enter text into the main document (or edit text if you are using an existing document). Enter and edit the *constant* text as in a standard Word document. When you reach a position in the document where you want Word to insert a field of *variable* data, click the **Insert Merge Field** button on the print-merge toolbar:

Word will open the Insert Merge Field dialog box. The **Print Merge Fields:** list box will contain a list of all of the fields of merge data you have specified, as explained in the previous section. To illustrate, if the example data document given in the previous section were attached to the main document, this list would contain the following items:

Choose the name of the field you want to insert, and click the OK button. Word will insert a special print-merge instruction into your document consisting of the name of the selected field surrounded by chevron characters.

Dear «customer»:

Continue to enter and edit the main document, using the same method for inserting any additional merge fields that are required. Figure 18.6 illustrates a completed main document, which uses the three merge fields defined in the example data document.

To view the print-merge instruction as described, make sure that the **View/Field Codes** menu option is *not* enabled.

Before printing copies of the document, make sure you have entered *all* required records into the data document and have saved you work on disk. To switch to the data document, simply click the **Edit Data File** button on the print-merge toolbar.

PRINTING PERSONALIZED DOCUMENTS

To print a merge document:

1. Open the main print-merge document.
2. Click the **Merge-to-Printer** button at the top of the document window. Word will now open the Print dialog box.
3. Specify the desired number of copies, range of pages, and other print options.
4. Click OK to begin printing.

To print the copies of your merge document, first open the main print-merge document, and then click the **Merge-to-Printer** button in the print-merge toolbar at the top of the window.

Word will open the Print dialog box described in Chapter 17. Before clicking OK to begin printing, you can set the number of copies, the range of pages you want to print, and other print options. The

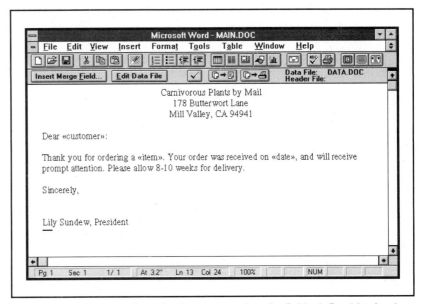

Figure 18.6: An example main document using the fields defined in the data document of Figure 18.4

Copies: box, however, deserves some explanation. Word always prints at least one copy of the document for each record it finds in the data document. If the value **1** is entered into the Copies: box (the default), Word will print one copy using the first record, one copy using the second record, and so on. If, however, **2** is entered into this box, it will print two identical copies using the first record, then two identical copies using the second record, and so on.

Figure 18.7 illustrates the three copies that would result from printing the example print-merge documents that have been given.

CHECKING THE
DOCUMENT OR PRINTING TO A FILE

If you want to check your documents for errors before printing, follow the instructions given here.

Before printing the copies of your merge document, you can have Word check the main document and data document for technical errors. First, open the main document, then click the **Check** button

Carnivorous Plants by Mail
178 Butterwort Lane
Mill Valley, CA 94941

Dear Venus Horn:

Thank you for ordering a plant. Your order was received on 5/21/90, and will receive
prompt attention. Please allow 8-10 weeks for delivery.

Sincerely,

Lily Sundew, President

Carnivorous Plants by Mail
178 Butterwort Lane
Mill Valley, CA 94941

Dear John Cobra:

Thank you for ordering a plant. Your order was received on 5/23/90, and will receive
prompt attention. Please allow 8-10 weeks for delivery.

Sincerely,

Lily Sundew, President

Carnivorous Plants by Mail
178 Butterwort Lane
Mill Valley, CA 94941

Dear Sally Huntsman:

Thank you for ordering a book. Your order was received on 5/23/90, and will receive
prompt attention. Please allow 8-10 weeks for delivery.

Sincerely,

Lily Sundew, President

Figure 18.7: The printed copies resulting from merging the main document of Figure 18.6 with the data
document of Figure 18.4

on the print-merge toolbar at the top of the main document window:

Word will inspect each instruction and inform you if there is a problem (for example, if a field name contains an invalid character or if the data document cannot be opened).

As an alternative to directly printing the merge document, you can have Word send all copies to a new document, separating each copy with a section break. To do so, click the **Merge-to-Document** button on the print-merge toolbar above the main document:

After creating the new document, Word will automatically open it, so that you can view its contents. The new document is not automatically saved to disk, though; after examining it, you can either save it to print later or discard it.

SETTING PRINT-MERGE OPTIONS

There is an alternative way of printing merge documents that allows you to set several output options. First, open the main merge document. Then, rather than clicking one of the buttons on the print-merge toolbar, choose **File/Print Merge**. Word will display the Print Merge Setup dialog box. Click the **Merge** button and Word will open the Print Merge dialog box, as shown in Figure 18.8.

You can choose one of the following options from the **Merge Results** area:

    Merge to Printer
    Merge to New Document
    Only Check for Errors

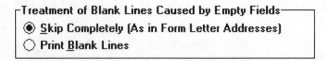

Figure 18.8: The Print Merge dialog box

Each of these options has the same effect as clicking the corresponding button on the print-merge toolbar. **Merge to Printer** prints copies of the merge document, **Merge to New Document** writes the copies to a new document, and **Only Check for Errors** checks the main and data documents without producing output.

You can also tell Word how to handle blank lines by selecting one of the following options:

┌─**Treatment of Blank Lines Caused by Empty Fields**─────
◉ **Skip Completely (As in Form Letter Addresses)**
○ **Print Blank Lines**

For example, if you are using the print merge command to print mailing labels, you may have defined a field for the company name. If a particular record has no company name, though, the field will be left blank. If you choose the **Skip Completely** option (the default), Word will not leave a blank line on the actual mailing label. If, however, you choose **Print Blank Lines**, Word will leave a blank line corresponding to the empty field.

Finally, you can specify exactly which records you want Word to print, in one of two ways. First, you can specify the *range* of records to print by selecting one of the options in the **Print Records** area of the Print Merge dialog box:

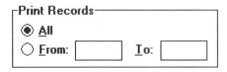

The **All** option (the default) prints every record in the data document. To have Word print only a specified range of records, select the **From:** option, and then enter the number of the first record to print into the **From:** box, and the number of the last record to print into the **To:** box. (The records in the data document are numbered, beginning with 1.) For example, the following choices would print six documents, using data records 5 through 10:

◉ **From:** `5`   **To:** `10`

If desired, you can specify *several* rules in the Record Selection dialog box and combine them using the *and* and *or* logical operators. See the *Microsoft Word User's Guide* for more information on specifying rules for record selection.

Second, you can have Word choose which records to print according to rules that you specify. To set rules, click the **Record Selection** button. Word will open the Record Selection dialog box (Figure 18.9). To specify a single rule, choose a field name from the **Field Name:** list box, choose a relational operator from the **Is:** box, enter a value into the **Compared To:** box, and click the **Add Rule** button.

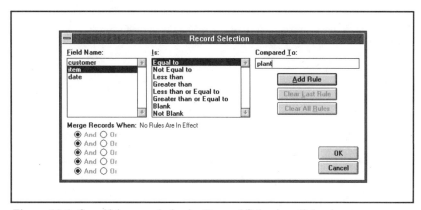

Figure 18.9: Specifying a rule in the Record Selection dialog box

To illustrate, the rule specification shown in Figure 18.9 would cause Word to print only records in which the **item** field is equal to **plant**. If this rule were applied to the example print-merge document given previously in the chapter, Word would print only the first two documents shown in Figure 18.7.

When you have completed specifying the desired rule or rules, click OK to return to the Print Merge dialog box. (Note that Word displays the total number of rules you have defined at the bottom of the Print Merge dialog box.)

When you have set all desired options, click OK in the Print Merge box. Word will now display the familiar Print dialog box and you can proceed as described previously in the chapter (in the section ''Printing Personalized Documents'').

Part

IV

Document Templates

A template is the framework upon which a document is built. A document template is a great timesaver. Once you have set up a template for a particular type of document, documents you create based upon this template automatically acquire all features assigned to the template, such as formatting, styles, repetitious text, and other important elements.

19

An Overview
of Document Templates

CHAPTER 19

A DOCUMENT TEMPLATE RESIDES IN A SPECIALLY formatted disk file, which is named with the DOT file extension and is stored in the Word for Windows program directory on your hard disk (usually, \WINWORD).

All new Word documents are based upon a specific document template. As you have seen, when you create a new document by selecting **File/New**, you can select the name of the document template.

If you want to find out the name of the document template for the current document, choose **File/Template**. The name will be displayed in the **Attach Document To:** box.

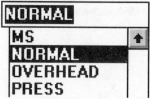

The new document automatically acquires all of the features assigned to the document template. The Word for Windows package includes a variety of templates, including NORMAL, ARTICLE, FAX, MEMO1, and many others. NORMAL is a general-purpose template, and the others are designed for specific types of documents.

The template NOR-MAL, as it is supplied by Microsoft, does not contain any text. Thus, all new documents based upon it are initially empty.

In this chapter, you will learn the following facts about templates and methods for managing them:

- The document features that can be assigned to templates
- The special properties of the NORMAL template
- The relationship between the document and the document template
- How to change the template assigned to a document
- How to create a new template or modify an existing one

FEATURES THAT CAN BE ASSIGNED TO TEMPLATES

The following features can be assigned to a document template, and are automatically acquired by all new documents based upon the template:

- Text and text formatting
- Styles
- Glossary entries
- Macros
- Toolbar, menu, and keyboard assignments

TEXT AND FORMATTING

A template can contain text or graphics. When you create a new document based upon the template, Word automatically inserts all text or graphics from the template into the new document, together with any character or paragraph formatting that is assigned to the text. A template can also be assigned section or document formatting features, which are likewise automatically acquired by all new documents based upon the template.

For example, a template used for creating letters might contain the heading, salutation, and other elements common to all letters you write. Such common text is known as *boilerplate text*.

STYLES

 Styles are discussed in Chapter 20.

A *style* is a collection of character and paragraph formatting features that is identified by name and can be applied to paragraphs in a document. Style definitions can be assigned to a template; any new document based upon the template automatically acquires these definitions, so that you can use these styles when formatting the document.

GLOSSARY ENTRIES

Glossaries are discussed in Chapter 21.

Each template has its own *glossary*, which can store one or more blocks of text or graphics (known as *glossary entries*). A glossary entry is identified by name, and can be inserted anywhere within a document. A document has access to all entries contained in the glossary belonging to the document template.

MACROS

 Macros are discussed in Chapter 22.

A *macro* stores a series of keystrokes and mouse actions. You can have Word automatically execute these keystrokes and mouse actions by *running* the macro. Macros are identified by name, and are stored in a document template. While you are working on a document, you can run any of the macros assigned to the document template.

TOOLBAR, MENU, AND KEYBOARD ASSIGNMENTS

Chapter 23 discusses how to create custom Toolbar, menu, and keyboard assignments.

You can add or remove buttons from the Toolbar, assigning the desired command to each button; you can remove commands from or add commands to the default menus; and you can specify the keystrokes that execute specific commands or execute macros that you have created. Toolbar, menu, and keyboard assignments are stored in a document template and are automatically available while you are working on any document based upon the template.

NORMAL AND OTHER TEMPLATES

Later in the chapter, you will see how to change the document template after a document has already been created.

In this section, you will learn some of the special properties of the NORMAL template. When you create a new document by using the **File/New** command, Word initially suggests NORMAL as the document template. You can, of course, pick another template from the list.

Also, when you start Word without specifying a document name, or create a document by clicking the **New button** on the Toolbar, Word automatically creates a new document using NORMAL as the document template. Thus, NORMAL is the default document template.

When the document template is NORMAL, the document simply acquires all the features that have been assigned to NORMAL (those features initially assigned by Microsoft, as well as any features you have explicitly assigned). For example, the initial NORMAL asignments include settings for print orientation (e.g., portrait or landscape), type font and point size, and top and bottom margins. When the document template is *not* NORMAL, the document acquires all the features assigned to that document template, *plus* any of the following features assigned to the NORMAL template that are not duplicated by the selected template:

- Glossary entries

- Macro definitions

- Toolbar customizations

- Keyboard assignments

- Menu assignments

Accordingly, the NORMAL template is known as the *global* template, because it affects *all* documents, even those assigned different document templates. Note, however, that if there is a conflict between an element belonging to NORMAL and an element belonging to the document template, the element belonging to the selected template *overrides* the feature belonging to NORMAL. In other words, the assigned template takes precedence over the global template. For example, if the document template is LETTER, and if both LETTER and NORMAL have a glossary entry named *head* (and the entries have different text), inserting **head** will produce the text belonging to the *LETTER* glossary entry rather than that belonging to NORMAL.

Also, if you have assigned the same keystroke to both LETTER and NORMAL, and you have associated the keystroke with different commands, pressing the keystroke will issue the command assigned to *LETTER* rather than that assigned to NORMAL.

THE RELATIONSHIP BETWEEN A DOCUMENT AND ITS TEMPLATE

As you have seen, when a *new* document is created, it acquires all features that belong to the template it is based upon. After a document has already been created, however, what is the relationship between the document and the document template? Does changing the template affect the document? Does changing the document affect the template?

In answering these questions, the features can be divided into two groups:

- Text, graphics, formatting, and styles

- Glossary entries and macros, and Toolbar, menu, and keyboard assignments

TEXT, GRAPHICS, FORMATTING, AND STYLES

When a new document is created, it acquires all text, graphics, formatting, and styles belonging to the template upon which it is based. These elements are copied into the new document, where they are stored *separately* from the template. Thus, if you later change one of these elements within the template, the document is *not* automatically affected. Likewise, if you edit the text or graphics within the document, or change the formatting or styles, the document template is *not* automatically affected.

However, as you will see later in the chapter (in the section "Modifying a Template"), you can explicitly copy elements between a document and a template in the following two ways:

- When you change certain formatting features in the document, you can copy these changes to the document template by clicking the **Use as Default** button within the Formatting dialog box.

- You can transfer styles from a document to the document template, or transfer styles from a specified template to the current document, using the **Format/Style** menu command.

GLOSSARY ENTRIES AND MACROS, AND TOOLBAR, MENU, AND KEYBOARD ASSIGNMENTS

When you create a new document, it acquires all glossary entries and macros, and Toolbar, menu, and keyboard assignments belonging to the global template (NORMAL) *and* those belonging to the

You will learn how to make changes to a template later in the chapter, in the section "Modifying a Template."

document template (assuming that the document template is not NORMAL). Unlike the features described in the previous section, however, glossary entries, macros, and Toolbar, menu and keyboard assignments are stored within the template (or templates) and *not* within the document itself. Therefore, if you later add, remove, or modify any of these features within a template, the changes immediately affect all documents based upon the template. (Changing one of the features in NORMAL affects *all* documents.)

CHANGING THE TEMPLATE ASSIGNED TO A DOCUMENT

You can assign a *different* template to a document, at any time after the document has already been created, through the following steps:

1. Select **File/Template**; Word will display the Template dialog box.

2. Type the name of the desired template into the **Attach Document To:** box, or choose a template name from the list. If the template is not in the Word directory (\WINWORD), you must specify the full path name.

Changing the document template *after* the document has already been created does *not* alter the document text, formatting, or style definitions. These elements are acquired from a template only when the document is first created, and they are stored separately within the document itself.

In contrast, when you assign a new template, the document immediately acquires the glossary entries, macros, and Toolbar, menu, and keyboard assignments defined in the new template (since these elements are stored in the template and not in the document itself).

CREATING OR MODIFYING A TEMPLATE

Microsoft supplies a large number of useful templates with the Word for Windows package. You can also create new templates or modify existing ones to suit your exact needs.

CREATING A NEW TEMPLATE

To create a new template:

1. Choose **File/New**.
2. Select the **Template** option within the New dialog box.
3. Enter all text or graphics and assign all features you want the template to store.
4. Choose the **File/Save** command to save the template. Be sure to specify the DOT extension in the file name you enter, or omit the extension.

To create a new template, issue the **File/New** menu command and select the **Template** option within the New dialog box.

Like a document, a new template is based upon an existing template, and automatically acquires its features. You should therefore choose from the **Use Template:** list box the template that most closely matches the one you want.

You can now assign all desired features to the template. As you have seen, you can assign text and text formatting features to a template. You can also assign the following:

- Styles

- Glossary entries

- Macros

- Toolbar, menu, and keyboard assignments

Instructions for assigning these features are given in the remaining chapters of this part of the book. When you have added all desired features, save the template using **File/Save** or **File/Save As**, or by clicking

If you enter a description into the **Title:** box of the document summary information for a template, Word will display this description whenever you select the template name in the **New** dialog box, making it easier to identify the template when creating a new document. See Chapter 26 for information on setting the document summary information.

the **Save button** on the Toolbar. Enter a file name for the template into the **File Name:** box.

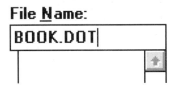

The template name should have the DOT file extension; if you do not include an extension in the name you type, Word will automatically supply the DOT extension. If you do not specify a directory name, Word will place the template file in the Word directory (\WINWORD) on your hard disk. It is best to place the template in this directory, since Word automatically lists all templates found in this directory when you create a new document.

Alternatively, you can create a new template by opening an existing template, modifying it, and then saving it under a new name. Use the following steps:

1. Choose **File/Open** or click the **Open button** on the Toolbar. Word will display the Open dialog box.

2. Select the **Document Templates (*.dot)** item from the **List Files of Type:** list, so that Word will display the names of all templates within the current directory.

3. Use the Open dialog box to find and open the desired document template.

4. Make the desired modifications to the template.

5. Save the modified version under a new name by choosing the **File/Save As** menu command, entering a name for the new template into the **File Name:** box, and clicking the OK button. Be sure to give the file the DOT extension (or omit the entire extension). Word will automatically save the file as a document template, and place it within the Word directory (that is, \WINWORD, unless you specify a different path in the file name).

Finally, you can create a new template by opening an existing *document,* making any desired modifications, and then saving the file in the template format under a new name. By using an existing document, you can take advantage of text you have already entered, and definitions you have already specified. Open and modify the document as explained previously. To save the modified version as a template, perform the following steps:

1. Issue the **File/Save As** menu command.

2. Type a *new* name for the template into the **File Name:** box. Be sure to give the file the DOT extension (or omit the entire extension).

3. Choose the **Document Template (*.dot)** item from the **Save File as Type:** list box (see Figure 19.1).

4. Click the OK button.

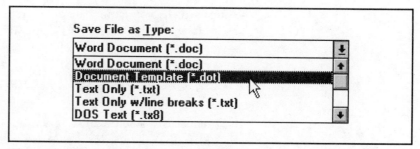

Figure 19.1: Choosing the document template format for saving a file

MODIFYING A TEMPLATE

To modify a template, use one of the following methods:

- To modify the template directly, open the template file using **File/Open**, make any desired changes, and then save the file.

- To indirectly modify formatting features within a template, click the **Use as Default** button when you are assigning these features to a document that is based upon the template.

- To indirectly change the style definitions in a template, use the **Format/Style** command to merge styles from the current document to the template (or select the **Add to Template** option when you define a style).

- To alter a glossary entry, macro, or Toolbar, menu, or keyboard customization within a template, define and save the feature within a document that is based upon the template.

To modify a template, you can either open and modify the template file itself, *or* you can make changes while working on a document *based upon* the template and then save these changes to the template.

Modifying a Template Directly

To modify a template directly, use the following steps:

1. Open the desired template using the **File/Open** menu command, or by clicking the **Open button** on the Toolbar. (See the instructions for opening a template given in the section "Creating a New Template").

2. Make the desired modifications using the techniques presented in this book.

3. Save the template by choosing the **File/Save** menu command or by clicking the **Save button** on the Toolbar.

Modifying a Template through a Document

You can also modify a template indirectly by making changes to a document *based upon* the template. The technique for modifying a template through a document depends upon the specific feature you want to change.

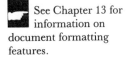 See Chapter 13 for information on document formatting features.

After changing certain formatting features within a document, you can copy these changes to the document template by clicking the **Use as Default** button within the dialog box.

The following are the menu commands that permit you to save changes to the document template:

- **Format/Character**
- **Format/Language**
- **Format/Page Setup**

When you click the **Use as Default** button, Word will save—within the document template—all features that have been entered into the dialog box. (If the document template is not the global template, NORMAL, you do *not* have the option to save the changes to NORMAL.)

To alter text, graphics, or any other forms of formatting belonging to a template, you must edit the template directly, as described previously in the chapter.

See Chapter 20 for information on defining styles.

Style definitions are stored within each document. If you add, delete, or modify a style definition, the change is saved together with the document itself, and does not automatically affect the document template.

As you will see in Chapter 20, however, you can transfer styles from a document to the document template, or transfer styles from a specified template to the current document. These operations are performed through the **Format/Style** menu command.

If the document template *is* NORMAL, then only the **Global** option can be selected.

As you have seen, glossary entries, macros, and Toolbar, menu, or keyboard customizations are stored within a template; saving one of these features, therefore, always modifies a template. When you define one of these features, however, you can specify whether you want to save it within the global template (NORMAL), or within the document template (if it is not NORMAL). For example, when saving a Toolbar customization (as explained in Chapter 23), you can choose one of the following two options:

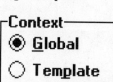

If you select the **Global** option, Word will save the feature in the NORMAL template, and if you choose the **Template** option, it will save the feature in the document template.

When you save a glossary entry or macro, Word will normally display a prompt to find out if you want to save the item in the global or document template. You can modify this behavior, however, by choosing **File/Template** and selecting one of the following options in the Template dialog box:

```
┌─Store New Macros and Glossaries as─────────┐
│  ○ Global (Available to All Documents)      │
│  ○ With Document Template                   │
│  ● Prompt for Each New                      │
└─────────────────────────────────────────────┘
```

If you choose one of the first two options, Word will automatically save the feature you are defining either in the global (NORMAL) or document template, without prompting you.

Note that when you make any change that affects a template, Word instantly transfers the changes to the specified template, and any document based upon the template will immediately be affected. To make these changes *permanent,* however, you must write them to the template file on disk. If you close the document, or quit the program, Word will prompt you to save any changes you have made to a template. Alternatively, you can save the changes at any time by choosing the **File/Save All** menu command.

20

Defining Styles
to Simplify Formatting

A STYLE IS A COLLECTION OF CHARACTER AND paragraph formatting features that is identified by name and can be applied to one or more paragraphs in a document. For example, you might create a style named **quote** that contains the formatting features you normally apply to paragraphs of quoted text.

Using styles can save you time in two important ways. First, you can assign an entire set of formatting features to a style and then apply these features to a paragraph through a *single* command. Say you have assigned the following formatting features to the style **quote**: $1/2''$ left indent, $1/2''$ right indent, and small capital characters. Whenever you need a paragraph formatted in the style of **quote**, you can simply issue the appropriate command rather than applying each of these formatting commands individually.

Second, if you *change* a style belonging to a document, the change is immediately applied to all text throughout the document that has been assigned the style. You do not need to go through the entire document and reformat each applicable paragraph. For example, if you decide that you want to indent quoted text by $3/4''$ rather than $1/2''$, and you want the characters to be bold, you can simply make these changes to **quote**; Word will instantly apply the changes to all paragraphs that have been assigned the **quote** style.

In this chapter, you will first learn about the predefined styles available in a new document. You will then learn how to apply a style, how to define a new style, and how to alter, delete, or rename an existing style.

THE PREDEFINED STYLES

When you open a new document, various predefined styles are normally available; the exact collection of predefined styles depends upon the document template you selected when you created the document. If the document is based upon the NORMAL template (and if you haven't altered this template), it will possess a set of predefined styles known as *standard* styles.

The standard styles are listed in Table 20.1. As you can see in this table, Word automatically assigns these styles to various elements within the document. For example, it assigns the style **Normal** to ordinary document text, the style **footer** to footers, and the style **toc 1** to top-level items in tables of contents. The third column of Table 20.1 lists the style descriptions as they appear in the Style dialog box. These style descriptions are explained later in the chapter (the exact description you see may differ slightly, depending upon your version of Word).

Table 20.1: The Automatic Word Styles

STYLE	USE	DESCRIPTION
annotation reference	Annotation reference marks (see Chapter 25)	Normal + Font: 8 Point
annotation text	Annotation text (see Chapter 25)	Normal +
footer	Footer text (see Chapter 10)	Normal + Tab stops: 3″ Centered; 6″ Right Flush
footnote reference	Footnote reference marks (see Chapter 10)	Normal + Font: 8 Point, Super-script 3 Point
footnote text	Footnote text (see Chapter 10)	Normal +
header	Header text (see Chapter 10)	Normal + Tab stops: 3″ Centered; 6″ Right Flush
heading 1	Top-level outline heading (see Chapter 24)	Normal + Font: Helv 12 pt, Bold Underline, Space Before 1 li, Next Style: Normal

Table 20.1: The Automatic Word Styles (continued)

STYLE	USE	DESCRIPTION
heading 2	Level 2 outline headings	Normal + Font: Helv 12 pt, Bold, Space Before 0.5 li, Next Style: Normal
heading 3	Level 3 outline headings	Normal + Font: 12 Point, Bold, Indent: Left 0.25″, Next Style: Normal Indent
heading 4	Level 4 outline headings	Normal + Font: 12 Point, Underline, Indent: Left 0.25″, Next Style: Normal Indent
heading 5	Level 5 outline headings	Normal + Bold, Indent: Left 0.5″, Next Style: Normal Indent
heading 6	Level 6 outline headings	Normal + Underline, Indent: Left 0.5″, Next Style: Normal Indent
heading 7	Level 7 outline headings	Normal + Italic, Indent: Left 0.5″, Next Style: Normal Indent
heading 8	Level 8 outline headings	Normal + Italic, Indent: Left 0.5″, Next Style: Normal Indent
heading 9	Level 9 outline headings	Normal + Italic, Indent: Left 0.5″, Next Style: Normal Indent
index 1	Top-level index item (see Chapter 11)	Normal +
index 2	Level 2 index item	Normal + Indent: Left 0.25″

Table 20.1: The Automatic Word Styles (continued)

STYLE	USE	DESCRIPTION
index 3	Level 3 index item	Normal + Indent: Left 0.5″
index 4	Level 4 index item	Normal + Indent: Left 0.75″
index 5	Level 5 index item	Normal + Indent: Left 1″
index 6	Level 6 index item	Normal + Indent: Left 1.25″
index 7	Level 7 index item	Normal + Indent: Left 1.5″
index heading	Headings for index sections	Normal +
line number	Line numbers (see Chapter 14)	Normal +
Normal	Ordinary document text	Font: Tms Rmn 10 pt, Languagn English (US), Flush Left
Normal Indent	Text following outline heading level 3 and higher	Normal + Indent: Left 0.5″
toc 1	Top-level table of contents item (see Chapter 11)	Normal + Indent: Right 0.5″, Tab stops: 5.75″...; 6″ Right Flush
toc 2	Level 2 table of contents item	Normal + Indent: Left 0.5″ Right 0.5″, Tab stops: 5.75″...; 6″ Right Flush
toc 3	Level 3 table of contents item	Normal + Indent: Left 1.0″ Right 0.5″, Tab stops: 5.75″...; 6″ Right Flush

Table 20.1: The Automatic Word Styles (continued)

STYLE	USE	DESCRIPTION
toc 4	Level 4 table of contents item	Normal + Indent: Left 1.5″ Right 0.5″, Tab stops: 5.75″ . . .; 6″ Right Flush
toc 5	Level 5 table of contents item	Normal + Indent: Left 2.0″ Right 0.5″, Tab stops: 5.75″ . . .; 6″ Right Flush
toc 6	Level 6 table of contents item	Normal + Indent: Left 2.5″ Right 0.5″, Tab stops: 5.75″ . . .; 6″ Right Flush
toc 7	Level 7 table of contents item	Normal + Indent: Left 3.0″ Right 0.5″, Tab stops: 5.75″ . . .; 6″ Right Flush
toc 8	Level 8 table of contents item	Normal + Indent: Left 3.5″ Right 0.5″, Tab stops: 5.75″ . . .; 6″ Right Flush

Notice in the descriptions of the styles that all of the standard styles are based upon the style **Normal**. This means that these styles have all of the features of **Normal** *plus* the additional features specified. Also, the description

> Normal +

denotes that the style is based upon **Normal** without any additional features.

Here are some examples to clarify the style descriptions. The description for the **toc 2** style for tables of contents

> Normal + Indent: Left 0.5″ Right 0.5″, Tab stops: 5.75″ . . .; 6″ Right Flush

means that it is based upon **Normal** (10-point Tms Rmn, flush left), and that it has left and right indents at 1/2", and custom tab stops. The first tab, 5.75" from the left margin, uses the leader character- . . . (period characters) instead of blank spaces. The second tab is 6" from the left margin, with the flush right style.

Similarly, the **heading 2** style for outlines

> Normal + Font: Helv 12 Point, Bold, Space Before 6pt, Next
> Style: Normal

means that it is based upon **Normal** with several additional features. The font is 12-point bold Helv instead of 10-point Tms Rmn, and each second-level heading is preceded by 6 points of vertical space (before the paragraph). In addition, the paragraph that follows the heading (next style) has the **Normal** style. Note that outline headings in levels 3 to 9 use Normal Indent as the next style—that is, **Normal** with a 1/2" left indent.

Later in the chapter, you will see how to modify an standard style, thereby changing the formatting of all document text assigned the style.

APPLYING STYLES

To apply a style to the selected paragraph, use one of the following methods:

- Choose **Format/Style**, select the desired style from the **Style Name:** list, and click the **Apply** button.

- Select the desired style from the style list at the left end of the ribbon.

- Press **Ctrl-S** and type the name of the style at the prompt.

- Press the shortcut key for the style, if one has been defined.

All paragraphs in a document have an associated style. Unless you apply an alternative style, Word assigns the **Normal** style to paragraphs of ordinary text or graphics. In this section, you will learn how to change the style of a paragraph by explicitly applying another style.

You can apply a predefined style, or one that you have defined while working on the document. There are three basic methods:

- The **Format/Style** command
- The ribbon
- The **Ctrl-S** key combination or the style shortcut key

Before learning about each of these methods, you should know about a feature that makes it easier to work with styles: the *style area*. The style area displays the name of the paragraph style adjacent to each paragraph. If you choose **Tools/Options**, select the **View** category, and enter a measurement other than 0 into the **Style Area Width:** box, Word will display a style area to the left of the text within the window. The style area has the width specified in the Style Area Width box. Figure 20.1 illustrates a window with a style area that is 0.75″ wide.

Note also that you can print a description of each of the document styles by choosing **File/Print** and selecting the **Styles** item from the **Print:** list box (Figure 20.2).

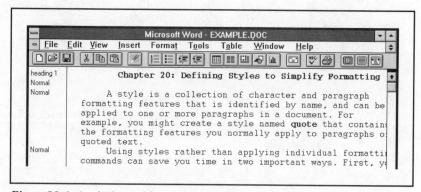

Figure 20.1: A window with a style name area

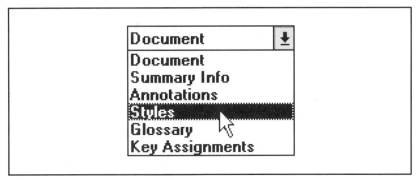

Figure 20.2: The Print list box

USING THE FORMAT/STYLE COMMAND

To apply a style using **Format/Style**, first select the paragraph or paragraphs you want to change. If you want to assign a style to a single paragraph, you can simply place the insertion point within the paragraph and choose Format/Style. Word will display the Style dialog box, illustrated in Figure 20.3. Alternatively, you can open the Style dialog box by pressing **Ctrl-S** twice, or by double-clicking within the style area (if it is displayed).

You can now type the name of the style you want to apply into the **Style Name:** box. Alternatively, you can select a style name from

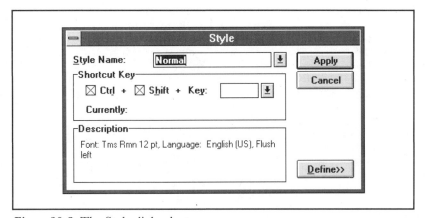

Figure 20.3: The Style dialog box

the **Style Name:** list. This list will display the names of all styles you have defined, all standard styles currently used in the document, and the names of a few standard styles that may not be in use (**Normal**, **heading 1**, **heading 2**, and **heading 3** are always displayed). To have Word list *all* of the standard styles given in Table 20.1, press **Ctrl-Y**. To apply the specified style to the selection, click the **Apply** button.

To practice assigning a style, you can select a paragraph of text in your document (which will have **Normal** unless you have previously applied another style). Then, choose Format/Style; type Normal Indent, the name of a standard style, into the Style Name box; and click the Apply button. Notice that the paragraph becomes indented, since **Normal Indent** is defined with a 0.5″ indent. This is not a very impressive demonstration of the power of using styles, since the style was defined with only a single feature (in addition to the features of **Normal**). Keep in mind, however, that a style could be defined with *many* formatting features, all of which could be instantly assigned to a paragraph by simply applying the style. Remember also that you can later globally reformat *all* paragraphs in a document having a particular style by simply redefining this style.

Note that when the Style dialog box is first displayed, the Style Name box initially contains the name of the style currently assigned to the selected paragraph. Typically, you then select or type the name of a different style. If, however, you leave the original style name in the Style Name box, and then click the Apply button, Word will *reapply* this style to the paragraph; this will remove any formatting applied to the paragraph other than that belonging to the style.

To restore all paragraph formatting in the selected paragraph to the features defined by the style, press **Ctrl-Q**. To restore the character formatting of the selected characters to the features defined by the style, press **Ctrl-spacebar**.

To illustrate this process, consider the following scenario: You select a paragraph that is assigned **Normal**, and then press **Ctrl-E** to apply the *centered* alignment format. You later select the paragraph again and use Format/Style to reapply **Normal**. Word will remove the centered paragraph alignment, and will restore the *left* alignment, since this feature is part of the definition of **Normal**.

Note finally that when you apply a new style to a paragraph, the resulting character formatting is sometimes difficult to predict. If the entire paragraph, or a large portion of it, has been assigned a specific character formatting feature, such as italic, applying the new style will *replace* this feature with the character formatting defined for the style. If, however, a character formatting feature has been applied to only a relatively small portion of the paragraph, assigning a style will leave the character formatting intact.

USING THE RIBBON

If the ribbon is visible, you can apply a style to the current selection by typing the name of the desired style into the style box at the left end and pressing Enter. To place the insertion point within this box, either click inside the box with the mouse or press **Ctrl-S**.

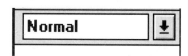

Alternatively, you can select a style from the pull-down list:

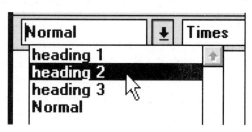

The style is applied as soon as you select it within the list; you do not need to press Enter. The list contains the names of all standard styles used within the document, all styles you have defined for the document, plus a few standard styles that may not be in use (**heading 1**, **heading 2**, and **heading 3**).

If you specify the name of the style that is already assigned to the selected paragraph, and if that paragraph has been assigned formatting that does not belong to the style, Word will display a message box asking if you want to redefine the style based upon the selection. If you click the **No** button, Word will *reapply* the style to the selection, as described in the previous section. If, however, you click **Yes**, Word

If the ribbon is not currently displayed, you can display it by choosing **View/Ribbon**. Using the ribbon is discussed in Chapters 15 and 16.

The style list on the ribbon, unlike the list within the Style dialog box, cannot be made to display *all* standard styles.

will modify the style based upon the formatting features of the selection. For more information on redefining styles, see "Defining Styles Using the Ribbon or Keyboard" later in this chapter.

Also, if you enter a new name (one not already assigned to an existing style), Word will create a new style based upon the selection. This method is also described in "Defining Styles Using the Ribbon or Keyboard."

USING THE KEYBOARD

Pressing **Ctrl-S** *twice* opens the Style dialog box.

You can also apply a style to the current selection by pressing **Ctrl-S**. Type the name of the desired style at the prompt that Word displays within the status bar:

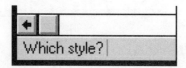

If the ribbon is visible when you press Ctrl-S, Word will place the insertion point inside the style box at the left end of the ribbon rather than displaying a prompt within the status bar.

When specifying a style by pressing Ctrl-S while the ribbon is not displayed, you must type the correct style name; you do not have the benefit of a list of valid style names. Otherwise, specifying a style through this keyboard command is exactly the same as applying a style by using the style list on the ribbon.

USING THE SHORTCUT KEY

If a style has been assigned a *shortcut key,* you can simply press this keystroke to apply the style to the selected paragraph or paragraphs. Initially, none of the standard styles have shortcut keys. Later in the chapter, you will learn how to assign a shortcut key to a standard style or to a style you have created.

Note that if you press the shortcut key for the style already assigned to the current paragraph, Word neither reapplies the style nor changes the style definition. Rather, it simply ignores the command.

DEFINING STYLES USING FORMAT/STYLE

In the next two sections, you will learn how to define styles, so that you can create new styles or modify existing ones. In this section, you will learn how to define styles using the **Format/Style** command, and in the next section, you will learn how to define styles using the ribbon or keyboard.

You can use Format/Style to perform the following tasks:

- Create a new style

- Modify, rename, or delete an existing style

- Copy styles between the document and other documents or templates

When you choose Format/Style, Word will display the Style dialog box, which was illustrated in Figure 20.3. To define one or more styles, you should click the **Define** button. Clicking this button will expand the Style dialog box to reveal several additional options. The expanded dialog box is shown in Figure 20.4.

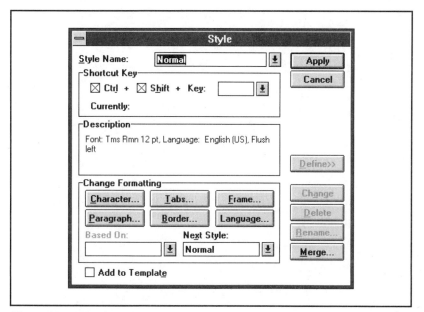

Figure 20.4: The Style box, with the Define options visible

CREATING A NEW STYLE

To create a new style:

1. Choose **Format/Style**. Word will open the Style dialog box.

2. Type a name for the style into the **Style Name:** box.

3. Assign all desired paragraph and character formatting features by using the appropriate keyboard commands, or by clicking one of the buttons in the **Change Formatting** area to open a formatting dialog box.

4. Click the **Add** or **Apply** button.

To define a new style, first type the name you want to assign the style into the **Style Name:** box within the Style dialog box:

<u>S</u>tyle Name:	quote	⬇

The style name can contain up to 20 characters, and can include space characters. Be sure that you do not type the name of an existing style (either one you have defined, or one of the standard styles listed in Table 20.1).

Initially, the new style is assigned all of the features of the paragraph that was selected when you chose **Format/Style**. You can now freely add or remove individual formatting features. Notice that Word displays a description of the style within the **Description** area near the center of the dialog box:

┌─**Description (by example)**─────────────────┐

Normal + Small Caps, Indent: Left 0.5" Right 0.5"
Justified

└──────────────────────────────────────┘

As you add or remove features, Word updates this description.

Assigning Formatting Features to the New Style

To assign a formatting feature to the new style, you can use a keyboard command or a dialog box, just as if you were formatting a paragraph within a document. To apply a paragraph formatting feature with the keyboard, you can issue any of the commands (except **Ctrl-S**) described in Chapter 15, in the section "Using the Keyboard." For example, if you press **Ctrl-E**, the style will be assigned the centered paragraph alignment style, and the word *Centered* will be added to the style description.

To apply a character formatting feature with the keyboard, you can issue any of the commands described in Chapter 16, in the section "Using the Keyboard."

To assign formatting features using a dialog box, click one of the following six buttons displayed in the **Change Formatting** area of the Style dialog box:

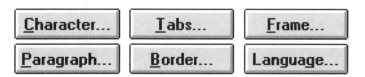

Clicking a button will open the corresponding formatting dialog box. Once the dialog box is open, select the desired features as if you were formatting a regular text selection.

Unfortunately, you can't use the ruler or ribbon to apply formatting. Remember, however, that the new style you are defining is initially assigned all of the formatting features of the paragraph that was selected when you chose **Format/Style**. Therefore, *before* choosing this command, you can assign all desired formatting features directly to the selected paragraph, freely using the ruler or ribbon. (If you want a character formatting feature to be assigned to the style, you must assign it to *all* characters in the selected paragraph.)

Specifying the Base and Next Styles

A style is usually *based upon* another style. This means that the style has all of the features currently assigned to the base style, *plus* all features specifically assigned to the style. Many styles are based upon

Normal. For example, consider the following style description:

Normal + Small Caps, Indent: Left 0.5″ Right 0.5″ Justified

This style is based upon **Normal**; it therefore has all of the features currently assigned to **Normal**. The style *also* has the Small Caps character formatting feature, both left and right half-inch margin indents, and justified paragraph alignment. Note that any feature explicitly assigned to the style overrides a conflicting feature assigned to the base style. For example, a paragraph assigned the style just described would be justified, even though the **Normal** style specifies flush left alignment.

If a base style is modified, all styles based upon it will instantly reflect the change. For example, if all styles defined for a document are based upon **Normal**, and if you assign **Normal** the Courier font rather than the Tms Rmn font, all text in the document (including headers, footnotes, and other elements) will instantly be converted to the Courier font, except for any text assigned a style that specifies another font or text explicitly formatted with another font.

The **Based On:** box contains the name of the current base style (if the style you are defining does not have a base style, this box is blank):

Based On:

| Normal | ↓ |

If you want to change the base style, type the name of the desired style into the Based On box, or select a style from the pull-down list. If you do not want to base the style you are defining on another style, leave this box blank.

You can also specify a *next style*. The next style is the style that Word automatically assigns to a paragraph inserted *following* a paragraph assigned the style you are defining. Usually, the next style is the same as the style you are defining, so that paragraphs you type one after the other will have the same style. It is sometimes useful, however, to have Word assign the next paragraph a different style.

Consider, for example, the **heading 1** standard style, which is designed for creating document headings and is described in Table 20.1.

This style is assigned **Normal** as the next style. Therefore, when you press Enter after you have finished typing a heading assigned the **heading 1** style, the next paragraph will be assigned the **Normal** style. This feature is convenient, since a title is typically followed by normal text, and not by another title.

When you are defining a new style, the **Next Style:** box is initially empty. If you leave it empty, Word will make the next style the *same* as the style you are defining. If you want to specify a different next style, type the style name into the Next Style box, or select a style name from the pull-down list.

Assigning a Shortcut Key

You can also assign a *shortcut key* to a style, so that you can apply the style to selected paragraphs by simply pressing the keystroke. To assign a shortcut key to the style you are defining, choose one of the keys from the **Key:** list box:

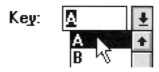

You can also select the **Ctrl** option, the **Shift** option, or both options, to include one or both of these keys in the keystroke. For example, if you make the following selections when defining the style **quote**,

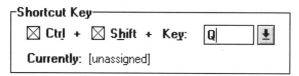

you will be able to apply this style to selected paragraphs by pressing Ctrl-Shift-Q.

If the keystroke you designate is already assigned to another style or Word function, Word indicates this assignment following the **Currently:** label; if you accept the keystroke, Word will *reassign* the keystroke to your style. If the keystroke is currently unassigned, Word displays **[unassigned]** following this label. If you choose both the Ctrl and the Shift options, your chances of finding an unassigned keystroke are much better.

If you select a letter key, such as **N**, in the Key box, you must also choose the Ctrl option.

Adding a Style to the Template

If you select the **Add to Template** option at the bottom of the Style dialog box, Word will copy the new style definition to the document template, so that the style will be available both within the current document *and* within any new documents based on the same template.

Completing the Definition

Click the **Add** button to define the new style based upon the features you have specified. The dialog box will remain open so that you can continue to work with styles. Alternatively, you can click the **Apply** button to define the style, apply it to the selected paragraph, and close the dialog box.

MODIFYING, DELETING, OR RENAMING A STYLE

To modify, delete, or rename a style:

1. Choose **Format/Style** to open the Style dialog box.
2. Select the name of the style you want to change from the **Style Name:** list.
3. To modify the style, apply the desired formatting features and other options, and click the **Change** button.
4. To delete the style, click the **Delete** button.
5. To rename the style, click the **Rename** button.
6. Click the **Close** button when you have completed working with styles.

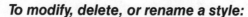

You can *modify* a standard style, but you cannot delete it or rename it.

In addition to creating a new style, you can use the Style dialog box to modify, delete, or rename an existing style. If the Style dialog box is not currently displayed, open it by choosing **Format/Style**. Click the **Define** button to expand the Style dialog box to reveal all options.

When the Style dialog box is first opened, the **Style Name:** box contains the name of the style assigned to the currently selected paragraph. (If, however, the selection encompasses paragraphs with different styles, this box will be blank.)

If you leave the original style name in the Style Name box, or if you select another style from the pull-down list, the **Description** area will display the definition of the style. In this case, any changes you make in the Style dialog box are added to the current definition of the style. If, however, you *type in* the name of an existing style, the Description area will display all of the formatting features of the currently selected paragraph. In this case, any changes you make in the Style dialog box are added to the format of the selection. Thus, by typing in a style name, you can use the selection as a model for the modifications you want to make to the style.

To modify the style, you can now specify any formatting feature as described in the previous sections. You can also change the base style and the next style, or assign a shortcut key (or change the existing shortcut key).

If you select the **Add to Template** option, the changes you make will be applied to the style within the current document *and* within the document template.

When you have completed specifying the features of the style you are modifying, click the **Change** button to redefine the style and leave the dialog box open. To redefine the style, apply it to the current selection, and close the dialog box, click the **Apply** button.

To *delete* the style named in the Style Name box from the current document (provided it is not a standard style), click the **Delete** button. Clicking this button does *not* delete the style from the document template if it exists there; to delete it from the template, you must open the template file and delete it through the Format/Style command.

Finally, you can rename the style (provided it is not a standard style) by clicking the **Rename** button. Word will display a dialog box that allows you to specify the new name.

Click the **Close** button to remove the Style dialog box when you have finished working with styles.

MERGING STYLES

To merge styles:

1. Click the **Merge** button within the Style dialog box to open the Merge Styles dialog box.

2. To copy all styles *from* the current document *to* a template, select either the document template or the global template (NORMAL.DOT) from the **File Name:** list, and click the **To Template** button.

3. To copy all styles *from* another document or template *to* the current document, select the source document or template from the File Name list, and click the **From Template** button.

4. Click OK.

Remember that when you first create a new document, it acquires a *separate copy* of all styles defined in the document template. You can later change the styles stored in the document without affecting the template, or change the styles in the template without affecting the document. Therefore, the document and its template do not necessarily have the same styles.

As you saw in the previous section, you can copy a new or modified style definition to the document template by selecting the **Add to Template** option within the Styles dialog box. In this section, you will learn how to copy *all* document styles to the document template or to the global template (NORMAL). You will also learn how to copy styles from a template or another document *to* the current document.

Begin by clicking the **Merge** button:

Word will display the Merge Styles dialog box, shown in Figure 20.5.

You can now either copy all styles from the current document to a document template, or copy all styles from a template or other document to the current document.

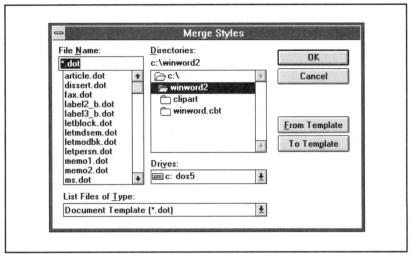

Figure 20.5: The Merge Styles dialog box

When copying styles, a copied style with the same name as an existing style in the target document or template will *replace* the existing style, and a style with a new name will be *added* to the target's styles.

When you first open the Merge Styles dialog box, the current directory should be \WINWORD (or the directory in which you installed Word), in which Word stores document templates. To change to another directory, use the **Drives:** and **Directories:** list boxes as described in Chapter 3.

To copy all styles from the current document to a template, click the **To Template** button within the Merge Styles dialog box, observing the following guidelines:

- If the **File Name:** box does *not* contain a specific template file name when you click the To Template button (or if it contains the name of the document template), Word will automatically copy all styles defined in the document to the document template.

- You can have Word copy all styles from the current document to the global template (NORMAL), whether or not NORMAL is the document template. To do this, select NORMAL.DOT from the **File Name:** list.

- If the File Name box contains the name of a template or document other than the document template or NORMAL, the To Template button is grayed and cannot be clicked. Thus, the Merge Styles dialog box allows you to transfer styles only to the document or global template.

To copy all styles from a template or other document to the current document, click the **From Template** or **OK** button, observing the following guidelines:

- To quickly copy all styles from the document template to the current document, simply click the From Template button. Make sure, however, that the File Name box does not contain the name of a specific template or document; otherwise, styles will be copied from the specified file. (It can contain a *general* name, such as *.DOT.)

- To copy all styles from another document or template, first switch to the appropriate directory and select the name of the document or template using the **Directories:** and **Drives:** list boxes as described in Chapter 3. Then click either the From Template or OK button.

DEFINING STYLES USING THE RIBBON OR KEYBOARD

To create or modify a style based upon the formatting of the selected paragraph:

1. Press **Ctrl-S** or click on the style list at the left end of the ribbon.

2. To create a new style, type an original name for this style and press Enter.

3. To modify the existing style of the selected paragraph, type the name of this style and press Enter (if you are using the ribbon, the name will already be displayed; simply press Enter).

You can create a new style or alter an existing one based upon the character and paragraph formatting features of an existing paragraph. This method is useful for quickly creating a new style, or for altering an existing one, after you have already applied the desired formatting commands to a paragraph. Also, it enables you to see how the formatting commands look and to make sure they are correct before assigning them to a style. A final advantage of this method is that it allows you to apply formatting features using the ruler or ribbon.

Once you have created a new style by example, you can later enhance the style, if desired, through the **Format/Style** command.

The first step is to apply the desired character and paragraph formatting to a paragraph in your document. When choosing the paragraph you want to use as an example, keep in mind the following guidelines:

- If you are creating a new style, you can use *any* paragraph as an example. It makes sense, however, to choose one that is as close as possible to the desired format.

- If you want to modify an existing style, you must use a paragraph that is assigned this style.

Note that if a given character formatting feature varies within the paragraph, Word will use the feature applied to the majority of the characters. For example, if some characters are assigned the Helv font, but most are assigned the Courier font, Word will assign the Courier font to the style you define.

Next, make sure that the insertion point is within the example paragraph, or that you have selected part or all of this paragraph (if the selection encompasses more than one paragraph, Word will use the settings of the *first* paragraph within the selection to define the style).

If the ribbon is *not* currently displayed, simply press **Ctrl-S**. Word will display the following prompt within the status bar:

Which style?

If the ribbon *is* displayed, either press Ctrl-S or click within the style box at the left end of the ribbon. Word will place the insertion point within this box.

Next, type the name you want to assign to the new style you are defining and press Enter. Word will immediately add the new style to your document. If you are creating a new style, you should type a name that is not already used for a style defined within the document or for one of the standard styles listed in Table 20.1.

To modify a style using the method described in this section, you must first select (or place the insertion point within) a paragraph that has been assigned this style.

The name of the style will be displayed in the ribbon unless the current selection encompasses two or more files formatted with different styles.

If you want to *modify* the style assigned to the selected paragraph, follow these steps:

1. If the ribbon *is* displayed, click in the style list at the left end of the ribbon. The name of the style of the selected paragraph will appear in the style box within the ribbon. Press Enter. If the ribbon is *not* displayed, press **Ctrl-S**. Then type the name of the style of the selected paragraph at the prompt within the status bar and press Enter.

2. Word will ask you if you want to redefine the style based upon the selection. Click the **Yes** button. (If you click the **No** button, Word will *reapply* the style to the selected paragraph, eliminating any formatting features you have manually added.) Note that if you type or select the name of an existing style *other* than the one assigned to the selected paragraph, Word will apply the specified style to the paragraph, replacing both the original style and any formatting you have manually applied.

21

Using the Glossary
to Save Typing

CHAPTER *21*

YOU CAN USE THE *GLOSSARY* TO STORE BLOCKS OF text or graphics. Each block—termed a *glossary entry*—is identified by name and can be retrieved and placed in any document. You can save time by storing frequently used blocks as glossary entries and inserting them when required, rather than retyping text or importing a picture each time it is needed. Unlike the Windows Clipboard, which will store blocks temporarily, a glossary provides permanent storage and can hold many entries.

In this chapter, you will learn how to store a selection in the glossary and how to insert a glossary entry into your document. Also, you will learn how to use a special glossary entry known as the *Spike*.

STORING A SELECTION IN A GLOSSARY

To define a glossary entry:

1. Select the block you want to store in the glossary.
2. Choose **Edit/Glossary**.
3. Type a name for the entry in the **Glossary Name:** box.
4. Click **Define**.

To define a glossary entry, you must select at least one character before choosing **Edit/Glossary**.

To store a block of text or graphics in a glossary, first select the desired block. Next, choose **Edit/Glossary**. Word will display the Glossary dialog box, illustrated in Figure 21.1. Type a name for the new glossary entry into the **Glossary Name:** box. A glossary name can be from 1 to 31 characters in length and can include spaces.

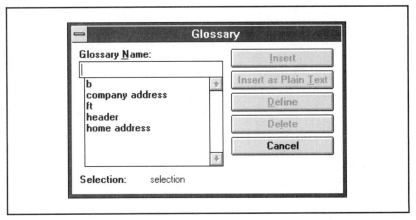

Figure 21.1: The Glossary dialog box

Before redefining an existing entry, Word will display a message box, allowing you to decide whether you want to redefine the entry.

At the bottom of the dialog box, Word displays the text that will become the contents of the glossary entry. You will actually see only the first 38 characters of the selection, the remainder being represented by an ellipsis (. . .).

If you type the name of an existing glossary entry (or select one from the pull-down list), Word will *redefine* the entry using the current selection.

Remember that glossary entries are stored in the document template, not with the document itself. When you add an entry, it immediately becomes available to all documents based upon the same template.

Click **Define** to store the selection in the glossary under the specified name. Word may then display the dialog box shown in Figure 21.2, asking you to specify the context of the new glossary entry. Select **As Global** to store the entry in the global template (making it available for all documents), or select **In Template** to store it in the document template.

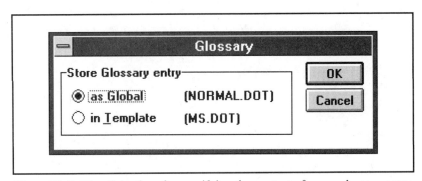

Figure 21.2: The dialog box for specifying the context of a new glossary entry

Word will not display this dialog box if the document template is the global template. Also, it will not ask you to specify the context if you have chosen either **Global** or **With Document Template** in the Template dialog box (opened through **File/Template**, which was explained in Chapter 19). If you have chosen either of these options, Word will store the selection without prompting you.

While the Glossary dialog box is open, you can delete a glossary entry by typing its name into the **Glossary Name:** box or by selecting from the list box and clicking **Delete**.

 If the document template is the global template, Word will simply print the global template entries.

You can print a list of available glossary entries by choosing **File/Print** and selecting **Glossary** from the **Print:** list box (see Figure 21.3). Word will print the name of each glossary entry, along with its contents. It will print the entries in the document template, followed by those in the global template.

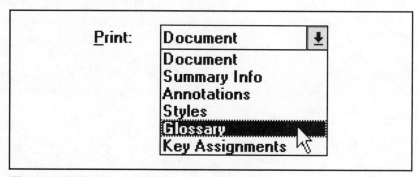

Figure 21.3: The Print: list box

INSERTING A GLOSSARY ENTRY INTO A DOCUMENT

To insert a glossary entry:

1. Place the cursor where you want to insert the entry.

2. Choose **Edit/Glossary**.

3. Select the name of the desired entry from the **Glossary Name:** list.

4. To insert the text *and* formatting, click the **Insert** button. To insert text only, without formatting, click **Insert as Plain Text**.

5. Rather than performing steps 2 through 4, you can simply type the name of the desired glossary entry and press **F3**.

You can insert a glossary entry at the cursor using either a dialog box or a keyboard command.

To insert a glossary entry using a dialog box, choose **Edit/Glossary**. Word will display the dialog box shown in Figure 21.1. Either type the name of the desired glossary entry into the **Glossary Name:** box or select a name from the list, as shown in Figure 21.4.

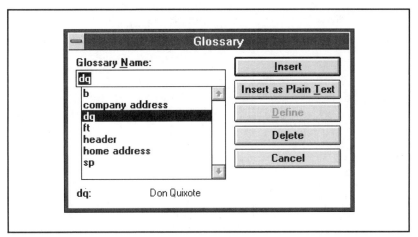

Figure 21.4: Selecting a glossary entry in the Glossary dialog box

When the entry name has been typed in or selected, Word displays the contents of the entry below the list. Word displays the first 38 characters of the entry and represents the remainder with an ellipsis (...). Click **Insert** to place the specified entry in your document.

Note that a glossary entry contains not only characters but also formatting. When you click **Insert**, Word inserts both the characters and the formatting. Alternatively, you can click **Insert as Plain Text** to insert only the characters, without formatting information. In this case, the inserted text will be assigned the formatting of the surrounding text at the insertion point.

To insert a glossary entry using the keyboard, type the name of the entry right where you want it to go and press **F3**. Word will replace the glossary's name with its contents. Alternatively, you can select a glossary name before pressing F3.

USING THE SPIKE

To store several selections in a single glossary entry:

1. Select a block of text and press **Ctrl-F3** to remove it from your document and store it in the special glossary called the **Spike**.

2. Repeat step 1 for any additional selections you want to move to the Spike.

3. To insert *all* selections currently stored in the Spike, place the insertion point at the desired position and press **Ctrl-Shift-F3**. The Spike will be cleared and its contents inserted into the document.

Normally, when you store a selection under the name of an existing glossary entry, it replaces the former contents of the entry. Word, however, provides a special glossary entry called **Spike**, which allows you to store multiple blocks of text or graphics and then insert them all at once (somewhat like the spike for storing notes on your desk).

To add a block to the Spike, select the block and press **Ctrl-F3**. The block is *removed from the document* and added to the Spike. You can continue to store additional selections in the Spike with this same method.

To insert the current contents of the Spike, place the insertion point at the desired position and press **Ctrl-Shift-F3**. All entries in the

Spike will be inserted as a single block in the order they were added to the Spike. Also, the Spike will be emptied; therefore, using **Ctrl-Shift-F3**, you can insert the Spike contents only once.

You can, however, insert the Spike's contents repeatedly by choosing **Edit/Glossary** and selecting the name **Spike**, or by typing the word **Spike** into your document and then pressing **F3**.

22

Writing Macros to Save Work

YOU CAN USE MACROS TO RECORD A SERIES OF EDITING or formatting actions. You can then repeat these actions at any time by running the macro. Macros are really new Word commands that you create. Creating macros to perform complex or routine tasks can be a great time-saver.

In this chapter, you will learn how to record, edit, and run a macro.

RECORDING A MACRO

To record a macro:

1. Choose **Tools/Record Macro**. Word will open the Record Macro dialog box.
2. Enter the name you want to assign the macro and a keystroke for executing the macro, along with a description.
3. Click OK the begin recording.
4. Perform the exact sequence of actions you want to be included in the macro.
5. Choose **Tools/Stop Recorder** when you have finished the steps. This will end recording.

Windows provides a Macro Recorder that allows you to record and run macros in one or more Windows applications. You can use it along with Word's macro feature. See the *Microsoft Windows User's Guide* for information.

The easiest way to create a simple macro is to record your actions as you perform them. To begin recording your actions, choose **Tools/ Record Macro**. Word will display the dialog box shown in Figure 22.1.

Type the name you want to assign the macro into the **Record Macro Name:** box. Word proposes the name Macro1 for the first macro you record, Macro2 for the second, and so on. You can accept these names or enter more descriptive names of your own. A macro name may not contain space characters.

Figure 22.1: The Record Macro dialog box

Next, specify a keystroke to run the macro. To assign a keystroke, choose one of the keys from the **Key:** list box.

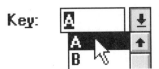

You can also select **Ctrl**, **Shift**, or both to include them in the keystroke. For example, if you make the following selections,

the keystroke combination to run the macro you are recording will be **Ctrl-Shift-M**.

If the keystroke you designate is already assigned to another macro or command, Word indicates this after the **Currently:** label; if you accept the keystroke, Word will *reassign* the keystroke. If the keystroke is unassigned, Word displays [unassigned] following this label. If you choose both the Ctrl and the Shift options, your chances of finding an unassigned keystroke are much better. If you select a letter key, such as **N**, in the **Key:** box, you *must* choose the Ctrl option.

Before recording the macro, you can enter a description into the **Description:** box. Word will later display your description if you select the macro from the Macro dialog box. The description can help you choose an appropriate macro. If you add a macro to a menu (as described in Chapter 23), Word will display the description in the status bar when the menu item is highlighted. You can change this description at any time.

When you are ready to begin recording, click the OK button. Word may then display the dialog box shown in Figure 22.2, asking you to specify the context of the new macro. Select **As Global** to store the macro in the global template (making the macro available to all documents), or select **In Template** to store it in the document template. Word will not display this dialog box if the document template *is* the global template. Also, it will not ask you to specify the context if you have chosen either **Global** or **With Document Template** in the Template dialog box (opened through **File/Template**, which was discussed in Chapter 19). If you have chosen either of these two options, Word will store the macro in the specified template without prompting you.

> Remember that macros, like glossary entries, are stored within the document template, not the document itself. When you define a macro, it immediately becomes available to all documents based upon the same template.

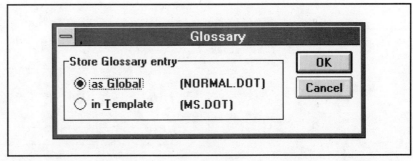

Figure 22.2: The dialog box for specifying the context of a new glossary entry

Word will then remove the dialog box and display the letters **REC** in the right side of the status bar to let you know that your actions are being recorded.

Now perform the series of actions you want to store in the macro. You can perform almost any editing action or Word command. Note, however, that you cannot record mouse actions, except for choosing menu commands, selecting options in dialog boxes, or clicking buttons on the Toolbar.

When you have finished the actions you want to record, choose **Tools/Stop Recorder**. Word will stop recording the macro without displaying a dialog box. It will also remove the **REC** indicator from the status bar.

If you have created or modified one or more macros, Word will prompt you to save your changes to the appropriate template when you quit the program.

Once you start recording a macro, **Record Macro** *on the* **Tools** *menu is replaced with* **Stop Recorder**.

AUTOMATIC MACROS

If you assign one of the following names to a macro that you have created, Word will run the macro *automatically* whenever the appropriate situation arises:

Although Word runs automatic macros automatically, you can run them manually using any of the methods described later in the chapter.

- AutoExec
- AutoExit
- AutoOpen
- AutoNew
- AutoClose

You can prevent Word from running an automatic macro if you hold down **Shift** while performing an action that would normally activate the macro.

AutoExec

If you assign a macro the name **AutoExec**, the macro will run automatically when you start Word. For example, if you want to open a specific document each time you start Word, you could create a macro as follows:

1. Choose **Tools/Record Macro**. Type **AutoExec** into the **Record Macro Name:** box, and enter a description if desired. You do not need to define a keystroke.

To define an
AutoExec macro,
make sure that **With
Document Template** has
not been selected in the
dialog box displayed by
File/Template, since you
need to specify the *global*
context.

2. Click the OK button to begin recording, and select the global context for saving the macro, if prompted. Word will then remove the dialog box.

3. Using **File/Open**, open the file you want to appear each time you start Word.

4. Choose **Tools/Stop Recorder**.

Note that you can *prevent* Word from running AutoExec by including the /m switch in the command line when you start the program:

```
winword   /m
```

AutoExit

If you assign a macro the name AutoExit, the macro will run automatically whenever you quit Word. You can record in this macro any final tasks you want to perform each time you quit Word. This macro should also be stored in the global template.

AutoOpen

If you name your macro AutoOpen, it will run automatically whenever you open an *existing* document. It does not run when you open a new document.

If you choose **In Template** when you start recording through **Tools/ Record Macro**, the macro will run only when you open a document that has the *same* document template as the document in which you recorded the macro. If you choose **As Global**, the macro will run when you open *any* document.

AutoNew

If you name your macro AutoNew, it will run whenever you open a *new* document. It does not run when you open an existing document.

If you choose **In Template** when you start recording, the macro will run only when you create a new document that has the *same* document template as the document in which you recorded the macro. If you choose **As Global**, the macro will run when you create *any* new document.

AutoClose

A macro named AutoClose will run whenever you close a document. Quitting Word or quitting Windows before closing the document will also trigger this macro.

If you choose **In Template** when you start recording, the macro will run only when you close a document that has the *same* document template as the document in which you recorded the macro. If you choose the **As Global** option, the macro will run when you close *any* document.

MODIFYING A MACRO

To modify a macro:

1. Choose **Tools/Macro**. Word will open the Macro dialog box.

2. Specify which macros you want Word to list by choosing an option in the **Show** area of the Macro dialog box.

3. Select the name of the macro from the **Macro Name:** list.

4. To edit, delete, or rename the macro, click the appropriate button.

5. To add a macro description or change the existing, enter or edit the text in the **Description:** box.

6. Click the **Close** button (which will be labeled **Cancel** if you haven't performed an operation or have only edited the description).

To modify a macro that you have recorded, choose **Tools/Macro**. Word will open the Macro dialog box, illustrated in Figure 22.3.

Once Word opens the Macro dialog box, the first step is to select the name of the desired macro from the **Macro Name:** list. Before

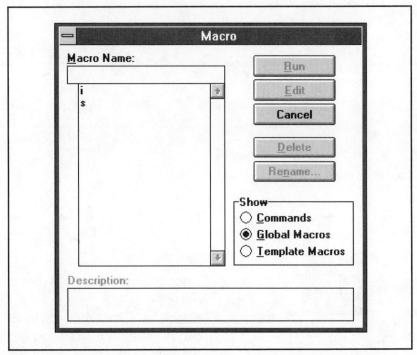

Figure 22.3: The Macro dialog box

selecting a name, however, you must make sure that the appropriate
context is selected in the **Show** area.

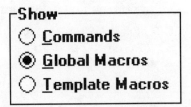

If **Global Macros** is selected, Word will display all macros that were
assigned the global context when they were recorded. If **Template
Macros** is selected, Word will show only the macros that were
assigned the Template context when they were recorded. If you select

Commands, Word will display a long list of basic Word commands, rather than macros you have defined yourself.

If you click **Edit**, Word will open a special window for editing the selected macro. (If you type a new macro name into the **Macro Name:** box before clicking the Edit button, you can write a new macro from scratch, rather than recording it). Editing or creating a macro in this window, however, requires knowledge of Word's macro programming language, WordBasic. This language allows you to include Word commands as well as control structures, and to create sophisticated macros; however, it is beyond the scope of this book. For information on using WordBasic, see the *Microsoft Word for Windows Technical Reference*. To exit the macro-editing window, click on the control box at the top right of the menu bar.

To delete the selected macro, click **Delete**. To assign the macro a new name, click **Rename** and type the new name at the prompt.

To edit the macro description, place the insertion point within the **Description:** box by clicking in this box or pressing **Alt-I**. You can modify the text using normal editing operations (the change you make will be saved even if you then click the Cancel button).

To remove the Macro/Edit dialog box, click the **Cancel** or **Close** button (the Cancel button becomes the Close button if you have deleted or renamed a macro).

If you understand WordBasic, in addition to editing and creating your own macros, you can also change the behavior of basic Word commands. Choose **Commands** in the **Show** area, select the Word command you want to modify, and click **Edit**.

RUNNING A MACRO

To run a macro, use one of the following methods:

- Press the shortcut assigned to the macro, if any.
- Choose **Tools/Macro**, select the macro, and click the **Run** button.
- If you have assigned a macro to a menu or Toolbar button (as described in Chapter 23), you can simply choose the menu item or click the button.

When you want to run a macro, simply type the shortcut key you assigned when you recorded it. If you didn't assign a shortcut key, or if you want to see a list of available macros, choose **Tools/Macro**. Word will display the Macro dialog box, shown in Figure 22.3. Type the name of the macro you want to run into the **Macro Name:** box or select the name from the list. Word displays the description (if any) of the macro in the **Description:** box.

Click **Run** when you are ready to run the macro. When you run a macro, Word performs all of the recorded actions; it does not, however, display any dialog boxes used while recording the macro, unless additional information is required through a dialog box.

You can start Word and have it automatically run a macro by including the /m flag on the command line. For example, if you have created a macro called **Initialize**, you could start Word and run this macro by using the following command line:

```
winword   /mInitialize
```

> If you have defined a macro named **AutoExec**, including the /m flag in the command line prevents this macro from running automatically upon starting Word.

> Do not insert a space character between /m and the name of the macro to execute.

RUNNING A MACRO THROUGH A MENU COMMAND OR TOOLBAR BUTTON

As you will see in Chapter 23, you can assign a macro you have created to a Word menu; the name of the macro will appear on the menu, and you can run it by simply choosing the menu item. You can also assign a macro to a button on the Toolbar. Then you can run the macro by clicking the button.

23

Customizing Word Features

CHAPTER **23**

IN THIS CHAPTER, YOU WILL LEARN HOW TO customize your working environment in Word. You will learn how to modify the Toolbar, how to add or remove commands or macros from Word menus, how to assign keystrokes to commands or macros, and how to change a wide variety of other Word features.

Keep in mind, though, that the techniques and descriptions presented throughout this book are based upon the original program options. Therefore, you might want to finish working through the book before you undertake any major modifications of the interface.

THE GENERAL METHOD

To set Word options:

1. Choose **Tools/Options**.
2. Select the desired category of options from the **Category:** list.
3. Make any desired changes in the Options dialog box.
4. Choose another category to set additional options, click OK or Close to accept all options set and close the dialog box, or click Cancel to close the dialog box without making any changes.

The following sections in this chapter discuss each of the categories in the **Category:** list. The chapter focuses on customizing the Toolbar, menus, and keyboard interface. Most of the other categories of options are discussed elsewhere in the book, and are briefly summarized here.

CUSTOMIZING THE TOOLBAR

To change a button on the Toolbar:

1. Choose the **Toolbar** category in the Options dialog box.

2. Select the global or template context from the **Context** area.

3. Specify the position on the Toolbar you want to alter by choosing the current item from the **Tool to Change:** list.

4. To assign a macro, choose **Macros** in the **Show** area and select the desired macro from the **Macros:** list.

5. To assign a Word command, choose **Commands** in the **Show** area and select the desired command from the **Commands:** list.

6. To assign a blank space, choose the **[space]** item from the **Macros:** or **Commands:** list.

7. Select the desired button from the **Button:** list (unless you are assigning a space).

8. Click the **Change** button.

Word alows you to add, remove, and change buttons on the Toolbar. You can even assign a new button to run a macro (as explained in Chapter 22) or execute a basic Word command (such as opening the Find dialog box), and you can also change commands associated with existing buttons.

To customize the Toolbar, choose the **Toolbar** icon in the **Category:** list. The Options dialog box will then appear, as shown in Figure 23.1.

Toolbar assignments are stored in a document template, not in the document itself. Therefore, any changes you make will instantly affect all documents based upon the template.

First, make sure that the desired context is selected in the **Context:** box. Select **Global** to affect all documents, or **Template** to affect only documents based upon the template that is attached to the current document.

Next, specify the position on the Toolbar you want to change by selecting an item from the **Tool to Change:** list. The Toolbar consists of a sequence of buttons and spaces.

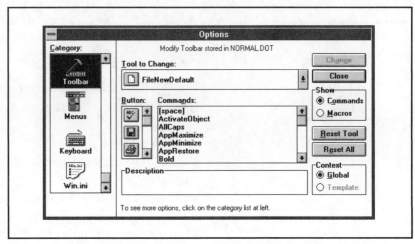

Figure 23.1: The Options dialog box with the Toolbar category selected

If the document template is the global template (NORMAL.DOT), then **Template** will not be available.

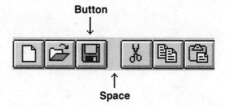

The Tool to Change list displays the buttons and spaces currently displayed on the Toolbar, in order from left to right. To change the command associated with a button, or to replace a button, select the button in the Tool to Change list.

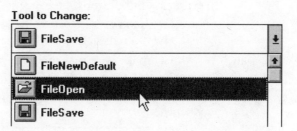

To replace a space with a button, select the space in the Tool to Change list.

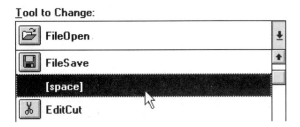

Once you have selected the desired Toolbar position, the next step is to choose the macro or command you want to assign to the position. If you want to assign a macro you have written, choose **Macros** in the **Show** area and select it from the **Macros:** list. If you want to assign a Word command, choose **Commands** in the **Show** area and select it from the **Commands:** box. If you want to assign a space to the Toolbar position, select **[space]** in the Macros or Commands list.

Notice that as you select each macro or command a description of it appears in the **Description:** box.

Next, choose the button you want to place at the designated position by selecting the button from the **Button:** list. Notice that the list contains many button styles to choose from in addition to those on the default Toolbar.

The **Reset Tool** button restores the tool that is currently selected, and **Reset All** restores *all* buttons to the initial default configuration.

When you have finished specifying the change, click **Change**, and Word will amend the toolbar. For example, the settings shown in Figure 23.2 would add a button to the right end of the Toolbar (replacing an existing space), with a macro I have named **SaveIt**. This macro saves the current position of the cursor; hence the choice of the piggy-bank icon.

You can now make additional changes to the Toolbar, choose another option category in the **Category:** list, or click the Close button to remove the Options dialog box.

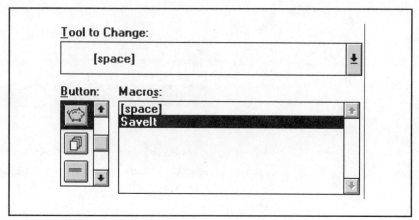

Figure 23.2: Options for adding a button to the Toolbar

MODIFYING THE MENUS

Word allows you to customize the default menus. You can customize the menus for all documents or for just a specific template. You can add a macro or standard Word command to any menu. You can also remove any of the standard menu items or change the menu text. Initially, the menus contain only a few of the many Word commands. You can display additional commands that you use frequently or remove those you seldom use. Also, adding a macro to a menu provides a convenient way to run it without having to remember the keystroke assigned to it.

To customize the menus, choose **Menus** in the **Category:** list of the Options dialog box. The Options dialog box will then appear as shown in Figure 23.3.

When you are working with a document that is not based upon the global template, menu changes applied to the document template override changes applied to the global template in the following ways:

- If you add a menu item to the global template, it will initially appear in all documents. If, however, you then explicitly remove it from a nonglobal document template (using **Delete**), it will no longer appear in any document based upon this template.

- If you remove a menu item from the global template, it will initially be removed from all documents. If, however, you

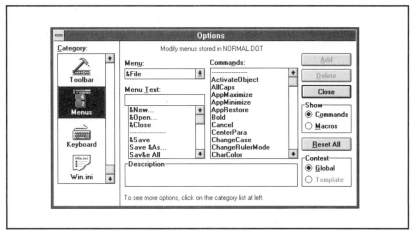

Figure 23.3: The Options dialog box with the Menus category selected

then explicitly add it back to a nonglobal document template (using **Add**), it will reappear in documents based upon this template.

ADDING A MACRO OR COMMAND TO A MENU

To add an item to a menu:

1. Select the **Menus** category in the Options dialog box.

2. Choose **Global** in the **Context** area to change *all* menus or **Template** to change only the menus for documents based upon the document template.

3. To add a macro, choose **Macros** in the **Show** area and then select the desired macro from the **Macros:** list.

4. To add a standard Word command, choose **Commands** in the **Show** area and then select the desired command from the **Commands:** list.

5. From the **Menu:** list, select the menu you want to alter.

6. If desired, edit the menu text in the **Menu Text:** box.

7. Click the **Add** button.

If the docu-
ment template is
the global template
(NORMAL.DOT),
then **Template** will not
be available.

First, select the appropriate option from the **Context** area. Choosing **Global** will add the item to the menu for any document. If the document template is not the global template, you can choose **Template**; in this case, the item will appear on the menu only when you are working with a document based upon the same template as the current document.

Next, to add a macro to a menu, choose **Macros** in the **Show** area and select the name of the macro from the **Macros:** list. To add a standard Word command to a menu, choose **Commands** in the **Show** area and select the name of the command from the **Commands:** list box. When you select a particular macro or command, a description (if available) appears in the **Description** area at the bottom of the dialog box. Notice that the first item in the list is a horizontal line, called a *separator*. This item is not an actual command or macro; rather, selecting it allows you to insert a horizontal line after the last menu item. Thus, you can separate existing menu items from those you subsequently add.

Then, choose the Word menu where you want to place the new command. Select the name of the desired menu from the **Menu:** list.

The **Menu Text:** box contains the actual text that will be displayed on the menu. When you select the name of a command or macro from the Commands or Macros list, Word automatically enters this name into the Menu Text box. If you want to change the text of the menu item, edit the contents of this box.

In the Menu Text box, the ampersand character (**&**) is not actually printed as part of the menu text. Rather, it underlines the following character. For example, typing the text

Menu Text:

&Spike

would result in the menu item

Spike   Ctrl+F3

with S underlined. Underline only one character in the text of the menu item. Then, when the menu with the item is open, you can choose the item by pressing the underlined character. If, however, two or more items on a given menu have the same underlined character, pressing the character will not choose either of the items; rather, it will move the highlight to the *next* item with the character. To choose the item, you must press Enter. Therefore, assign each menu item a unique underlined character.

Click **Add** to complete the menu assignment. You can then make additional menu changes, choose another option category, or click **Close** to remove the Options dialog box.

The command or macro will generally be added to the end of the specified menu, with two exceptions: first, it will go *before* a list of files at the end of the File or Window menu; second, if you reinstate a standard menu item, it is placed in its former location.

REMOVING OR MODIFYING A MENU COMMAND

To remove or change the text for a menu item:

1. Select the **Menus** category in the Options dialog box.
2. Choose **Global** in the **Context** area to affect all menus or **Template** to affect only the menus for documents based upon the document template.
3. Select a menu from the **Menu:** list.
4. Select a menu item from the **Menu Text:** list.
5. To remove the item, click **Delete**.
6. To change the text displayed on the menu, edit the contents of the **Menu Text:** box, and **Add**.

If you want to change the command or macro that is executed by a menu item, you must first remove the item, and then add a replacement menu item, which executes the desired command or macro, as described in the previous section.

You can remove or modify any item on a Word menu. First, in the **Context** area, choose **Global** to remove or modify an item on all menus or **Template** affect only menus for documents based upon the same template as the current document.

Next, in the **Menu:** list, select the Word menu containing the item you want to remove or change. Word will now list all items on this menu in the **Menu Text:** list. Select the desired item from this list.

To remove the item from the menu, click **Delete**. To change the text displayed on the menu item, edit the contents of the Menu Text box. To accept your changes, click **Add**.

If the docu-
ment template is
the global template
(NORMAL.DOT),
then **Template** will not
be available.

RESTORING THE DEFAULT MENUS

After you have made one or more changes to Word menus, you
can *restore* the default Word menus by following these steps:

1. Choose **Global** to restore all menus or **Template** to restore
   menus only for documents based upon the same template as
   the current document.

2. Click **Reset All**.

CHANGING THE KEYBOARD INTERFACE

Word also allows you to customize the key combinations used to
issue standard Word commands or macros. You can perform the following basic operations:

- Assign a keystroke to a specific command or macro. Once
  you have made this assignment, pressing the keystroke will
  execute the command or run the macro.

- Remove a keystroke assignment from a command or macro.
  Once you have removed the assignment, pressing the keystroke will no longer execute the command or macro.

- Restore the default keyboard assignments. This will eliminate any keyboard changes you have made.

You can employ these operations, for example, to assign a convenient
keystroke to a Word command that you use frequently. Also, you might
want to change the shortcut key for a macro you have created (or assign
a keystroke if you did not do so when recording it).

To perform one of these operations, select the **Keyboard** icon in the
Category: list of the Options dialog box. The Options dialog box will
then appear as shown in Figure 23.4.

The next step is to choose the context for the change. Choosing
Global in the **Context** area will affect the keyboard configuration
for all documents. Choosing **Template** will only affect the keyboard

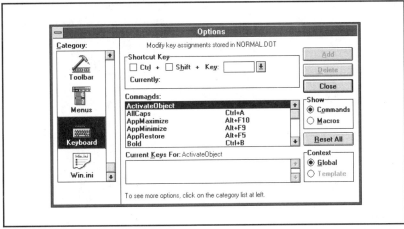

Figure 23.4: The Options dialog box with the Keyboard category selected

You can print a list of current keyboard assignments by choosing **File/Print** and selecting the **Key Assignments** item from the **Print:** pull-down list. You will obtain a list of key assignments you've made, not including Word's default key assignments.

configuration for those documents based upon the template that you have changed.

ASSIGNING A KEYSTROKE TO A COMMAND OR MACRO

To assign a keystroke:

1. Select the **Keyboard** category in the Options dialog box.

2. Choose **Global** in the **Context** area to affect all menus or **Template** to affect only the menus for documents based upon the document template.

3. To assign a keystroke to a macro, choose **Macros** in the **Show** area and then select one from the **Macros:** list.

4. To assign a keystroke to a Word command, choose **Commands** in the **Show** area and then select one from the **Commands:** list.

5. Specify the desired keystroke using the options in the **Shortcut Key** area.

6. Click **Add**.

Several different keystrokes may be assigned to a single command or macro, providing alternative methods for running it. Of course, a given keystroke may be assigned to only a single command or macro.

To assign a keystroke to a macro, choose **Macros** in the **Show** area and select one from the **Macros:** list. To assign a keystroke to a built-in Word command, choose **Commands** and select one from the **Commands:** list. Word will display all of the keystrokes currently assigned to the selected command in the **Current Keys For:** list at the bottom of the Options dialog box.

To specify the keystroke you want to assign, first choose one of the keys from the **Key:** list box in the **Shortcut Key** area.

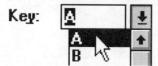

You can also select **Ctrl**, **Shift**, or both, to include them in the keystroke. For example, if you make the following selections,

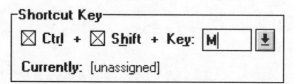

the selected macro will run when you press **Ctrl-Shift-M**.

If the keystroke you designate is already assigned, Word will indicate this assignment following the **Currently:** label; if you accept the keystroke, Word will reassign your new keystroke to the selected macro or command. If the keystroke is currently unassigned, Word will display **[unassigned]** following this label. If you choose both the Ctrl and the Shift options, your chances of finding an unassigned keystroke are much better. If you select a letter key, such as **N**, in the Key: box, you must choose the Ctrl option.

To assign the keystroke, click the **Add** button. The specified keystroke will be assigned to the command and will appear in the **Current Keys For:** box.

You can now make continue to work with keyboard assignments, choose another options category, or click the Close button to remove the Options dialog box.

Once you have completed these steps, pressing the assigned keystroke will execute the designated command or macro. When you quit the program or choose **File/Save All**, Word will prompt you to save any changes to the appropriate template file.

REMOVING A KEYSTROKE ASSIGNMENT

To remove a keystroke assignment while the Options dialog box displays the keyboard options, do the following:

Word has preassigned Alt-key combinations to certain commands. You cannot remove these preassigned Alt-key keystrokes from commands.

1. Select the command or macro from the **Commands:** or **Macros:** list as described in the previous section. A list of all keystrokes currently assigned will appear in the **Current Keys For:** list.

2. Select the keystroke you want to remove from the **Current Keys For:** list.

3. Click **Delete**.

RESTORING THE ORIGINAL KEYBOARD ASSIGNMENTS

Be careful using **Reset All**, since it will remove all keyboard assignments you have made.

To restore all keyboard assignments to the default values, click **Reset All**. Word will immediately restore all original keyboard assignments within the global template (if **Global** is selected) or in the document template (if **Template** is selected). Word will remove all keystrokes that you have assigned. Word will warn you before actually resetting the keyboard assignments, giving you the opportunity to cancel the operation.

SETTING OTHER OPTIONS

There is no **Reset All** option to restore the default settings.

This section will briefly summarize the other categories of options you can select through **Tools/Options**. Most of them are set through check boxes, with an occasional text box (for entering a numeric value or text) or list (for selecting an item). The illustrations in this section show Word's initial default settings.

SETTING THE VIEW OPTIONS

The view options affect the way Word displays your documents. To set these options, select the **View** icon in the **Category:** list of the Options dialog box. The view options are illustrated in Figure 23.5.

Window Options

OPTION	EFFECT
Horizontal Scroll Bar	Displays the horizontal scroll bar.
Vertical Scroll Bar	Displays the vertical scroll bar.
Status Bar	Displays the status bar at the bottom of the window.
Style Area Width	Entering a nonzero measurement displays a style area having the specified width (see Chapter 20).

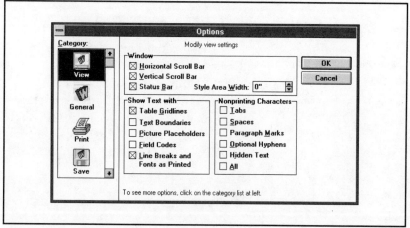

Figure 23.5: The Options dialog box with the View category selected

Show Text with Options

OPTION	EFFECT
Table Gridlines	Displays a box around each cell in a table (these lines do not print; see Chapter 8).
Text Boundaries	Marks all margins, headers, footers, and framed paragraphs in Page Layout view (see Chapter 17), to make these objects easier to identify.
Picture Placeholders	Displays empty rectangles on the screen in place of all pictures, to make scrolling faster (see Chapter 9).
Field Codes	Displays field instructions rather than the results of fields. For example, Word would display {TOC} rather than an actual table of contents.
Line Breaks and Fonts as Printed	Displays line breaks at the same positions where they will occur on the printed page; also, displays the fonts that will actually be used to print the document.

Nonprinting Characters Options

OPTION	EFFECT
Tabs	Displays tabs as right arrows (see Chapter 3).
Spaces	Displays normal spaces as small centered dots, and nonbreaking spaces as degree symbols (see Chapter 3).
Paragraph Marks	Displays paragraph marks, newline characters (Chapter 3), and end-of-cell marks in tables (Chapter 8).
Optional Hyphens	Toggles the display of nonbreaking hyphens (as a special character) and optional hyphens (see Chapter 17).

OPTION	EFFECT
Hidden Text	Displays characters formatted as hidden text with a dotted underline (see Chapter 16).
All	Displays *all* of the nonprinting characters listed above.

SETTING THE GENERAL OPTIONS

The general options affect the way you enter and edit text in Word. To set these options, select the **General** icon in the **Category:** list of the Options dialog box. The general options are illustrated in Figure 23.6.

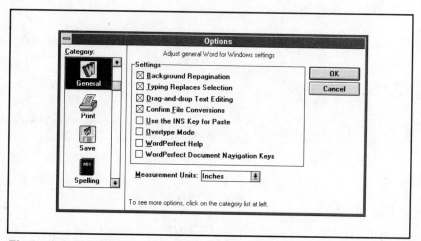

Figure 23.6: The Options dialog box with the General category selected

Settings Options

OPTION	EFFECT
Background Repagination	Updates the positions of page breaks in the document whenever the program is not carrying out another command. If you disable this option, you can repaginate whenever required by choosing **Tools/Repaginate Now** (see Chapter 3).

OPTION	EFFECT
Typing Replaces Selection	Erases selected text or graphics when you type a key or issue the paste command (see Chapter 3).
Drag-and-drop Text Editing	Enables the drag-and-drop methods for copying, moving, and linking selections with the mouse (see Chapter 5).
Confirm File Conversions	Allows you to specify the format of a file you are opening that is not in standard Word-document format.
Use the INS key for Paste	Pressing the Insert key will paste the contents of the Clipboard.
Overtype Mode	Word will initially be in overwrite mode (as described in Chapter 3); you can still toggle this mode off and on by pressing the Ins key (unless the **Use the INS key for Paste** option has been enabled).
WordPerfect Help	Allows you to use WordPerfect keys to issue commands and learn how to perform the operations using Word commands.
WordPerfect Document Navigation Keys	Permits you to navigate through your document using WordPerfect keystrokes.
Measurement Units	Select the default unit of measurement used in Word (see Appendix C).

HELP FOR WORDPERFECT USERS

WordPerfect Help caters to WordPerfect users by allowing them to use standard WordPerfect keystrokes to execute equivalent tasks in Word. WordPerfect users can also gradually accustom themselves to the Word interface by using WordPerfect keystrokes and viewing the WordPerfect help that Word generates to show them how to perform those tasks using Word commands.

To access WordPerfect help, choose **Help/WordPerfect Help**. Word will display the Help for WordPerfect Users dialog box, shown in Figure 23.7. There are several different ways you can use this dialog box.

First, you can select a WordPerfect command from the **Command Key:** list. As soon as you select a command, Word displays a brief description of the method for accomplishing the task using standard *Word* commands. For example, Figure 23.8 illustrates the information displayed if you select the **Bold** command in the Command Key list. (If you want more detailed information, click **Word Help**, which activates the standard Word help facility). Next, choose **Help Text** in the **Help Options** area to display instructions or **Demo** to have Word automatically perform the task on your document. Then, click OK; Word will remove the dialog box and execute your command.

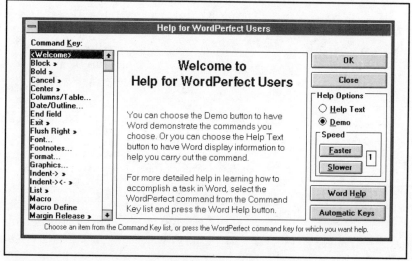

Figure 23.7: The Help for WordPerfect Users dialog box

Second, you can simply press a WordPerfect keystroke while the dialog box is open. Word will immediately remove the dialog box and either display instructions (if you have chosen the **Help Text** option) or automatically execute the command (if you have chosen **Demo**). For example, if you press **F6** (the WordPerfect keystroke for bold), Word will remove the dialog box and either display information on

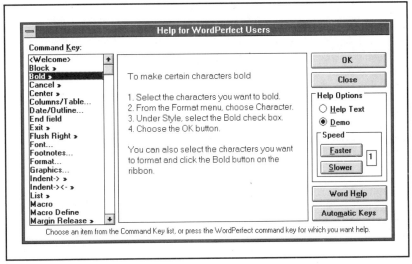

Figure 23.8: Information displayed on the Bold command

When you activate automatic WordPerfect help or WordPerfect navigation keys, the normal functioning of these keystrokes within Word is disabled; you will not be able to use these keystrokes as described in this book until you deactivate these features.

Word's bold commands or automatically apply the bold format. (You can adjust the speed at which Demo operates by clicking the **Faster** and **Slower** buttons).

The third way you can use the dialog box is to click **Automatic Keys**. Then, after you click OK or Close to return to your document, Word will *automatically* invoke WordPerfect help (either HelpText of Demo) whenever you issue a WordPerfect keystroke. Choosing **Demo** and clicking **Automatic Keys** in the Help for WordPerfect Users dialog box effectively remaps the Word keyboard interface to match that of WordPerfect. It will remain this way until you disable Automatic Keys.

Automatic Keys also enables WordPerfect navigation keys. For example, if you are working on a document and press Home and then up arrow, Word will move the insertion point to the top of the window as in WordPerfect; pressing these keys in Word moves the cursor to the beginning of the line above. Note that Word always carries out a navigation keystroke; it does *not* display information, even if you have selected **Help Text** in the Help for WordPerfect Users dialog box.

To disable automatic help and navigation keys for WordPerfect, choose **Help/WordPerfect Help** and click **Disable Automatic**.

Although you can enable automatic WordPerfect help through the **WordPerfect Help** option of the **Tools/Options** command, you must issue the **Help/WordPerfect Help** command to control whether Word carries out actions or merely displays help information in response to WordPerfect keystrokes.

Alternatively, you can enable or disable WordPerfect automatic help or navigation keys using the following method: Choose **Tools/Options**, and select the **General** category, as described in the previous section. Turn automatic help on or off by clicking **WordPerfect Help**. Turn the navigation key feature on or off by clicking **WordPerfect Document Navigation Keys**.

SETTING THE PRINT OPTIONS

The print options control the way Word prints your documents. To set these options, select the **Print** icon in the **Category:** list of the Options dialog box. The print options are illustrated in Figure 23.9. See Chapter 17 for more information on printing.

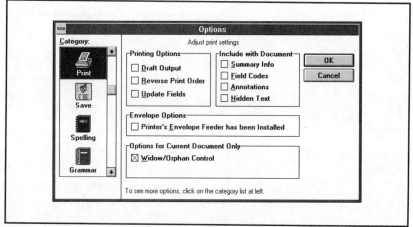

Figure 23.9: The Options dialog box with the Print category selected

Printing Options

OPTION	EFFECT
Draft Output	Prints using a single font and indicates character formatting with underline text; also, it will print pictures as empty rectangles.

OPTION	*EFFECT*
Reverse Print Order	Prints the pages of a document from last to first; this option is useful for older laser printers that stack paper in reverse order.
Update Fields	Updates all fields (such as a table of contents or date) immediately before printing the document.

Include with Document Options

OPTION	*EFFECT*
Summary Info	Word will print the document's summary information on a separate page (see Chapter 26).
Field Codes	Word will print field instructions rather than the results of fields. For example, Word would print {TOC} rather than an actual table of contents.
Annotations	Word will print annotations at the end of the document, after starting a new page (see Chapter 25). Selecting this option automatically enables **Hidden Text** because annotations are formatted as hidden text.
Hidden Text	Word will print characters formatted as hidden text (see Chapter 16).

Envelope Options

OPTION	*EFFECT*
Printer's Envelope Feeder has been Installed	Word will use the printer's envelope feeder when printing envelopes through **Tools/Create Envelope**.

Options for Current Document Only

OPTION	EFFECT
Window/ Orphan Control	Word will not insert a page break between a single line at the beginning or end of a paragraph.

SETTING THE SAVE OPTIONS

The save options determine the way Word saves documents on disk. To set these options, select the **Save** icon in the **Category:** list of the Options dialog box. The save options are illustrated in Figure 23.10. See Chapter 3 for information on saving documents.

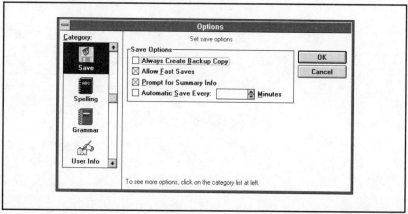

Figure 23.10: The Options dialog box with the Save category selected

Save Options

OPTION	EFFECT
Always Create Backup Copy	When you save a document on disk, Word will preserve the previous saved version of the document, assigning it the same name as the current version, but with the .BAK extension. Selecting this option prevents you from selecting **Allow Fast Saves**.

OPTION	EFFECT
Allow Fast Saves	Word will save the document on disk in a format that is bulkier but that permits faster saving.
Prompt for Summary Info	The first time you save a new document, Word will automatically prompt you for document-summary information (see Chapter 26).
Automatic Save Every:	Word will periodically save your document. Enter into the box the desired number of minutes between saves.

SETTING THE SPELLING OPTIONS

The spelling options control the way **Tools/Spelling** checks spelling. To set these options, select the **Spelling** icon in the **Category:** list of the Options dialog box. These options are illustrated in Figure 23.11. See Chapter 7 for a full explanation.

Ignore Options

OPTION	EFFECT
Words in UPPERCASE	The spelling checker will ignore words in all capital letters (it will, however, check text formatted with **All Caps** or **Small Caps**).
Words with Numbers	The spelling checker will ignore *all* words that combine letters and numbers (the checker always ignores words consisting of numbers and a single letter, such as **20A**, whether or not this option is enabled).

Custom Dictionaries Option

This list allows you to select the custom dictionary or dictionaries that Word will use when checking the spelling in your document.

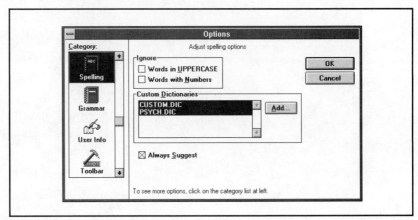

Figure 23.11: The Options dialog box with the Spelling category selected

Always Suggest Option

Selecting this option provides a list of alternative spellings when it encounters an unknown word. If the option is not selected, you must click the **Suggest** in the Spelling dialog box to obtain this list.

SETTING THE GRAMMAR OPTIONS

The grammar options control the behavior of the **Tools/Grammar** command. To set these options, select the **Grammar** icon in the **Category:** list of the Options dialog box. These options are illustrated in Figure 23.12. See Chapter 7 for a full explanation.

Use Grammar and Style Rules Options

OPTION	EFFECT
Strictly (All Rules)	Word will enforce *all* grammar and style rules.
For Business Writing	Word will not enforce all of its rules; rather, it will apply a set of rules more appropriate for business writing.
For Casual Writing	Word will enforce even fewer rules; it will use a set of rules appropriate for informal writing.

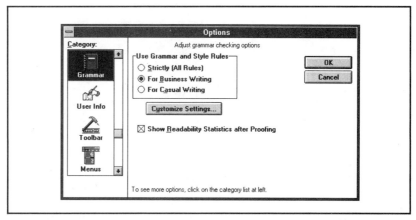

Figure 23.12: The Options dialog box with the Grammar category selected

Customize Settings Button

Click this button to open a dialog box for setting the exact set of grammar and style rules that the grammar checker employs.

Show Readability Statistics after Proofing Option

If you enable this option, the grammar checker will display statistics on the overall readability of your document (after it completes the spelling check).

SETTING THE USER INFO OPTIONS

The user info options supply data on the user of the program. To set these options, select the **User Info** icon in the **Category:** list of the Options dialog box. These options are illustrated in Figure 23.13.

Name: Box

This box shows the user's name. This name is automatically inserted into the **Author** field of the document-summary information (see Chapter 26). It is also used to determine access to locked documents (see Chapter 3).

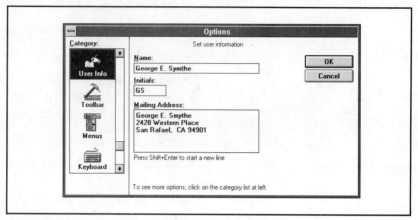

Figure 23.13: The Options dialog box with the User Info category selected

Initials: Box

The initials entered into this box are used to identify annotations.
See Chapter 25.

Mailing Address: Box

Tools/Create Envelope uses the address entered here for printing
return addresses. You can modify it here or in the Create Envelope
dialog box. See Chapter 17.

SETTING THE WIN.INI OPTIONS

The Win.ini options change the information Word stores in the
Windows initialization file, WIN.INI. To set these options, select
the **Win.ini** icon in the **Category:** list of the Options dialog box. These
options are illustrated in Figure 23.14.

For information on making changes to the WIN.INI file, see the
Microsoft Word User's Guide.

Application: List Box

Select from this list the section of the WIN.INI where you want to
make changes.

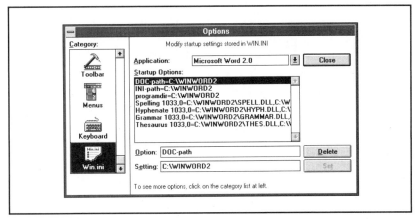

Figure 23.14: The Options dialog box with the Win.ini category selected

Startup Options: List Box

Select from this list the specific line of initialization information you want to change. Each line contains an option, followed by an = sign, followed by a setting for the option.

Option: Box

Displays the option selected in the **Startup Options:** list.

Setting: Box

In this box, you can edit the setting for the option selected in the **Startup Options:** list.

Part
V

Working with Multiple or Complex Projects

Now that you have learned basic editing and formatting techniques, as well as how to use the time-saving features that can be incorporated into document templates, this part of the book presents techniques that will assist you with more complex and larger-scale projects.

In Chapter 24, you will learn how to use Word's outline view to make large documents more manageable. In Chapter 25, you will learn how to add annotations and mark revisions—two features that help you keep track of changes to a document, and make it easier for several people to work on the same document. In Chapter 26, you will learn how to manage collections of documents. Finally, in Chapter 27, you will learn how to use Object Linking and Embedding (OLE) to incorporate elements from other Windows applications into your document.

24

Outlining Your Documents

WORD'S OUTLINE VIEW CAN HELP YOU CREATE AND organize a document. Outline view provides you with an overview of the structure of the document. You can vary the amount of document detail that is shown, and you can quickly rearrange large blocks of text within the document. You can also use outline view to quickly find particular topics within a large document.

When you use outline view, the outline is not separate from the document. Rather, outline view is merely a unique way of looking at and working with the document. Any changes made in outline view are reflected in all other document views, since they are changes made to the document itself.

In this chapter, you will learn how to examine and organize your document in outline view, how to have Word automatically number your outline headings, and how to create a table of contents directly from outline headings.

WORKING WITH OUTLINE VIEW

To view a document as an outline:

1. Either create a new document, or open an existing one.

2. Choose **View/Outline**.

3. Organize the document by converting body text to outline headings, by converting headings to body text, or by promoting or demoting the level of headings, as described later in the chapter.

4. To switch out of outline view, choose either View/Normal or **View/Page Layout**.

To switch into outline view, choose **View/Outline**. To turn off outline view, choose either the **View/Normal** command to switch into Normal view, or the **View/Page Layout** command to switch into Page Layout view. Figure 24.1 illustrates a short document in outline view. Notice that Word displays a row of buttons at the top of the window. This is the *outline tool bar;* the use of each of the buttons in this bar is discussed later in the section.

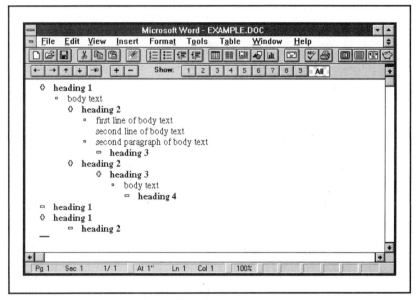

Figure 24.1: A document in outline view

You can change the formatting features of a particular heading level by redefining the corresponding standard style (**heading 1**, **heading 2**, and so on). You cannot, however, change the amount a heading is indented in outline view, since this feature is determined by the heading level alone.

A document in outline view has two types of paragraphs: *outline headings* and *body text.*

An outline heading is a paragraph that has been assigned a specific type of standard style; the style determines the heading level. A top-level heading is assigned the **heading 1** standard style, a second level heading is assigned the **heading 2** style, and so on. The style for the lowest possible heading level is **heading 9**. In outline view, a top-level heading is aligned with the left margin; levels 2 through 9, however, are successively indented, so that each heading level is placed farther to the right than the preceding heading level. In other document views, the indent of a heading depends upon its paragraph formatting.

A paragraph of body text within an outline is one that has *not* been assigned an outline heading style (that is, a paragraph assigned a style other than **heading 1**, **heading 2**, and so on).

The term *subtext* refers to all subordinate headings (headings at lower levels), plus all body text, that immediately follow an outline heading. For example, in Figure 24.1, the subtext belonging to the first top-level heading consists of five subordinate headings and four paragraphs of body text—that is, everything up to the next heading at the same level. The second top-level heading has no subtext.

Notice also in Figure 24.1 that Word marks all headings that have subtext with a large plus icon, all headings without subtext with a large minus icon, and all paragraphs of body text with a small square icon. These icons are called *paragraph icons*. Later in the chapter, you will see several ways that you can manipulate a paragraph by using the mouse in conjunction with the paragraph icon.

You can create a new document in outline view, or you can work with an existing document in this view. If you open a new document and then immediately switch into outline view, the document will consist of a single top-level heading containing the insertion point. Each time you press Enter, Word will insert another top-level heading beneath the one containing the insertion point, and it will move the insertion point to the beginning of this heading (in the same manner that Word inserts new paragraphs when you type text into a document in other views).

If you have already created a document in another view, and then switch into outline view, the document will initially consist of only body text (unless you have previously applied a heading style to one or more paragraphs).

In this section, you will learn the following techniques:

- How to select text in outline view.

- How to promote or demote outline text; that is, how to change the level of a heading or convert between a heading and body text.

- How to collapse or expand an outline heading; that is, how to hide or reveal various amounts of subtext belonging to a heading.

- How to quickly move a heading—together with varying amounts of its subtext—within the document.

- How to use outline view to rapidly find a topic within a document.

You will learn both mouse and keyboard methods for each of these operations. The keyboard methods are sometimes more efficient, and some of them can be used to manage outline headings when you are not in outline view.

SELECTING IN OUTLINE VIEW

The first step in performing many of the operations discussed in this chapter is to select the appropriate text within the outline. In general, you can use any of the basic selection methods discussed in Chapter 5. The following, however, are some unique features of selecting when in outline view:

 Notice that when the mouse pointer is on top of the paragraph icon, it becomes a four-pointed arrow.

- You can select a heading together with all of its subtext (whether expanded or collapsed) by clicking the paragraph icon or by double-clicking in the selection bar next to the paragraph.

- You can select one or more characters within a paragraph using a standard selection method (for example, by pressing an arrow key while holding down Shift). However, as soon as you extend the selection past a paragraph boundary, both adjoining paragraphs are selected.

PROMOTING AND DEMOTING OUTLINE TEXT

FAST TRACK

To change the level of the selected heading or body text, use one of the following methods:

- To promote the selection click the **left-arrow** button on the outline toolbar or press **Alt-Shift-Left-arrow**.

- To demote the selection, click the right-arrow button or press **Alt-Shift-right-arrow**.

■ Drag the paragraph icon to the left or to the right to promote or demote a single paragraph.

Using promoting and demoting techniques, you can change the level of a heading, convert body text to a heading, or convert a heading to body text.

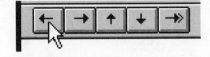 Notice that a *higher* heading level has a *smaller* number.

The first step is to select the block of text in the outline that you want to promote or demote. You can select one or more headings or paragraphs of body text. To promote or demote a single heading or paragraph of body text, simply place the insertion point anywhere within the paragraph.

When you promote a heading (level 2 through level 9), it is assigned the next higher level. It is also moved to the left, together with any body text that immediately follows it (whether or not the body text is included in the selection). For example, a level 3 heading (assigned the style **heading 3**) becomes a level 2 heading (it is reassigned the style **heading 2**).

Demoting a heading (level 1 through level 8) has the opposite effect. The heading is assigned the next lower level and is indented farther to the right, together with any body text that immediately follows it.

If you promote a paragraph of body text, it is converted to a heading having the same level as the heading immediately above it. If you demote a paragraph of body text, it is converted to a heading that is one level lower than the heading immediately above it.

Note, however, that to convert body text to a heading, the selection *cannot* contain a heading; if the selection contains a heading, body text can be moved, but it remains body text.

Once you have selected the desired block, you can use any of the following methods to promote or demote the selection:

• Use the buttons on the outline toolbar. To promote the selection, click the **left-arrow button** on the outline toolbar.

- To demote the selection, click the **right-arrow button** on the outline toolbar.

- Press **Alt-Shift-left-arrow** to promote the selection, or press **Alt-Shift-right-arrow** to demote it.

- To promote a heading together with all of its subtext, drag the paragraph icon (the hollow plus sign preceding the heading level) to the left.

- To demote a heading and its subtext, drag the paragraph icon to the right. Notice that as soon as you click on a paragraph icon, Word automatically selects the heading together with all of its subtext. You therefore cannot use this method to promote or demote multiple headings or a heading without all of its subtext.

- To promote or demote a heading or body text, you can simply assign it the desired style, using any of the methods described in Chapter 20. For example, to demote a top-level heading one level, you can assign it the **heading 2** style.

As you have seen, you can convert body text to a heading by simply promoting or demoting it. To convert a selected heading to a body text, you can use one of the following methods:

- Click the **double-right-arrow button** within the outline toolbar.

- Press **Alt-Shift-5** (the 5 must be on the numeric keypad, and Num Lock must be off).

- Assign the heading the **Normal** style, or some style other than **heading 1** through **heading 9**.

COLLAPSING AND EXPANDING HEADINGS

To collapse or expand the outline, use one of the following methods:

- To collapse or expand the selected heading(s) by one level, click the − or + button on the outline toolbar.

- To collapse or expand the selected heading(s) by one level, press the − or + key on the numeric keypad.

- To collapse or expand the entire outline to a particular level of heading, click one of the numeric buttons on the outline tool bar to indicate the desired level.

- To expand the entire outline completely, click the **All** button on the outline toolbar. Click this button again to collapse the outline to level 9.

- To show only the first line of each paragraph of body text, press **Alt-Shift-F**. Press this key again to show all lines of body text.

To *collapse* a heading means to hide some or all of the subtext belonging to the heading. To *expand* a heading means to make visible subtext that was previously hidden. You can collapse and expand individual headings, or headings throughout the entire document.

Collapsing and Expanding Individual Headings

To collapse one or more headings, perform the following steps:

Rather than selecting a single heading, you can simply place the insertion point within it.

1. Select the desired heading or headings.

2. Click the − button on the outline toolbar,

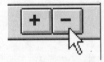

press the minus key (−) on the numeric keypad, or press **Alt-Shift-minus** (using the minus key above the letter keys, *not* the one on the keypad).

Notice that Word partially underlines a heading that is partly or fully collapsed, to let you know that the heading has hidden subtext.

Word will collapse the heading by one level; that is, it will hide the lowest-level subordinate heading that is currently visible. Note that body text is considered to be at a lower level than a level 9 heading. For instance, if the heading is fully expanded and includes body text, the first time you perform this step, all body text under the heading or under any of its subordinate headings is hidden.

3. Repeat step 2 for each additional level you want to collapse. If you continue to collapse levels, eventually only the heading itself will be visible.

Alternatively, you can double-click the paragraph icon next to the heading. If the heading is fully expanded, Word will completely collapse it (that is, it will hide all its subtext). If, however, it is partially or fully collapsed, Word will fully expand it.

To expand one or more headings, perform the following steps:

Rather than selecting a single heading, you can simply place the insertion point within it.

1. Select the desired heading or headings.

2. Click the + button on the outline toolbar, press the plus key (+) on the numeric keypad, or press **Alt-Shift-plus** (using the plus key above the letter keys, *not* the one on the keypad).

    Word will expand the heading by one level; that is, it will reveal the highest level of subtext that was previously hidden. For example, if a level 2 heading is completely collapsed, performing this step will display all level 3 subordinate headings that belong to it.

3. Repeat step 2 for each additional level you want to expand. If you continue to expand levels, eventually all subtext will be visible.

Alternatively, if the heading is fully or partially collapsed, you can fully expand it by double-clicking the paragraph icon belonging to the heading.

Collapsing and Expanding the Entire Outline

By clicking the appropriate numbered button on the outline toolbar, you can collapse or expand headings throughout the entire outline.

If you click the button numbered 1, Word will display only top-level headings; all headings with levels 2 through 9, as well as all body text, will be hidden. If you click the button numbered 2, Word will display all headings with levels 1 or 2, and everything will be hidden; if you click the button numbered 3, Word will display all headings with levels 1, 2, or 3; and so on. Clicking the button numbered 9 will reveal all headings, but no body text. Finally, clicking the **All** button will cause Word to display *all* headings and all body text (that is, the entire outline will become visible). Clicking the All button again causes Word to display headings through level 9 (as if you had clicked the button labeled 9). In other words, the All button toggles the outline between the completely expanded view and the level 9 view.

Rather than clicking a numbered button, you can press the Alt-Shift-*number* combination, where *number* is a number between 1 and 9 indicating the heading levels you want visible. You must press a number key on the top row of the keyboard, rather than a number key on the numeric keypad. For example, pressing **Alt-Shift-3** is the same as clicking the button numbered 3. Also, pressing **Alt-Shift-A**, or simply pressing the * key on the numeric keypad, is the same as clicking the All button.

Unless body text is already visible, you will not immediately see the effect of pressing **Alt-Shift-F**.

Finally, if you press **Alt-Shift-F**, Word will display *only the first line* of each paragraph of body text throughout the outline. Word indicates the presence of the hidden lines of body text by terminating each first line with an ellipsis (...). Pressing **Alt-Shift-F** again causes Word to display all lines of body text.

MOVING A HEADING AND ITS SUBTEXT

In outline view, you can easily move any of the following objects:

- A heading
- A heading together with some or all of its subtext
- Several headings, together with their subtext
- One or more paragraphs of body text

By moving headings together with their subtext, you can quickly rearrange a document.

The first step is to select the outline text you want to move. To move a single heading or paragraph of body text, you can simply place the insertion point anywhere within the paragraph. If you select a heading without its subtext, Word will move the heading, but will leave the subtext in its current position. If, however, a heading is completely collapsed, Word will always move both the heading and all of its subtext.

You can now use one of the following methods:

- Click the **up-arrow button** on the outline toolbar to move the selection up in the outline.

- Click the **down-arrow button** on the outline toolbar to move the selection down in the outline.

- Press **Alt-Shift-up-arrow** to move the selection up, or **Alt-Shift-down-arrow** to move it down.

- Drag a paragraph icon either up or down. Using this method, you can move only a single paragraph of body text, or a heading together with all of its subtext.

USING OUTLINE VIEW TO FIND TOPICS

If your document contains outline headings, you can use outline view to help you find a specific topic.

1. Choose **View/Outline** to switch to outline view.

2. Collapse the outline so that only the desired level of headings is shown.

3. Scroll through the document to find the desired topic. You can scroll quickly, since only the headings are displayed.

4. When you find the desired location in the document, place the insertion point at this position.

5. Switch out of outline view. Word will display the beginning of the document.

6. Press **Shift-F5** to scroll instantly to the position of the insertion point.

Alternatively, you can locate a desired position in your document by activating outline view in a separate window pane. Use the following steps:

See Chapter 26 for more information on working with split windows.

1. While working on a document in normal editing view, divide the window into two panes by dragging the split bar down to the approximate center of the screen.

2. Activate outline view in the pane containing the insertion point by choosing **View/Outline**. Notice that the *other* pane remains in normal editing view.

3. Collapse the outline to the desired level of headings.

4. Scroll through the outline to find the desired topic. Notice that the other pane (in normal editing view) automatically scrolls to the same position in the document viewed through the pane in outline view.

5. Once you have found the desired topic, you can remove the outline pane, if desired, by dragging the split bar all the way to the top of the window (if the outline pane is on top), or to the bottom of the window (if the outline pane is on the bottom).

NUMBERING OUTLINE HEADINGS

FAST TRACK

To number outline headings:

1. Expand or collapse the headings to reveal the level of headings you want to number.

2. Select the group of headings you want to number.

3. Choose **Tools/Bullets and Numbers**.

4. Select the desired numbering format, starting number, and indent.

5. Click OK.

Word will number only paragraphs that are currently displayed.

You can have Word automatically number the headings within your outline. You should first collapse or expand the headings within your document to reveal the portions of the outline that you want to number. Next, select the headings within your document that you want to number (if there is no selection, Word will number only the paragraph containing the insertion point). If the selection contains only headings, or both headings and body text, Word will number only the headings. If, however, the selection contains only body text, Word will number each selected body text paragraph.

Once you have selected the desired portion of the document, choose **Tools/Bullets and Numbering**. Word will display the Bullets and Numbering dialog box. Select the **Outline** option at the top of the dialog box.

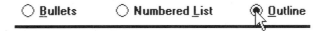

The Bullets and Numbering dialog will then appear as shown in Figure 24.2.

First, select the desired numbering style from the **Format:** list. Notice that when you select a style, Word illustrates the style in the **Sample** box. If you select **Learn by Example**, Word will model the numbering style after any numbers already contained within the outline.

Choose the **Auto Update** option if you want Word to automatically maintain the outline numbers in the correct sequence as you add, delete, or move outline headings. (If, however, you insert a new paragraph, it is not automatically numbered; you have to issue the Tools/Bullets and Numbering command again.) Automatic numbering always begins with 1 or A; you cannot control the starting number. Also, you can have only one sequence of numbers in a document (for example, you could not number top-level headings 1, 2, 3, and so on in more than one location in the document).

If you do *not* select the Auto Update option, Word will insert numbers that must be manually updated. If you delete, insert, or rearrange one or more paragraphs, you must update the numbering by issuing the Tools/Bullets and Numbering command again. With

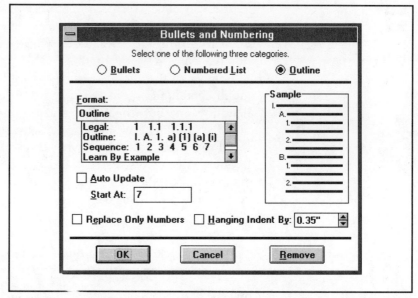

Figure 24.2: The Bullets and Numbering dialog box with the Outline option selected

manual numbering, however, you can choose the starting number, and you can have more than one numbering sequence in the same document.

Enter a value into the **Start At:** box if you want to change the starting outline number that is displayed there.

Select the **Hanging Indent By:** option to have Word indent all of the selected paragraphs (this will indent even paragraphs of body text that are not numbered). In each paragraph, all lines will be indented except the first line. To adjust the amount of the indent, change the value in the box following the **Hanging Indent By:** label.

If you are *renumbering* an outline, or a portion of it, you can choose the **Replace Only Numbers** option to have Word update the number in front of each paragraph that is already numbered, without adding numbers to unnumbered paragraphs within the selection.

To *remove* any existing numbering from the selected paragraphs, click the **Remove** button.

When you are ready to apply the numbering, click the OK button.

CREATING A TABLE OF CONTENTS FROM OUTLINE HEADINGS

In Chapter 11, you learned how to create a table of contents from entries manually inserted into the document. If you have included outline headings in your document, you can also create a table of contents directly from these headings, without the need to manually insert table of contents entries. Once you have finished adding outline headings to your document, use the following steps to create a table of contents from these headings:

1. Place the insertion point at the position in your document where you want the table of contents.

2. Choose **Insert/Table of Contents**. Word will display the dialog box shown in Figure 24.3.

3. Select the **Use Heading Paragraphs** option within the Table of Contents dialog box.

4. Select the **All** or **From:** option.

   Select **All** if you want Word to include all outline headings in the table of contents. Select the **From:** option if you want Word to use only the outline headings within a range of levels, and enter the starting and ending levels into the **From:** and **To:** boxes. To use a single level, you can type the same number into both boxes.

   You can use the From option to create several tables within a single document. For example, if you use outline levels 1 through 5 for topic headings, and outline level 6 for figure captions, you could create a general table of contents by specifying outline levels 1 through 5, and *also* create a table of figures by specifying level 6 headings.

5. Click the OK button. Word will insert the table of contents at the position of the insertion point.

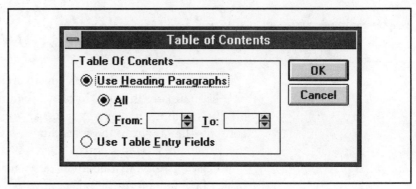

Figure 24.3: The Table of Contents dialog box

25

Adding Annotations and Marking Revisions

CHAPTER 25

THIS CHAPTER PRESENTS TWO FEATURES THAT HELP
you work with other writers and editors and develop final versions
of your documents: annotations and revision marks. Annotations
allow you or another writer to add comments to a document. Revision marks help you keep track of changes made to a document.

ADDING ANNOTATIONS

To insert an annotation:

1. Place the cursor where you want the annotation reference.
2. Choose **Insert/Annotation**. Word will open a separate pane for annotation text.
3. Type your comments into the annotation pane.
4. Close the annotation pane by clicking Close at the top of the pane.

Using annotations, you can add comments to a document without inserting them directly into the document text. Each annotation is labeled with the initials of the person who wrote it. Thus, if several people are working on the same document, annotations allow them to exchange comments and ideas on a manuscript without altering the manuscript.

Like a footnote, an annotation consists of two elements: the annotation mark and the annotation text. The annotation mark contains the initials of its creator and an identification number. It is inserted into the document text, but is formatted as hidden text, so it normally will not appear on the printed copy.

The annotation should be placed in the portion of the document that it pertains to.

The annotation text is displayed in a separate window pane and is *not* part of the document itself. The annotation text begins with the same mark that is inserted in the document to assist you in finding the text that goes with a particular mark.

Figure 25.1 illustrates a document containing annotations and an open annotation pane.

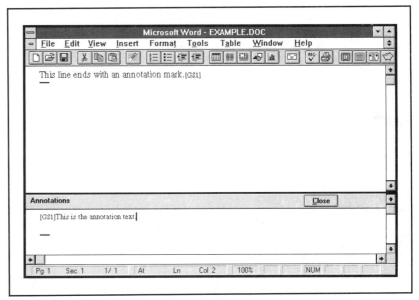

Figure 25.1: A document containing annotations

The following are steps for adding annotations to a document:

When an annotation pane is open, Word automatically turns on **Hidden Text**, so that you can see any annotation marks in the document. Even if the annotation pane is not open, you can show hidden text by choosing **Tools/Options** and selecting the **View** category.

1. Choose **Insert/Annotation**. Word will open an annotation window pane and automatically insert the annotation mark into both the document (formatted as hidden text) and the annotation pane.

   The initials added into the annotation mark are the initials entered when you installed Word. You can change the author's initials at any time by choosing **Tools/Options**, selecting the **User Info** category, and typing replacement characters in the **Initials:** box.

If another person works on your document using a different copy of Word, the annotations entered by this person will contain his or her initials. You can thus identify the writer of an annotation.

Notice that the annotation mark also contains a number. All annotations by the same person are numbered sequentially, starting with 1. If annotations are subsequently inserted or deleted, Word maintains the correct numbering.

2. Now type the text for the annotation directly into the annotation pane. To move the insertion point back and forth between the annotation pane and the document pane, press **F6** or click in the desired pane.

3. Once you have entered the annotation text, you can either leave the window open or close it. To close the annotation pane, drag the split bar to the top or the bottom of the window, or turn off **View/Annotations**.

When you insert an annotation, **View/ Annotations** is automatically turned on. You can manually turn it off to remove the annotation pane. If the annotation pane is not visible, you can manually turn it on to display it.

You can later edit the annotation. First open the annotation pane, if necessary, by turning on **View/Annotations** or by pressing the **Ctrl** key while dragging the split bar down the window. You can then use standard techniques to edit the annotation text.

You can copy annotation text into the document itself using any of the techniques for copying text explained in Chapter 5.

You can delete an annotation by selecting the annotation mark in the document and pressing Del. Word will remove both the annotation mark and its associated text.

You can also move an annotation by simply moving the annotation mark. To move the annotation mark, cut and paste it as described in Chapter 5.

CHANGING ANNOTATION FORMATTING

Annotation marks are assigned the standard style **annotation reference** and paragraphs of annotation text are assigned the standard style **annotation text**. (The features of these styles are listed in Table 20.1 in Chapter 20.) You can thus change annotation formatting by redefining the standard style.

FINDING ANNOTATION MARKS AND READING ANNOTATIONS

You can use the Word Go To command to move the insertion point to a specific annotation mark in your document. Follow these steps:

1. Choose **Edit/Go To** or press **F5**.

2. At the prompt, type **a** to go to the *next* annotation mark, or **a** and a number to go to a specific annotation mark.

Here are several examples using Go To:

INSTRUCTION	*MOVES CURSOR TO*
a4	The fourth annotation within the document
a+3	The third annotation mark after the cursor
a−2	The second annotation before the cursor
a	The next annotation in the document

Notice that the annotation pane is linked with the document pane. When you scroll through the document, Word automatically scrolls the text in the annotation pane. Likewise, if you scroll through the annotation pane, Word automatically scrolls the document pane.

PRINTING ANNOTATIONS

Normally, annotations do not appear on the printed copy of the document. By selecting appropriate print options, however, you can print the document together with its annotations, or even print just the annotations.

You can print both the document and the annotations as follows:

1. Choose **File/Print**.

2. Click **Options** in the Print dialog box. Word will display the Options dialog box.

3. Select **Annotations** in the **Include with Document** area of the Options dialog box.

Notice that selecting **Annotations** automatically selects **Hidden Text**; since annotations are formatted as hidden text, they must be made visible. Selecting just **Hidden Text**, however, does not necessarily make annotations visible.

4. Click OK in the Options dialog box, and then click OK in the Print dialog box to begin printing.

Word will print all hidden text, including annotation marks, printing annotation text after the document text. Each annotation will include the page number of the annotation mark, the creator's initials, and the i.d. number.

To print only the annotations, perform the following steps:

1. Choose **File/Print**.

2. Select **Annotations** from the **Print:** pull-down list in the Print dialog box.

3. Click OK to begin printing.

Each annotation will include the page number of the mark, plus the initials of the writer and the i.d. number.

LOCKING A DOCUMENT

Menu commands and options that change the document's content are displayed in gray and cannot be selected.

If you *lock* a document when you save it, only you or someone using your copy of Word will be able to modify the document. People using other copies of Word will be able to add annotations, but will not be able to modify the document.

Use the following steps to lock a document:

1. Choose **File/Save As**.

2. Click **File Sharing** in the Save As dialog box.

3. Select **Lock File for Annotations** in the File Sharing dialog box.

4. Click OK in the File Sharing dialog box and again in the Save As dialog box. Word will save the document under its original name, as a locked document.

You can later unlock the document by saving it with **File/Save As** and turning off **Lock File for Annotations** before saving the file. Only the author of the document can lock or unlock it.

How does Word know who the author of the document is? When you first ran the Word program, you entered an author's name. When you save a new document, Word stores this name in the document.

If a document is locked, and the author's name in the document does not match the author's name in the current copy of Word, you cannot change the document. You can defeat this mechanism, however, by changing the author's name stored in the program to match that in the document. To change the name, choose **Tools/Options**, select the **User Info** category, and then enter another name into the **Name:** box (see Chapter 23).

MARKING REVISIONS

When you print a document, all revision marks will appear on the printed copy, unless you have disabled their display.

You can manually format text as strikethrough characters using **Format/Character**. Such text is not considered by Word as being deleted.

You can have Word mark all additions or deletions in a document, either as you go along or by comparing the current document with a previous version.

Word marks changes in your documents as follows:

- It places a vertical line in the margin adjacent to the change. This line is known as a *revision bar.*

- If you delete text, Word leaves the text in the document, but formats it as strikethrough characters.

  | ~~This line has been deleted. It is marked using strikethrough characters.~~

- If you add new text, Word marks it in a prespecified manner (for example, by formatting it as underlined characters). If desired, you can prevent Word from marking new text.

Figure 25.2 illustrates a paragraph containing revision marks.

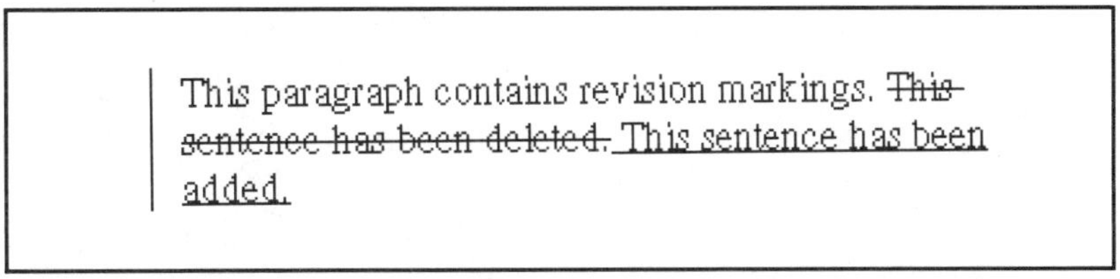

This paragraph contains revision markings. ~~This sentence has been deleted.~~ This sentence has been added.

Figure 25.2: Text with revision marks

As you will see later in the chapter, you can *remove* revision marks, either accepting or undoing the marked changes.

MARKING CHANGES AS YOU MAKE THEM

To mark revisions in your document as you make them, use the following procedure:

1. Choose **Tools/Revision Marks**. Word will open the Revision Marks dialog box, shown in Figure 25.3.

2. Select **Mark Revisions**.

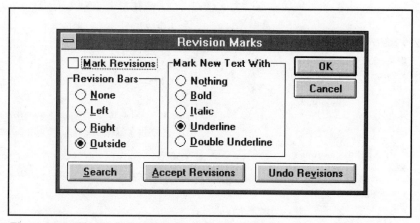

Figure 25.3: The Utilities/Revision Marks dialog box

3. Choose the type of revision bars you want Word to display by selecting an option from the **Revision Bars** area.

4. Choose an option specifying the way you want Word to mark new text from the **Mark New Text With** area.

5. Click the OK button. Word will begin marking all insertions or deletions within the current document.

The **Revision Bars** options have the following effects:

OPTION	*EFFECT*
None	Revision bars are eliminated
Left	Revision bars are printed in the left margins
Right	Revision bars are printed in the right margin
Outside	Revision bars are printed in the left margin on even- numbered (left-hand) pages and in the right margin on odd numbered (right-hand) pages

Note that even if you choose the **Right** or **Outside**, the revision marks will be displayed in the left margin in *Normal* view. They will appear in the designated margin in *Page Layout* view, *Print Preview,* and on the printed copy.

The **Mark New Text With** options have the following effects:

OPTION	*EFFECT*
Nothing	New text is not marked (if you have enabled Revision Bars, Word will display and print a revision bar adjacent to the new text)
Bold	New text is formatted as bold characters
Italic	New text is formatted as italic characters
Underline	New text is formatted as underlined characters
Double Underline	New text is formatted as double-underlined characters

Note that you can later open the Revision Marks dialog box and change either **Revision Bars** or **Mark New Text With**. Any change you make will affect not only subsequent markings, but also all markings already made.

Although you can choose the type of revision bars and the marking style for new text, deleted text is always marked with strikethrough characters.

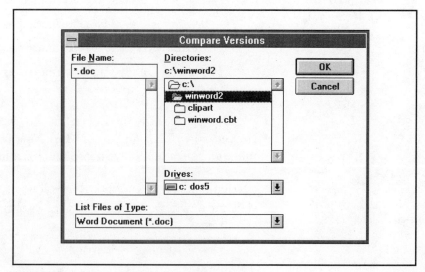

Later in the chapter, you will see how to remove the existing markings, either permanently implementing the changes or undoing them.

You can stop revision marking by selecting the **Tools/Revision Marks** again, turning off **Mark Revisions**, and clicking OK. Word will no longer mark revisions; however, any markings made previously will remain intact.

COMPARING WITH A PREVIOUS VERSION OF THE DOCUMENT

Rather than marking changes as you make them, you can mark changes in a document as compared to a previous version of it stored in a disk file. Use the following steps:

1. Choose **Tools/Compare Versions**. Word will display the Compare Versions dialog box, illustrated in Figure 25.4.

2. Select the former version of the document, using the list boxes as described for **File/Open** in Chapter 3 (by now these boxes should be quite familiar).

3. Click the OK button.

Word will mark all characters *added* to the previous version by formatting them as underlined text, unless you have specified a different

Figure 25.4: The Compare Versions dialog box

marking style. Also, Word marks each paragraph containing added text with a revision mark.

Unfortunately, Word does not indicate text that was deleted in the current version. Also, Word is sometimes over zealous in marking added text. For example, if you inserted text at the beginning of a paragraph, it marks the *entire* paragraph as new text.

SEARCHING FOR REVISIONS

You can find revision marks in your document as follows:

1. Issue **Tools/Revision Marks**.

2. Click the **Search** button in the Revision Marks dialog box. Word will highlight the first revision mark it finds and will leave the dialog box open. If you have selected text, Word searches from the beginning of the selection. When Word reaches the end of the document, it asks you if you want to continue searching from the beginning; click **Yes** to continue the search.

3. To search for the next revision mark, click **Search** again.

When you search for revisions using the Revision Marks dialog box, Word highlights either new or deleted text. Alternatively, you can search specifically for new text using the following method:

1. Choose **Edit/Find**. Word will display the Find dialog box.

2. Delete any text in the **Find What:** box.

3. Type **Ctrl-N** to find new text.

4. Click the **Find Next** button.

ACCEPTING OR UNDOING REVISIONS

To accept or undo marked revisions:

1. Choose **Tools/Revision Marks**.

2. To incorporate revisions and remove revision marks, click **Accept Revisions**.

3. To lose all revisions and remove the marks, click **Undo Revisions**.

Clicking **Accept Revisions** has the following effects:

- Text marked for deletion with strikethrough is removed. (Word does *not* delete text you have formatted as strikethrough with **Format/Character**.)

- Text that is marked as new is inserted into the document, with the marking removed.

- Revision bars are removed from the margins.

Clicking **Undo Revisions** has the following effects:

- Text marked to be deleted with strikethrough is left in the document, but the strikethrough formatting is removed.

- Text that is marked as new is deleted.

- Revision bars are removed from the margins.

26

Managing Collections
of Documents

AFTER WORKING WITH WORD FOR A WHILE, YOU may acquire a large collection of documents. In this chapter, you will learn how to use Word's document retrieval facility to help you find documents and perform operations on groups of documents. You will then learn how to manage Word windows so that you can work with several open documents at the same time.

RETRIEVING DOCUMENTS

Using the **File/Find File** command, you can obtain a list of Word documents or files in other formats that match a specified set of search criteria. For example, you can obtain a list of all documents written by a particular author; or a list of all documents created within a certain range of dates. Once you have obtained the list, you can use the File/Find File dialog box to perform any of the following operations:

- Sort the list of documents
- Preview documents or view other document information
- Open documents on the list
- Print documents on the list
- Delete documents on the list
- Copy documents on the list
- Edit the summary information for documents on the list

OBTAINING A LIST OF DOCUMENTS

To search for documents:

1. Choose **File/Find File**.
2. Click the **Search** button in the Find File dialog box.
3. In the Search dialog box, specify the type of file you want to find, the directories you want to search, and any other search criteria you want to use to narrow the search.
4. Click the **Start Search** button.

For more information on DOS directories and an explanation of the *current Word directory,* see Appendix B.

To obtain a list of documents matching a set of search criteria, choose **File/Find File**. The first time you issue this command, Word constructs a list of all documents within the Word directory. Subsequently, when you choose this command, Word compiles a list of all documents matching the criteria specified the last time you issued the command. Constructing a list can be a lengthy process; if you want to stop it, click the **Cancel** button or press Esc. When Word finishes compiling the list of files (or if you abort the search), it displays the Find File dialog box, which is illustrated in Figure 26.1. The **File Name:** list within the Find File dialog box contains the names of all documents obtained in the search (if you stopped the search, the list will contain only the files found before the search was aborted).

To obtain a list of documents matching a specific set of criteria, click the Search button. Word will now open the dialog box shown in Figure 26.2.

Indicate the type of file you are searching for by selecting an item from the **Type:** list box (the default type is Word Document (*.doc)). When you select a file type from this list, Word automatically copies the appropriate specification into the File Name text box.

Alternatively, you can enter a file name directly into the File Name box, using the * or ? wildcard characters if you want to specify a group of files (see Appendix B for information on using wildcard characters).

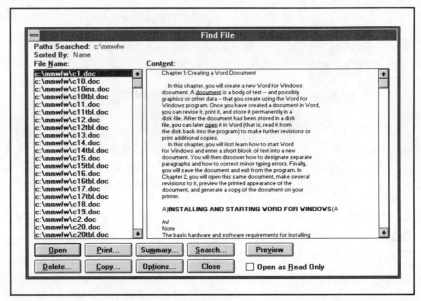

Figure 26.1: The Find File dialog box

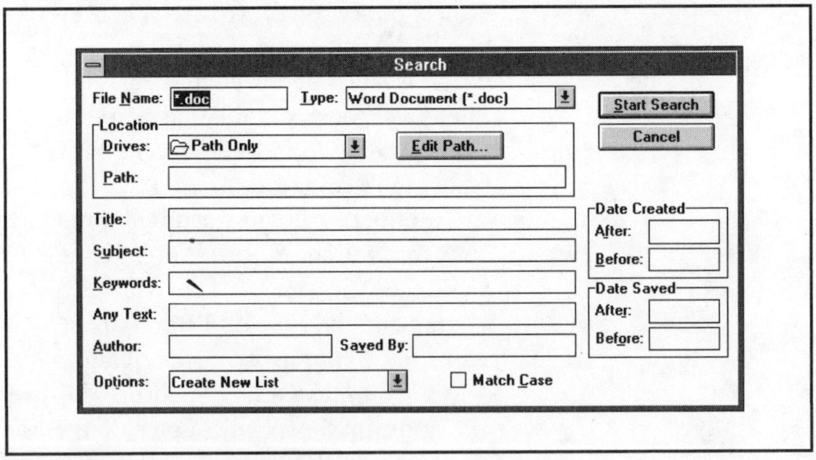

Figure 26.2: The Search dialog box

Next, specify the disk directory or directories you want Word to search, by using the controls within the **Location** area of the Search dialog box.

To search one or more specific directories, choose the **Path Only** item from the **Drives:** list (this is the default choice). If you leave the

Path: box empty, Word will search the current directory. If you want to specify one or more specific directories, you must enter them into the Path box. You can type the directory path for each directory you want to search directly into this box, separating each path with a semicolon. However, the easiest way to specify one or more directories is to click the **Edit Path** button, and then construct a list of paths using the Edit Path dialog box that Word then displays (Figure 26.3). To add a directory to your list, use the familiar **Drives:** and **Directories:** list boxes displayed within the Edit Paths dialog to select a directory path, and then click the **Add** button. When you have added all desired directories to the list, click the **Close** button to return to the Search dialog box. Word will then insert your list into the Path box in the Search dialog box.

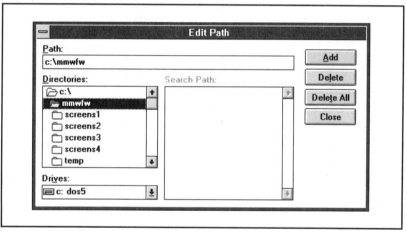

Figure 26.3: The Edit Path dialog box

If you select an item in the Drives list other than Path Only, Word ignores any information entered into the Path box.

To search an entire disk drive, select the desired drive from the Drives list box. You can also select the **All Local Drives** or **All Drives** option from this list to search all hard drives on your computer, or all hard drives on your network.

You can specify additional search criteria by entering the appropriate text into one or more of the other text boxes within the Search dialog box. The other criteria you can specify are summarized in Table 26.1. Notice that many of these criteria are based upon items contained in the document summary information. For example, if you type **Ivan** into

To learn how to read and edit the summary information belonging to any document, see "Editing Document Summary Information" later in this chapter.

the **Author** box in the Search dialog box, Word will list only files that contain the name *Ivan* in the Author field of the document summary information.

Table 26.1: Optional Search Criteria

SEARCH CRITERIA	EFFECT
Title	Lists documents that have this text within the Title box of the document summary information.
Subject	Lists documents that have this text within the Subject box of the document summary information.
Author	Lists documents that have this text within the Author box of the document summary information.
Keywords	Lists documents that have this text within the Keywords box of the document summary information.
Saved By	Lists documents that have this text within the Last Saved By field of the Statistics dialog box.
Any Text	Lists documents that contain this text (see Table 26.2 for special characters you can enter).
Date Created	Lists documents created within the range of dates specified in the From and To boxes.
Date Saved	Lists documents last saved within the range of dates specified in the From and To boxes.

If you do not specify any of the criteria listed in Table 26.1, Word will list all files that conform to the name and directory specifications entered into the File Name, Drives, and Path boxes. If you specify one or more of the criteria in Table 26.1, Word will *combine* the criteria.

For example, if you enter the following specification into the File Name box,

    *.doc

select the Path Only option within the Drives box, leave the Path box empty, and enter the following name into the Author box,

    T. Jones

Word will list the names of all documents that are in the current Word directory *and* are written by T. Jones. If, in addition to specifying an Author criteria, you also entered the following word into the **Keywords:** box

    nasturtium

Word would list the names of all documents that are in the current directory, are written by T. Jones, *and* contain the keyword *nasturtium* in the Keywords field of the document summary information.

Note that the text you enter into a criteria box need only match a *portion* of the text in the corresponding box of the document summary information. For example, entering **T** into the Author box of the Search dialog box would match documents with any of the following names in the Author field of the document summary information: T. Jones, John Tussey, or Tomaso Albinoni.

Note also that entering characters into the Any Text box causes Word to search for text within the document itself, rather than within the document summary information.

When you type text into a text box within the Search dialog box (other than the File Name box, the Path box, or the date boxes), you can enter one or more of the special characters described in Table 26.2. For example, if you entered the following expression into the Any Text box, Word would search for documents containing the word *Partridge* and the word *Sophia* (the two words do *not* need to be together in the document):

    Partridge & Sophia

Table 26.2: Special Characters for Document Search Criteria

CHARACTER	EFFECT
?	Matches any single character (for example, **a?e** would match *abe, ace, age,* and so on).
*	Matches any group of one or more characters (for example, **a*** would match *a, t, ace, apple,* and so on).
^	Treats the following special character as a normal character (for example, **^?** would match a question mark).
, (comma)	Means "or" (for example, entering **bat, cat** into the Keywords box would cause Word to search for documents that have either *bat* or *cat,* or both, within the Keywords box of the document summary information).
&	Means "and" (for example, entering **bat & cat** into the Keywords box would cause Word to search for documents that have both *bat* and *cat* within the Keywords box of the document summary information).
~ (tilde)	Means "not" (for example, entering **~ bat** into the Keywords box would cause Word to search for documents that do *not* have the word *bat* within the Keywords box of the document summary information).

If you select the **Match Case** option within the Search dialog box, Word will search for the exact combination of uppercase and lowercase letters entered into the Any Text box. If the Match Case option is not selected, Word will ignore the case of all letters when searching for text within documents. The Match Case option does not affect criteria other than that specified in the Any Text box.

You can also control the way Word constructs the list of files by selecting one of the items in the Options list at the bottom of the

Search dialog box:

The **Create New List** option (the default) causes Word to build an entirely new list by searching through all of the files matching the File Name and **Location** specifications. If you select **Add Matches to List**, Word will search in the same manner, but will *add* any files it finds to the files already listed in the Find File dialog box. If you select the **Search Only in List** option, Word will search through only the files already listed in the Find File dialog box (and then list only the files that meet all current search criteria).

When you have specified all desired criteria and options within the Search dialog box, click the **Start Search** button. Word will compile a list of all documents that meet your specifications. It will remove the Search dialog box, and display the list of documents within the Find File dialog box. You can now select one or more of these files and perform any of the operations described in the following sections.

To close the Find File dialog box, click the **Close** button. The next time you open the dialog box, Word will display the same set of documents. If changes have occurred within the search directories, Word will perform the search again and display an updated version of the list. It will use the same criteria previously entered into the Search dialog box. You can work with this list, or you can obtain a new list of files by clicking the Search button and revising the search criteria.

SORTING THE LIST

Word remembers the sorting order you specify, and uses it the next time you choose the **File/Find File** command.

Once Word has built a list of documents, you can sort this list. To do so, first click the **Options** button in the Find File dialog box. Word will open the Options dialog box, illustrated in Figure 26.4. Now choose one of the options within the **Sort Files By** area to specify the desired sorting order (these options are explained in Table 26.3), and click the OK button. Word will immediately sort the files displayed in the Find File dialog box according to the newly specified sorting order.

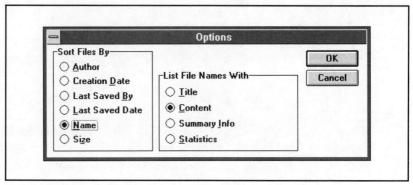

Figure 26.4: The Options dialog box

Table 26.3: File Sorting Orders

SORT OPTION	EFFECT
Name	Sorts files alphabetically by file name.
Author	Sorts files alphabetically by Author field of document summary information.
Creation Date	Sorts files chronologically by date of creation.
Last Saved Date	Sorts files chronologically by date of most recent save.
Last Saved By	Sorts files alphabetically by name of the user who most recently saved each file.
Size	Sorts files from smallest to largest.

PREVIEWING DOCUMENTS

To choose the type of file information displayed in the Find File dialog box:

1. Click the **Options** button.

2. Choose an option within the **List File Names With** area of the Options dialog box.

3. Click OK.

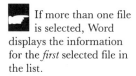 If more than one file is selected, Word displays the information for the *first* selected file in the list.

Word can display several types of information on each selected file that is listed in the Find File dialog box. This information can assist you in finding the desired file or files. To specify the particular type of information that Word displays, click the **Options** button at the bottom of the Find File dialog box. Word will display the Options dialog box. Choose one of the options within the **List File Names With** area:

```
┌─List File Names With──────────────────┐
│  ○ Title                              │
│  ○ Content                            │
│  ◉ Summary Info                       │
│  ○ Statistics                         │
└───────────────────────────────────────┘
```

If you choose the **Title** option, Word will display the **Title** field of the document summary information next to each document shown in the Find File dialog box. If you have selected a sort order other than **Name**, Word will also list the associated information for each file. For example, if you are sorting by author, Word will list the document author in addition to the title.

If you choose the **Content** option (the default), Word will display the actual text of the selected file. The text will appear in the **Content:** box within the Find File dialog box in a small but legible font. If desired, you can use the scroll bars in this box to scroll through the entire document. If the file is in a format Word recognizes, it automatically displays the text; if the document is in an unfamiliar format, you can click the **Preview** button within the Find File dialog box to force Word to display the text (if you have selected a program or other binary file, the results may appear quite strange!).

If you choose the **Summary Info** option, and if the selected file is a standard Word document, Word will display the document summary information for the document. If you choose the **Statistics** option, it will display the document statistics (including information such as the total number of words). Both the document summary information and the document statistics are discussed later in the chapter, in the section "Editing the Document Summary Information."

OPENING DOCUMENTS

To open one or more documents listed in the Find File dialog box, first select the name or names from the **File Name:** list. To select a single name, click on it; to select several names, hold down the **Ctrl** key while clicking each name. Next, click the **Open** button. Word will remove the Find File dialog box and will open the selected documents, each one in a separate window.

You can also open a single file and remove the dialog box by double-clicking the file name.

PRINTING DOCUMENTS

You can print one or more files in the **File Name:** list by selecting the file or files, and then clicking the **Print** button. Before printing the files, Word will display the Print dialog box. The options you enter into this dialog box will affect all of the documents printed (Word displays the dialog box only once, before printing the first document).

DELETING DOCUMENTS

You can delete one or more files in the **File Name:** list by selecting the files, and then clicking the **Delete** button. Word will display a message box asking you to confirm the deletion of the files. After performing the deletion, Word leaves the Find File dialog box open.

COPYING DOCUMENTS

To copy the selected file or files to another directory, click the **Copy** button at the bottom of the Find File dialog box. Word will open the Copy dialog box, illustrated in Figure 26.5. Use the **Drives:** and **Directories:** list boxes, in the usual manner, to select the destination directory. When you click OK, Word will copy the selected files to this directory, under the same names.

You cannot open more than nine documents at the same time (this is the maximum number of open windows).

You must copy a file to a different directory from its current location. You cannot specify a new file name when copying.

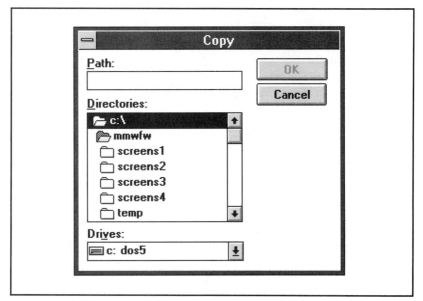

Figure 26.5: The Copy dialog box

EDITING THE DOCUMENT SUMMARY INFORMATION

To edit the document summary information for a document listed in the Find File dialog box:

1. Select the document.
2. Click the **Summary** button.
3. Edit any of the fields displayed in the **Summary Info** dialog box.
4. Click OK.

As you saw in Chapter 1, when you first save a new document, Word automatically prompts you for document summary information (unless you have turned off the Prompt for Summary Info option through the Save category of the Tools/Options command). Word stores the document summary information in the disk file, together with the document text.

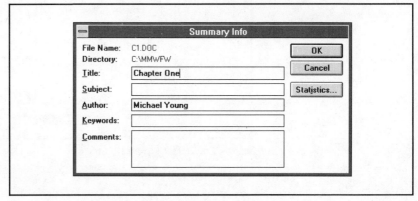

You can also add or revise the document summary information for the current document by choosing the **File/Summary Info** command.

You can add or revise the document summary information for a document within the **File Name:** list of the Find File dialog box by selecting the name of the document and clicking the Summary button. Word will display the Summary Info dialog box, which is illustrated in Figure 26.6. This is the same dialog box that is automatically displayed when you first save a new document and you are prompted for summary information. Opening the Summary Info dialog box for a document does not cause Word to open the document itself.

Figure 26.6: The Summary Info dialog box

Table 26.4 summarizes each of the items you can enter into this dialog box. You can enter up to 255 characters for each item.

You cannot update the document statistics through the **File/Find File** command.

If you click the **Statistics** button within the Summary Info dialog box, Word will display the Document Statistics dialog box, which shows a variety of information on the current document. An example of a Document Statistics dialog box is illustrated in Figure 26.7.

Note that the three items at the bottom of the dialog box, following the label **As of last update:**, may not contain the current correct values. If an item does not contain an up-to-date value, it is displayed in gray letters. To update all items, you must *open* the document, and then either print the entire document, or choose **File/Summary Info**, click the Statistics button, and then click the **Update** button.

Once you have opened a document, you can print the document summary information, either by itself or together with the document. To print the document summary information alone, select the **Summary Info** item from the **Print:** list box within the Print dialog box. To print

Table 26.4: Document Summary Items

ITEM	PURPOSE
Title	A title for the document. You can enter a more descriptive name than that provided by the file name (which can be only eight characters long).
Subject	A description of the content of the document.
Author	The name of the writer of the document. Word initially inserts the name from the Your Name box in the Utilities/Customize dialog box. If desired, you can enter another name.
Keywords	One or more words, each of which describes an important topic or term covered in the document. The words should be separated by a space. Supplying keywords makes it easy to find the desired document through the File/Find command (you can enter a keyword into the Keywords box within the Search dialog box).
Comments	Free-form notes on the document for future reference.

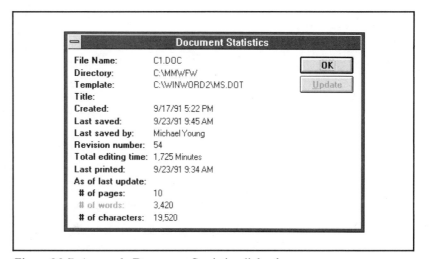

Figure 26.7: A sample Document Statistics dialog box

the document summary information together with the document, choose the Document item from the Print list box, click the **Options** button, and check the **Summary Info** option within the Options dialog box.

As you have seen, supplying document summary information for a document is optional. However, providing this information can make it easier to find a specific document using the File/Find File command as described previously in the chapter.

WORKING WITH WINDOWS

In this section, you will learn how to work with Word's various windows. Specifically, you will learn the following techniques:

- How to work with the Word window

- How to work with a document window

- How to open and manage several documents at the same time

- How to work with a single document in several windows

- How to split a window

If you need more information on any of these methods, read the *Microsoft Windows User's Guide.*

Before reading this section, you should be familiar with the following basic Microsoft Windows techniques for manipulating a window:

- Maximizing, minimizing, and restoring a window

- Moving a window on the screen

- Adjusting the size of a window

THE WORD WINDOW

The term *Word window* refers to the main window displayed by Word. The Word window contains the following elements:

- A title bar at the top of the window containing the label **Microsoft Word**. If the active document window is maximized (expanded to fill the entire area within the Word window), this title bar also contains the name of the active document.

- The Word control icon,

  which opens into the Word control menu (see Figure 26.8).

- Minimize and maximize (or restore) icons

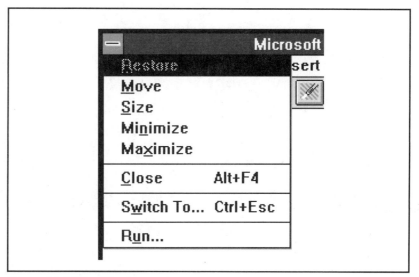

Figure 26.8: The Word control menu

- The menu bar. If the active document window is maximized, the document control menu icon for this window is placed at the left end of the menu bar.

- The status bar (provided that the **Status Bar** option is checked within the **View** category of the **Tools/Options** command).

The Word window may contain one or more document windows. It is the *parent* of these windows, which means that the document windows are always contained within the boundaries of the Word window.

When you first run the Word program, the Word window is maximized so that it fills the entire screen. You can restore it to a window that fills only a portion of the Windows screen by clicking the restore icon:

You can now move the Word window anywhere on the screen, and you can adjust its size. If you click the minimize icon (the downward-pointing triangle) on the Word window, it is reduced to the program icon:

DOCUMENT WINDOWS

Each open document is displayed within a *document window*. A document window is a *child* of the Word window, meaning that it is always contained within the boundaries of the Word window. A document window contains the following elements:

- A title bar at the top of the window containing the name of the document. If the document window is maximized, it shares a title bar with the main Word window; the shared title bar contains both the label **Microsoft Word** and the name of the document.

- The document control icon,

If the document window is maximized, the document control icon will be displayed at the left end of the menu bar belonging to the Word window; otherwise, it is displayed at the left end of the title bar belonging to the document window.

which opens into the document control menu (Figure 26.9).

- A maximize icon (an upward-pointing triangle), unless the window is already maximized.

- A vertical scroll bar, provided that the **Vertical Scroll Bar** option is checked within the **View** category of the **Tools/Options** command.

- A horizontal scroll bar, provided that the **Horizontal Scroll Bar** option is checked within the **View** category of the **Tools/Options** command.

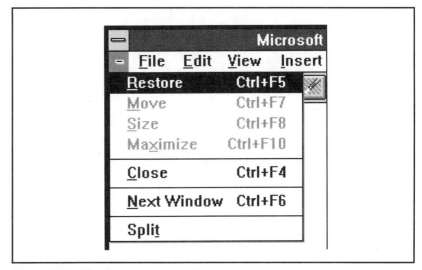

Figure 26.9: The document control menu

When you first run Word and open a document, the document window is maximized, meaning that it fills the entire available space within the Word window. To reduce the document window so that it fills only a portion of the Word window, choose the **Restore** item on the document control menu.

When the document window is no longer maximized, you can move it or change its size, using standard techniques. However, the document window always remains within the boundaries of the Word window.

OPENING SEVERAL DOCUMENT WINDOWS

When you open a document within Word, the document you are working on (if any) is not closed. Rather, Word opens an *additional* document window. If you choose **Window/New Window**, Word will

If a single document is displayed in more than one window, the title bar of each document window is numbered to identify the particular window.

When several documents are open at the same time, you can easily exchange text among them using the Windows Clipboard, as described in Chapter 5.

open another window containing the *same* document you are currently working on. At a given time, Word can contain up to nine open document windows.

The document window you are working within is known as the *active document window*. Its title bar is highlighted, it contains the insertion point (or selection), and menu commands act upon it. You can switch among open document windows (that is, activate the next open document window) by pressing **Ctrl-F6**, or by choosing the name of the desired document from the Window menu. You can also switch between windows by clicking the mouse in the window you wish to make active (if it is visible on the screen).

You can arrange the document windows within the Word window so that you can view more than one of them at a time. Use the standard techniques for moving and changing the size of windows to arrange them in a convenient pattern. If the active window is currently maximized, you will first have to reduce its size by choosing the **Restore** command from the document control menu.

Alternatively, you can choose the **Window/Arrange All** command. Word will automatically arrange the open document windows so that you can view all of them at the same time.

To close the active window, double-click the document control icon, choose the **Close** item from the document control menu, or press **Ctrl-F4**. If the current document is contained in more than one window, this command will close the current window, but *not* the document itself (that is, all other windows containing the document remain open). Alternatively, if you choose **File/Close**, Word will close the current document by closing *all* windows containing the document.

SPLITTING A WINDOW

If you want to see two views of the same document, it may be easier to split the active document window rather than opening a new window. When a window is split into two panes, you can scroll independently in each pane, and you can edit the document in either pane. To move the insertion point from one pane to another, press the F6 key or simply click in the other pane.

To split a window using the mouse, drag the split bar (the black bar at the top of the vertical scroll bar) down the window to the point where you want to split the window. You can adjust the size of the panes at any time by dragging the split bar to a new position. To remove the split, drag the split bar all the way to the top or the bottom of the window.

27

Using OLE: Object Linking and Embedding

THE LATEST VERSION OF WORD FOR WINDOWS provides an unprecedented set of features for combining information from a variety of sources within a single document. The mechanism that makes this integration of information possible is known as *Object Linking and Embedding,* or *OLE.* This chapter first introduces you to some of the general features of OLE. It then discusses the basic techniques for using Object Linking and Object Embedding for enhancing your Word documents.

AN INTRODUCTION TO OBJECT LINKING AND EMBEDDING

See Chapter 5 for information on cutting and pasting text, and Chapter 9 for information on cutting and pasting graphics.

You have already seen how to use the Windows Clipboard to cut or copy text or graphics from other applications and then paste the data into a Word document. When you paste *text* from another application, the text becomes a normal part of the Word document, and can be displayed and edited in the same manner as any other text. When you paste *a drawing, chart, or other complex data* into a document, however, Word does not have the facilities to allow you to edit the information (except for simple scaling and cropping). Without OLE, if you needed to change the information, you needed to reactivate the source application, edit the source data, and then copy and paste it into the Word document. Fortunately, the new Object Linking and Embedding mechanism allows you to freely insert these types of information from any application that supports OLE, *and* makes it easy to *update* the information.

OLE is actually *two* separate mechanisms: Object Linking and Object Embedding. If you insert information using Object Linking, the data is stored both within the source application and within the Word document, and a link is established between the two documents. Whenever you change the information in the source application, it is updated within your document, either automatically or through a simple command.

If you use Object Embedding, the imported information is stored *only* within the Word document. Word, however, maintains a connection between this information and the source application. If you simply double-click on the object, the source application is instantly activated to allow you to edit the information using all of the tools provided by that application.

A document that contains information from a variety of source documents, and uses OLE to automate the updating of this information, is termed a *compound document*. The remainder of the chapter shows you how to use Object Linking and Object Embedding to create compound documents within Word.

OBJECT LINKING

To insert linked information into a Word document:

1. Run the application that is the source of the data, and select the information you want to insert into Word.
2. Choose the **Copy** command on the **Edit** menu *of the source application.*
3. Activate Word and place the insertion point at the position where you want to insert the information.
4. Choose the **Paste Special** command from *Word's* **Edit** menu.
5. Select the desired data format in the Paste Special dialog box and click the **Paste Link** button. The information will be inserted into the document and the link established.
6. To update the information, change it within the source application. Word will automatically make the same change to the data within your document.

The *source application* is also known as the *server*, and the *destination application* (Word, in this discussion) is also known as the *client*.

You can insert information from another Windows application into a Word document in such a way that Word will *update* the information in your document whenever the information is changed within the source application. To do this, the source application must support either the OLE standard, or the older *DDE* standard (*Dynamic Data Exchange*). Inserting information in this way is known as *Object Linking*.

Note that Word and the source program must both be running in Windows in order to preserve the link. If you close the Word document, and then later reopen it, Word will ask you if you want to reestablish the link to the source application. If the source application is not running when you attempt to update linked data, or to reestablish a link, Word will display an error message; if you do not open the source application at this point, the data will appear in the document, but will no longer be linked and will not be automatically updated.

OBTAINING THE INFORMATION

Word can also serve as a *source* of linked data. In this case, you would copy the text or graphics from Word, and then use the destination application's **Paste Link** (or equivalent) command to insert the data and establish a link with Word. For details, see the documentation provided with the specific destination application.

To insert linked information into a Word document, the first step is to run the source application and either create or open the document containing the desired information. You should then select the portion of the document you want to insert into your Word document, and choose the **Copy** command, which is usually on the application's **Edit** menu. This command will transfer the selected data, as well as all required information for establishing the link, into the Windows Clipboard.

For example, if you wanted to insert a portion of a Microsoft Excel spreadsheet into a Word document, first run Excel and open or create a spreadsheet containing the desired data. Then, select the spreadsheet cells you want to insert into the Word document and select **Copy** on the Excel **Edit** menu. Figure 27.1 illustrates an example of a portion of a spreadsheet in Excel that has been selected and is ready to be copied into the Clipboard.

Remember to save the source document to disk so that it is available later for updating.

INSERTING THE INFORMATION

Once you have copied the information from the source program into the Clipboard, activate Word and place the insertion point at the document position where you want to insert the linked information. Then, choose **Edit/Paste Special** to open the Paste Special dialog box, which is illustrated in Figure 27.2.

After the Paste Special dialog box has been opened, you should first select the desired data format from the **Data Type:** list. Usually, Clipboard data is stored in several formats; each of these formats will be listed in the **Data Type:** list. Note that when you select certain formats, the **Paste Link** button in the Paste Special dialog box is disabled

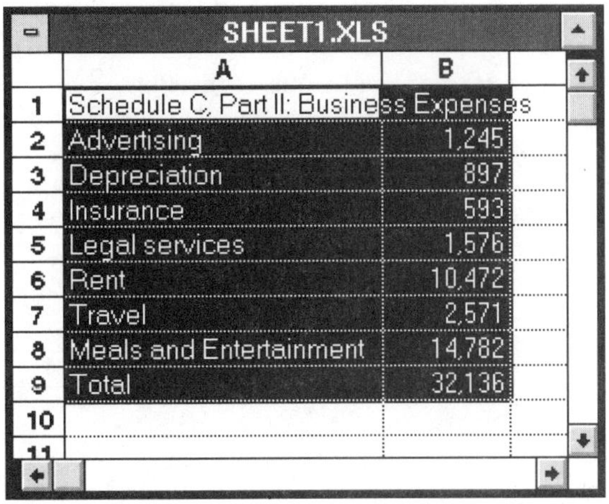

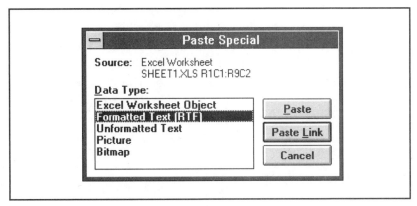

Figure 27.1: An example Excel spreadsheet

Figure 27.2: The Paste Special dialog box

⊙ Although you may be able to edit the information within Word after pasting and linking a block of data (specifically, if the data consists of text), you should not do so, because your edits will be lost whenever Word *updates* the data by matching it to the data in the source document.

(that is, displayed in gray letters), indicating that you cannot establish a link using the selected format. Therefore, make sure that you select a format that enables the Paste Link button.

Next, click the **Paste Link** button. Word will remove the Paste Special dialog box, insert the selected data into your document, and establish a link between the data in the source application and the copy of the data in the Word document. Subsequently, whenever you change the data within the source application, Word will implement the same change to the linked data within your Word document.

To illustrate this process, consider the example Excel spreadsheet presented in the previous section. If you copied the selection illustrated and then switched to Word and issued the Edit/Paste Special command, the Data Type list would contain the following formats:

```
Data Type:
┌─────────────────────────────────┐
│ Excel Worksheet Object          │
│ Formatted Text (RTF)            │
│ Unformatted Text                │
│ Picture                         │
│ Bitmap                          │
│                                 │
└─────────────────────────────────┘
```

In this example, to establish a link, you must choose the **Formatted Text (RTF)**, **Unformatted Text**, **Picture**, or **Bitmap** item (choosing the **Excel Worksheet Object** would *embed* an object, as discussed later in the chapter), and then click the **Paste Link** button. If you select **Formatted Text (RTF)**, Word will create a table in your document and insert all text contained within the selected spreadsheet cells into the cells of the table, maintaining the original formatting (font, size, and so on) of the characters in Excel. The result of selecting this option is illustrated in Figure 27.3.

Choosing the **Unformatted Text** option would simply insert the characters from the spreadsheet, without creating a Word table and without preserving the original character format. Choosing either the **Picture** or **Bitmap** format would insert the data as a picture, which would contain all of the original text as well as any graphic elements (lines, circles, and so on) contained in the spreadsheet cells (in the example, there are no graphic elements in the cells).

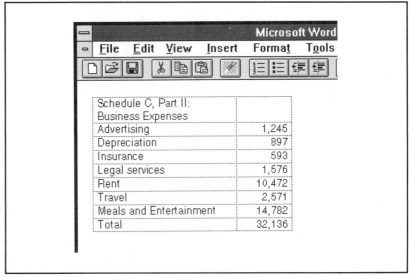

Figure 27.3: Excel spreadsheet of Figure 27.1, paste-linked into a Word document

In this example, any change made to the spreadsheet (including changes made by Excel when it recalculates the total) would automatically be transferred to the copy of the spreadsheet in Word.

EDITING THE LINK

To change the properties of one or more objects you have pasted and linked into a document—or to force Word to update an object—choose the **Edit/Links** menu command. Word will display the Links dialog box, which is shown in Figure 27.4.

First, select the link or links you want to change or update from the **Links:** list. The description of each link includes the source application, the source document name and directory path, and other information. To select a single link, click on it; to select several links, click on each one while holding down the **Ctrl** key.

To change the type of link, choose either the **Automatic** or **Manual** option:

Update: ⦿ **A**utomatic ◯ **M**anual

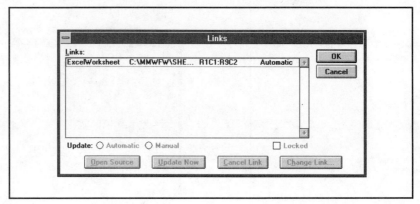

Figure 27.4: The Links dialog box

The **Automatic** option causes Word to automatically update the linked object as soon as the source document is changed and the data is available (this is the default option, initially selected for all new linked objects you insert). If you choose the **Manual** option, the linked object will not be updated until you choose the Edit/Links menu command, select the object in the Links list, and click the **Update Now** button.

To *prevent* Word from updating the selected link or links, choose the **Lock** option; the link will not be updated until you turn this option off. To open the source application for the selected link, click the **Open Source** button. To remove the link, so that the selected object will no longer be updated, click the **Cancel Link** button.

To change the source application for the link, the source document, or the location of the link within the source document, click the **Change Link** button, and enter the desired values into the dialog box that Word displays.

OBJECT EMBEDDING

You can also insert information created by another Windows application into a Word document using *Object Embedding*. With object embedding, unlike object linking, the data is stored *only within your document*; the data is *not* linked to a separate copy within the source application.

When you insert an embedded object, Word stores the name of the source application. You can later double-click on the object and Word will automatically open the source application and allow you to edit the object using the tools provided by this application.

To use object embedding, the source application must support OLE; older applications that support only DDE cannot be used to embed objects.

In this section, you will first learn how to enter information into a freestanding application, such as Microsoft Excel, and then embed the information in a Word document. You will then learn how to use the special utilities that are included with the Word for Windows package to embed drawings, charts, and other objects into your Word documents.

EMBEDDING OBJECTS FROM FREESTANDING APPLICATIONS

To embed an object from a freestanding OLE application:

1. Run the source program and select the information you want to insert into your Word document.

2. Choose the **Edit/Copy** (or equivalent) command from the menu of the source program.

3. Switch to Word and place the insertion point at the document position where you want to display the information.

4. From Word, choose the **Edit/Paste Special** menu command.

5. In the Paste Link dialog box, select whichever format description contains the word *object*, and click the **Paste** button. The information will now be displayed in your document.

6. To scale, crop, move, or copy the embedded object, use the same methods employed for managing pictures (described in Chapter 9).

7. To edit the embedded object, double-click on it to activate the source application. When you finish editing it, exit the source application and respond *Yes* if it asks you if you want to update the embedded object.

In this section you will learn how to embed—into a Word document—information created in a freestanding application that supports OLE. The first step is to run the source application and open or create the document containing the information you want to embed. Next, select the desired information and use the source application's **Edit/Copy** command to copy the selection to the Windows Clipboard.

For example, to embed an Excel chart in a Word document, run Excel and open the window containing the desired chart. The chart must be in its own window, not displayed within a spreadsheet, as shown in Figure 27.5. Then, select the chart by issuing Excel's **Chart/Select Chart** menu command.

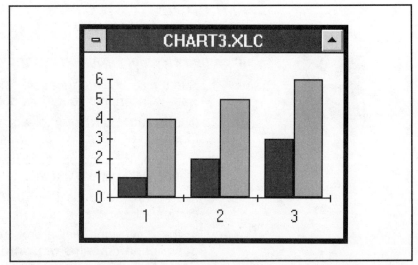

Figure 27.5: A chart in Excel, to be copied to the Windows Clipboard and then embedded in a Word document

Once the desired data has been copied to the Clipboard, activate Word and place the insertion point at the document position where you want to insert the information. Next, issue the **Edit/Paste Special** menu command. From the **Data Type:** list in the Paste Special dialog box, select the format that has the word *object* in its description, and then click the **Paste** button. Word will now embed the object into your document.

For example, to embed the Excel chart shown in Figure 27.5, switch to Word and place the insertion point at the position in the document where you want to display the chart. Then, choose Edit/ Paste Special, select **Excel Chart Object** from the Data Type list, and click the Paste button. The chart will now be displayed in your document, as shown in Figure 27.6.

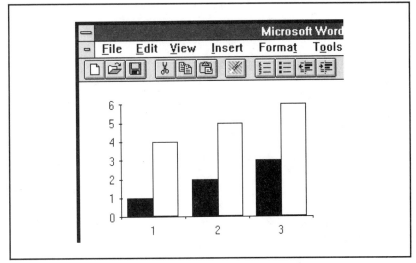

Figure 27.6: An Excel chart embedded in a Word document

Like a picture, you can select an embedded object together with adjoining text. In this case, the embedded object is simply highlighted, without sizing handles.

Once an object has been embedded in your application, you can select it by clicking on it. Word will draw a border, which will contain eight sizing handles. You can then scale or crop the object by dragging the handles in exactly the same manner described for pictures in Chapter 9 (hold down the Shift key to crop). You can also copy or move an embedded object by selecting it and using the standard cut, copy, and paste commands.

Unlike *linked* data, you cannot edit an *embedded* object even if it consists only of text.

Except for scaling or cropping, you cannot edit an embedded object using Word commands (even if the linked object consists of textual data, such as spreadsheet numbers). To edit the object, you must activate the source application and use the editing tools provided by that program. Fortunately, this is an easy task. Simply double-click on the embedded object (or select it and choose **Edit/ Object**). Word will automatically run the source application and cause it to open a window displaying the object. You can now freely edit the object using the facilities of the source application. When you have finished editing it, simply close the source application. The source application may ask if you want to *update* the object within Word (in this case, click **Yes**), or it may simply update the object automatically. The source program's window will then disappear and you will see the results of your editing displayed in the Word document.

Note that an embedded object consumes more memory than normal text or graphics. If you no longer need the embedding features—that is, if you no longer need to use the source application's editing tools—you can convert an embedded object into normal Word-document text or graphics. To do this, select the embedded object, and then press **Ctrl-Shift-F9**.

EMBEDDING WORD AND WORD UTILITIES OBJECTS

To embed an object using a utility supplied with Word:

1. Place the insertion point at the document position where you want to display the object.

2. Choose **Insert/Object**.

3. Select the type of object you want to embed from the Object dialog box, and click OK. Word will automatically run the source program.

4. Create the desired drawing, chart, or other information using the facilities of the source program.

5. Exit the source program, and respond *Yes* if it asks you if you want to update the Word document. The object will now appear in your document.

6. To scale, crop, move, or copy the embedded object, use the same methods employed for managing pictures (described in Chapter 9).

7. To edit the embedded object, double-click on it to activate the source program. When you finish editing it, exit the source program and respond *Yes* if it asks you if you want to update the embedded object.

The Word for Windows package includes a special collection of utility programs that you can use to create different types of objects to embed in your Word documents. These "embed" utilities (which, incidentally, can only be run from within Word) are briefly described in Table 27.1. Installing the utilities is optional. If you want to install a utility that is not currently on your system, run the *Setup* program again, choose the **Custom Installation** option, and select the utility you want.

Table 27.1: Word Utilities with Object Embedding

Equation Editor	Allows you to create or edit mathematical expressions, employing numbers and a wide variety of ready-to-use mathematical symbols.
Microsoft Draw	Provides tools for creating and editing simple drawings (see Chapter 9).
Microsoft Graph	Creates a variety of different types of charts, based upon numeric data you either type into the utility or import from other sources. This tool is useful for presenting data graphically within your documents.
Microsoft WordArt	Creates special effects with text. You can type or paste in a block of text, and then select from a variety of special fonts (named after cities in Washington state), styles (for slanting, bending, and otherwise manipulating the text), and other features. This tool is convenient for creating logos or headlines in your documents.

The **Object Type:** list will also display any freestanding OLE applications (such as Excel) that you have installed on your system. You can use the **Insert/ Object** command as described in this section as an alternative to the method for embedding objects described in the previous section.

To embed an object using one of these utilities, first place the insertion point at the position in your document where you want to display the object. You can then insert a Microsoft Draw object by clicking the **Draw button** on the Toolbar:

or you can insert a Microsoft Graph object by clicking the **Graph button**:

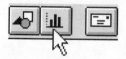

To use one of the utilities not represented on the Toolbar, place the insertion point where you want to embed the object, and choose the **Insert/Object** menu command. Word will open the Object dialog box, illustrated in Figure 27.7. The **Object Type:** list within this dialog box will display the different types of objects you can insert (the actual items appearing in this list depend upon which OLE programs you have installed). Select the type of object you want to embed and click the OK button. Word will now run the appropriate utility.

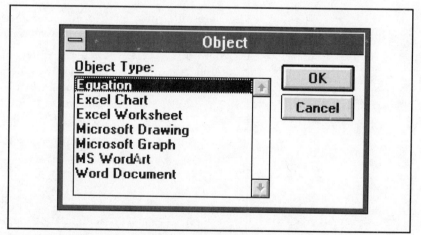

Figure 27.7: The Object dialog box

For example, if you select the **MS WordArt** item in the Object Type list and click OK, Word will open the WordArt utility window, as shown in Figure 27.8.

Once the utility window has opened, you can freely use any of its tools to create the object you want to embed: an equation, drawing, chart, or special text, depending on which utility you are using.

When you have completed creating the object, simply exit the utility program, using any of the standard methods. The utility may then ask you if you want to update the object in your Word document; respond *Yes* to embed the new object.

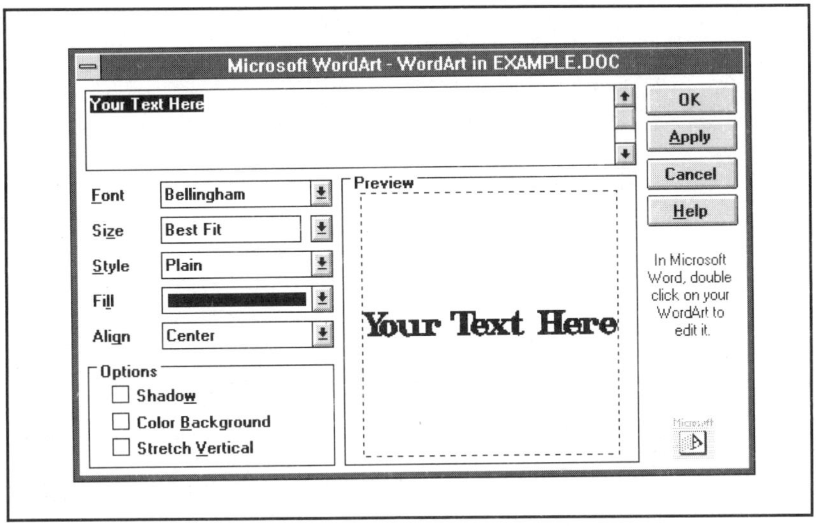

Figure 27.8: The WordArt utility

When using one of the embedding utilities, you *update* the object in the Word document rather than *saving* it in a disk file. Remember that an embedded object is stored only within your document. To save your work permanently, you must save the entire document on disk.

If you cut or copy a selection from a Word document into the Clipboard, you can embed it instantly by choosing **Edit/Paste Special** and selecting the **Microsoft Word Object** format. The resulting embedded-object icon will "contain" the contents of the Clipboard.

To edit an object once it has been embedded in your document, you must double-click on the object icon (or select it and choose **Edit/Object**) to reactivate the source application, as described in the previous section.

You can also scale or crop the object by selecting the icon and dragging a sizing handle, and you can move or copy it using the cut, copy, and paste commands. These are the same techniques used for pictures, which were discussed in Chapter 9.

You may also have noticed the **Word Document** item displayed within the Object Type list of the Object dialog box. Rather than embedding a drawing, chart, or other item within the document, choosing Word Document actually embeds an entire Word document within the *current* document. If you choose this item and click OK, Word will open a separate document window. You can then enter and format text and graphics into this window in the same manner as creating a normal Word document. When you have finished entering this information, however, rather than saving your work in a separate disk file, you simply close the window. Word will then ask you if you want to update your original document. If you click the **Yes** button, Word will then embed the document object within the current document.

When you embed a document object, Word does not display the text and graphics contained within the object; rather, it simply displays the Word program icon, as shown in Figure 27.9. You can later double-click on this icon to open a separate window containing the embedded document object so that you can edit its contents. You might use embedded document objects in this way to create a single master document that allows you to quickly access any member of a set of embedded documents by double-clicking the appropriate icon.

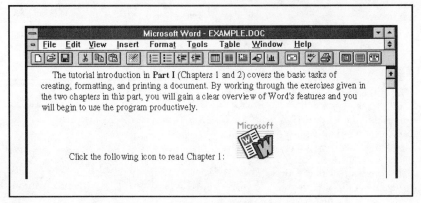

Figure 27.9: A Word Document Object embedded in a document

Appendices

Installing Word for Windows

APPENDIX *A*

USING WORD SETUP

To install Word for Windows, follow these steps:

1. Place the Word **Setup** disk in drive A.

2. Start Windows if it is not already running.

3. Choose **File/Run** from the Windows Program Manager.

4. Type **A:SETUP** into the **Command Line:** box.

5. Click the OK button.

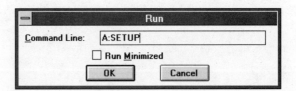

The Word Setup program will now begin running, guiding you through the entire installation process.

The Setup program first asks you to specify the name of the hard-disk directory where you want to install Word. If desired, you can simply accept the default directory, \WINWORD. (Unless you have good a reason for not doing so, accept the default directory, since it is used in the examples in this book.)

Setup then displays the dialog box illustrated in Figure A.1, asking what type of installation you want it to perform.

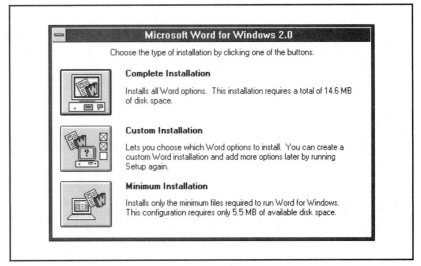

Figure A.1: Options for selecting the type of installation

COMPLETE INSTALLATION

If you click **Complete Installation**, Setup will install all of Word's features, including the proofing tools (spelling, grammar, thesaurus, and hyphenation), the online help information, the tutorial lessons, and utilities for creating graphics, equations, charts, and text effects.

CUSTOM INSTALLATION

If you click **Custom Installation**, you will be able to specify exactly which features you want Setup to install. Setup will display the

If you have limited space on your hard disk, choose **Custom Installation** or **Minimum Installation**. If you choose **Custom Installation**, the Setup Options dialog will display the space available on your disk and the total space required for the features selected for installation.

If you have selected **Custom** or **Full**, Word asks you if you would like information on its WordPerfect Help system.

The first time you run the Setup program, you *must* choose the **Microsoft Word** option, which installs the basic files required to run Word.

Microsoft Word Setup Options dialog box, which is shown in Figure A.2. To install an entire group of features, check the box next to the description of the features you want:

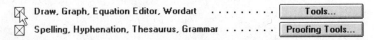

To choose exactly which features you want to install within a group, click the button to the right of the description:

Setup will then display another dialog box allowing you to select specific features belonging to the group.

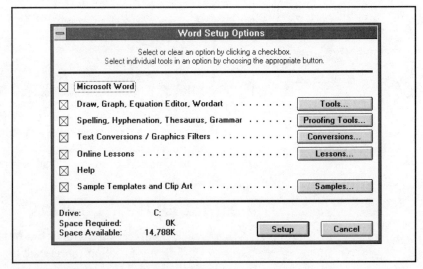

Figure A.2: The Setup Options dialog box

Table A.1 describes each of the program features you can select when performing a custom installation. When you have specified all the features you want installed, click **Setup** to continue with the installation.

You can run the Setup program at any time to install additional features (be sure to choose **Custom Installation**). Once the installation is complete, you can run Setup again simply by double-clicking on the **Setup** icon in the **Word for Windows** group of the Program Manager.

Table A.1: Custom Installation Features

FEATURE	INSTALLS...
Microsoft Word	Installs the basic files needed to run Word. You must select this option the first time you install Word.
Draw, Graph, Equation Editor, WordArt	Utilities for creating and editing objects that can be embedded in Word documents: Draw for graphics, Graph for charts, Equation Editor for mathematical expressions, and WordArt for manipulated text (for creating special text effects).
Spelling, Hyphenation, Thesaurus, Grammar	Features for proofing your documents: Spelling for checking your spelling, Hyphenation for automatic hyphenation, Thesaurus for finding synonyms, and Grammar for checking you grammar and writing style.
Text Conversions/ Graphics Filters	Files for opening documents that are not in standard Word for Windows format (**Text Conversions**) and for inserting pictures from graphics files (**Graphics Filters**). When you click **Conversions**, you can select which formats you want.
Online Lessons	An interactive tutorial for learning Word. If you click **Lessons**, you can choose **Getting Started** (basic tasks), **Learning Word** (more advanced techniques and features unique to Word), or both.
Help	Word's online help, accessed by pressing **F1** or choosing items from the **Help** menu.
Sample Templates and Clip Art	Templates you can use to quickly create specific types of documents (**Sample Templates**) and files containing graphics you can insert into your documents as pictures (**Clip Art**). If you click **Samples**, you can select template, clip art, or both.

MINIMUM INSTALLATION

If you click **Minimum Installation**, Word will install only the files that are required to run Word, without prompting you to choose specific options. If you select this type of installation, many of the features described in this book will be missing. If desired, however, you can run Setup again to install additional options.

NETWORK INSTALLATION OPTIONS

The Setup program also provides options for installing Word on a network.

If you run Setup from a floppy-disk drive and specify a network path as the destination program directory, Setup will display the **Server Installation** button rather than the **Minimum Installation** button. Choose this option to install all of Word's features (including a copy of the Setup program) on the network server.

If you then run the Setup program from the network drive where Word was installed, Setup will display **Workstation Installation** in place of Minimum Installation. Choose this option to install the files required to run Word on a network workstation.

The Setup program next asks you whether you want it to update your AUTOEXEC.BAT file, stating the changes it wants to make. Click Yes unless you want to update AUTOEXEC.BAT manually with an ASCII text editor.

COMPLETING THE INSTALLATION

Once you have selected the desired type of installation (and, for a custom installation, have chosen the specific features you want installed), Word will proceed with the installation, prompting you for each program disk as it is required.

After the installation process is finished, you can start Word by double-clicking the **Microsoft Word** icon that the installation program has placed in the Program Manager.

B

Understanding the DOS File System

APPENDIX *B*

MICROSOFT WINDOWS—AND WORD FOR WINDOWS—run under the DOS operating system, and they use the DOS file system. When you read or write Word documents or other files, therefore, it is important to understand how DOS organizes files. In this appendix, you will learn about DOS file directories and how to specify the full path name of a file. You will then learn about the current disk and directory, and how to specify the partial path name of a file. Finally, you will discover how to specify a group of files by using *wildcard* characters within the file name.

HOW FILES ARE ORGANIZED

Your computer has one or more disk drives. For example, it may have two floppy disk drives, known as drive A and drive B, and a hard disk drive, known as drive C.

Each disk drive contains a primary storage area, known as its *root directory*. The root directory can contain one or more files (such as Word documents or other applications); it can also contain other directories. Like the root directory, each of these other directories can store files and additional directories. Figure B.1 illustrates a simple collection of files and directories on drive C and shows the tree-like structure that results from the ability to store directories within other directories.

The root directory is always present on a disk drive. When you install a program such as Word for Windows, it creates one or more additional directories. You can also create or remove directories yourself using DOS or the Windows File Manager.

For instructions on creating or removing directories, see a DOS handbook, or the *Microsoft Windows User's Guide*.

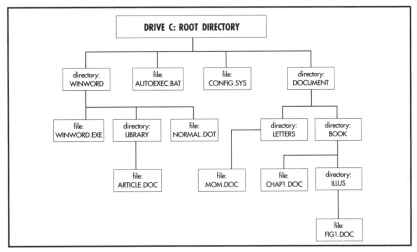

Figure B.1: A simple directory structure

SPECIFYING FULL PATH NAMES

The full path name for a file specifies both the name of the file and the exact location of the file within the computer's directory structure. A full path name begins with the drive specification, then indicates each of the directories containing the file, and finally supplies the file name.

The details of typing a full path name are best explained by giving some examples. As the first example, the full path name for the file AUTOEXEC.BAT in Figure B.1 would be the following:

```
C:\AUTOEXEC.BAT
```

The **C:** indicates that the file is on drive C; the \ character represents the root directory; and **AUTOEXEC.BAT** is the name of the file. This path name thus indicates that the file AUTOEXEC.BAT is in the root directory on drive C.

As another example, the full path name for the file ARTICLE.DOC in Figure B.1 would be

```
C:\WINWORD\LIBRARY\ARTICLE.DOC
```

As in the previous path name, the *first* \ indicates the root directory. The subsequent \ characters, however, are simply separators between directory or file names. This path name indicates that the file ARTICLE.DOC is in the LIBRARY directory, which is in the WINWORD directory, which is in the root directory of drive C.

SPECIFYING PARTIAL PATH NAMES

When Word prompts you for a file name (for example, when you choose **File/Open**), you can always specify the full path name of the desired file. If, however, you understand the concept of the current drive and current directory, you can save time when typing a file name.

At any given time, Word considers one of the disk drives in your system as the *current drive*. If a file is on the current drive, you do not have to specify the drive in the path name. For example, if drive C is the current drive, you can fully identify the file WINWORD.EXE of Figure B.1 through the following name:

> You can change the current drive by double-clicking the name of the desired drive within any Word dialog box that provides a list of drive names.

    \WINWORD\WINWORD.EXE

Since this path name does not contain a drive specification, Word assumes the current drive (C).

Just as you can omit the name of the current drive from any file name, so can you omit the name of any drive's *current directory*. For example, if the current directory on drive C is the DOCUMENT directory (refer to the example file structure in Figure B.1), you could specify the file CHAP1.DOC with the name

> You can change the current directory by double-clicking the name of the desired directory within any dialog box that lists directory names.

    C:BOOK\CHAP1.DOC

You could use this specification from any drive as long as you know that the current directory on drive C is the DOCUMENT directory. (Of course, if you're on drive C to begin with, you don't need the **C:** in front of the specification.) Notice that in this example you have omitted not only the current directory on the drive (**DOCUMENT**), but also the backslash after the **C:**. You can do this because you already know that the DOCUMENT directory is a subdirectory of the root.

USING WILDCARDS IN FILE NAMES

You can specify an entire *set* of files by including one of the *wildcard* characters, ? or *, within a file name. The ? character stands for *any single character.* For example, the name

CHAP??.DOC

indicates any file name beginning with the characters CHAP, followed by any two characters, followed by the .DOC extension (such as CHAP01.DOC or CHAP05.DOC).

The * character stands for any number of characters (0 or more). For example, the name

C*.DOC

indicates any file name beginning with C and having the .DOC extension (such as CHAP03.DOC, CATS.DOC, or C.DOC).

You can use a wildcard character when entering the name of a file into a Word dialog box, to obtain a list of all files matching the name. For example, if you entered the name

*.TXT

into the **File Name:** box within the Open dialog box, Word would list all files in the current directory having the .TXT extension.

Entering Measurements
in Word

APPENDIX C

MANY OF THE WORD DIALOG BOXES REQUIRE YOU to enter measurements. If you specify the measurement in the *default unit,* you can simply type the number, and you do not have to indicate the units. For example, if the default unit of measurements is inches, you can simply type the number **8.5** into the **Width:** box in the Page Setup dialog box; Word will interpret this value as inches and will automatically add the abbreviation for inches (") after you click the OK button (as you will see the next time you open the dialog box).

You can set the default unit used for measurement boxes by issuing the **Tools/Options** command, choosing the **General** category, and then selecting the desired unit from the **Measurement Units:** list box.

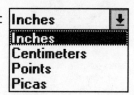

For certain text boxes, however, Word always uses a specific default unit, regardless of the default you specify with Tools/Options. For example, the default unit for specifying paragraph spacing (through the **Format/Paragraph** command) is always lines (li).

You can enter a value into a text box in a unit other than the default unit for that text box; however, you must specify the desired unit using the correct abbreviation for this unit. For example, if the current default unit for a text box is inches, you could enter a value in centimeters by including cm after the number, as in the following example:

    2.54 cm

The next time you open the dialog box, you will discover that Word has converted all measurements to the default unit.

Table C.1 provides the abbreviation for each of the units used by Word. For each unit, it also gives the equivalent number of each of the other units, to help you convert from one unit to another. For example, the table indicates that 1 inch is equal to 2.54 centimeters, 6 lines, 6 picas, or 72 points.

Table C.1: Abbreviations and Conversion Factors for Measurements Used in Word

UNIT	ABBREVIATION	CENTIMETERS	INCHES	LINES	PICAS	POINTS
Centimeters	cm	1	.39	2.38	2.38	28.35
Inches	" *or* in	2.54	1	6	6	72
Lines	li	.42	$1/6$	1	1	12
Picas	pi	.42	$1/6$	1	1	12
Points	pt	.035	$1/72$	$1/12$	$1/12$	1

Index

E

F

SYBEX

FREE BROCHURE!

Complete this form today, and we'll send you a full-color brochure of Sybex bestsellers.

Please supply the name of the Sybex book purchased.

_____

How would you rate it?

_____ Excellent   _____ Very Good   _____ Average   _____ Poor

Why did you select this particular book?

_____ Recommended to me by a friend

_____ Recommended to me by store personnel

_____ Saw an advertisement in _____

_____ Author's reputation

_____ Saw in Sybex catalog

_____ Required textbook

_____ Sybex reputation

_____ Read book review in _____

_____ In-store display

_____ Other _____

Where did you buy it?

_____ Bookstore

_____ Computer Store or Software Store

_____ Catalog (name: _____)

_____ Direct from Sybex

_____ Other: _____

Did you buy this book with your personal funds?

_____ Yes   _____ No

About how many computer books do you buy each year?

_____ 1-3   _____ 3-5   _____ 5-7   _____ 7-9   _____ 10+

About how many Sybex books do you own?

_____ 1-3   _____ 3-5   _____ 5-7   _____ 7-9   _____ 10+

Please indicate your level of experience with the software covered in this book:

_____ Beginner   _____ Intermediate   _____ Advanced

Which types of software packages do you use regularly?

_____ Accounting	_____ Databases	_____ Networks
_____ Amiga	_____ Desktop Publishing	_____ Operating Systems
_____ Apple/Mac	_____ File Utilities	_____ Spreadsheets
_____ CAD	_____ Money Management	_____ Word Processing
_____ Communications	_____ Languages	_____ Other _____
		(please specify)

Which of the following best describes your job title?

_____ Administrative/Secretarial   _____ President/CEO

_____ Director   _____ Manager/Supervisor

_____ Engineer/Technician   _____ Other _____
                                                             (please specify)

Comments on the weaknesses/strengths of this book: _____

_____

_____

_____

_____

Name _____

Street _____

City/State/Zip _____

Phone _____

PLEASE FOLD, SEAL, AND MAIL TO SYBEX

SYBEX, INC.
Department M
2021 CHALLENGER DR.
ALAMEDA, CALIFORNIA USA
94501

SYBEX

SEAL

Common Word Commands (continued)

Command	Key Combination	Menu Item
Help, Show Index	Alt-H, *then* I	Help/Index
Hyphenate Selection	Alt-O, *then* H	Tools/Hyphenate
Index, Compile and Insert	Alt-I, *then* I	Insert/Index
Index Entry, Define	Alt-I, *then* E	Insert/Index Entry
Insert Document Contents	Alt-I, *then* L	Insert/File
Insert Page, Column, or Section Break	Alt-I, *then* B	Insert/Break
Macro, Record	Alt-O, *then* R	Tools/Record Macro
Macro, Run or Edit	Alt-O, *then* M	Tools/Macro
Maximize Document Window	Alt-hyphen, *then* X *or* Ctrl-F10	Document Control/Maximize
Maximize Word Window	Alt-Spacebar, *then* X	Word Control/Maximize
Minimize Word Window	Alt-Spacebar, *then* N	Word Control/Minimize
Move Document Window	Alt-hyphen, *then* M *or* Ctrl-F7	Document Control/Move
Move Word Window	Alt-Spacebar, *then* M	Word Control/Move
New Document, Create	Alt-F, *then* N	File/New
Next Document Window	Alt-hyphen, *then* N *or* Ctrl-F6	Document Control/Next Window
Number Paragraphs or Outline	Alt-O, *then* B	Tools/Bullets and Numbering
Object, Edit	Alt-E, *then* B	Edit/Object
Object, Insert	Alt-I, *then* O	Insert/Object
Open Document	Alt-F, *then* O *or* Ctrl-F12	File/Open
Options, Set	Alt-O, *then* O	Tools/Options
Outline Document View	Alt-V, *then* O	View/Outline
Page Numbers, Print at Top or Bottom of Page	Alt-I, *then* U	Insert/Page Numbers
Page Layout Document View	Alt-V, *then* P	View/Page Layout
Page Setup	Alt-T, *then* U	Format/Page Setup
Paragraph, Format	Alt-T, *then* P	Format/Paragraph
Paste Contents of Clipboard	Alt-E, *then* P, Ctrl-V, *or* Shift-Ins	Edit/Paste
Paste Link	Alt-E, *then* S	Edit/Paste Special
Picture, Insert	Alt-I, *then* P	Insert/Picture
Picture, Format	Alt-T, *then* R	Format/Picture
Position Paragraph or Picture	Alt-I, *then* F	Insert/Frame
Print Document	Alt-F, *then* P *or* Ctrl-Shift-F12	File/Print
Print Merge	Alt-F, *then* M	File/Print Merge
Print Preview Document View	Alt-F, *then* V	File/Print Preview
Printer Setup	Alt-F, *then* R	File/Print Setup
Repaginate	Alt-O, *then* A	Tools/Repaginate Now